BYTE-SIZE FLASH MX

ADVENTURES IN DESIGN OPTIMIZATION

Geneviève Garand
David Hirmes
Cody Lindley
Kip Parker
Keith Peters
Robert Reich
Roy Tanck

APress Media, LLC

BYTE-SIZE FLASH MX ADVENTURES IN DESIGN OPTIMIZATION

© 2002 Apress
Originally published by friends of ED in 2002

First Printed December 2002

Trademark Acknowledgements

friends of ED has endeavored to provide trademark information about all the companies and products mentioned in this book by the appropriate use of capitals. However, friends of ED cannot guarantee the accuracy of this information.

ISBN 978-1-59059-211-3   ISBN 978-1-4302-5207-8 (eBook)
DOI 10.1007/978-1-4302-5207-8

Since this book is all about bytes, we have chosen to use the following standard and correct abbreviations throughout the text. Kilobytes will be abbreviated KB. The capital K denotes the use of the binary thousand, 1,024 (as opposed to the decimal thousand, 1,000, which is represented by a lower case k), and the capital B denotes bytes rather than bits (represented rather by a lower case b). Megabytes will likewise be abbreviated MB.

CREDITS

Authors

Geneviève Garand

David Hirmes

Cody Lindley

Kip Parker

Keith Peters

Robert Reich

Roy Tanck

Reviewers

Kristian Besley

Steve McCormick

Sam Riggs

Jon Steer

Jeremy Thomas

Mike Urwin

Commissioning Editor

Jim Hannah

Technical Editors

Julie Closs

Steve Rycroft

Alan McCann

Project Manager

Richard Harrison

Graphic Editor

Katy Freer

Indexer

Simon Collins

Proof Readers

Chris Matterface

Mel Orgee

Cathy Succamore

Geneviève Garand

My dream was to become a filmmaker but now, I am an interface designer. I studied in Communication and I finally discovered new media! After two years of work as a Web Designer for an interactive agency in Montréal, Canada , I returned to University and conceived 3weeksinApril.com, an experimental web site that explores new ways of navigation and features an engaging narrative. Since then, I used with my passion for art and interactive design to produce work that is both technologically advanced and creatively inspired.

Cody Lindley

Cody-Lindley = new array [Not so well spoken but full of spoken words, Moody, cleaner than most, shy, private, 26, inquisitive, thinker, 193 pounds, worrier, designer, programmer, husband, Macintosh, half full, man, son, kind, dog owner, brother, graduate, Idaho, Texas, Alabama, Oregon, homebody, Washington, Mt. biker, climber, honest, explorer, athlete, Christian, 6 foot, brown hair, brown eyes, American, www.codylindley.com, pride, rogue writer, buzz cut, Patagonia, beautiful wife, patient, computers, www.idahostatesman.com, snowboarder, home owner, loyal, pizza, dyslexic, hard headed, cold not hot, April 28th, winter, photography, facial hair, pricey not cheap, task driven, movies, beer, friend not foe];

David Hirmes

David Hirmes is a Flash developer living in Brooklyn, New York

Kip Parker

Born: 31.01.73   Live: London

Having previously worked as a van driver, nanny, ice cream seller, sandwich maker and band manager, in 1997 I started making web sites. I'm self-taught, and have managed to avoid getting qualifications for anything, though I do have a clean driving licence. I now work through my own company Hi-Rise Limited and in collaboration with Anthony Burrill as Friendchip, which was established by accident in 1998. Friendchip's first commercial job was for the inventors of electronic music Kraftwerk, and we've gone on to work largely with bands and music companies. Friendchip also exhibit in art galleries, as well as making an occasional interactive installation. Hi-Rise Limited does a wide range of work, from children's spelling games to large and serious database driven sites. In all my work, I try to condense ideas into something simple and playful.

Creating sound and graphics with code allows you to be surprised by your own work. Computers put things together in a way that no human would, occasionally creating something unexpectedly beautiful or, more often, unexpectedly humorous.

Keith Peters

I've been addicted to computers since 1986, when I got my hands on a used Commodore 128. I've always been interested in both computer graphics and various programming languages. I found Flash to be the ideal medium for creating graphics with code. In my personal experimental site, www.bit-101.com, I try to see just how far I can push Flash and ActionScript.

I want to thank my wife, Kazumi, the most important person in my life.

Her support and love have made this all possible.

Roy Tanck

I got into computer graphics at an early age and soon knew that was what I wanted to do with my life. After graduating from the Utrecht School of Arts in 1997, I spent several years photoshopping website designs together and have started using Flash more intensively during the past couple of years. I'm currently employed by Bright Alley in Hilversum, where I'm part of a team that creates innovative e-learning solutions. Within this environment, Flash is a great tool. In my spare time I try to update my personal homepage, www.weefselkweekje.com, as often as I can.

Robert B. Reich

Robert lives in Hamburg, Germany. His first creative steps were made with an Amiga by learning Assembler and entering the german Demo Scene at the age of 14.

The goal – which fuels the scene – was always to create the coolest graphical effect with limited resources.

During his studies in Berlin, he got his first insight into what drives the Internet, and he jumped on the new media train.

His first touch with Flash came with websites like thevoid.co.uk, what was nearly the same work like the early scene days, only with less codework to do.

Inspired by this, Flash became his medium of choice, alongside HTML and serverside driven website creation.

At the same time, the development of his first Content Management System for Flash began.

After working for SalonDigital.de and the online section of Macup publishing house, he now works as freelancer for several firms.

Welcome 1

1 Generative Experiments 5

2 A Byte-size Bitmap Gallery 43

6 City Blossom   175

7 Beyond the City Limits 207

8 Using JavaScript with Flash MX 243

9 Separating Form and Function:Flash and XML 279

Index 333

CONTENTS

WELCOME

Byte-Size Flash MX: Adventures in Design Optimization

Here's the myth: "If you want Flash, you've got to wait."

Five years of all-singing all-dancing introductory movies that take half an hour to load have worn users down into a "broadband-or-forget it" attitude. Say it ain't so!

It ain't so.

This book has been specially designed to ingrain excellent optimization tips and tricks into the user's mind. You *can* deliver JPEG photographs quickly through Flash. You *can* create fully interactive animations. You *can* deliver sound in 2k. You *can* create entire sites that load instantaneously. You *can* experiment and deliver amazing effects, and all at light-speed!

We're very proud of this collection. Some of the hottest designers from around the world have pulled their optimization tricks out of the bag, and here they reveal all in the form of clear and concise demonstrations.

You'll learn to create an animated photo gallery, a website, and a drawing application where you can *record* your work. You'll learn to produce animations through numbers, and you'll find out how to create amazing and amusing sound toys. It's all here!

This book could save you money

OK, so everyone wants their files to load quickly. Sure, we can do that for you, no problem. But speed is not always of the essence here. These tips and techniques are *so much* more important than that.

Countless sites have disappeared over the years because they've used up too much bandwidth, and become victims of their own popularity. Service providers hit their customers in the pocket, and all too often, they have to call it a day. *Don't let this happen to you!*

A quick note: the file size of this introduction (while it still lived on a computer) was 24KB. The average size of the download files we create in this book is under 4KB. Need we say more?

The Science Part

Layout

The code in this book is written as it appears in the final files, with one exception: the Continuation symbol (➡) denotes where a line of code is too wide to fit on our page. If you're typing it in, you should continue on the same line.

Source files

Believe it or not, we figured it would be a bit dumb if we included a CD with this book (and hiked the price). As all the files are so tiny, it makes a whole lot of sense to keep them on our website. You may download them from:

www.friendsofed.com/books/flash_mx_titles/byte_size/

As with all friends of ED titles, this book is backed up with free, fast, and friendly technical support from our editors. If you have a query or problem, mail support@friendsofed.com, and we will get back to you as soon as possible.

If you have any comments about this book, good, bad, or ugly, we're keen to hear from you. Mail feedback@friendsofed.com and have your say!

There's a host of other features at friendsofed.com that may interest you – interviews with top designers, samples from our other books, and a message board where you can post your questions, discussions and answers.

Display your talents!

1 GENERATIVE EXPERIMENTS

ROY TANCK

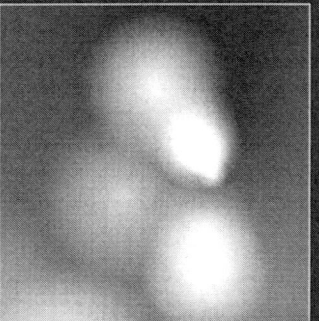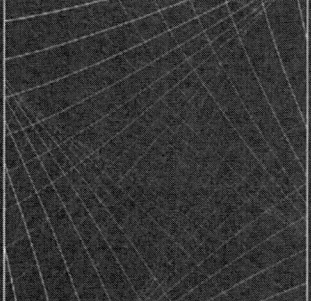

Drawing sophisticated shapes and animating them can make your Flash projects pretty bandwidth heavy. So why draw things by hand when you can script them? Indeed, some really cool effects can be created through the use of ActionScript alone.

The modular and reusable nature of Flash MX allows you to use graphics you've drawn as often as you like. By giving each of the copies different colors, sizes, and even behavior you can create some wonderful effects. Complex movements can often be described in only a few lines of code. Using a little high school math you can also add randomness to your work, and including user interactivity features can make things even more interesting.

One technique I particularly like and that combines many of these advantages is that of creating a particle system. In 3D computer animation software, particles are used to simulate natural phenomena like fire and smoke. Such particle systems use what's known as an *emitter* that continually creates new particles, essentially acting like a fountain spraying out the particles.

In the first few examples in this chapter I'll use the mouse position as my emitter. All particles can have their own behavior and can be subject to 'physical' entities like wind and gravity. They will generally have a limited lifespan, and eventually they'll disappear. Because there are usually many particles, together they can look like a single object. By setting the properties of the particles, this object can look and move like fire, smoke, clouds, water, and so on. Remember, all particles are copies of the same object, so only one is needed to create the effect – this original object is duplicated almost endlessly. Movie clips are ideal for this, because they can be *cloned* into any number of instances very easily, and can have scripts assigned to their instances to create specific behaviors.

Add to these techniques the drawing API in Flash MX, which also enables you to do everything with ActionScript alone, without having to *manually* draw anything on the stage at all. You can create new movie clips, draw complex shapes into them and assign scripts to their instances. Movies constructed like this will generally have only one frame, with a stop action in it. I personally prefer to use keyframe animation in many cases. The freedom to change the animation in a convenient interface outweighs the disadvantage of its inherently large file size – having to adjust parameters in a script to shorten an animation is a lot less intuitive then removing a few frames from a timeline.

In this chapter I'll try to give some examples of what I mean by generative experiments, and I'll discuss some of the code needed. Like the examples for the rest of this book, all of the relevant code can be downloaded from www.friendsofed.com for you to play around with.

Circles

This movie is a very simple example of just how easy it can be to create a nice visual effect using ActionScript. It simply creates expanding circles where the mouse pointer is – open up `circles.swf` and try it out:

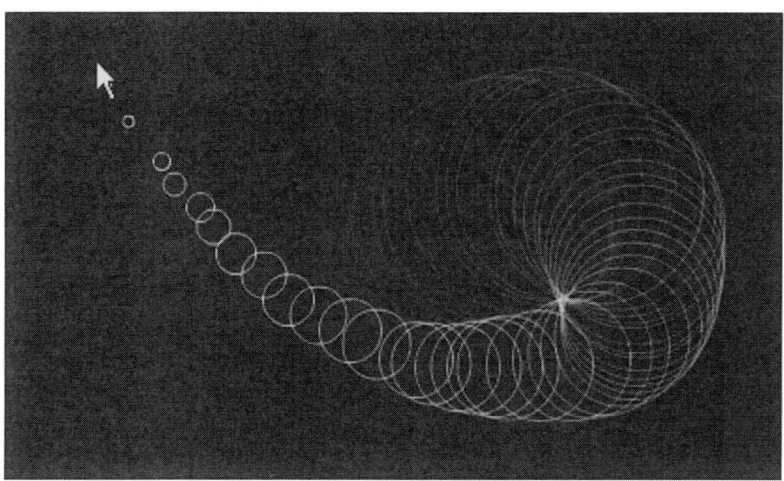

Now let's see how it works – the first frame on the main timeline in `circles.fla` contains all the code that we need. This code is commented throughout for clarity – but don't worry if you don't understand something the first time around, we'll follow it with a detailed description:

```
c = 10;
this.createEmptyMovieClip("blank_mc", 1);
blank_mc.onEnterFrame = function() {
    // step 1: Where's the mouse pointer right now?
    currx = _root._xmouse;
    curry = _root._ymouse;
    // step 2: If it's not in the same location it was last
➡time...
    if (!(prevx == currx && prevy == curry)) {
        // step 3: Create a new instance of "mc"
        _root.attachMovie("mc", "mc"+c, c);
        // step 4: Place the instance at the mouse pointer's
        // position and set size of new instance
        with (_root["mc"+c]) {
            _x = currx;
```

```
      _y = curry;
      _width = 0;
      _height = 0;
    }
    // step 5: Create an enter frame action
    // for each new duplicated mc
    this._parent["mc"+this._parent.c].onEnterFrame =
➡ function() {
      // Set variable to count the number of frames played
      this.i++;
      // Increase circle by (x) pixels
      this._width += 1.4;
      this._height += 1.4;
      // Decrease alpha by (x) amount
      this._alpha -= 100/60;
      // If frame reaches 60, remove mc
      if (this.i>=60) {
        this.removeMovieClip();
      }
    };
    // step 6: Increase the c used for instance names
    _root.c++;
  }
  // step 7: Store where the mouse was, so we can compare
  // that info to the position in the next program cycle
  prevx = currx;
  prevy = curry;
};
```

This might look complicated, but it's really quite simple when we break it down. In the Library of this file there's a movie clip called mc.

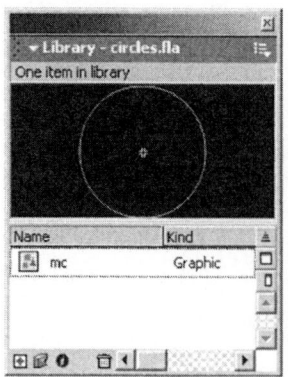

It contains a simple hairline circle that we'll use to create the expanding circles. As you can see, at the start of the code I've declared a counter variable c to use when creating instances. Next we'll need to create an empty movie clip that is going to control all the circles. I could have done this by creating an empty movie clip in the Library and dragging it to the stage, but I used the createEmptyMovieClip method instead because now all the information concerning the creation and use of blank_mc is in one place.

Next I created an `onEnterFrame` function for the blank movie clip. Because the movie clip is playing, this code runs every frame, so in this case, with the document's frame rate set to 30 fps, it'll run 30 times per second. It checks whether the mouse has moved, and if so it uses `attachMovie` to create a new instance of `mc`. To be able to attach that Library item to our movie, its linkage settings need to be set to Export for ActionScript:

Linkage Properties ☒

Identifier: `mc`

Linkage: ☑ Export for ActionScript
☐ Export for runtime sharing
☐ Import for runtime sharing
☑ Export in first frame

URL:

OK
Cancel
Help

Every one of the instances also needs a name that's different from the other ones if we want to control them with our ActionScript. That's why I've used `"mc"+c` as the second argument for `attachMovie` – this represents the new instance name for the created object. Since the counter is incremented every frame, no two movie clips will have the same name. Instead, they will be called `mc10`, `mc11`, and so on.

The new instance is moved to the current mouse position. I want the circles to start small and grow larger, so I set the initial size of the movie clip to zero (`_width = 0` and `_height = 0`). Next I've declared an `onEnterFrame` function for the newly created circle. It increases the object's size, and decreases its opacity on each new frame. I decided that I wanted to make every particle last for 60 frames, and grow to be 84 pixels in size (`1.4 x 60` frames). At the same time I wanted them to go from 100 percent opacity to being completely transparent – subtracting 100/60 from their opacity on each new frame achieves this. This way, the newest circles will be the smallest one on the screen, and every previous one will have expanded slightly. The longer an instance has been around the further along it'll be in its 60 frame scripted animation.

To make sure the movie doesn't become overcrowded with transparent movie clips that still demand processing time, I put a simple check in the `onEnterFrame` event that checks for how long the object has been around and removes it if necessary. Since one is created every frame, and they 'live' for 60 frames, there will be a maximum of 60 instances in the movie at any given time.

As you've probably noticed, I'm using very short variable names. I'm also keeping the amount of spaces in the code to a minimum. These factors all affect the file size of the SWF that's generated. Comments are not exported, so I generally prefer to use them to explain that `c` stands for `counter` if need be, instead of giving `c` a more comprehensible name.

1

You may also have noticed the following statement in the code:

```
with (_root["mc"+c]) {
```

The `with` statement is a great tool if you want to change a lot of properties in one object at once. In the example, I used it to change a newly created circle's position and size. Using the name of the circe enclosed within the brackets is an efficient way of addressing the right object. All objects inside a movie clip can be referenced just like the elements in an array of data. So, similar to the use of `array[i]`, you can directly address a movie clip that's within another movie clip using the generalization `parentclip[childclip]`.

Because there's basically just one real movie clip in this movie and all the rest is done by scripting, the finished SWF file is extremely small – just over 500 bytes! The script could have been even simpler if it didn't check whether the current mouse position was identical to the previous one. However, I hope you'll agree that it's a lot more beautiful this way.

In early versions of this movie I used a keyframe animation to expand the circles. This is a great way to decide how long you want your objects to live, and how big you want them to grow. Once I decided on the 60 frames, 84 pixels in size, and the fact that I didn't want any ease in or out within the motion, I switched to ActionScript. After I scripted the movement and removed the keyframe animation the movies were reduced by about 50%.

The result is a very simple example of a particle system. The mouse acts as the particle emitter, the instances of `mc` are the particles, and a short piece of code defines their simple behavior.

Smoke

The great thing about `circles.swf` is that it can very easily be changed into something that looks quite different – like smoke for instance. In `smoke.fla` I've simply changed the graphic of the circle outline from the previous example into a circle shape filled with a radial gradient from solid white in the center to transparent at the edge.

Keeping the same code as `circles.fla` creates a pretty neat smoke-like effect, with the mouse pointer as the source of the smoke.

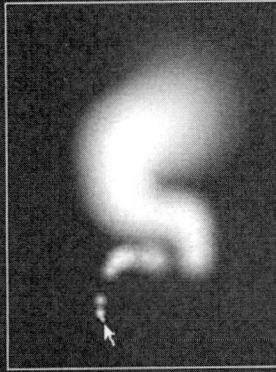

1

Dynamic characters

The ActionScript we've written so far will essentially duplicate anything you can throw at it! Here's another variation – try dyn_char1.fla, in which I've used a capital letter A as the graphic symbol to create quite an eerie text effect.

To make this movie look more exciting I added a little rotation. I made the A spin by adding a little to its rotation property every frame. Also, I wanted every new instance to have a slightly bigger initial rotation than in the previous design. These changes were implemented by amending the code in steps 4 and 5 as follows (the new lines are highlighted in bold):

```
// step 4: Place the instance at the mouse pointer's
// position and set size of new instance
with (_root["mc"+c]) {
  _x = currx;
  _y = curry;
  _xscale=0;
  _yscale=0;
  _rotation=_parent.counter;
}
// step 5: Create an enter frame action
// for each new duplicated mc
this._parent["mc"+this._parent.c].onEnterFrame =
function() {
    // Set variable to count the number of frames played
    this.i++;
    // Increase symbol by (x) pixels
    this._xscale+=4;
    this._yscale+=4;
    this._rotation-=3;
    // Decrease alpha by (x) amount
    this._alpha -= 100/60;
    // If frame reaches 60, remove mc
    if (this.i>=60) {
      this.removeMovieClip();
    }
};
```

Another thing I had to change was the code that sets the instance's size. Because the A clearly isn't a circular shape like the ones I used earlier, setting its width and height directly will deform it. Only with a circle are the width and height identical at any degree of rotation. Here I've switched to using _xscale and _yscale instead. I decided on adding four percent to them every frame after playing around with different values for a while. Setting this to other values will have great impact on the overall effect, so it usually takes me quite a while to decide on the most aesthetically pleasing value. The same goes for the three degrees with which I increment the rotation.

If this movie has been running for 100 frames, the *counter* variable will be 110, since it had an initial value of 10. The newly created instances will then be rotated by an angle that depends on what number the counter is at when they are created. I used an initial value of 10 for the counter so the first instance would not be created at depth 0, but at depth 10 (so that it wouldn't interfere with anything).

Note that the A graphic was *broken apart* (Modify > Break Apart) to save file size (sometimes that helps with single characters that are used only once), but nevertheless the file now weighs in at about 600 bytes – test it out.

1

Now try another subtle variation of the graphic – keeping the same rotation, but changing the A to a simple line will again create a totally different effect. In dyn_char1.fla I've changed the movie's background color to white and drawn a black line to make the whole thing look a little like an interactive drawing made on paper.

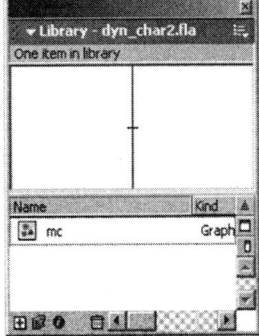

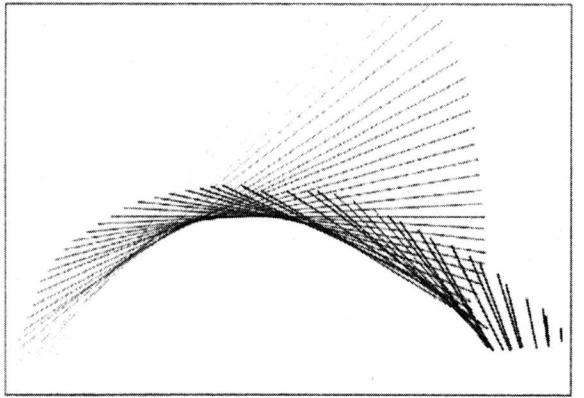

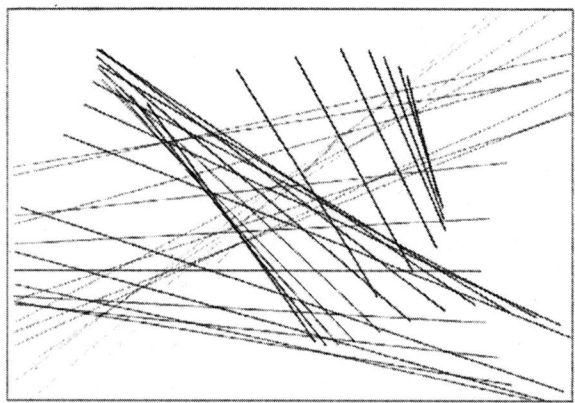

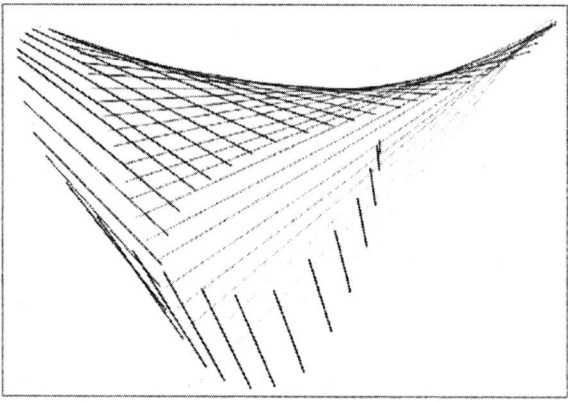

I've also increased the value that changes the instance's sizes from 4 to 15 to make the lines grow much faster:

```
this._xscale += 15;
this._yscale += 15;
```

Test the FLA to see the finished effect.

Because we're now using lots of alpha effects, we're making things hard on the Flash Player. Even though these are tiny movies, the user will need a fast computer to play them back at a decent frame rate – especially the smoke variation of our code. And even then, full screen is not a practical option. I generally use small playback sizes for movies like this to achieve higher frame rates.

When you think about the amount of work the Flash Player has to do, it's not surprising that using alpha slows down playback. Partial transparency means the player will have to calculate every screen pixel's color by analyzing what objects cover that pixel, and what their alpha setting is. From this it has to calculate the pixel's color. These calculations take up a lot of time and slow down the movie's playback. By decreasing the amount of pixels (that is, the playback size), the amount of calculations is drastically reduced. For instance, it's worth remembering that a 200 x 200 pixel movie has only a quarter the amount of pixels a 400 x 400 pixel movie has – that's 25% less rendering that your processor has to do!

Another trick is setting the movie's playback quality to low. This will often generate lots of horrible *jaggies*, but sometimes it works. There are no hard edges in the smoke.swf movie that we looked at earlier, so setting the quality to low will hardly affect the display quality. Actually, when I tried it I couldn't spot any difference at all, except in playback speed.

Basically there are two ways to set the quality – the first is to change it in the object and embed tags used to run the movie from an HTML web page. The great thing about this is that you could actually make different pages that display the same movie at different qualities. This is the most flexible solution, but it only applies to movies viewed online on a web page.

The second approach is to add the line _quality="low" to the code, preferably in the first frame. This will force the Flash Player into low quality mode. If you're planning to load the movie you're making into another project using loadMovie, you should realize that this technique also affects the parent movie's quality.

Realistic smoke

To create a more realistic smoke effect, let's add some behavior to the particles we create. This movie again uses an empty movie clip to make a new instance of a movie clip every frame. This time I didn't make it check whether the mouse had moved, because I wanted some serious smoke, even without mouse activity. I also wanted the instances to move once they were created. To simulate real smoke I wanted them to move upwards like particles in a column of smoke. Finally, I wanted them to spread out a little.

Take a look at `smoke2.swf` to see the effect that we're going to learn how to create:

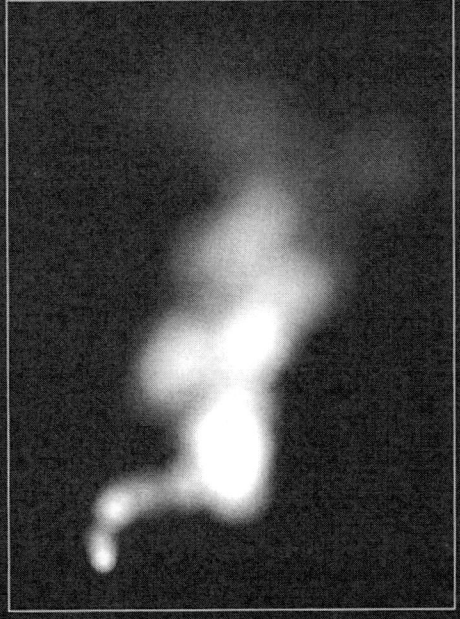

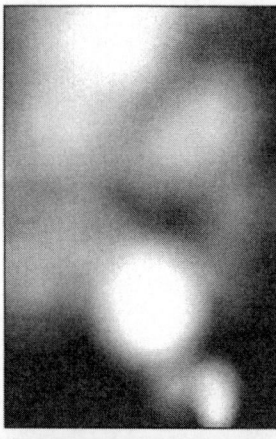

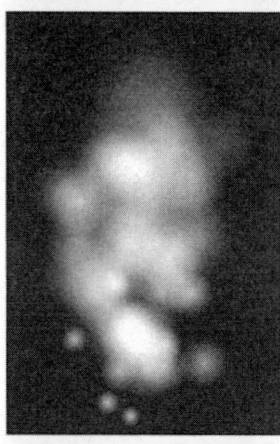

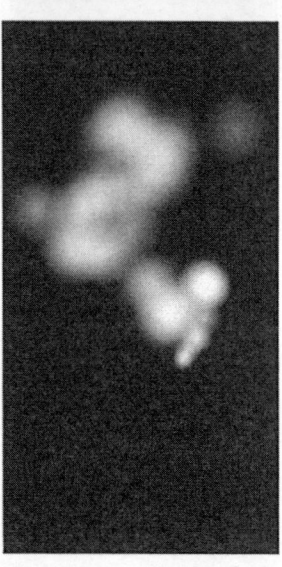

To create this effect, every particle now has its own `onLoad` and `onEnterFrame` event scripts, which makes the code look like this:

```
// set playback quality to low
_quality="low";
// create controller mc
this.createEmptyMovieClip("mc",1);
mc.c=10;
mc.onEnterFrame=function(){
   // attach new instance every frame
   this._parent.attachMovie("particle","p"+this.c,this.c);
   // set initial values for new instance in onLoad
   this._parent["p"+this.c].onLoad = function(){
      this.wl=50+50*Math.random(); // wavelength for sine
      this.ampl=0; // amplitude for sine
      this.as=2*Math.random(); // speed for amplitude change
      this.sp=2+2*Math.random(); // speed for upward motion
      this.bx=_root._xmouse;// set base x coord to mouse pointer
      this._y=_root._ymouse; // set base y coord to mouse pointer
      this._x=this.bx;
   }
   // fire off the onLoad function
   this._parent["p"+this.c].onLoad();
   // onEnterFrame function for new instance
   this._parent["p"+this.c].onEnterFrame=function(){
      // calculate new coords
      this._x=this.bx+(this.ampl*Math.sin((this._y)/this.wl));
      this._y-=this.sp;
      // increase amplitude of wave to make the smoke spread out
      this.ampl+=this.as;
   }
   // increase counter for levels
   this.c++;
}
stop();
```

As noted above, in this example I'm not only using an `onEnterFrame` function, but also an `onLoad` event script. The problem with using `onLoad` in conjunction with `attachMovie` is that by the time the `onLoad` action is declared the event has already passed! That's why I'm 'firing off' the `onLoad` function *by hand* as it were. I could also have declared a regular function to do the same things that `onLoad` now does. The reason I'm using an `onLoad` function even though it doesn't really work like one is that the event handler `onLoad` perfectly describes what it is used for – that is, to set initial values.

As you can see, later in the code I've used a sine wave to determine the object's x position:

```
this._x=this.bx+(this.ampl*Math.sin((this._y)/this.wl));
```

This way you can create a beautiful, fluent motion – sine waves are ideal for such natural dynamics.

Typically, this math function is used like this:

```
outcome = amplitude*Math.sin(input/wavelength);
```

In this example, the *amplitude* variable controls how large the values for *outcome* will get. Without *amplitude*, *outcome* would be between 1 and -1, so if you'd set *amplitude* to 1000, *outcome* would be between -1000 and 1000.

The default *wavelength* is 2 times the mathematical number Pi (which is approximately 3.14). So to create waves longer than 6.28 pixels (which is a little short for most uses), we can use the *wavelength* variable. Setting it to 100 will make our wave repeat every 628 pixels.

To put things in motion we'll need to change the value of *input* regularly. That's why I generally use the program counter as *input*.

In this movie, the values of the *wavelength* (wl) and the *amplitude* (ampl) are set in the onLoad event for each instance. These variables are set to random values to make every particle move along a different path. The onLoad event is also used to set _y and bx to the mouse's position, so the particle will appear there. The bx variable is used as an offset for the sine wave, which determines _x. Ultimately, _x will vary between bx+ampl and bx-ampl.

Because I've set the wave's amplitude to zero when it's created, the first _x value will equal bx. To make sure the smoke spreads out from the mouse pointer's position upward, I've added the as variable (which stands for *amplitude speed*), a random number by which the amplitude of the wave is increased every frame. This way, the further away from its point of origin a particle gets, the bigger the wave will get. Once created, every bit of smoke will follow its own path upwards, sway sideways and eventually delete itself.

One major difference between earlier movies and this one is that in this case I've used a little timeline animation to control the way the particles grow over time. The motion is now far more complex, and I've used several keyframes to make it grow quickly at first, then more slowly and fade out towards the end. I've also used **ease in** on two of those keyframes. The resulting animation would be very hard to script, and when done it would be even harder to modify. As we'll see in the next example, modifying only this short keyframe animation can make the resulting movie look quite different.

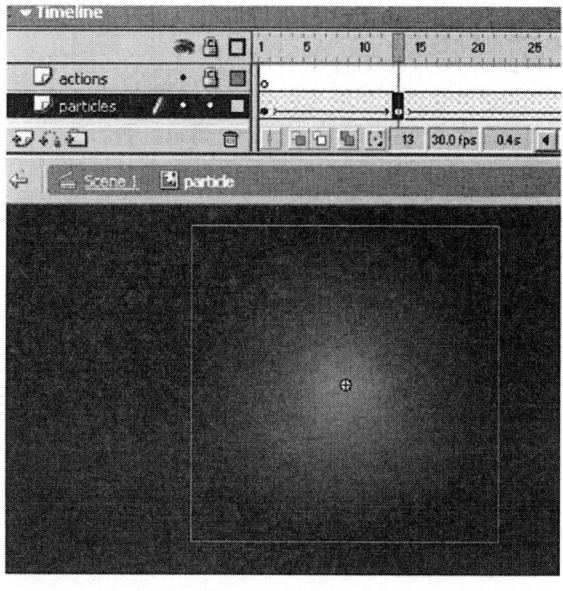

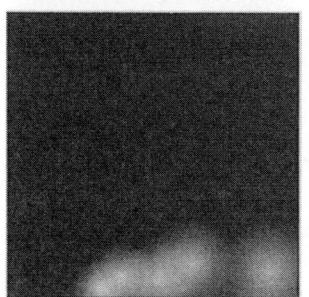

For the same reason, I've moved the code that removes the movie clip instances from the main timeline to within the movie clip. At the last frame of the particle's timeline there's now a simple `this.removeMovieClip` action. This again makes it easier to control the effect, since all you need to do to have the particles live longer is add frames to their timeline.

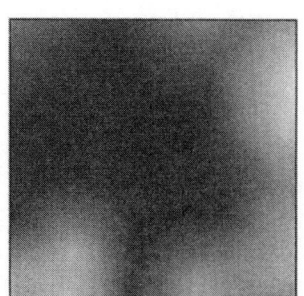

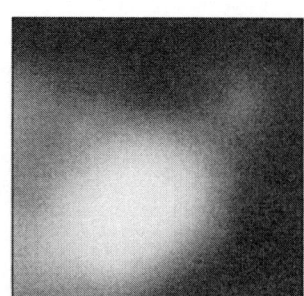

Fire

As with earlier examples, `smoke2.swf` can be made to look quite different by changing the shapes and the animation in the particles. For instance, in `fire.fla` I've simply added some tint effects to the keyframes of the particle motion tween to make them start out bright yellow, and turn red before they disappear. This will hopefully have the effect of making the animation look like a fire, especially if you make the particles a little smaller towards the end of their life. They'll look more like sparks that way. Increasing the length of the animation makes for a larger flame.

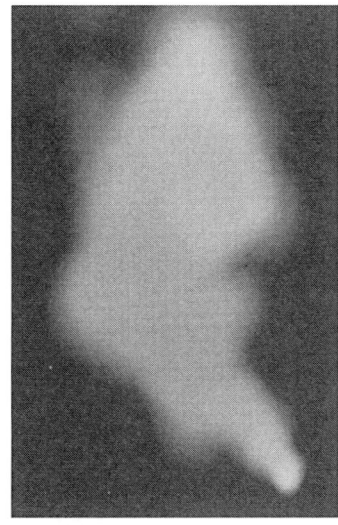

Again, both `smoke2.swf` and `fire.swf` benefit from setting the playback quality to `low`. These two movies actually look better with a low quality setting. For some reason the Flash player renders small errors and strange artifacts at its high setting – perhaps it's just too crowded with so many objects so close to each other. At `low`, the smoke is smooth as silk, and the movie plays at a much higher frame rate.

Both of these movies are still under 2 KB, even with the additional frame tweening. The export size report feature of Flash (File > Publish Settings... and select Generate size report on the Flash tab before testing your movie) isn't very helpful in determining which parts of the movie take up most of that space, but an educated guess would suggest that less than half of it is the code. The graphic is only 82 bytes, but the movie clip incorporates the animation – keyframes, regular frames, and especially tweens, all take up finite amounts of file space. As I said earlier, if I had really wanted to save every last byte I could probably have done the keyframe animation from ActionScript as well, but that would take away all the fun of changing the keyframe animation to achieve different effects.

Next, open up `fire_letters.swf` to see what the design looks like with the graphic symbol replaced by a dynamic text field. Check out the Property inspector with the graphic's text field selected and you'll see it's got a variable name (in the Var input field) linking the text to a random character:

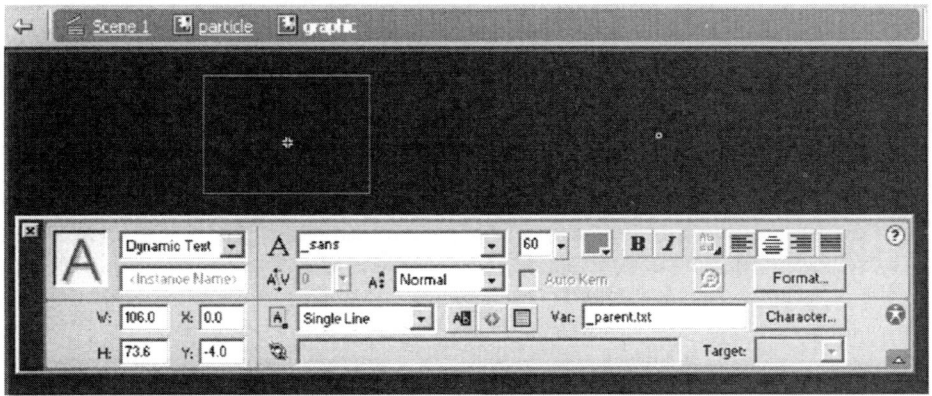

And voila, a cool text effect:

The first thing I changed to create this effect was that I added a line at the beginning of the previous code. All it does is declare a string variable that contains all lowercase characters. We'll use `str` so that we can randomly pick a single character from it for every particle.

```
// create string to randomly select characters from
str="abcdefghijlklmnopqrstuvwxyz";
```

The dynamic text field I put in the graphic displays the value of a variable called `txt`. In the part of the code that initializes the new particles, there's a line that selects a random character from `str` and puts it in `txt`:

```
this.txt=str.substr(Math.floor(_root.str.length*Math.random()
➥ ),1);
```

Here I'm using `Math.floor` to make sure I'm getting integer numbers from the random function. This number is then used to extract a character from `str` using the `substr` function. The main difference between `Math.floor` and `Math.round` is that `Math.floor` doesn't round (hey, simple right!). For example, `Math.floor(1.99)` will produce `1`. Let's say you want an integer between zero and five. If you'd used `Math.round(5*Math.random())`, the outcome of `5*Math.random()` would have to be below 0.5 for the result to be zero. This means you would have only half as much chance of getting a zero as you'd have of getting a 1 (0.5 to 1.4999). This is where `Math.floor` comes in useful. If the outcome is anywhere between 0 and 0.99999, the result will be zero. And since it doesn't really interpret the value but simply throws away everything after the point it probably even executes slightly faster than `Math.round`.

To create this effect I had to include all lowercase characters of the font used in the movie. This increased the file size to an *enormous* 3.65 KB! Not including the font outlines would make the characters appear aliased, but would save about 2.5 KB of file size. Since 4 KB is not a big download by far, and it looks so much better this way, I decided to include them.

Fireworks

Up until now I've used empty movie clips to create new instances on every frame. Now, `fireworks.swf` does things differently. Instead of the movie making new objects, in this case the user will have to use the mouse to get things going – try it out for yourself to see what I'm talking about.

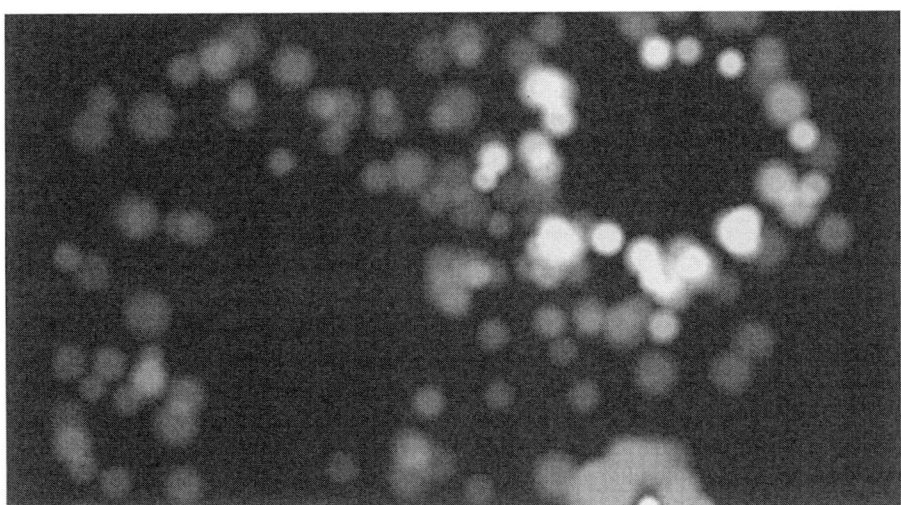

Let's see how this was constructed – take a look at `fireworks.fla`. I've created an empty movie clip and attached an `onMouseDown` event script to it. This way, the user will be able to click anywhere within the movie to start this script. Once he or she does so, a new instance of a movie clip called `arrow` is created. What I want to happen next is that this arrow starts at the bottom of the screen, flies to where the user clicked and explodes like fireworks. Here's the start of the code from frame 1 of the main timeline:

```
_quality="low";
ct=10;
this.createEmptyMovieClip("clickSensor",1);
clickSensor.onMouseDown=function(){
    // when clicked, create new instance of "arrow".
    this._parent.attachMovie("arrow","a"+ct,ct);
    this._parent["a"+ct].onLoad=function(){
        this.tx=_root._xmouse;
        this.ty=_root._ymouse;
        this._x=_root._xmouse+(Math.random()*200-100);
        this._y=400;
    }
    this._parent["a"+ct].onLoad();
```

As you can see, I've set the `arrow`'s `_y` property to 400, which places it at the bottom of the screen. I've also picked a random x coordinate, which is within 100 pixels of the mouse's x coordinate. The arrow is created in those coordinates.

Next, as with most fireworks, we'll want each arrow to shoot up into the sky. That's why I've stored the mouse's position in the tx and ty variables. That's where we want the arrow to go, since it's where the user clicked the mouse. These target coordinates will be used in the onEnterFrame event to move the arrow towards that point. The code to do that is pretty straightforward:

```
this._parent["a"+ct].onEnterFrame=function(){
    // move this arrow
    this._x+=0.08*(this.tx-this._x);
    this._y+=0.08*(this.ty-this._y);
```

This is a great trick for doing smooth motions with lots of *easing out*. As you can see, _x is increased by 8 percent of the way it has to go. This happens every frame, and the distance to its target will be getting smaller and smaller. 8% of that remaining distance will subsequently also be getting smaller, which makes the motion ease out very nicely.

The next part checks whether the arrow is within one pixel of its destination. That's close enough for us, as it will take a long time for the distance to become exactly zero. If the arrow is where it should be, a number of things will happen – first, a random color value is calculated. I've created a short function to do this, which I'll explain later on. This color will be used for the explosion. Next, the variable a is assigned a random value between 15 and 50. This will be the number of sparks in the explosion. I made this random so the explosions would all look different. Finally, the sparks are created and each is placed at the location of the explosion. The color value is also passed to each spark:

```
    // check if it's at its destination yet (or almost)
    if(Math.abs(this.tx-this._x)<1&&Math.abs(this.ty-
this._y)<1){
        // if so, choose color for sparks
        this.cv=newSparkColor();
        // random amount of sparks
        this.a=Math.random()*35+15;
        // make instances of sparks
        for(this.i=0;this.i<this.a;this.i++){
            this.t="s"+ct; // temp string for instance name
            this._parent.attachMovie("spark",this.t,_root.ct);
            _root.ct++;
            this._parent[this.t]._x=this._x; // pass _x to
            ➥spark
            this._parent[this.t]._y=this._y; // pass _y to
            ➥spark
            this._parent[this.t].col=this.cv; // pass color
```

Each spark again has event code to make it move. The onLoad event sets the instance's color to the one it got from the arrow that created it. The object's size and opacity are set to random values to make the sparks look less alike:

```
// onLoad function for spark, which sets
// initial values for movement
this._parent[this.t].onLoad=function(){
  this._alpha=Math.random()*50+50;
  this._xscale=this._yscale=Math.random()*50+65;
  this.c=new Color(this);
  // set color
  this.c.setRGB(this.col);
  // random total speed
  this.sp=(Math.random()*10)+10;
  // random direction
  this.angle=(2*Math.PI)*Math.random();
  // calculate x speed
  this.xs=this.sp*Math.sin(this.angle);
  // calculate y speed
  this.ys=this.sp*-Math.cos(this.angle);
  // constant for gravity
  this.gr=0.1;
  // gravity increase per frame
  this.grInc=Math.random()*0.08+0.06;
  // frame counter
  this.c=1;
};
// fire the onLoad
this._parent[this.t].onLoad();
```

As you can see, I used a random initial speed (sp) and direction (angle) for each spark, and calculated the resulting x and y speeds using sine and cosine functions. Every spark will blast off in its own direction, with its own individual speed. This makes the shape of the explosion completely random. The spark's onEnterFrame code is used for its motion:

```
// onEnterFrame function for spark,
// which moves it along
this._parent[this.t].onEnterFrame=function(){
  this._x+=this.xs;
  this._y+=this.ys+this.gr;
  this.xs=this.xs*0.8;
  this.ys=this.ys*0.8;
  this.gr+=this.grInc;
  this._alpha=0.948*this._alpha;
  this.c++;
  if (this.c>60) {
    this.removeMovieClip();
  }
};
```

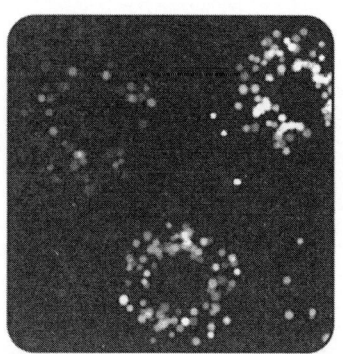

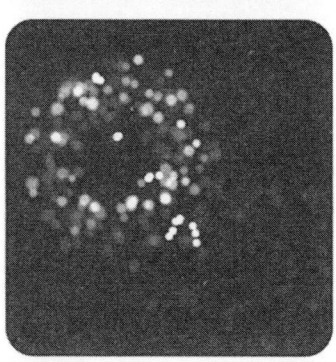

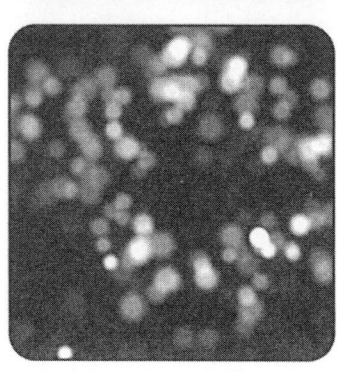

Here, xs and ys are the spark's random initial x and y speeds – these are applied to the object, and then decreased by 20% every frame to make the motion ease out. The initial speeds are quite high values to make it all look like a real explosion. They can be anywhere from 10 to 20 pixelsper frame. If a specific spark's x speed is set to 20 it starts out traveling horizontally at a speed of 600 pixels per second!

Lastly, I've added a gravity effect to the whole design – every spark is moved downwards by gr pixels every frame, where gr is initially set to 0.1 as we saw earlier. It's then increased every frame to make the sparks fall faster over time. I'm using a random number between 0.08 and 0.14 to increase this so all sparks will fall at different speeds. We need to use small numbers here to keep them from falling too fast.

At the same time, I'm decreasing the sparks' opacity. After trying different values for a while, I found that multiplying them by 0.948 makes them disappear completely in exactly 60 frames. At the end of the chunk of code above, there's a line that checks whether the counter has reached 60 frames, and should be removed.

After all this is done, we have no more need for the arrow, so we can remove it, and then we need to remember to increase the program's counter.

```
        }
        // arrow no longer needed
        this.removeMovieClip();
      }
    };
    // increase counter
    _root.ct++;
};
```

To calculate the colors for the explosions, I've written a short function. It takes no input, but returns a color value, stored in a single number. To do that I first need 3 values, representing the color's red, green and blue values. These values need to be between zero and 255. If they are all indeed 255 the color will be white, if they're 0 the color will be black. I've made sure the r, g and b values for the color are all above 115 to make sure the sparks in the explosion are not going to be darker than the background is.

Once I have these three values I put them into one number by using complicated binary stuff (actually the bitshift operator, you can look this up in Flash's documentation if you want to know more about it), and return that value. Storing a color this way is more efficient than using the regular 0xff00ff syntax, and makes for shorter code:

```
function newSparkColor() {
    r = Math.random()*140+115;
    g = Math.random()*140+115;
    b = Math.random()*140+115;
    return (r << 16)+(g << 8)+b;
}
```

All this adds up to a 1.04 KB interactive fireworks simulation. It creates a new arrow for every click – that arrow is then launched and explodes. Each of these explosions has a random color, and no two explosions are the same. The user can click anywhere and any number of times. All this is done using just one graphic symbol for both the arrow and the spark. Everything else is achieved by scripting!

Bubbles

In this next example I've tried to simulate bubbles floating through water. To achieve this I added several 3D effects. First of all, the movement of the bubbles is calculated using a three dimensional coordinate system. This is then used to change the actual screen position, and things like alpha and scale. On top of that, I've tried to simulate a *depth of field* effect, whereby only objects at a certain depth are completely in focus – objects that are nearer or further away appear to be slightly blurred. This is a cinematic effect used to emphasize the depth in a certain scene, exactly what I wanted for this movie. But more about that later, let's focus on getting the 3D movement right for now.

First of all, to give you a flavor of what we're working towards, open up `bubbles.swf` and have a play around with it.

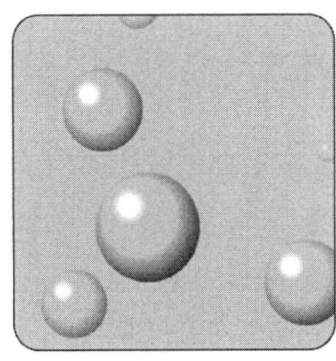

In this case I've again used an empty movie clip to create the `bubble` objects. The only difference is that this one doesn't spawn a new instance every frame. Instead, it contains code that creates bubbles randomly every once in a while. This is done to keep the amount of bubbles on the screen limited. I used randomness instead of creating new bubbles at equal intervals to make things more interesting. It's nice to have groups of bubbles fly by, and then see none at all for a while.

The first part of the code sets some constants we'll need:

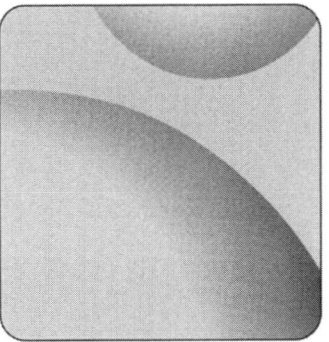

```
// set global constants
centerx = 150; // screen center x
centery = 150; // screen center y
pval = 300; // strength of perspective
c = 0; // counter to keep track of depths
```

The `centerx`, `centery`, and `pval` variables are all set on the root timeline so they can easily be accessed from anywhere in the movie. `centerx` and `centery` contain the coordinates for the movie's center and are used as the vanishing point for the perspective, while `pval` controls the strength of the perspective used in the 3D calculations. This movie is designed to run at 300 x 300 pixels.

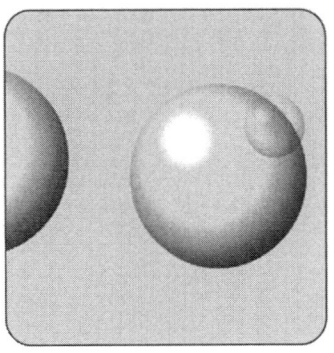

Next, we create an empty movie clip that blows bubbles:

```
// create empty movie clip to control stuff
this.createEmptyMovieClip("mc",1);
// make one instance to start with
newInst();
// onEnterFrame code for controller that randomly creates
➡bubbles
mc.onEnterFrame = function() {
    // chance of 1 in 120 that new instance is created.
    if(Math.floor(120*Math.random())==0){
        newInst();
    }
    // increase counter
    c++;
};
```

I'm using a function called newInst (defined below) to create the new instances for me. This enables me to easily make one instance right away. I've done this to make sure that something will appear as soon as possible. As you can see, the onEnterFrame event is also used to create new instances, but the chance of this happening are only 1 in 120. So statistically this should happen about once every four seconds at the movie's playback rate of 30 frames per second. To make sure that there will be at least one bubble right away I've put in the extra call to the newInst function.

This doesn't mean that this first bubble will be visible right away. In fact, all bubbles are created off screen and, as soon as they're created, they'll start floating upwards. I've again used sine waves to create nice, fluid motions:

```
// function to create new instance and attach event scripts
function newInst() {
    this.attachMovie("bubble","b"+c,c+10);
    this["b"+c].onLoad = function() {
        // hide the bubble for now
        this._visible = false;
        // set initial values
        this.bx = 300*Math.random()-150; // base x coord for
        ➡sine
        this.y = 400; // initial y coord
        this.bz = 300*Math.random()-150; // base z coord for
        ➡sine
        // randomize counter for sine
        this.cnt = 5000*(2*Math.PI)*Math.random();
        this.wl = 8; // wavelength for sine calculations
```

```
        this.amp = 120; // amplitude for sine wave
        this.ysp = -1; // speed y direction (minus for upward
        ➡motion)
    };
    // start the onLoad script manually
    this["b"+c].onLoad();
```

The onLoad event sets up the variables needed for the motion. Many of these are old friends from previous examples. I've added a special counter called cnt to use as input for the sine function. ysp is a constant value that's used for the upward motion. I've set it to -1 to have the bubbles move upwards at an average speed of 1 pixel per frame. The actual speed will depend greatly on how far away from the camera the object is.

Next, let's get those bubbles moving:

```
    // the onEnterFrame code moves the ‹bubble
    this["b"+c].onEnterFrame = function(){
        // change the x,y,z coords
        this.x=this.bx+(this.amp*Math.sin(this.cnt/this.wl));
        this.y+=this.ysp;

this.z=this.bz+((this.amp/2)*Math.sin(this.cnt/this.wl));
        // increase counter on which sine and cosine are based
        this.cnt+=0.05;
        // call the function that applies 3D effects to this
        ➡bubble
        m3d(this,this.x,this.y,this.z);
        // check whether this instance is off screen, if so
        ➡delete it
        if(this._y<-200){
          this.removeMovieClip();
        }
        // now that it's in place, let the bubble show
        this._visible=true;
    };
}
```

The first part above calculates the new values for x, y and z. I've used a sine wave in both the x and z directions. This means the bubbles will not only sway sideways, but also towards and from us. I've made the amplitude in the z direction half of what the x amplitude is to make sure the effect is not too strong. For the upward motion I'm using a constant speed.

Once we have the new x, y, and z values, the m3d function (again, defined below) is called to move the bubble to the newly calculated position. I've added a little check to see whether the object has left the screen. The bubbles can get quite big, especially those that are close to the 'virtual camera', so I've checked this by quite a large margin. Only when the object's y coordinate has become smaller than -200 (that is, 200 pixels above the movie's 'view port') is it considered to have left the screen. If that's the case, the bubble is burst!

The m3d function does the actual work of displaying that 3D movement on the screen. It takes the *virtual* x, y and z coordinates and calculates at what position each bubble should be placed on the screen to make it look like they're in that 3D spot. It also sets the bubble's alpha and scale to make bubbles that are further away appear smaller and more transparent. Here's what this important function looks like:

```
// this function does the 3d stuff
function m3d(obj,x,y,z){
    // calculate perspective value
    ps=_root.pval/(_root.pval+z);
    // change the object's properties
    with(obj){
        // set 2d coords
        _x=centerx+(obj.x*ps);
        _y=centery+(obj.y*ps);
        // set scale and alpha
        _xscale=100-(z/2);
        _yscale=100-(z/2);
        _alpha=100-(z/2);
    }
}
```

I'm not a real trigonometry wizard, so I've borrowed some 3D code from an example by Brandon Williams (thanks Brandon!). As you can see, the distance of the object to the camera, z, is used in calculating every aspect of its appearance. I've divided z by 2 when calculating the alpha and scale. The value of z is initially somewhere between -150 and 150, so if I subtracted that from 100, the alpha could be negative and the object would disappear completely. This way most objects are visible even if they're really close or very far away. I usually play with these numbers until the result looks just right.

So far we've only used the position, size, and transparency of the objects to simulate depth. As I told you earlier, I wanted to simulate depth of field as well. Take a look at bubbles2.fla to see that the way I've done this is by setting a variable called f (for focal point) at the first frame of the movie:

```
f = -50; // initial focus
```

Bubbles with a z coordinate that exactly matches f will be completely in focus. The bigger the difference between a bubble's z coordinate and f the more blurred I want it to look.

Since there's no *object._blur* property in Flash MX, I had to come up with a way to make the bubbles appear blurry without any pixel-based calculations. Bitmap-based graphics programs usually blur images by having each pixel adopt a little of the color values of the pixels surrounding it, but obviously this can't be done in Flash because it's vector-based. I had to use another trick.

What I came up with is to have not one, but eight separate bubble graphics in each object. All eight are set to 15 percent alpha, and if you put them all exactly on top of each other, it'll look almost exactly like one regular bubble. If you vary the size of each of the eight instances very slightly, the bubble appears to become blurred.

So instead of attaching a bubble to the main timeline directly, I'm now creating an empty movie clip, and putting eight bubbles into that one. Here's what the modified newInst function looks like:

```
function newInst(){
    this.createEmptyMovieClip("b"+c,c+10);
    this["b"+c].onLoad = function(){
        // hide the bubble for now
        this._visible=false;
        // set initial values
        this.bx=300*Math.random()-150; // base x coord for sine
        this.y=400; // initial y coord
        this.bz=300*Math.random()-150; // base z coord for sine
        // randomize counter for sine
        this.cnt=5000*(2*Math.PI)*Math.random();
        this.wl=8; // wavelength for sine calculations
        this.amp=120; // amplitude for sine wave
        this.ysp=-1; // speed y direction (upwards)
        // create the blurring-instances
        for(i=1;i<9;i++){
            this.attachMovie("bubble","d"+i,i+10);
            this["d"+i]._alpha=15;
        }
        this.attachMovie("button","button",20);
        this["button"].onRelease = function(){
            this._parent._parent.f=this._parent.z;
        };
    }
    // run the onLoad script manually
    this["b"+c].onLoad();
```

This creates the empty movie clip and eight instances of `bubble` within it. I've also added a round invisible button of the same size to the objects. I wanted to make the movie interactive by letting the user focus on a specific bubble. All that the `onRelease` event for the button does is set the global variable `f` to the z coordinate of that bubble. The result will be that the bubble that was clicked will become completely in focus. This will also affect all the bubbles in the screen since their blurriness depends on `f`.

Next I needed to change the sizes of the bubble instances slightly to make them appear blurry. First, the `bl` value is derived from where the object is relative to the *focus* of the movie – so `bl` determines the strength of the blur effect. Next, I loop through all the instances to change their size. As you can see I've included the index `i` in this calculation to make the effect increase at higher instance numbers. This way the first instance has its size set to 100 percent plus `bl` times 1, the second instance is set to 100 percent plus `bl` times 2, and so on:

```
// the onEnterFrame code moves the bubble
this["b"+c].onEnterFrame = function(){
    // change the x,y,z coords
    this.x=this.bx+(this.amp*Math.sin(this.cnt/this.wl));
    this.y+=this.ysp;

this.z=this.bz+((this.amp/2)*Math.sin(this.cnt/this.wl));
    // increase counter on which sine and cosine are based
    this.cnt+=0.05;
    // call the function that applies 3D effects to this
bubble
    m3d(this,this.x,this.y,this.z);
    // set blur value and change instances accordingly
    this.bl=Math.abs((this.z-f)/40);
    for(i=1;i<9;i++) {
       this["d"+i]._xscale=100+this.bl*i;
       this["d"+i]._yscale=100+this.bl*i;
    }
    // check whether this instance is off screen, if so
delete it
    if(this._y<-200){
       this.removeMovieClip();
    }
    // now that it's in place, let's show the bubble
    this._visible=true;
};
}
```

Note that this version of the movie is still just over 1 KB in size. Like the earlier examples, all it does is make a number of instances of a single graphic. The trick is in what you do with those instances. In this case adding 3D animation to them has resulted in quite an interesting visual effect. I could have animated instances of the bubble using a regular timeline and keyframe animation, but in that case getting nice smooth motions would have been hard to do. The animation would also have looped. Sure, I could have used several movie clips all looping at different intervals, but still you would have probably noticed the same bubble floating by every once in a while. Using ActionScript I've made it completely random!

This *depth of field* effect is particularly hard to process for the Flash player. Every bubble now consists of eight layers with a lot of use of the alpha property. Setting the quality to low makes it look awful, so the only way to get decent performance is to display it at something like 200 x 200 pixels.

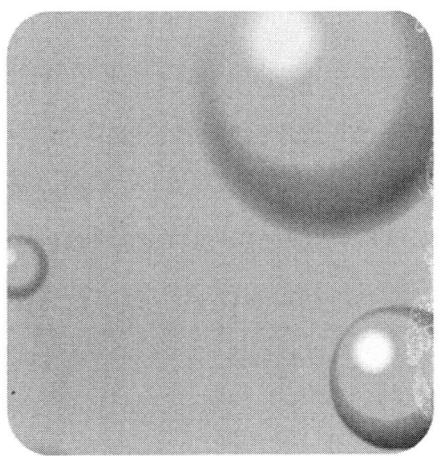

1

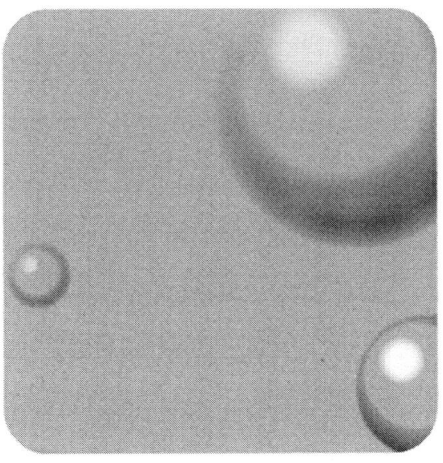

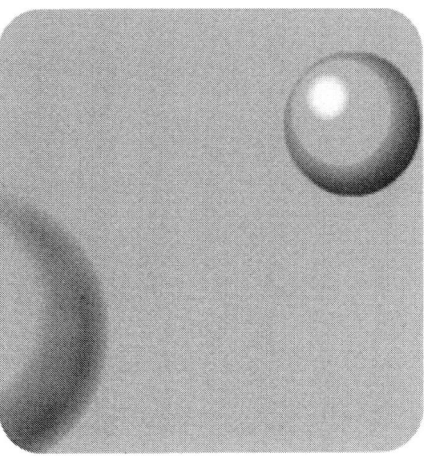

3D effects

Take a look at the file `outlines.swf`:

Having one collective outline around multiple circles is quite easy to do in Flash. Let's say you want a black outline around several white circles, like in this example. All you basically need to do is place white circles at high levels, and black ones at lower levels. Next you make sure the movement of the bottom black ones matches that of the top white ones, and make the black ones a little larger in size than the white ones are. Because the white circles are on higher levels and they're all the same color, they'll seem to form one shape when they overlap. The same goes for the black ones. Is that clear? Well, hopefully it will become clear after we look at the relevant code.

I decided it would be fun to use some 3D for this effect too, in an attempt to create an interesting mix of 3D and 2D. What I did was make the outlined circles move along 3D paths. The perspective makes the balls smaller as they move away from us, but the width of the outline remains the same to keep an overall 2D feel to the movie. Lastly, I wanted the 3D movement to be controlled by the mouse pointer's position, to incorporate some user interactivity.

Again, I used an empty movie clip to do all the calculations. All the circles are *remote controlled* from this one 'motor' that drives the movie. Here's what the code looks like (see also frame 1 of outlines.fla):

```
this.createEmptyMovieClip("mc",1);
mc.onLoad=function() {
    // some constant values
    lw = 20; // thickness of outlines
    centerx = 150; // screen center x
    centery = 150; // screen center y
    // constant value needed for angle translations
    pf = Math.PI/180;
    pval = 300; // strength of perspective
    // array of 3D points (x,y,z coords) - 'modeling' done
    ➥here
    p3d=new Array( {x:-80,y:-80,z:-80},
            ➥ {x:80,y:-80,z:-80},
            ➥ {x:80,y:80,z:-80},
            ➥ {x:-80,y:80,z:-80},
            ➥ {x:-80,y:-80,z:80},
            ➥ {x:80,y:-80,z:80},
            ➥ {x:80,y:80,z:80},
            ➥ {x:-80,y:80,z:80},
            ➥ {x:0,y:0,z:-113},
            ➥ {x:0,y:0,z:113},
            ➥ {x:-113,y:0,z:0},
            ➥ {x:113,y:0,z:0},
            ➥ {x:0,y:-113,z:0},
            ➥ {x:0,y:113,z:0});
    // array for screen positions (empty for now)
    p2d=new Array();
    for(i=0;i<p3d.length;i++) {
        p2d[i]={x:0,y:0};
    }
```

The coordinates I put in the p3d array represent 14 points located almost exactly on a sphere. I rounded the coordinates to the nearest integer number (I calculated these numbers by hand). By altering these coordinates, the balls can be put in all sorts of locations. Or you can make more, by simply adding to the array. Every element in the array consists of an x, y, and z coordinate. These store the object's position in the *virtual* 3D space. The center of that space has (0, 0, 0) as coordinates, and objects that are close to it will appear in the center of the screen.

The p2d array is where I keep the actual screen coordinates for all the objects. As you can see I've used p3d.length in the for loop to create an array with the same number of entries. Each entry in the p2d array consists of only an x and y coordinate, since it is used to store the 2D location of the objects. Every program cycle, the values in the p3d array are translated into 2D screen coordinates by some tricky trigonometry code, and stored in p2d. Even though there's quite a bit of math involved, the movie doesn't slow down very much – math calculations are handled quite well by the Flash Player.

The next thing we'll need to do is create the instances of the black and white circles. For this effect to work we'll need the four circles that make up one ball to be at distinctly different levels. That's controlled by the j variable. As you can see I'm using a nested loop here to create the instances:

```
// make instances of circles
for(i=0;i<p2d.length;i++){
    for(j=0;j<4;j++){

this.attachMovie("c","c"+i+"_"+j,i+(p2d.length*(j+1)));
        // color every even numbered circle black
        if(j%2==0){
            col=new Color(this["c"+i+"_"+j]);
            col.setRGB(0);
        }
    }
};
// start the onLoad code manually
mc.onLoad();
```

For every element in the p3d array, four instances of the c movie clip are created. The first one to be created will be called c0_0, which means it represents the first element of the p3d array, and it will be the bottom-most one. In the next loop, j will have increased to 1, and the instance created, c0_1, will be placed on a higher level than the first one. It still represents element number 0 from our array of points. This continues until all four instances are created, each on a higher level than the previous one. This process itself is then repeated to produce all the other balls, ending with the creation of c13_3, since there are 14 elements in p3d and I chose to create four circles for each ball.

The movie clip from which all objects are instantiated contains nothing more than a simple white circle – take a look in the Library of outlines.fla if you don't believe me. That's really all the graphics we'll need! Every even numbered circle, for instance c3_2, is then colored black, so we have alternating black and white ones. Since all the number 3 circles are now on top of everything else, they'll seem to merge when they overlap. The black circles are beneath them, so we'll only see them if they are bigger than the top ones. This is done in the last portion of the onEnterFrame code. First we'll need to connect the 3D rotation to the mouse's position:

```
// the onEnterFrame event moves things along
mc.onEnterFrame = function() {
    // set rotation by mouse pointer position
    xrot=(_root._ymouse-centery)/30;
    yrot=(_root._xmouse-centerx)/30;
    zrot=0;
```

Here, xrot, yrot, and zrot will control the rotation of our 3D coordinate system – xrot controls the rotation around the x-axis, a horizontal line through the center of the screen. This means that the objects will be moving up and down, as well as towards us and away from us, but not along the x-axis. This is why I made xrot depend on the mouse's y position, and vice versa. Unfortunately the mouse moves in a 2D field, so it's not possible to change all three variables using the mouse. I've set zrot to zero.

The next part of the code is an adaptation of a 3D engine by Brandon Williams. It converts the numbers in our p3d array to 2D, coordinated with the perspective calculated in. These are stored in the p2d array. The pval variable I declared in the onLoad portion of the code controls how strong the perspective will be. Setting it to 100 will give you an extreme wide-angle view of the objects. Higher values will give you a more modest perspective. I've set it to 300 in this case:

```
/********** start of 3D code **********/
// calculate sines
sina=Math.sin(xrot*pf);
cosa=Math.cos(xrot*pf);
sinb=Math.sin(yrot*pf);
cosb=Math.cos(yrot*pf);
sinc=Math.sin(zrot*pf);
cosc=Math.cos(zrot*pf);
// calculate 2d positions
for(i=0;i<p3d.length;i++){
    // apply x rotation
    rx1=p3d[i].x;
    ry1=p3d[i].y*cosa+p3d[i].z*-sina;
    rz1=p3d[i].y*sina+p3d[i].z*cosa;
    // apply y rotation
    rx2=rx1*cosb+rz1*sinb;
    ry2=ry1;
    rz2=rx1*-sinb+rz1*cosb;
    // apply z rotation
    rx3=rx2*cosc+ry2*-sinc;
    ry3=rx2*sinc+ry2*cosc;
    rz3=rz2;
    // set p3d value to rotated ones
    p3d[i].x=rx3;
    p3d[i].y=ry3;
    p3d[i].z=rz3;
    // calculate perspective
    psf=pval/(pval+rz3);
    tx=rx3*psf;
    ty=ry3*psf;
    // set coords in p2d array for screen positions
    p2d[i].x=centerx+tx;
    p2d[i].y=centery-ty;
}
/********** end of 3D code **********/
```

Once all the 3D stuff is done, I again loop through all the circles and set their positions and sizes. Setting the position of the objects is easy, but we need a little calculation to get the size right. The size depends on the object's z coordinate. The further away it is, the smaller it has to become. The simplest code to set the width, for example, would be `_width = maxsize - p3d[i].z`.

Since the z coordinate can be up to 113, I found that I also needed to divide them by five to get the effect right. Furthermore, I had to add the outline width to the size of circles. `lw` represents this width and was set in the `onLoad` event. We can use the `j` variable to do this, but simply adding `j*lw` to the sizes would make the top one the biggest, so we need to reverse the order by using `3-j`. For the top circles, `3-j` equals 0, so no extra size will be added. The smaller `j` is, the bigger the circle will become. I could've made `j` run up to a variable instead of 4, and make as many outlines as I wanted. I personally found the effect most striking using the four circles:

```
// move the instances
for(i=0;i<p2d.length;i++){
    for(j=0;j<4;j++){
        this["c","c"+i+"_"+j]._x=p2d[i].x;
        this["c","c"+i+"_"+j]._y=p2d[i].y;
        this["c","c"+i+"_"+j]._width=(65-p3d[i].z/5)+(lw*(3-j));
        this["c","c"+i+"_"+j]._height=(65-p3d[i].z/5)+(lw*(3-j));
    }
}
};
```

The whole movie, which basically consists only of the code and one circle, boils down to a 1.03KB movie. Not bad at all!

Spirograph

In all the previous examples, I've used at least a tiny little pre-drawn graphic to create effects. However, since we're trying to get file sizes down to their bare minimum, let's avoid using any pre-built graphics at all. Take a look at `spirograph.swf` – this is basically as simple a project as possible. The associated FLA file has only about 30 lines of script in the first frame, and absolutely nothing in its Library. Take a look at the stunning result:

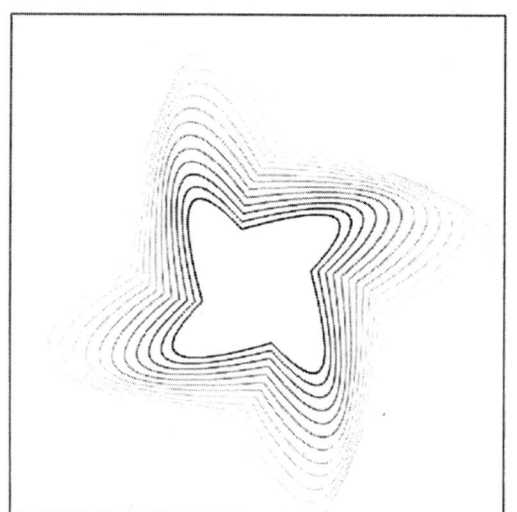
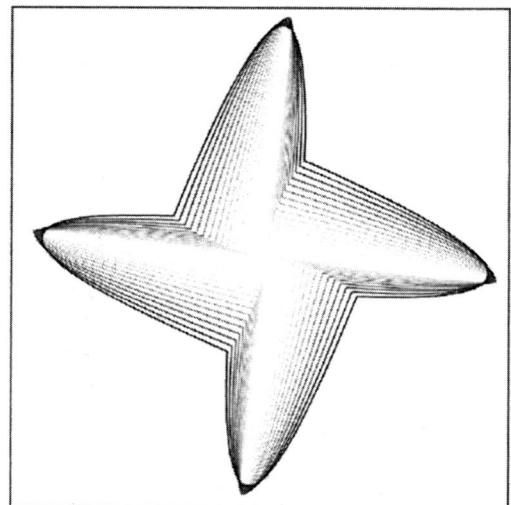
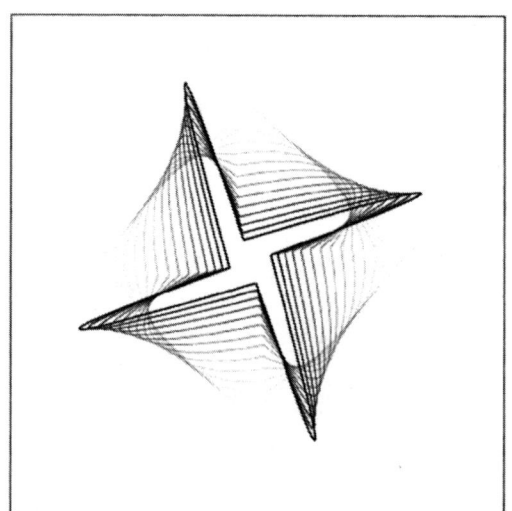
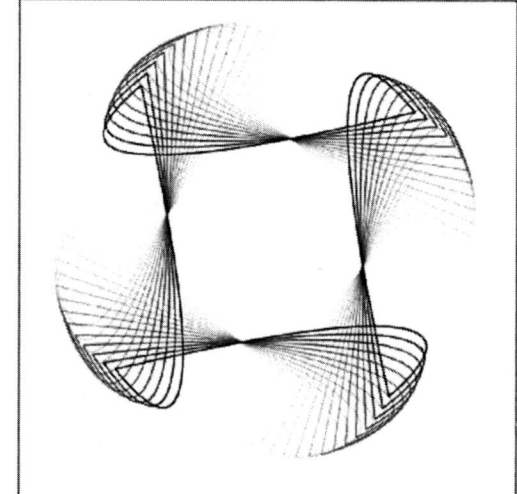

This movie originates from some experiments I was working on with scripted circles. What I basically did was take four points along a circle's outline, and use the `curveTo` method of the ActionScript drawing API to connect them.

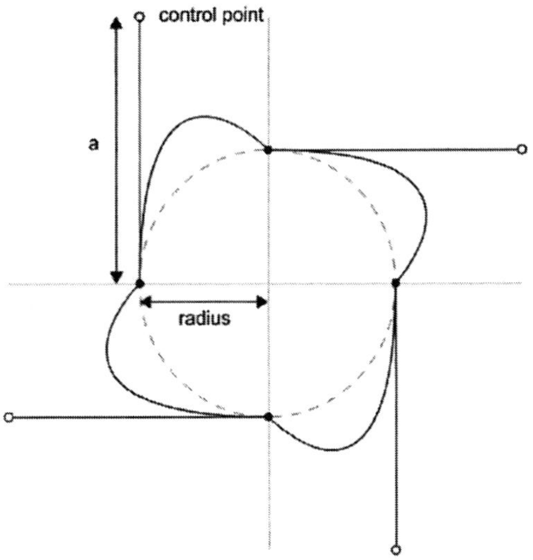

control point

a

radius

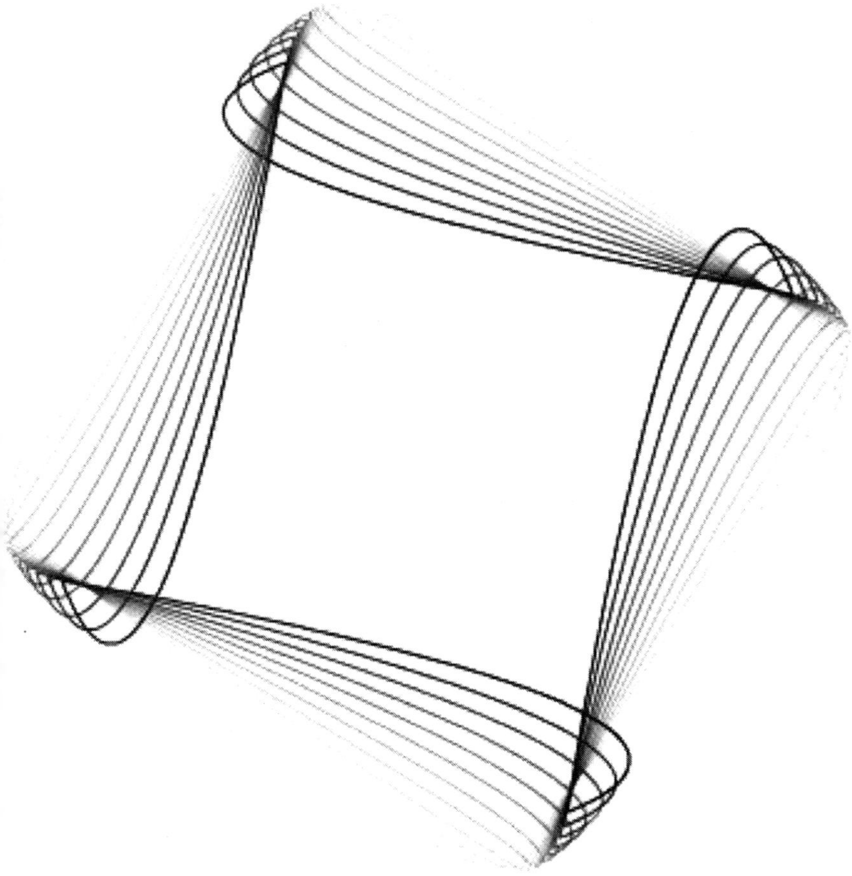

I made the coordinates of the control points of these curves depend on variables, so I could change them while searching for the perfect circle. I soon got distracted, however, when I noticed that changing these variables over time resulted in some very nice eye candy! Eventually my little experiment evolved into the following code (see also spirograph.fla):

```
// create empty movieclip to control mc
this.createEmptyMovieClip("mc",1);
c=0; // counter
// onEnterFrame script which creates new shapes
mc.onEnterFrame = function(){
    // create new empty movieclip
    this.createEmptyMovieClip("i"+c,c+10);
    with(this["i"+c]){
        // set this mc's position and rotation
        _x=200;
        _y=200;
        _rotation=360*Math.sin(c/103);
        // calculate new control point distance
        a=100+200*Math.sin(c/19);
        // calculate new radius
        r=50+50*-Math.sin(c/11);
        // draw the shape
        lineStyle(0,0,100);
        moveTo(0,-r);
        curveTo(a,-r,r,0);
        curveTo(r,a,0,r);
        curveTo(-a,r,-r,0);
        curveTo(-r,-a,0,-r);
    }
    // onEnterFrame script that fades out and removes the mc
    this["i"+c].onEnterFrame = function() {
        this._alpha-=0.2*this._alpha;
        if(this._alpha<=1){
            this.removeMovieClip();
        }
    };
    //increase counter
    c++;
};
```

The initial `onEnterFrame` event in this program creates a new empty movie clip in which to draw. It then places that movie clip at the center of the movie, and sets its rotation based on the sine value of the movie's counter, `c`. Remember that the outcome of the sine function has a value between `-1` and `1` at all times, so I had to multiply it by `360` to create a full 360 degree rotation. As you can see I'm using pretty weird values here as wavelengths for the sine waves: `103`, `19`, and `11` are prime numbers. Since these are not divisible by anything but themselves, this will let the movie run without repeating itself very often.

The `a` variable is used to place the control points in the `curveTo` actions, and it's basically the only thing left over from my original experiment to create a circle. It controls how far the control points protrude from the circle, and its value can be anywhere from -100 to 300, based on the sine of `c`. Next, `r` stands for radius, and controls the distance of the four points mentioned earlier to the center of the movie clip. Again, having this controlled by a sine value will make the shape seem to open up and close down very smoothly.

The code that actually draws the shape is pretty straightforward – it uses the `a` and `r` variables, and draws the curves between the points.

To make each new shape fade out and disappear eventually, I've added an `enterFrame` event to every new instance, which does this for us.

Note that this final size of this SWF is only 416 bytes – I love scripting in Flash MX! Well, I hope you've enjoyed this tour of some of my low calorie generative experiments. Now you should be ready to go out and create them for yourself!

1

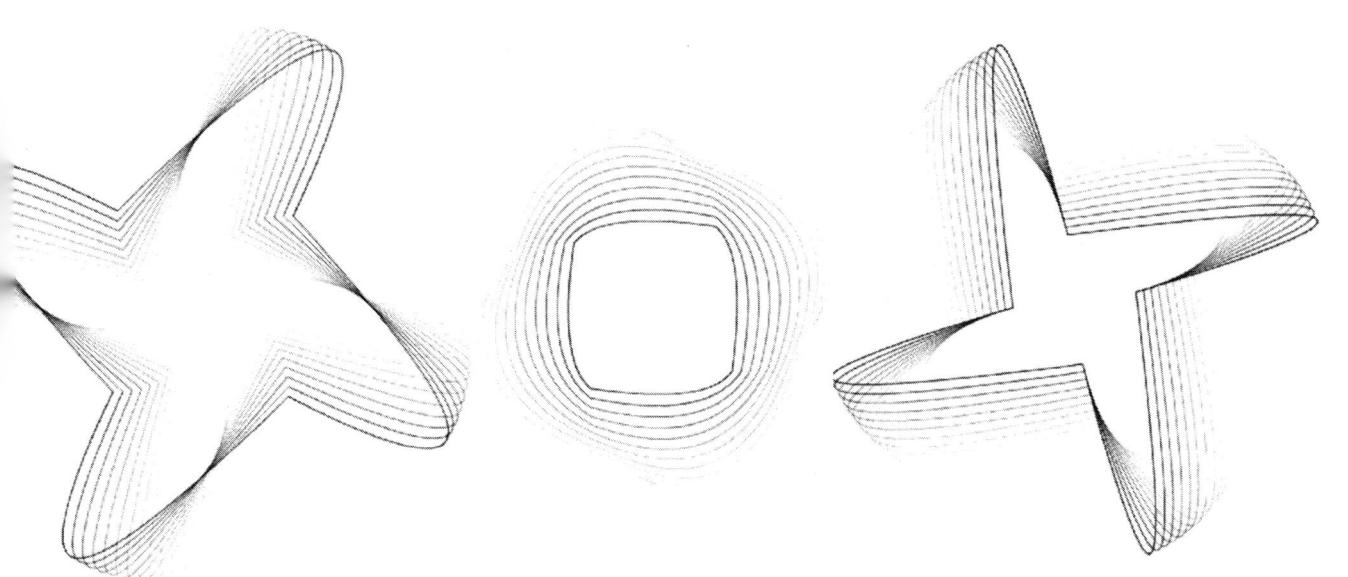

2 A BYTE-SIZE BITMAP GALLERY

CODY LINDLEY

There are a multitude of reasons that you might want to display pictures on your Flash site. Graphical elements add color and interest to your online content, whatever its subject matter, and while Flash's vector graphic capabilities are impressive, there are times when only a bitmap will do. What's more, there are many sites that aim to sell a product that the user needs to see before they would buy. In some cases, you may even be designing a site whose main purpose is to display or sell photos or other artwork. However, too often in Flash, using bitmapped images poses a problem in terms of bandwidth, as a few pictures can push the file size of your project through the roof. Accordingly, this chapter aims to show you how you can successfully produce Flash files and bitmaps that will overcome the bandwidth limitations that may have plagued your projects in the past.

Over the last couple of years I've spent numerous days, nights, and weekends, working at improving my Flash skills and learning how to optimize my designs. That's not to say I consider myself a master in these matters, but I have discovered some effective ways to get round the problems inherent in designing for the 56KB modem user, and these methods should stand you in good stead when you find yourself in this situation. I've logged in the hours on this subject, so you don't have to!

The very fact that you've purchased this book suggests that you've already started to ask the question that all Flash designers eventually ask themselves – how long will this Flash file take to download? A novice Flash user might well be guilty of being so blown away by the visually impressive effects that you can create in Flash, that they wait until the end of the project to ask this crucial question. In fact, that was the path I followed when I first started working with Flash. The good news is that as you gain experience of developing sites for the web, eventually every project will start by considering who the intended user is, and at what *bit rate* this user is connecting to the web . Even though broadband is starting to become more widespread, all too often the answer is that our target audience is mainly standard home users with a dial-up modem connection. So for the foreseeable future, this issue is not going to go away – we need to design with file size considerations at the front of our minds.

Pondering the image format

You can import a number of different file types into Flash, but if you have ever considered the question of download times, then you might know that, in terms of purpose or compression, all image formats are not created equal. So first of all, let's quickly review a few of the more common image file types you may want to incorporate into your Flash designs.

JPEGs

The JPEG is a bitmap image format – essentially the information for the color to be displayed on the screen is saved for every individual pixel. The creators of the JPEG format had one purpose in mind when creating this compression type – to compress images that are photographic (millions of colors) in quality, or have gradient-like color transitions. JPEGs were specifically designed to allow pictures with small file sizes to be delivered over the web, email, and FTP.

Because of this, the format is a **lossy** compression, meaning it will lose image quality when compressed. The amount of compression you apply, and therefore the amount of quality loss, is up to you. It is the best compression system for these specific types of images, so it is used by Flash to process bitmaps. A few things to remember about JPEGs are:

- Saving an image as a JPEG will always cause a loss of image quality. They lose quality every time they are opened, edited and then saved. Because of this, it's better to do your editing in a *lossless* format, and wait until you are happy with your image before saving it as a JPEG.

- Graphics programs do not have a standard setting for image compression, so the amount of compression you apply needs to be done on an image-by-image basis, with a bit of trial and error. For instance, a 30% quality JPEG from Photoshop and one from Fireworks will not necessarily come out the same.

- JPEGs require more processing power than a GIF file, so you should only use them for the image types they were designed for.

- JPEG images do not support transparency.

GIFs

Another commonly used image type for web compression is the GIF. Unlike the JPEG format, it was designed to compress images made up of solid color blocks. It makes the image file size smaller by saving the color information as data about groups of pixels, rather than for each individual pixel. They are commonly used for illustrations, logos, pixel art, and images with a transparent layer. An important thing to remember about a GIF is that when compressed its quality is **lossless**, meaning it does not lose image quality when compressed. It will, however, shrink in size when colors are removed, so we do this until we can no longer live with the end results. Again, we need to consider both file size and image quality.

If you need to create images that consist of blocky colors, you might well be better to consider creating them with the tools available in Flash, or another vector-based program (more on this later). But there are times, such as when you are designing a company website where the logo is already saved in GIF format, where you may need to import GIFs into Flash.

However, making elements that would normally benefit from the GIF compression format into vectors is a great way of cutting down file size, especially as you can then convert them to symbols. So think carefully about whether you really need that bitmap!

2

PNGs

I'm going say something that might shock you. Are you ready? Unless you are working with assets already created and saved by someone else, never import a GIF into Flash, or a JPEG for that matter. OK, calm down and let me explain... Flash will allow you to import PNG files, and I suggest you take advantage of this. The PNG format marries the attributes of the GIF compression and the JPEG compression together to create one very robust format. The PNG will allow a transparent layer, lossless compression, and lends itself kindly to images with millions of colors. Obviously, if an image starts out as a low quality GIF or JPEG, saving it as a PNG won't improve the quality of the image, but where this situation can be avoided, it should be. Need I say more? Well, I suppose you need to know *why* I only import PNGs into Flash.

Why import a lossy image into Flash, only to then have Flash compress it again, and by doing so incorporate another round of lossy compression? It's often been said that you should bring JPEGs into Flash at the highest quality possible. It's good thinking, but if you're going to do that, I say bring the highest quality image possible into Flash, and that isn't a JPEG. Once the lossless image is in the Flash environment, then we can start thinking about a lossy compression for it.

So, I import PNGs into Flash, and Flash then uses the JPEG format to compress these images upon publishing. PNGs in, JPEGs out! The secret to a small Flash file that contains bitmaps is in the compression controls available to us within Flash, not the compression that takes place before we import an image into Flash.

General rules for using bitmaps in flash

It's hard to have a discussion about JPEGs and Flash without touching on some general rules for using bitmaps with Flash. I wish I had some magical answer for decreasing the file size of a Flash file containing JPEGs. But since I have no wand and I know no magic, we're stuck with the cold hard reality that all Flash designers face every day.

The points I am about to highlight are just *general guidelines* for maintaining the smallest file size possible:

- Use bitmaps sparingly.

- All images should be imported into Flash as PNG files, and compressed using the JPEG format.

- Turn off smoothing for all JPEGs in the Properties panel, that is unless you like choppy animations.

- Don't resize an image to be larger in Flash than its original size when it was imported.

- Avoid animating a bitmap with the timeline.

- Compress JPEGs in Flash as small as possible while still being able to live with the image quality.

- Make everything a Library symbol, especially repetitive images.

- The actual dimensions of a Flash movie should be kept as small as possible.

- Try animating a mask or a vector graphic over the top of a bitmap, rather than the bitmap itself.

- Keep the amount of key frames that contain bitmaps to a minimum.

- Spread images over several frames. Don't line them up in one frame.

These well-known guidelines will help you get smaller Flash files and more fluent animation sequences, but don't be afraid to break some rules. What I mean is this: don't look at these as the definitive rules of bitmaps and Flash. Re-read the list and figure out ways to overcome the limitations. Fight the system! Indeed, designers break these rules all the time, and succeed at discovering a new process for overcoming bandwidth limitations in Flash. In fact, in an example towards the end of this chapter I'm going to show you how to happily break the first rule mentioned above – *use bitmaps sparingly* – I bet you can't wait!

Using JPEGs in the Library

Although with Flash MX we are given the ability to dynamically load JPEGs into our SWFs, there are times when you might want to use them from within your Flash environment. I still maintain that, where you can, it's a better idea to import PNGs at a high quality – from Macromedia Fireworks use PNG-32 and from Adobe Photoshop use PNG-24. Flash will handle the rest. But of course, there will be times when you need to use images that have been made by someone else and already saved as JPEGs.

JPEG is the default compression format for all images imported into Flash unless otherwise changed in the Library. This is good to know – if no changes are made from the Library at least your images are being compressed. What you need to know is just how much compression is being implemented. To answer this question let's open Flash and view the Publish Settings, accessed through the File menu:

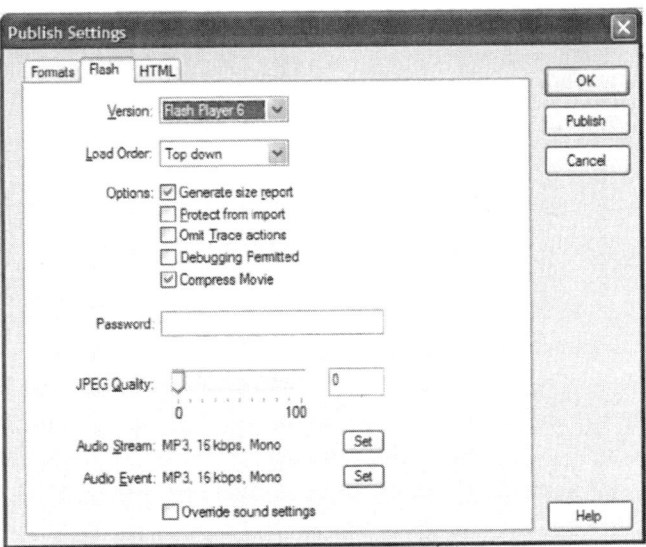

Located at the bottom of this window is a value slider that controls the compression applied to all images imported into Flash. A low percentage will add more compression to all bitmaps, and reduce file size. However, remember that while you might be reducing the overall file size of an entire Flash movie by compressing all imported images, the quality of the images is being sacrificed.

This feature is nice, but lacks options when you want to compress one particular JPEG more than another. The bottom line is that it's not the best answer for reducing overall file size. It's one answer, but you're reading this book looking for the best answer. For the most part, I rarely worry about this slider, and set the compression for my images through the Library on a case-by-case basis. This allows me to cut away every kilobyte possible on each individual image and, in most cases, reduce my overall file size significantly.

In a new Flash movie, open up the Library by hitting the F11 key. Import a few JPEGs into your movie, just so we can have a look at the settings:

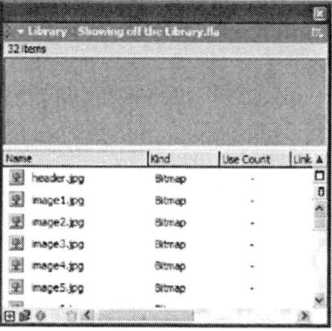

Looking at the Library will show you all the images that have been imported in to Flash. The images will appear in the Library by default when imported, or pasted from the clipboard, into Flash. By double-clicking on the image icon in the Library, you will be able to edit the properties of the bitmap:

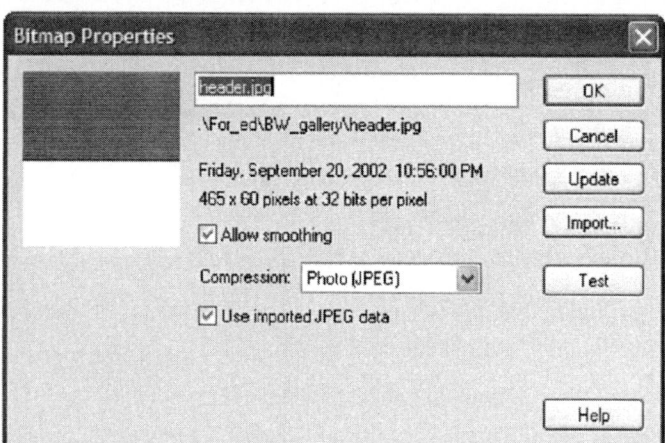

You can place the mouse over the image in the upper left-hand corner of the window and move the image around in this box for more accurate compression views.

For the most part, the first thing I do is uncheck Allow smoothing – this is particularly important if bitmaps are moving around the stage. Next, I will make sure the compression drop-down is set to JPEG. We need a lossy compression in order to shave off bytes from the file size. A lossless format may allow us to reduce the file size, but not by as much.

Next, make sure you uncheck the box Use imported JPEG data, or on a PC Use Document Default Quality, and by doing so a quality setting will appear. By un-checking this box you are overriding the compression settings for the entire Flash movie – the Publish Settings we saw earlier.

This is where things get a little arbitrary. At this point enter a Quality percentage between 0 and 100, 100 being the smallest amount of compression and 0 being all the compression that can possibly be applied to an image in Flash. Only you can decide how much compression you can live with. Make sure you balance this decision with the overall file size of the Flash movie and frame rate. I like to start at 60 percent and work my way down until the image quality is unacceptable, then use the last bearable setting.

You can use the Test button to check how the image is looking, but it's always a good idea to exit this window and view your image in the context of the whole Flash movie to make sure you can live with the quality of the animation sequence, or whatever, that you've created using the bitmap. You will find that a static bitmap will take less compression than an animated bitmap, as motion is more forgiving. An image that is standing still on the stage of a Flash movie is like a painting on a wall for critiquing.

I suppose we should have a discussion about tracing bitmaps. I really don't have much to say about this issue, as I think it's a design issue rather than one of compression. Personally, I trace a bitmap for an artistic look, or to use as a fill, and if I have to resize an image to larger than its original size when it was imported. Other than that, I really haven't found any particular benefit to tracing an image. If you've heard people saying that tracing a bitmap reduces the file size, well they're right. The other part of that conversation is that a traced image has a completely different image quality to a JPEG. So although tracing has its uses, it doesn't really help us when dealing with photograph-quality images.

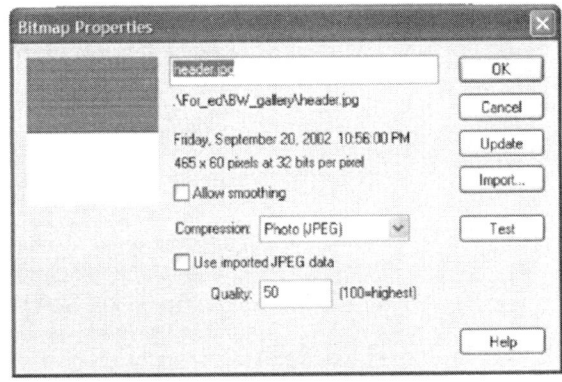

Bitmap image

Vector image (traced bitmap)

2

Dynamic loading capabilities

Using the dynamic loading capability of Flash MX to load JPEGs on-the-fly is undoubtedly the best way of dramatically reducing file size within Flash, and download times for the user.

Before Flash MX, we loaded external JPEGs by loading an external SWF file with a compressed JPEG embedded within the file. This was done because we wanted the main, or index, Flash movie to load very quickly and not get bogged down with bitmaps. The hope was that the user would wait around for these images to load when requested and thus break a huge Flash file of bitmaps into a few smaller SWF files that could be downloaded on demand. In fact, not much has changed with Flash MX. The idea is similar, and we are limited to pretty much the same restraints, but the process is easier. We no longer have to embed the JPEG in an SWF to break up their download. We simply download them straight into the Flash player for use with our movie.

If you haven't thought about it quite yet, just imagine what this means for backend programmers. Macromedia has pretty much given us the ability to create and manage our own dynamic designs. Incorporate this idea with some of the powerful features of ActionScript and (wow!) we have a genuine solution for updating the content and images of entire websites with a single application – Flash MX.

The drawback when it comes to dynamically loaded JPEGs is that everything I just told you about optimizing images in Flash... forget about it – none of it will work. In fact, if you take the JPEG compression slider and move it to zero in the export options it won't affect the image quality of an externally loaded JPEG in the slightest. That means the compression is left up to the image editing program of choice, which actually brings us a certain amount of clarity and simplicity. In this scenario, all of your fiddling around with compression should be done *before* the image is used by Flash.

Dynamically loading a JPEG

For the most part, loading a JPEG dynamically is not much different to loading a SWF file into a Flash movie. You need to know the name of the item you want to load, the path to the item, and the level you want to load the item to.

You can, if you wish, use the `loadMovie` method on the root timeline to load a JPEG. If you choose to do this, the bitmap will default to the x and y coordinates (0,0). These coordinates place a static image in the top left hand corner of the Flash stage. This is not particularly revolutionary, and it is extremely limited in its uses.

A much better idea is to load the JPEG into an *empty* movie clip placed on a particular level. You can then give the image a name and a home. Once there, you can use the name of its home (that is, the name of the newly created movie clip) to manipulate the image with ActionScript. Obviously, this gives us all sorts of options.

Calling the `createEmptyMovieClip` method on the root timeline will provide my image with a home, identified here by the name of `hold_my_image`:

```
this.createEmptyMovieClip("hold_my_image",1);
```

This creates a new movie clip on level 1. Then, I just tell the new movie clip which image to load:

```
hold_my_image.loadMovie("myimage.jpg");
```

I tell my `loadMovie` method to get the image called `myimage.jpg`. In this example, no path is specified so Flash will look for this image in the same directory as the movie that is calling the image file. Make sure you always put the image name in quotes and that the path is accurate. If my image file happened to be one directory up, I would either have to use an *absolute path* to the file, or write the path name as something like:

```
../myimage.jpg.
```

This tells Flash to access the file one directory up. All this shouldn't be a surprise because the issue of having the correct path arises when you use the `loadMovie` method to load an external SWF.

Because `myimage.jpg` lives in the `hold_my_image` movie clip, I can now manipulate my image just like any movie clip by calling the name of the movie clip and the property that I want to change:

```
hold_my_image._x=50;
hold_my_image._y=50;
```

Be aware that if an image is saved as a progressive JPEG, Flash will not load it into the Flash player. So check and make sure all JPEGs are non-progressive when compressed for Flash. Any time I am given an image as a JPEG, I always make sure it's non-progressive by opening it up in my favorite graphics application, and saving it again.

Animating JPEGs – timeline versus ActionScript

Animating an object (like a movie clip) with ActionScript is a far superior practice to animating a symbol with the Flash timeline. If you choose to use ActionScript to animate your symbols you will more than likely produce smaller Flash files, smoother animations, and more advanced animation sequences.

Just in case you haven't figured it out yet, making a bitmap (or just about anything) move across the screen with the timeline is taxing on the movie's frame rate as well as the overall file size. Because of this limitation with the Flash timeline, many designers have taken on the role of *rogue programmer extraordinaire*. Designers realized that by using ActionScript to animate bitmaps in Flash they could defy the large file sizes of the bitmaps and tame the choppy animation sequences produced by the timeline.

Consider for a minute how you would design in Flash if I told you to take 23 bitmaps and animate them so that they would appear on the Flash stage at random sizes, and then animate across the stage from right to left at random speeds and at random locations. Also, if a user were to roll over one of the bitmaps, the image would stop in its place, re-arrange its stacking order to the front of the screen and then on roll-off continue on its

2

animation path. Don't worry, this is not a task we must take on today – it's probably a little outside of our scope of interest. But if you had to, how would you accomplish such an animation? Could such a task be accomplished with a bitmap keyframe tween in the Flash timeline? I think you would find that *manually* creating such an animation with the timeline would be very tricky and at some point you'd need to turn to ActionScript for help. Truth be told, ActionScript is the secret to successfully using bitmaps in Flash while keeping the file size to a minimum. Without it, the intended user would never be able to handle 23 simultaneously animating bitmaps.

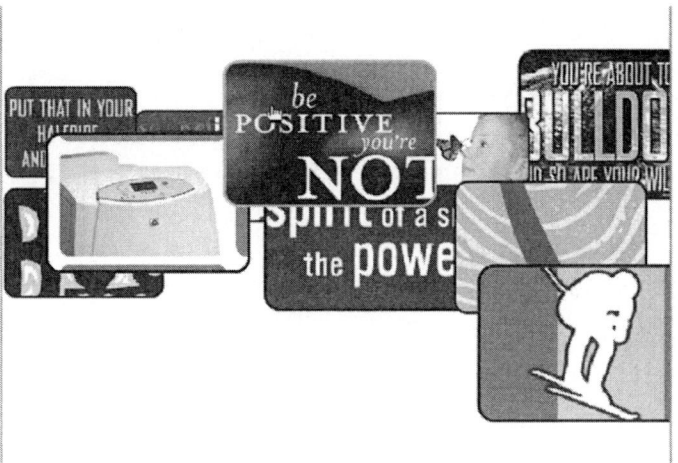

Just so you don't think I am all theory and no pudding, the above situation I describe was actually a design I created for a local advertising firm in Boise, Idaho. The work I did for this firm is included with this chapter's downloadable example files so you can see how I went about designing such an animation sequence with ActionScript. Open the file called `animation-example.fla` and take a look. Most of what I have learned about Flash has come from snooping around FLA files. I just get hold of one and tear it apart until I understand everything the author did. I'm providing my file so you may investigate in this manner if you wish to, and also to allow you to get an idea of the power of animating bitmaps with ActionScript.

You can also view this example online at www.oh-zone.com. Note that the FLA included here is only the portfolio section of the site, but it's a great example of what can be achieved with ActionScript that could never be accomplished with timeline-based animation. If you're still relying on the timeline to animate your bitmaps, your projects will surely be plagued by large file sizes, choppy animations, and a lot of unnecessary work.

Flash photo gallery

Now we're ready to get our hands dirty! I'd like to explain the process I went through to build a Flash photo gallery for the online department of a newspaper. Here are a few rules I set myself before I began:

- The entire Flash file should not be over 10 KB.

- No loading bars or fancy tricks to waste the user's time.

- The gallery will be designed for 56K modem users, and will display 31 JPEGs.

- Dynamically loading JPEGs will be used to stream content to the gallery.

- The user should be able to use the gallery by the time the first image downloads into the Flash player.

If you haven't already done so, open the `Photo_Gallery.html` file from the download files in a browser and get comfortable with the functionality of the gallery (`B&W/THE_MEAT/Photo_Gallery.html`).

Let's stop here for moment and discuss file size. At this point you should have a pretty good understanding of how the gallery works from the user's perspective. Before we go any further, let's take a look at the file size of `Photo_gallery.swf`. According to my operating system, the size of the file is around 9 KB. Well, actually it's less than that but I have included the size of `tool.swf` and `mask.swf` in this number because they are loaded into the `Photo_gallery.swf`. All together, the Flash files are incredibly small in file size. In comparison, the average 469x60 banner ad is about 12 KB, which should give a clue to the advantages of loading dynamic JPEGs. Note that I'm not trying to hide the fact the user still has to download the JPEGs – the size of the JPEGs are just not included with the Flash files because they are not imported into the Flash environment.

In simple terms, with these three Flash files I can successfully load and animate 31 JPEGs and still have an incredibly small Flash file for my end user to download. Let's see how it's possible...

2

File structure

Now you know how the end product functions, let's go back to the B&W folder and take a look at the file structure:

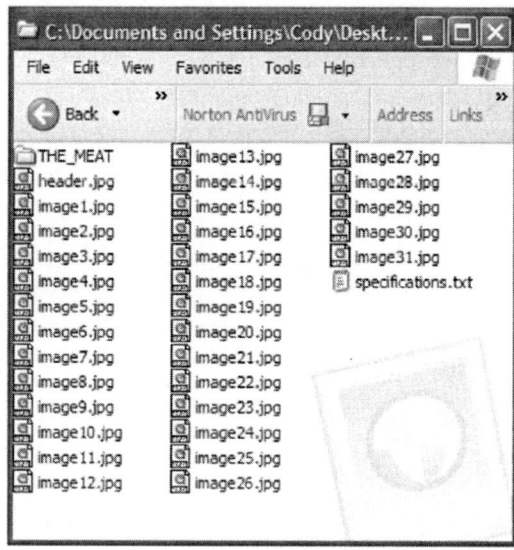

Inside this file you will find a folder named THE_MEAT, 32 JPEGs, and one text file called specifications.txt. Let's discuss these briefly.

The folder named THE_MEAT holds all the Flash files that make up the parts of the gallery. The contents of THE_MEAT folder include a mask.fla movie, a Photo_Gallery.fla movie, and a tool.fla movie along with the accompanying SWF, HTML, and projector files for each FLA.

Notice in the B&W folder that the JPEGs are named image1.jpg through to image31.jpg. The only image that is not named in this manner is header.jpg. This image is the header for the gallery and is loaded along with the gallery images, but remains present all the time the gallery is being viewed. The purpose of header.jpg being dynamically loaded is to allow the gallery to change depending on its desired audience. By replacing this image, along with the other JPEGs, you could tailor the Flash movie for a different audience, and display other work.

The one text file in the B&W folder will provide the gallery with the content information for the title of the gallery. Again, making it a separate text file means the gallery is easy to update by anyone. Loading a text file into Flash is a pretty simple practice to wrap your head around – we're just adding variables and values to the timeline. These values are updateable by making changes to the text file in a simple text editor like Notepad or SimpleText, without opening Flash.

Before we open the gallery in Flash we need to keep a couple of things in mind regarding the file structure:

- The images must be stored one level up from the contents of the THE_MEAT folder in order for the path in the ActionScript to find the images; this also applies to the text file. If we change the relationship between the file locations of the main gallery FLA and the files it will dynamically load, we must make sure to change the coding accordingly.

- The images must be named properly in order for the Flash file to recognize the file it needs to load. The naming process works like this:

    image + a number between 1 and 33 + .jpg.

If an image is named outside of these restraints, Flash will not recognize the image.

Next, we need to discuss the preparation of the images that are loaded for the gallery. But first, let's briefly talk about how Flash actually loads JPEGs. We are going to look at the process by which I created a very small Flash file that can be quickly loaded on to a user's machine from the Internet. Once the Flash file is loaded, the ActionScript starts loading my images into the duplicated movie clips and these create blank movie clips to hold the images. If we chose to import all the images into Flash, my initial movie would be a gigantic download. My intended user would more than likely have had to wait for the file to download had I taken that road.

However, in this example, because the images are being loaded dynamically, from the moment the first image appears the user has the ability to view the image at 100 percent. From what I have seen from testing the gallery on a few different 56K connections, the first image loads instantly and so the user never has to wait to start using the gallery. No waiting, no loading bars, and no tricks to waste the user's time.

Preparing the images for the gallery

The actual process for preparing a JPEG for the gallery can be done in any graphic editing software you like. I am going to use Macromedia Fireworks, but you can use whatever program you're comfortable with. Once you have a blank canvas in your graphics program, resize the canvas to be 465 pixels in width and 296 pixels in height. At this point I would make the entire stage a gray color or whatever color you would like. Now import your image for the gallery onto the stage and resize the image so all its parts are viewable on the canvas.

Once this is done, center the image on the stage and convert the entire document to grayscale. If you like, before compressing the image you can add a nice border around it, like I've done in the gallery sample I provided with this chapter's sample files. Now save the image as `image1.jpg`. Make sure you think carefully about the compression because we want the image's file size as small as possible. Repeat this process until you have 31 images named `image1.jpg` through to `image31.jpg`. Move the files to the correct folder and you're done.

Don't worry if you don't have 31 images to load into the gallery. If you like, you can load one JPEG or all 31 JPEGs. Flash will think there has been an error when it can't find all the images but your user will never be privy to that information. Only in the Flash application, upon testing the gallery, do you get this error in the Output window. In fact, even using my example, you will always get an error as there is no `image32.jpg` but Flash tries to load one. Again don't worry about it. The gallery will function fine whatever you do, so load one image or 31, it's your choice!

I'd also like to mention the importance of making the gallery easily updateable by non-designers. Since I was not going to be the one creating the images for this gallery once it was passed off to certain departments at the newspaper I designed some Adobe Photoshop droplets so that image preparation could be automated. The droplets will perform all the editing required for an image to appear in the gallery as seen with this example. The entire process is explained in a bonus document, called `Image_resize_programs.doc`, which has been included with this chapter's download files. If you have Photoshop 6, be sure to check these droplets out. Just make sure you read the word document first as there are some issues if you're using a Macintosh. Of course, droplets don't work in Photoshop 7, but you can accomplish something very similar using batch processing. Think creatively around problems like this, and your clients will love you.

The text file

The other element we want to load dynamically to fulfill our goal of a small, easily updateable gallery, is the text file. Loading a dynamic text file in Flash is a pretty simple concept to grasp – we use an external text file that is loaded into Flash with ActionScript in order to change the values of variables in the Flash movie without having to open the Flash application. That said, a dynamically loaded text file simply loads a list of variables and their values in the location that the file is called from. In the case of the gallery example, my `specifications.txt` file is loaded into the `_root` timeline.

The main thing to remember about writing a text file to be loaded into Flash is that after you have declared the first variable, each variable name after this will need to start with an ampersand (&). For example, take a look at the first couple of lines of the `specifications.txt` that is loaded into the gallery (and remember that Flash will ignore whitespace in a dynamically loaded text file):

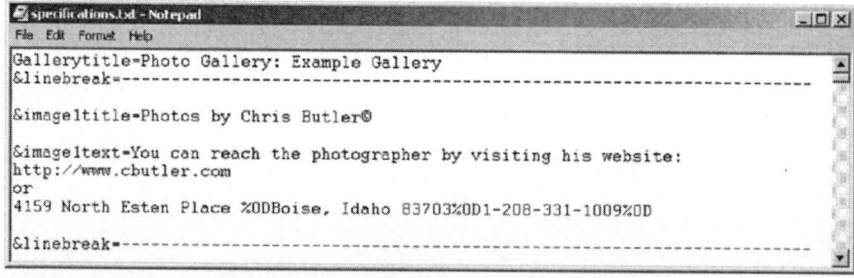

Notice that I put in a `linebreak` variable to keep my text file more readable. This is done for clarity, not because the `linebreak` variable is used in the gallery.

As you can see, apart from the line breaks I have declared three variables: `Gallerytitle`, `imagetitle`, and `imagetext`. If you look at their values, they are the same values that appear in the gallery if you click on the first image in the first column. In reality the `Gallerytitle` variable is always showing. The reason I chose to use this file to populate the text fields in my gallery was to keep the information easily updateable, such that even an inexperienced user could handle it – after all, it'd take very little training to edit a simple text file. In the text file I have included, the values are the same no matter which image is clicked on, but if you want to see how easy it is to change this, add in some names and information of your own.

The Flash gallery file

At this point, open the Flash gallery and take a look at the stage. At first glance the `Photo_gallery.fla` file might seem incomplete. If this seems odd just keep reading – I promise it will all make sense.

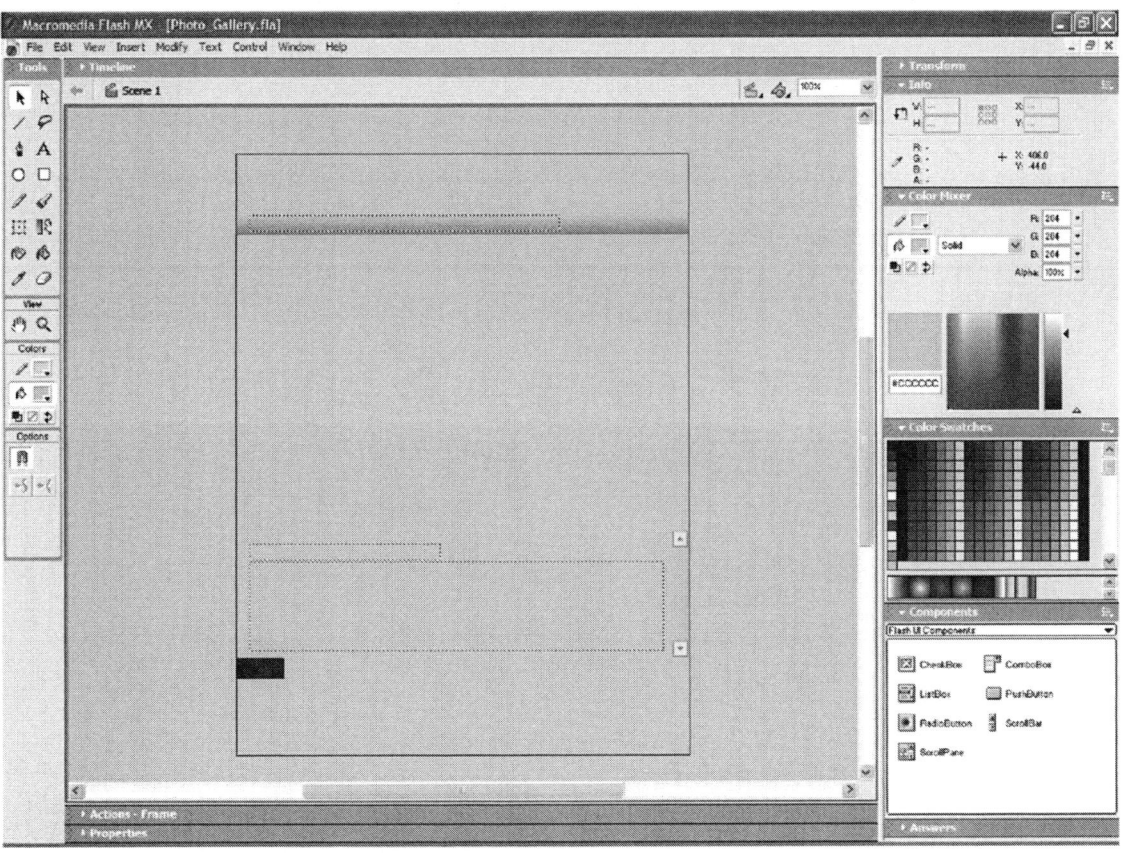

Let's just dive in and take a look at the items on the stage. Near the top you will notice a gradient – this is purely a design feature. On top of the gradient is a dynamic text field where the main title for the gallery will go once the text file (specifications.txt) has been loaded into the Flash player to provide this text field with the appropriate value.

Next, you will find two text fields more than halfway down on the Flash stage. The smaller text field is where the image title for each image will be loaded, and the larger text field is where any text accompanying an image will be loaded. If this is confusing, just preview the Flash file in the player for clarification on these two text fields. Rather than provide information for all the files in this example, I have provided a generic set of information, which will be displayed no matter which photo is being viewed, but again this could easily be changed to display whatever textual information you want. The values for these two dynamic text fields will also be loaded into Flash from the same text file that provides the gallery with a main title.

To the left of the two text boxes is a Flash component. Components are essentially complex movie clips – self-contained packages of functionality – with defined parameters that can be set up in the authoring environment, and a unique set of ActionScript methods that allow you to set parameters and additional options at runtime. Well, that was straight from the manual. A Flash component is similar to what a smart clip was in Flash 5, if that helps you understand components better. The component I used is from the Components window in Flash and was simply dragged to the stage and then given the proper name to target my dynamic text field named imagetext, which is the largest text field on the stage. After dragging the component to the stage you will see the Property inspector change to indicate the component parameters and this is where the value of the text field can be entered to attach the text scroller to the imagetext text field. That's all there is to the text scroller. Say it with me now: *components are very cool!*

Next, you will find a little black rectangle at the bottom of the canvas where the first thumbnail image would usually appear. Before I go much further, make sure you take a look at the timeline of Photo_gallery.fla and familiarize yourself with the layers shown below:

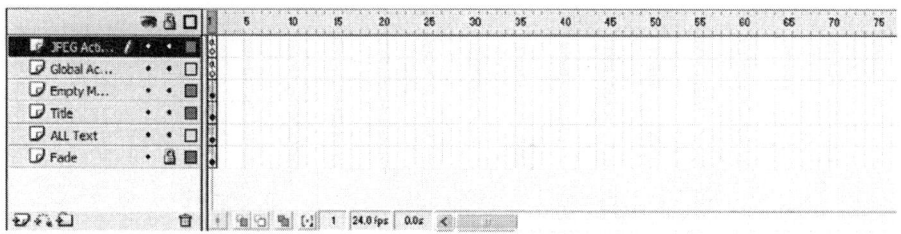

Global actions

For clarity I've separated Global Actions from JPEG actions (those that control the little black rectangle). Let's first look at the actions on frame 1 of the Global Actions layer. The first line sets the player so that the movie is always drawn at its original size and never scaled:

```
fscommand(allowscale, false);
```

Then I dim all the context menu items except About Flash Player:

```
fscommand(showmenu, false);
```

This method will load my `mask.swf` movie into level `1001`:

```
loadMovieNum("mask.swf", 1001);
```

This method will load my `tool.swf` movie into level `1004`:

```
loadMovieNum("tool.swf", 1004);
```

Then I create a new movie clip named `Holderheader`, placed on level `1000`:

```
this.createEmptyMovie clip("Holderheader", 1000);
```

Now I need to load the header JPEG into this empty movie clip:

```
Holderheader.loadMovie("../header.jpg");
```

Notice that I had to go one level up from where my Flash file is stored to find the image `header.jpg`.

This line loads the text file into the Flash player and places the variables and values that the `specifications.txt` file contains on the `_root` timeline:

```
loadVariables("../specifications.txt");
```

If you haven't done so already, locate `tool.swf` and `mask.swf` (from the same file directory as the `gallery.swf` file) and open them up in Flash. By viewing these files I am sure it will be obvious why they're loaded into the gallery. `tool.swf` is used for the tip that pops up when rolling over a thumbnail:

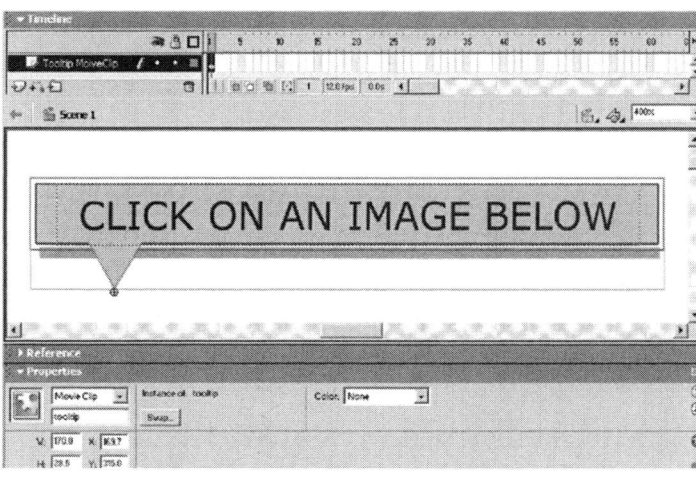

The `mask.swf` movie creates a mask that is laid over the top of the gallery, just to give it a little bit of structure:

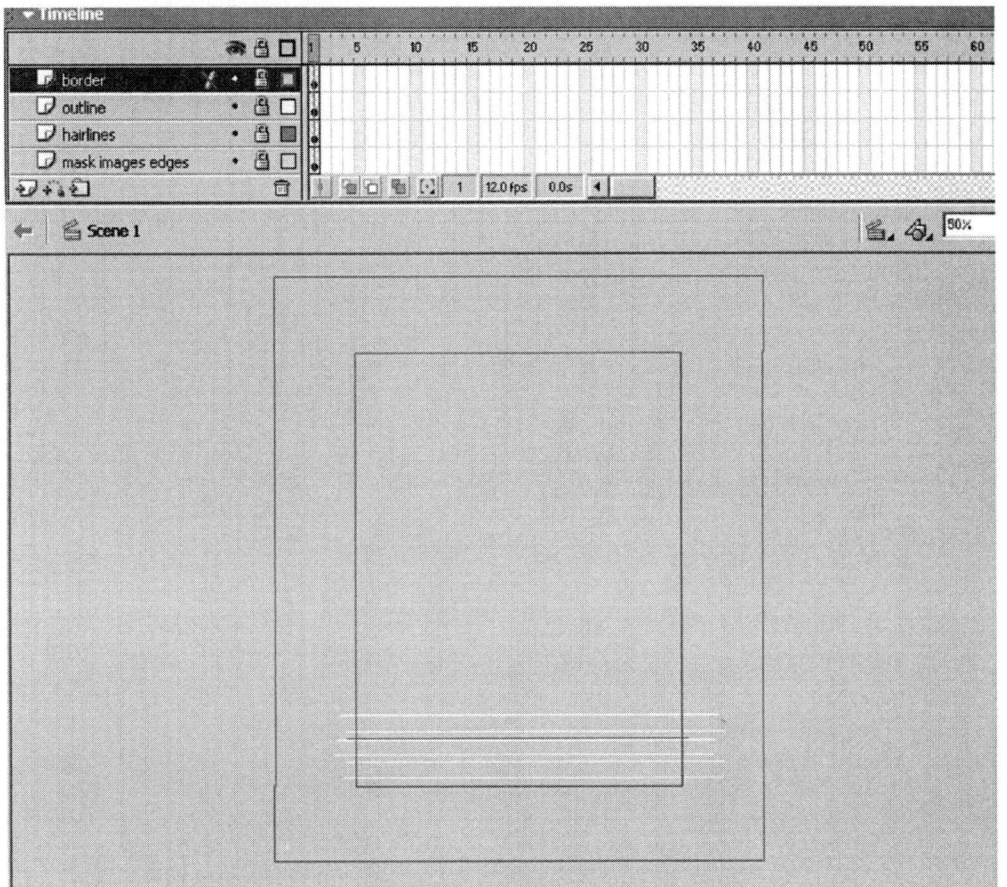

JPEG actions

Now, returning your attention to `Photo_gallery.fla`, select the little black rectangle on the stage. Notice the name of the movie clip in the Property inspector – `image1`. If you now open the Actions panel (press F9) you'll see that this movie clip does not have any actions attached to it. To see the actions that control our `image1` movie clip, return to the timeline and display the actions found on the JPEG Actions layer.

The first line is fairly self-explanatory, while the second line sets a variable called `num_images` to hold the value `34`:

```
stop();
var num_images = 34;
```

This value will be used in my `for` loop that follows, to duplicate the movie clip to hold each JPEG image:

```
for(var i=2; i<=num_images; i++) {
    duplicateMovie clip(_root.image1, "image"+i, i);
    _root["image"+i]._x = (_root["image"+(i-1)]._x)+42.4;
}
```

The loop starts with a value of 2 for i. I wanted to use movie clip `image1` (the one being duplicated) so all I really needed was 31 new movie clips plus the one already on the stage to make 32, the number of images I want to load.

When this movie clip is duplicated it renames each movie clip according to the value of i. So, on the first loop the initial duplicated clip will be called `image2` and placed on level 2. This is because during the first loop the value of i is 2. When the loop returns to the beginning, i is incremented, so that on the second loop the value is changed to 3, and so the next duplicated clip is called `image3` and placed on level 3. When the value of i is equal to the value of the `num_images` variable we set, 34, the loop will stop, and 32 new movie clips will have been created.

The last statement in the loop will place each of the duplicated clips in a row equally spaced apart. This statement is using the array access operator [ ] to call each duplicated movie clip and move its x position 42.4 pixels to the right from the last movie clip. At this point all the duplicated movies would be in a row spaced apart 42.4 pixels from the registration point of the x position, which is in the upper left-hand corner of the black rectangle. Notice that I do not create a dummy movie clip for duplication – the `image1` clip is part of the 32 clips. No waste here, thank you!

Then comes some code to reorganize my row of duplicated movie clips:

```
for (var i = 1; i<=num_images; i++) {
    if (_root["image"+i]._x>450) {
        _root["image"+i]._y += 32;
        _root["image"+i]._x -= 466.4;
        if (_root["image"+i]._y>532 & _root["image"+i]._x>450)
    {

            _root["image"+i]._y += 32;
            _root["image"+i]._x -= 466.4;
        }
    }
}
```

The movie clips must appear in three rows and eleven columns to fit on the screen. This code uses another `for` loop that will loop through each of the duplicated images and start a new row when the x position of a clip is located beyond 450 pixels from the left side of the movie stage. I need three rows so I have to use `if` statements in the loop to

2

decipher which clips would go into which row and when to start a new row. In other words, if a clip is located beyond 450 pixels, it's repositioned 32 pixels down and 466.4 pixels back to the left. Because I have three rows, I needed another `if` statement that would say if a clip is located beyond 450 pixels and vertically beyond 532 pixels then relocate the clip to another 32 pixels down and back to the left 466.4 pixels. In plain English, all I am saying is this – at this x position start a new row, and then if the clip is located vertically so far down the stage (y coordinates), then start another row.

So up to this point all we have done is duplicate the `image1` movie clip 32 times (the one that is there when you open Flash makes it 33 all together). These clips are then placed in a grid on the flash stage. The grid up to this point would just be 32 black rectangles spaced equally apart top to bottom and left to right, placed in three rows and 11 columns.

The image1 movie clip

Have you considered opening the `image1` clip and seeing what's on its timeline? Its contents are very important, as one would hope, seeing as I duplicated it 32 times with ActionScript. Let's check it out – all 33 movie clips are exactly the same, so if we look at one we'll find out what's in all of them. The one thing that is different about each clip is its name. This will come in pretty handy with the rest of the coding.

Double-click on the `image1` movie clip, and look at the timeline:

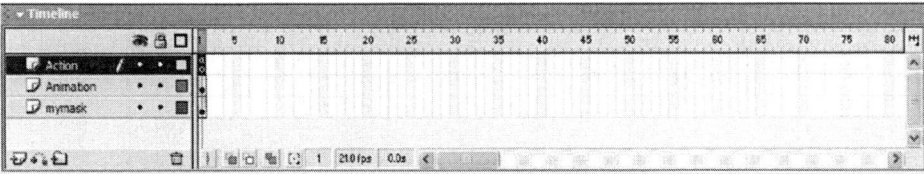

There are three layers named Action, Animation, and mymask (plus a working layer included in the version in the download files, which points out the position of another movie clip on the stage). Let's investigate the Action layer first, as this makes it easier to understand the function of the other two layers.

The set of actions we are about to look at will place each of the dynamically loaded JPEGs in its correct movie clip container and control the functionality of mouse events. We have 33 duplicated clips, and we now just need to load the correct JPEG into each of these clips. Let's break the code down to see how this is done. Remember that I need an empty clip to load each of my JPEGs into:

```
this.createEmptyMovieClip("imageholder", 0);
```

I then call my `imageholder` clip and load the correct JPEG into the empty clip:

```
imageholder.loadMovie("../"+this._name+".jpg");
```

How I determine which JPEG to load is by accessing the name of the current movie clip the code is located in, using `this._name`, and telling Flash to take the name of this clip and look one level up in the file structure for a JPEG with the same name. So for example, `image3.jpg` is loaded into a movie clip called `image3`.

Once the correct image is loaded I then resize the image by calling the empty clip I created to house the image and resizing it through its `_xscale` and `_yscale` properties:

```
imageholder._xscale = 8.7;
imageholder._yscale = 8.7;
```

This must be done because the JPEGs are loaded at the original size and must be taken down to a thumbnail size. Although this may seem counter-intuitive, doing things this way means that we only need to load one set of JPEGs, cutting down on download time.

Then we create two variables to hold the current x and y coordinates of this movie clip:

```
var x_pos = this._x;
var y_pos = this._y;
```

The next line sets a movie clip to act as a mask:

```
this.setMask(mymask);
```

The `setMask` method of Flash MX allows me to use a movie clip as a mask. This code sets the black rectangle (which is a movie clip called `mymask`) as a mask, and what it's masking is the current movie clip. That is why we see the black rectangle on the Flash stage, but when we view the SWF file the black rectangle becomes the mask and the loaded JPEG will show through. The point in having a mask is to have the effect of animating the image on the stage. By animating a mask over the top of the image I have worked around having to animate the actual bitmap. In doing so I have eliminated the need for extra keyframes on the timeline that animating a JPEG would produce, therefore cutting my file size.

The next section of code sets what we want to happen when the user puts the mouse over one of the thumbnail images:

```
this.onRollOver = function() {
    if (this._x>300) {
        _level1004.tooltip.gotoAndStop(2);
    }
    startDrag(_level1004.tooltip, true);
    _level1004.tooltip.name = _root[this._name+"title"];
};
```

2

This onRollOver method controls the tooltip timeline, which displays text in a pop-up box. The first part of the function moves the tooltip timeline to frame 2 on the images that are located past the x coordinates 300. In order to fully understand this, open up tool.fla, double-click on the tooltip movie clip and take a look at frame 2. This horizontal flip ensures the tool tip doesn't hang off the stage and become unviewable.

The if statement is only the first thing that happens in this onRollover event. Next I invoke the startDrag method to attach the tooltip movie clip in tool.swf to the thumbnail image (remember, we loaded tool.swf into level 1004 in the Global actions layer of the main timeline), and finally I pull the appropriate value from the dynamically loaded text file to fill the dynamic text field in the tooltip movie clip with the correct image title. So when the user rolls over an image, the text in the tool tip is the same text that appears in the image title text field.

Next I set what happens to the tool tip when the user rolls off the movie clip:

```
this.onRollOut = function() {
  _level1004.tooltip.gotoAndStop(1);
  _level1004.tooltip.stopDrag();
  _level1004.tooltip._x = 2000;
  _level1004.tooltip.name = "";
};
```

All I am doing here is undoing what I did in the above rollover, and then telling the tooltip movie clip to hide itself off stage. Then comes the all-important onRelease event that actually displays the full size image of the thumbnail that has been clicked on:

```
this.onRelease = function() {
  for (var i = 1; i<=_root.num_images; i++) {
    if (_root["image"+i]._y<500) {
      _root["image"+i]._y = _root["image"+i].y_pos;
      _root["image"+i]._x = _root["image"+i].x_pos;
      _root["image"+i].imageholder._xscale = 8.7;
      _root["image"+i].imageholder._yscale = 8.7;
      _root["image"+i].animate_mask.normal = 100;
    } else {
      this._x = 0;
      this._y = 81;
      this.imageholder._xscale = 100;
      this.imageholder._yscale = 100;
      this.animate_mask.normal = 1605;
      _root.imagetext.text = _root[this._name+"text"];
      _root.title.text = _root[this._name+"title"];
    }
  }
};
```

What I am doing here is using the same image for the thumbnail that I am using for the full size version that we want to view in the gallery. The user clicks on an image and the function loops through all the images and checks their y positions to find out which image is currently being displayed at full size. If the image is located above y coordinate 500 then it is the image in full size view, and it is moved back to the thumbnail view. When all the images have been checked, the `else` statement comes into play, and the movie clip that has been clicked on is scaled to 100 percent, moved up to the top and animated onto the stage.

In the last two lines of code I'm telling my text fields on the `_root` timeline (which I have named in the text field Properties window) to change text according to which thumbnail is clicked. If I click on the thumbnail with the instance name of `image12` it takes this name and adds `title` or `text` to it, which are names of variables that are loaded from the `specifications.txt` file. The values from these variables are then placed in the `title` or `imagetext` text fields on the `_root` timeline.

The mask

One part of the Flash file that we haven't looked at yet is the mask animation. I explained earlier that Flash MX allows me to turn a movie clip into a mask with the `setMask` method. As you know by now, the black square that you see when you open the gallery FLA is the movie clip I used to mask the JPEGs that are loaded into gallery. Because this mask is a movie clip too, I can control it with ActionScript just like any movie clip. So in the gallery, I apply a little bit of high school math to alter the x and y scale property of the `mymask` movie clip, using the `animate_mask` movie clip, in order to animate the mask over the top of an image. By animating the mask I in turn achieve an effect that looks to the viewer like I am animating the image itself. In reality the image isn't animating at all – the mask changing sizes just makes the image look as if it is animating.

2

Let's look at the code. If you double-click on the black rectangle in the `Photo_gallery.fla` file, you will be shown the timeline for the `image1` movie clip. If you look at the stage you should see an arrow that is pointing to an empty movie clip. Click once on this empty movie clip and view the code that is attached to the clip in the Actions panel. If you double-click on the movie clip you will not see anything, as the code is linked to the movie clip using the old techniqe of attached scripts, rather than remotely calling functions from the timeline. This code is placed on a movie clip and, as such, is usually called a movie clip controller. It controls the animation of the `mymask` movie clip.

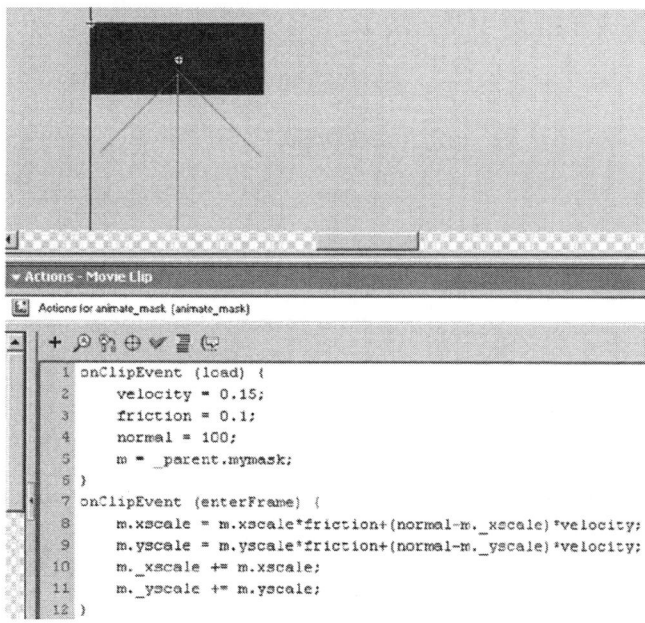

```
1 onClipEvent (load) {
2     velocity = 0.15;
3     friction = 0.1;
4     normal = 100;
5     m = _parent.mymask;
6 }
7 onClipEvent (enterFrame) {
8     m.xscale = m.xscale*friction+(normal-m._xscale)*velocity;
9     m.yscale = m.yscale*friction+(normal-m._yscale)*velocity;
10    m._xscale += m.xscale;
11    m._yscale += m.yscale;
12 }
```

The onClipEvent(load) will only execute once when the movie clip that the event exists on is loaded into the Flash timeline:

```
onClipEvent (load) {
```

Then I set how fast the animation accelerates:

```
velocity = 0.15;
```

And what slows the velocity of the animation over a period of timeline loops:

```
friction = 0.01;
```

Next I define the variable that sets the scale of the movie clip, so I can scale up the size of the mask when an image is clicked:

```
Normal = 100;
```

Then I use a variable to save the path to the movie clip that is being controlled:

```
m = _parent.mymask;
}
```

The next chunk of code runs on another clip event:

```
onClipEvent (enterFrame) {
    m.xscale = m.xscale*friction+(normal-m._xscale)*velocity;
    m.yscale = m.yscale*friction+(normal-m._yscale)*velocity;
```

This creates a loop that will execute each time the timeline enters the frame of the clip that the event lives on – this code is always looping. The animation effect changes because I change the value of the variable called normal in the equation each time a thumbnail is clicked. When the variable normal is equal to 100 you don't notice the effects of the following equation, but when normal is equal to 1605 this equation produces x and y scale properties that are used to animate the mymask movie clip:

The final lines of code change the scale of the movie clip:

```
    m._xscale += m.xscale;
    m._yscale += m.yscale;
}
```

They take my current value and add the value after the equal sign to create a new value – in other words they take the current x and y scale property of the mymask movie clip and then add whatever I put after the equal sign to create a new size. What appears after the equal sign is set by the preceding equation. Repeat this code a bunch of times like I have done with the onClipEvent, and you have animation!

Obviously, there are some definite areas for improvement and extension with this gallery. I'm working on a new version myself – maybe you should try to upgrade it to suit your own specific purposes too? Just dive right in, rework the code, or redesign the entire gallery. I'm sure you if you take the time to do so, it's inevitable that you'll learn something new about Flash and ActionScript along the way. Remember that this gallery was designed for the 56K user. So if you have any ideas on how to improve this design, give it a crack. Just remember – most of the world is still on a dial-up connection and, hey, even they deserve to play with some Flash designs.

3 DYNAMIC INTERFACES

KEITH PETERS

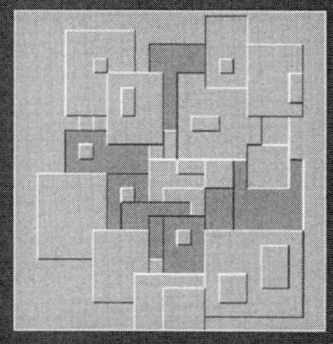 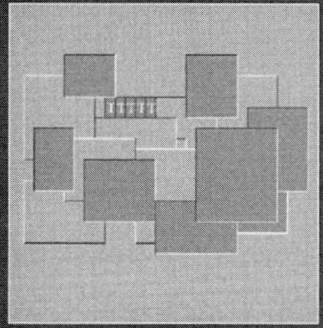 

I remember one of the first major Flash websites that a friend and I did. We had all kinds of tweens and cheesy text effects and a huge spinning globe – all rendered with frame-by-frame tweening. On top of that, we also had a 30 second MP3 music file.

The first version of the site came in at well over 500 KB. After some frantic optimizing, I managed to get it down to about 300 KB. My design partner said that was fine because the client's target audience were all assumed to be on broadband connections anyway. In the end, we threw a pretty lame looking preloader on it and called it a day!

A short while later I started seeing some really incredible scripted animations. This led me to find out more about this crazy ActionScript stuff. I remember the first time I created a really complex ActionScript file - I was already very impressed with the amount of real-time interaction that could be programmed into it. Then I looked at the size of the resulting SWF, "What? There must be some mistake! There's no way this could be only 6 KB!"

It slowly dawned on me that *ActionScript makes small files*! These days, I rarely create a single file that's larger than one or two kilobytes. The only exception would be when I need to embed a font or include some type of bitmap or sound file.

There are three features of Flash MX that greatly facilitate the making of small files.

The first one is the most direct and automatic - by default, Flash MX will compress your files when you publish them. This is done using the same routines that are used for many popular compression tools on the web. This feature can be found in the File > Publish Settings… dialog, but as I said, it's already set up to compress by default. So unless you disable it, your movie will be compressed. That was easy!

We'll be looking at the next two optimization features in this chapter. These are the `createEmptyMovieClip` method and the **drawing API**. But why are they so important? Well, these two features let you create content *on-the-fly*.

The `createEmptyMovieClip` method allows you to create an empty movie clip on stage where there was nothing before. This allows us to publish a seemingly blank movie – containing nothing but code.

The drawing API (**A**pplication **P**rograming **I**nterface) is a series of commands that allow you to draw with code. Here's a quick rundown on the commands we'll be using:

Drawing API method	Description
lineStyle(width, color, alpha)	Sets the width, color, and transparency of any lines drawn thereafter (color and alpha are optional parameters, with their defaults being black (0x000000) and 100%, respectively).
moveTo(x, y)	Moves the drawing position to the specified point, without drawing.
lineTo(x, y)	Draws a line from the current drawing position to the specified point.
beginFill(color, alpha)	Sets the color and transparency (optional) of the filled shape to be drawn.
endFill()	Signals that the shape is finished and can be filled.
clear()	Clears the current timeline of any previously drawn shapes.

Another way of looking at the difference between using ActionScript and the drawing API instead of manually drawing images in your designs is by considering that the API designs are automatically created at *runtime* whereas the manual technique involves pre-drawing at *author time*. Think about when you're creating a cheesy text effect tween, or a manual frame-by frame animation. Such designs are created at author time - the shapes of all the letters, their positions and rotations, alphas, and so on, for every frame, are all predetermined and stored in the file. That's a lot of information, which is why files with a lot of that stuff can become really large.

Now let's look at the other side of the coin – doing things at runtime. The user downloads the SWF, which just contains some code. The code tells the Flash player to create a movie clip, draw some content in it and then manipulates that clip with some more code. No graphical content needs to be downloaded at all, just the code - everything happens at runtime!

OK, this ActionScript does take up some file space, and of course it needs to be downloaded, but generally speaking, it's going to be a lot less than if you'd created all the graphics and tweens beforehand. This isn't always the case though. I recently experimented with making a completely scripted button – creating an empty movie clip, setting handlers for all the button events that would draw a different graphic for the over, up, down states. After working it over for a couple of hours, I got my scripted button down to less than 400 bytes. Then I made the same button the *old-fashioned* way in the authoring environment, and it came in at under 200 bytes!

The moral of the story is, if you find yourself writing very long code to make something relatively simple like a button, it's probably going to wind up bigger than if you made it in the authoring environment. However, by using loops and a few mathematical functions, we can often write very short code that creates very complex effects. That's where you're going to see some big difference in file size.

3

Creating a basic user interface with ActionScript

In this chapter, I'll demonstrate how we can use the drawing API to build a user interface for a website - with code alone. Rather than downloading any graphics or movie clips, the final SWF will contain only code to dynamically create my simple interface. Although this example will be pretty basic, the simplicity of the ActionScript that I'll use means that the design will be highly extensible.

The beauty of functions

All right, let's start using some of this stuff. Since my whole project is going to consist of code alone, **functions** are a great way to reduce the amount we use, and of using it efficiently.

A function is simply a series of statements with a name - you can call the named function, and it will run whatever code it contains. You can also send values to the function and return values back from the function. So, rather than typing in the same code over and over each time you need to perform a specific set of actions, you can put it into a function and save valuable space.

Essentially, functions in our ActionScript are just distinct reusable chunks of code.

In the following example I've made a function that creates a beveled panel for use in a website. This is just a few lines of code that I'll be able to use over and over to build up an entire interface background. The basic idea behind this function is to create an empty movie clip and draw in it a filled rectangle. The top and left edges will be white and the bottom and right will be black, giving that 3D feel to it. Open up ui01.fla from this chapter's download files - on frame 1 of the main timeline you'll find all of the code for this FLA file. Let's take a look at the makeBox function first:

```
function makeBox(x, y, w, h) {
    var box = createEmptyMovieClip("box"+boxCount,
    ➡ boxCount++);
    box._x = x;
    box._y = y;
    box.beginFill(0x999999);
    box.lineStyle(1, 0xffffff);
    box.lineTo(w, 0);
    box.lineStyle(1, 0x000000);
    box.lineTo(w, h);
    box.lineTo(0, h);
    box.lineStyle(1, 0xffffff);
    box.endFill();
    return box;
}
```

This function makes an empty movie clip using the relevant method. The arguments for this command are the name of the movie clip, and its depth. Depth determines whether an object will appear in front of or behind another. Higher depths will be seen in front of lower depths. This isn't so important for this project, but each movie clip must have a unique name and depth. Thus, we use boxCount to create the names, which will end up box0, box1, box2, and so on. Note that I only had to draw the first three lines – the final line will be drawn automatically with the endFill method. I just needed to specify the colors for beginFill and lineStyle to use.

Now all we have to do is issue our makeBox command with the x and y positions and width and height (w and h) as parameters. Here, we're declaring x and y as 20, the width as 530, and the height as 380:

```
makeBox(20, 20, 530, 380);
```

Here's the amazing result when we test this code:

3

OK, so it's not *that* impressive - but remember, this is just the tip of the iceberg!

We can even attach our function to a particular named movie clip we've just created, allowing us to store a reference to that clip, and later manipulate it - we can scale it, move it, and so on. For example, we could make it visible or invisible by simply replacing the previous line with the following code:

```
box1_mc = makeBox(20, 20, 530, 380);
box1_mc._visible = false;
//box1_mc._visible = true;
```

You could go as far as setting an onEnterFrame event handler to make our box grow into existence, like the following code seen in ui02.fla (we'll get more into onEnterFrame a bit later in the chapter):

```
box1_mc = makeBox(20, 20, 530, 380);
box1_mc._xscale = 0;
box1_mc._yscale = 0;
box1_mc.onEnterFrame = grow;
function grow() {
    if (this._xscale<100) {
        this._xscale++;
        this._yscale++;
    } else {
        this._xscale = 100;
        this._yscale = 100;
        delete this.onEnterFrame;
    }
}
```

Now, returning to our original function definition, makeBox is 14 lines of code. As mentioned earlier, this will take up some file space. If I was just going to create one or two panels, I probably would have simply drawn them in the authoring environment and been done with it. Remember, coding saves the most space when you are able to do the same thing over and over. Now that those functions are in place, you can make as many boxes as you want with just one line of code each - for instance, take a look at ui03.fla:

```
function makeBox(x, y, w, h) {
    var box = createEmptyMovieClip("box"+boxCount,
    ➥ boxCount++);
    box._x = x;
    box._y = y;
    box.beginFill(0x999999);
    box.lineStyle(1, 0xffffff);
    box.lineTo(w, 0);
    box.lineStyle(1, 0x000000);
    box.lineTo(w, h);
```

```
    box.lineTo(0, h);
    box.lineStyle(1, 0xffffff);
    box.endFill();
    return box;
}
box1_mc = makeBox(20, 20, 510, 360);
box2_mc = makeBox(40, 40, 470, 100);
box3_mc = makeBox(40, 160, 225, 200);
box4_mc = makeBox(285, 160, 225, 200);
```

Instead of making our user download three more movie clips, he just needs to download three more short lines of code. You can see that very soon the scales tip toward the advantages of ActionScript.

3

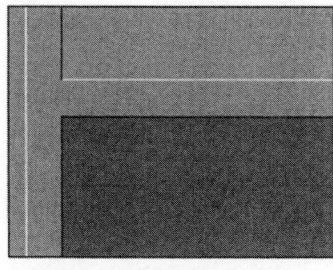

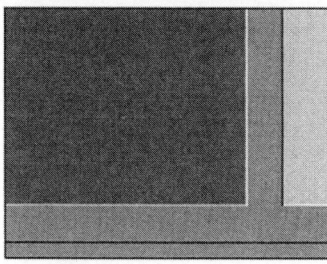

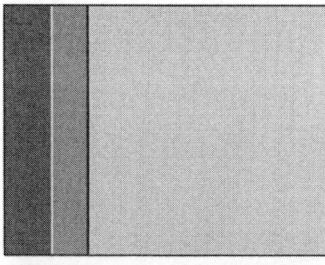

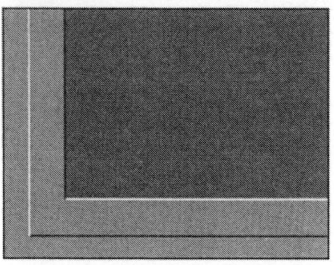

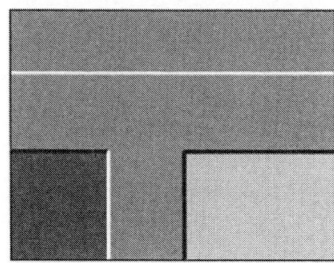

Next, instead of a panel that seems to protrude from the screen, I thought it might be nice to have an inset panel, and possibly one with a slightly darker fill for some contrast. Accordingly, I made the makeBox function a little more generic and gave it some additional parameters so you can choose the line and fill colors. Open up ui04.fla to check out these enhancements:

```
function makeBox(x, y, w, h, line1, line2, fill) {
    var box = createEmptyMovieClip("box"+boxCount,
    ➥ boxCount++);
    box._x = x;
    box._y = y;
    box.beginFill(fill);
    box.lineStyle(1, line1);
    box.lineTo(w, 0);
    box.lineStyle(1, line2);
    box.lineTo(w, h);
    box.lineTo(0, h);
    box.lineStyle(1, line1);
    box.endFill();
    return box;
}
```

Now you can make a few very simple functions that each make a different type of panel. All are based on makeBox:

```
function makePanel(x, y, w, h) {
    return makeBox(x, y, w, h, 0xffffff, 0x000000, 0x999999);
}
function makeInset(x, y, w, h) {
    return makeBox(x, y, w, h, 0x000000, 0xffffff, 0x999999);
}
function makeScreen(x, y, w, h, fill) {
    return makeBox(x, y, w, h, 0x000000, 0xffffff, fill);
}
```

See how, with just a few more lines of code, you have a lot more flexibility. Also notice that each of these functions passes on the reference to the created movie clip for later use, if needed.

With these additional functions, you can customize your interface even further:

```
box1_mc = makePanel(20, 20, 510, 360);
box2_mc = makeInset(40, 40, 470, 100);
box3_mc = makeScreen(40, 160, 225, 200, 0x666666);
box4_mc = makeScreen(285, 160, 225, 200, 0xcccccc);
```

Test `ui04.fla` to see the finished result:

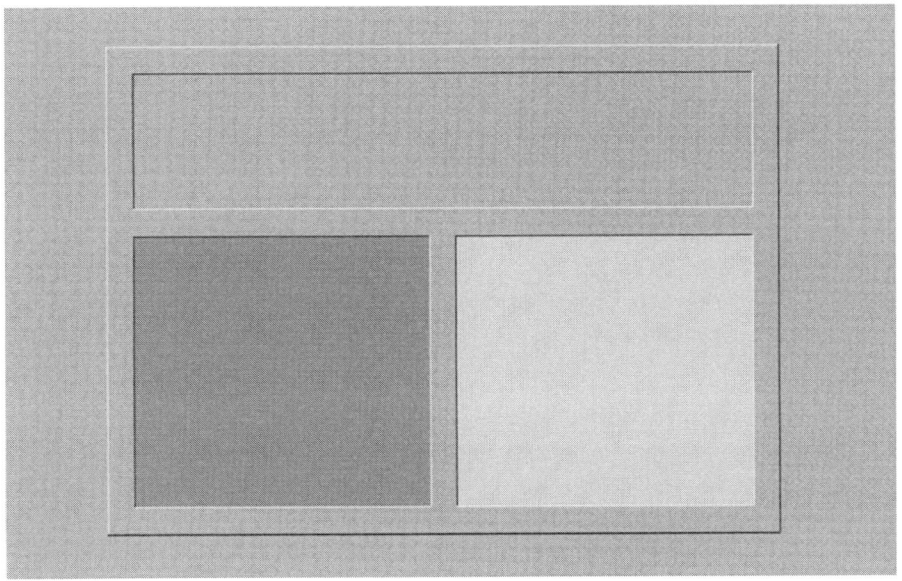

These boxes are pretty cool, but they really need some content. How about adding some basic text to our simple UI? This brings up another fantastic feature of Flash MX (yes, I've been holding out on you!) - just as you can create movie clips out of thin air, you can create text fields in the same way, using the `createTextField` command.

This takes just a bit more work than a movie clip. In the command itself, you need to name the text field, specify the depth, x and y positions, and the width and height. There are also a plethora of options you can specify individually - it's worth taking a look at this method with the internal ActionScript reference tool of Flash MX. For this example, I've kept it down to a couple of options: `wordWrap = true` and `selectable = false`. Then, I had the choice of going with the default text formatting or creating a customized format, which itself has more than a dozen optional parameters! Again, I've gone with the minimal option and just specified the font face, size, and color.

3

If you open up the file ui05.fla, you'll see that this new function that I've added, makeTextBox, takes care of all these options in about a half dozen lines. This sits on top of makeScreen giving a cool beveled background for the text. Here it is:

```
function makeTextBox(x, y, w, h, fill, fontFace, size,
➥ fontColor) {
    var box = makeScreen(x, y, w, h, fill);
    box.createTextField("display_txt", 100, 0, 0, w, h);
    box.display_txt.wordWrap = true;
    box.display_txt.selectable = false;
    box.display_txt.setNewTextFormat(new TextFormat(fontFace,
    ➥ size, fontColor));
    return box;
}
```

Let's go through it line by line. First, notice that I have the same parameters as makeScreen, plus the three format options I mentioned earlier. The first line simply calls makeScreen, assigning the returned object to a variable, box. Then, in box, I create a text field named display_txt. The next parameter is depth, which I kept high enough to stay on top of any other content that I might decide to put in here in the future. Then I set the x and y position of the text field to (0, 0). You might even want to push it out to (5, 5) to make a bit of a margin. If you do so, remember to reduce the next two parameters, width and height, by 10 so that you will have a margin on the bottom and right as well. The next two lines are obvious enough – I've just set the word wrap option to make text wrap to the next line, and made it so you can't select the text.

Then I created and assigned a text format in one quick line:

```
box.display_txt.setNewTextFormat(new TextFormat(fontFace,
➥ size, fontColor));
```

The textFormat object and its use is a subject which can seem pretty confusing to many. Most of the confusion seems to relate to the difference between the two commands, setTextFormat and setNewTextFormat. So I'll try to clarify here:

- setTextFormat - affects any existing text in the text field at the point it is defined.

- setNewTextFormat - affects any text which is added after it is defined.

A lot of the confusion comes when someone sets the format using setTextFormat and then adds some text. Since the format for *new* text has not been defined, the new text shows up as default black serif font. The setTextFormat was called before there was any text, so it didn't affect anything. Here, again in the name of keeping things simple, I set only the *new* text format, and do it right off the bat – before any text goes in there. That way, any and all future text that winds up there will have that format applied to it.

I could have created a variable to store the `textFormat` object in, and then used that in the `setNewTextFormat` command, like this:

```
boxFormat = new TextFormat(fontFace, size, fontColor);
box.display_txt.setNewTextFormat(boxFormat);
```

But I didn't expect to be needing it again, so I just created it right inside the command itself, as shown earlier.

Then of course I return the `box` object so I can access the movie clip we created. This is especially important now since I will need access to the inside of this clip so I can change the text. Here is how to create a couple of text boxes:

```
box3_mc = makeTextBox(40, 160, 225, 200, 0x666666, "_serif",
➡40, 0xffffff);
box4_mc = makeTextBox(285, 160, 225, 200, 0xcccccc, "_sans",
➡10, 0x000000);
```

And here's how I assign the text to them:

```
box3_mc.display_txt.text = "This is a big white SERIF font";
box4_mc.display_txt.text = "This is a little tiny SANS-SERIF
➡font";
```

In the above examples I used the device fonts `_sans` and `_serif`. You can specify any font you want to be displayed in the text box, but bear in mind that if you use a custom font that is not on the end user's system, Flash will try to choose a substitute, and the results may not be what you planned for your design. There is a solution for this – embedding the font in the text box. However, this would not only require more code to accomplish, but requires you to create a font symbol in the library and export it. This can add 20 KB or more to your final file size.

So, in the interests of keeping things small and fast, and knowing for sure what your text will look like on the end user's computer, I strongly suggest simply using a font that you are sure they will have. The device fonts `_sans`, `_serif`, and `_typewriter`, while not very exciting, are *always* available on any computer with the Flash player. You'll also be pretty safe with any standard font, such as Arial, Helvetica or Times.

3

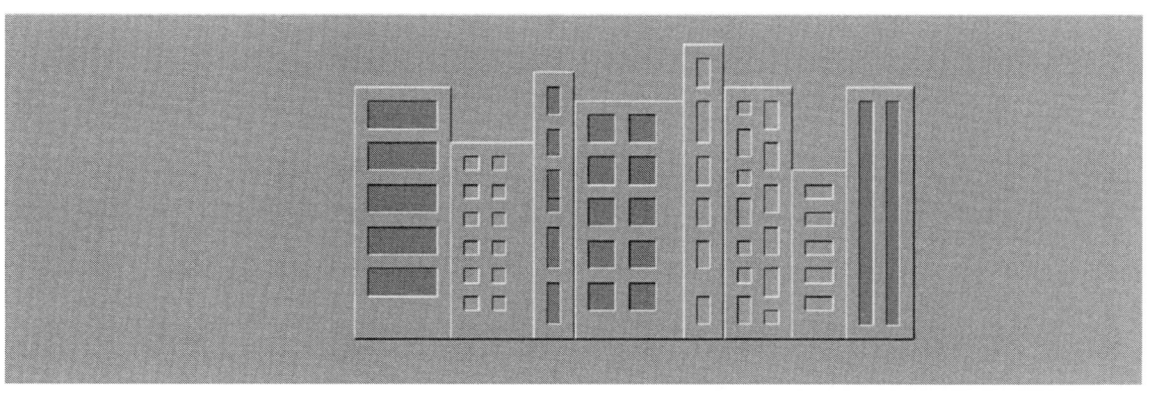

OK, in case things have gotten a bit confusing, and for the sake of completeness, here's what our code looks like so far:

```
function makeBox(x, y, w, h, line1, line2, fill) {
    var box = createEmptyMovieClip("box"+boxCount,
➥ boxCount++);
    box._x = x;
    box._y = y;
    box.beginFill(fill, 100);
    box.lineStyle(1, line1, 100);
    box.lineTo(w, 0);
    box.lineStyle(1, line2, 100);
    box.lineTo(w, h);
    box.lineTo(0, h);
    box.lineStyle(1, line1, 100);
    box.lineTo(0, 0);
    box.endFill();
    return box;
}
function makePanel(x, y, w, h) {
    return makeBox(x, y, w, h, 0xffffff, 0x000000, 0x999999);
}
function makeInset(x, y, w, h) {
    return makeBox(x, y, w, h, 0x000000, 0xffffff, 0x999999);
}
function makeScreen(x, y, w, h, fill) {
    return makeBox(x, y, w, h, 0x000000, 0xffffff, fill);
}
function makeTextBox(x, y, w, h, fill, fontFace, size,
fontColor) {
    var box = makeScreen(x, y, w, h, fill);
    box.createTextField("display_txt", 100, 0, 0, w, h);
    box.display_txt.wordWrap = true;
    box.display_txt.setNewTextFormat(new TextFormat(fontFace,
    ➥ size, fontColor));
    return box;
}
box1_mc = makePanel(20, 20, 510, 360);
box2_mc = makeInset(40, 40, 470, 100);
box3_mc = makeTextBox(40, 160, 225, 200, 0x666666, "_serif",
➥40, 0xffffff);
box4_mc = makeTextBox(285, 160, 225, 200, 0xcccccc, "_sans",
➥10, 0x000000);
box3_mc.display_txt.text = "This is a big white SERIF font";
box4_mc.display_txt.text = "This is a little tiny SANS-SERIF
➥font";
```

And remember, you can also open up `ui05.fla` from this book's downloadable code files. Here's what the movie looks like when we test it - it's a little under 700 bytes so far:

One final suggestion before we move on – take all the functions above and copy them into a text file named `interface.as`, or use the downloaded file supplied with this chapter's code files, and store it on your hard disk in the same directory you'll be making your files. Then, in the beginning of any new file you want to use the functions with, type:

```
#include "interface.as"
```

Note that there's *no* semicolon on the end! This will make all the functions available to you, just as if the were typed into the Actions panel directly. Check out `ui06.fla` to see this technique in action.

You can then create all the panels, insets, screens and text boxes you want. Note, that this doesn't reduce the size of the file at all, as the functions will still be pulled in at compile time. But it makes your workspace a little easier to manage and you don't have to worry about retyping or cutting and pasting those functions into a new file each time. Just #include them!

3

Adding interactivity to the UI

Up to now, the functions we've created have required you to manually input the numbers for the position and sizes of the boxes. This might work for you if you have a very visual and mathematical mind, or if you want to draw it all out on graph paper beforehand. But I thought it would be a lot easier to have a visual, mouse-oriented way of saying, "I want a box to go from here to here," and then to have Flash figure out the numbers for me.

Well, that shouldn't be too hard actually. All we really need to know is when and where the mouse was clicked, and when and where it was released. We can get those numbers by taking the values of _xmouse and _ymouse at the time we press or release the mouse button. Then we can act when it's pressed and released by defining the onMouseDown and onMouseUp handlers.

This was my general strategy in starting out with this next example:

- Define the onMouseDown handler to capture the mouse position at that time.

- Define the onMouseUp handler to capture the mouse position at that time.

- Also have the mouseUp handler call a function that will create the box.

I saved this example as ui07.fla. First off, I simply included the functions that we covered earlier:

```
#include "interface.as"
```

I knew that I only really needed two points to define a box, so I called them x1, y1 and x2, y2. I set up onMouseDown function to define x1, y1:

```
onMouseDown = function(){
    x1 = _xmouse;
    y1 = _ymouse;
}
```

Simple enough! Next, onMouseUp does essentially the same thing, then calls our function to draw the box:

```
onMouseUp = function(){
    x2 = _xmouse;
    y2 = _ymouse;
    makePanel(x1, y1, x2-x1, y2-y1);
}
```

Remember that makePanel requires the starting point and a width and height. To get the width and height, I subtracted the first point from the second.

Now you can go ahead and draw panels all over the place using your mouse! Feel free to experiment by making insets, screens, and text boxes instead of just panels. In the following code I used the mouse functions to create a text box and automatically add some text to it.

```
#include "interface.as"
onMouseDown = function(){
    x1 = _xmouse;
    y1 = _ymouse;
};
onMouseUp = function(){
    x2 = _xmouse;
    y2 = _ymouse;
    myTextBox_mc = makeTextBox(x1, y1, x2-x1, y2-y1, 0x666666,
    ➥ "_serif", 12, 0xffffff);
    myTextBox_mc.display_txt.text="Look at that! Dynamically
    ➥ created text boxes";
};
```

This just adds the extra parameters needed to make a text box, and then assigns some text to it.

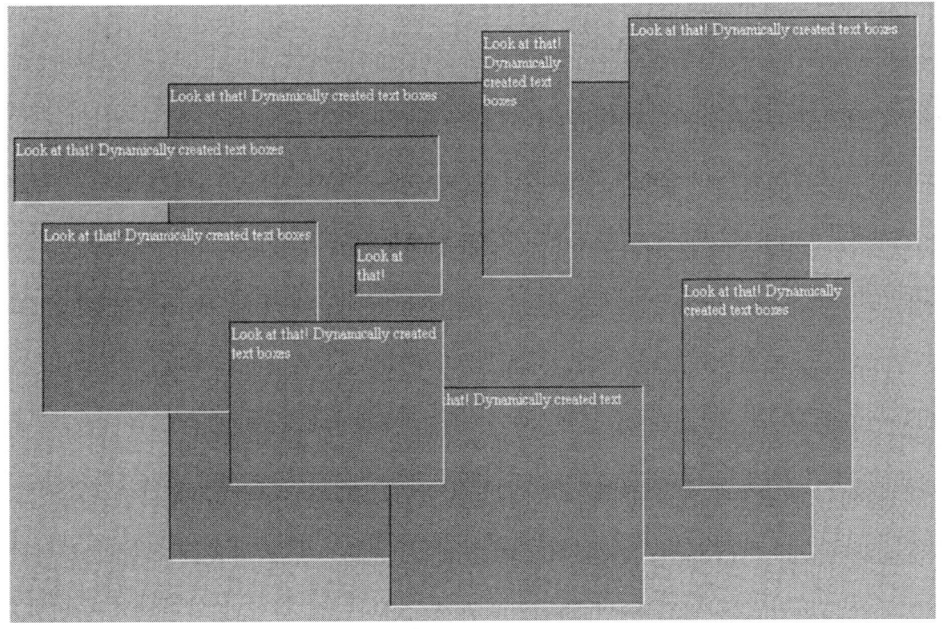

3

Enhancing the drawing functions

Now that the basics were working nicely, it was time to improve upon my dynamic user interface design, piece by piece.

First, although I was now drawing with the mouse, it wasn't quite as *visual* as I really wanted - mainly because I couldn't really see what I was drawing until *after* I released the mouse. What I needed was an interim shape to be drawn to give me an idea of what would eventually go there - like you might find in any drawing application. This is called **rubberbanding**.

The idea is simple - you just draw a shape, and erase it over and over so you have a continuous outline of where you started and where you are. And I've even given you a hint here regarding how we're going to do this - whenever you think about functionallty that needs to be 'continuous', or is repeated 'over and over', you should think onEnterFrame.

More specifically, for the rubberbanding in this example, I created an empty movie clip located on a very high level (10000 - so it would appear above any other screen content), and named it rb_mc. Then, I made a new function called rubberBand that gets assigned to onEnterFrame when the mouse is clicked, and is deleted when the mouse is released. Have a look at the new code in ui08.fla:

```
#include "interface.as"
createEmptyMovieClip("rb_mc", 10000);
onMouseDown = function () {
    x1 = _xmouse;
    y1 = _ymouse;
    onEnterFrame = rubberBand;
};
onMouseUp = function () {
    rb_mc.clear();
    delete onEnterFrame;
    x2 = _xmouse;
    y2 = _ymouse;
    myTextBox_mc = makeTextBox(x1, y1, x2-x1, y2-y1, 0x666666,
    ➥ "_serif", 12, 0xffffff);
    myTextBox_mc.display_txt.text = "Look at that! Dynamically
    ➥created text boxes";
};
function rubberBand() {
    rb_mc.clear();
    rb_mc.lineStyle(1, 0, 30);
    rb_mc.moveTo(x1, y1);
    rb_mc.lineTo(_xmouse, y1);
    rb_mc.lineTo(_xmouse, _ymouse);
    rb_mc.lineTo(x1, _ymouse);
    rb_mc.lineto(x1, y1);
}
```

As you can see if you test this code, when you click the mouse the `rubberBand` function starts executing on every frame. This clears the screen of any previously drawn lines, sets a line style as 1 pixel, black, 30% alpha (I don't want it too dark as it's just a hint), and draws a rectangle from the first point clicked to the current mouse position:

When you release the mouse, it first clears the `rb_mc` clip and stops the `rubberBand` function from running, then calls the chosen box drawing function:

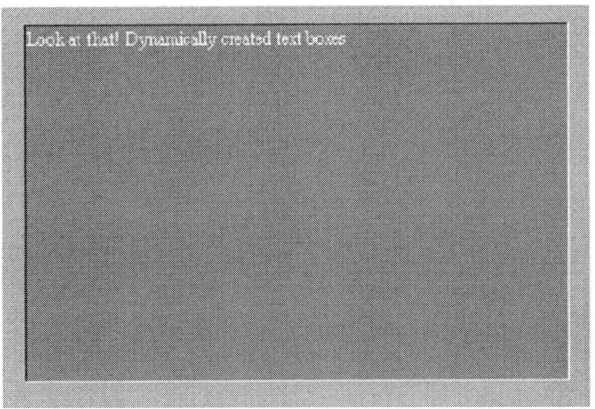

I was on a roll! But, after a bit of playing with this example, I found an ugly bug. Everything worked fine as long as I clicked and dragged down and to the right and released. But if I happened to drag upwards, or to the left of the original point, my box would somehow appear inverted:

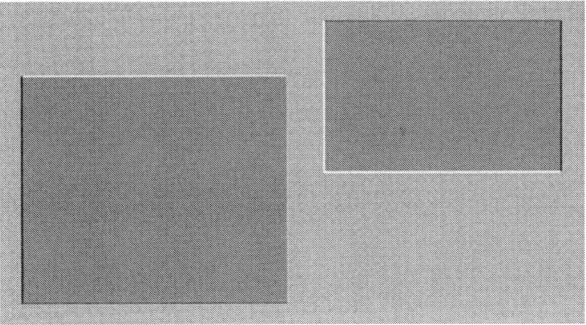

3

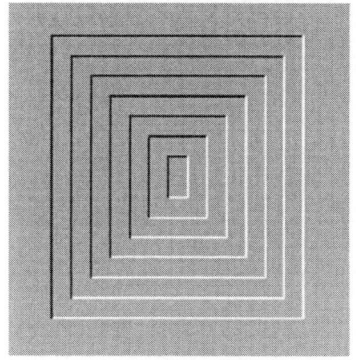

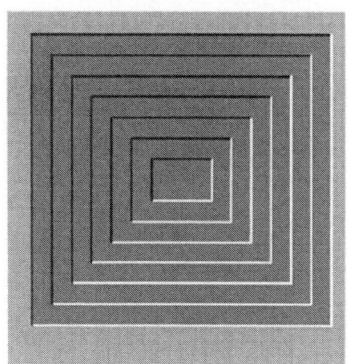

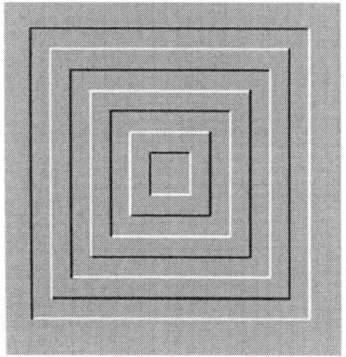

To fix this problem, I had two choices: I could either figure out which point was which and draw the box appropriately, or I could simply restrict the mouse control such that it would not allow a box to be drawn this way. After mulling it over, I decided the second option was a bit simpler. This took a couple lines in both the rubberBand function and the onMouseUp function. If the final value of either _xmouse or _ymouse was less than the original point, it would substitute the original point instead. Again, this had to be done for both the rubber band preview and the final box. Here's what the enhancements I came up with look like (you can see this code in action in ui09.fla):

```
#include "interface.as"
createEmptyMovieClip("rb_mc", 10000);
onMouseDown = function () {
    x1 = _xmouse;
    y1 = _ymouse;
    onEnterFrame = rubberBand;
};
onMouseUp = function () {
    rb_mc.clear();
    delete onEnterFrame;
    x2 = _xmouse<x1 ? x1 : _xmouse;
    y2 = _ymouse<y1 ? y1 : _ymouse;
    if (x1 != x2 && y1 != y2) {
        myTextBox_mc = makeTextBox(x1, y1, x2-x1, y2-y1,
        ➥ 0x666666, "_serif", 12, 0xffffff);
        myTextBox_mc.display_txt.text = "Look at that!
        ➥ Dynamically created text boxes";
    }
};
function rubberBand() {
    rb_mc.clear();
    rb_mc.lineStyle(1, 0, 30);
    rb_mc.moveTo(x1, y1);
    xtemp = _xmouse<x1 ? x1 : _xmouse;
    ytemp = _ymouse<y1 ? y1 : _ymouse;
    rb_mc.lineTo(xtemp, y1);
    rb_mc.lineTo(xtemp, ytemp);
    rb_mc.lineTo(x1, ytemp);
    rb_mc.lineto(x1, y1);
}
```

Here I've used a very cool and often poorly understood coding feature called a **tertiary operator**. It goes something like this:

```
condition ? do_this_if_true : do_this_if_false;
```

This is a very compact form of an `if/else` statement. The following pseudo-code would do exactly the same thing:

```
if(condition){
    do_this_if_true;
} else {
    do_this_if_false;
}
```

Personally, I don't use this technique too much, but in a case like this where I had to make four separate comparisons, it makes things a lot neater.

So, the code in question:

```
x2 = _xmouse<x1 ? x1 : _xmouse;
```

Essentially means this:

```
If _xmouse is less than x1, then x2 = x1.
If not, x2 = _xmouse.
```

Just as an extra touch, I also added the following `if` statement before drawing anything:

```
if (x1 != x2 && y1 != y2) {
```

This essentially says that Flash will only draw a box if `x1` doesn't equal `x2`, and `y1` does not equal `y2`. In other words, you can't draw a zero pixel high or wide box.

If you test that out, you'll see that you can't draw to the left or above the first point you click. So our bug's pretty much been swatted!

Now, on to another minor annoyance - say I drew a box on the left of the stage, then wanted to draw one beside it. My eyesight is pretty good, but it took a bit of work to get it lined up pixel-perfect. What I wanted next was a kind of *snap-to-grid* feature so I could casually draw boxes approximately where they should go and they'd all line up just right.

In the Flash authoring environment itself, I set my grids to 10 pixels (I was never quite sure what the logic of having 18 pixels as a default was!). To do this, I dug up a little trick for rounding off numbers. Say you want to round to the nearest multiple of ten. What you do is take your starting number, divide it by ten, round it off, then multiply by ten.

Take 14 as an example. 14 divided by 10 is 1.4. Round that off, and and you have 1, then multiply by 10, and you're left with 10. Easy! Similarly, starting with 16, 16/10 = 1.6, rounded is 2, times 10 is 20.

3

Here's how it looks in Flash, applied to mouse coordinates:

```
x1 = Math.round(_xmouse/10)*10;
y1 = Math.round(_ymouse/10)*10;
```

Now, when you click on the point (123, 218) for example, your starting point will actually be rounded off to (120, 220). It took a little work to fit in these code adjustments, but the result was pretty nice - test ui10.fla to see for yourself. Here's what the new code looks like:

```
#include "interface.as"
createEmptyMovieClip("rb_mc", 10000);
onMouseDown = function () {
    x1 = Math.round(_xmouse/10)*10;
    y1 = Math.round(_ymouse/10)*10;
    onEnterFrame = rubberBand;
};
onMouseUp = function () {
    rb_mc.clear();
    delete onEnterFrame;
    xRound = Math.round(_xmouse/10)*10;
    yRound = Math.round(_ymouse/10)*10;
    x2 = xRound<x1 ? x1 : xRound;
    y2 = yRound<y1 ? y1 : yRound;
    if (x1 != x2 && y1 != y2) {
        myTextBox_mc = makeTextBox(x1, y1, x2-x1, y2-y1,
        ➥ 0x666666, "_serif", 12, 0xffffff);
        myTextBox_mc.display_txt.text = "Look at that!
        ➥Dynamically created text boxes";
    }
};
function rubberBand() {
    rb_mc.clear();
    rb_mc.lineStyle(1, 0, 30);
    rb_mc.moveTo(x1, y1);
    xRound = Math.round(_xmouse/10)*10;
    yRound = Math.round(_ymouse/10)*10;
    xtemp = xRound<x1 ? x1 : xRound;
    ytemp = yRound<y1 ? y1 : yRound;
    rb_mc.lineTo(xtemp, y1);
    rb_mc.lineTo(xtemp, ytemp);
    rb_mc.lineTo(x1, ytemp);
    rb_mc.lineto(x1, y1);
}
```

This just makes another couple of interim variables, xRound and yRound, and uses them where I previously had _xmouse and _ymouse. It also rounds the original onMouseDown points. Now, as long as you have just a minimal amount of hand/eye coordination, you can have all your windows lined up just perfectly and make some pretty neat layouts.

These enhancements were all coming along just fine, but there was still plenty of room for further improvements. The most obvious drawback was that you could only draw one type of box. I'd been drawing tons of text boxes, but if I wanted to draw another kind of box instead, I had to exit the program and change the source code! Obviously that had to change.

First, I made four buttons, giving them each a highlighted Down state to indicate the selection, and put them on the far left of the stage. I made these buttons visually correspond to the four different types of boxes I could make, and named the instances: panel_btn, inset_btn, screen_btn, and textBox_btn. Open up ui11.fla to follow along with this example:

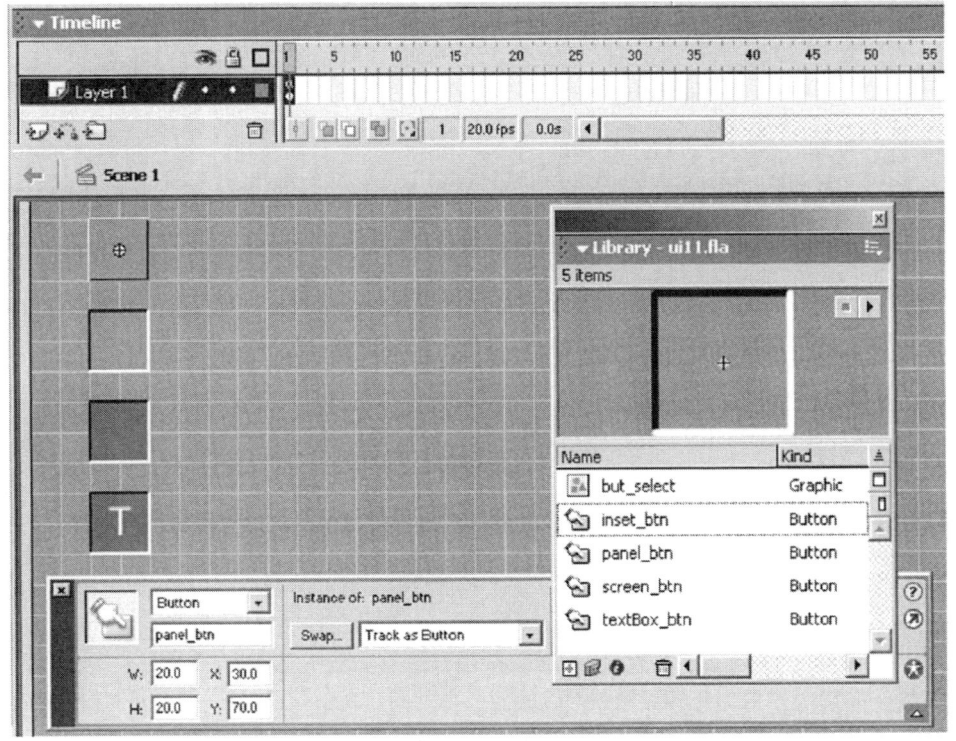

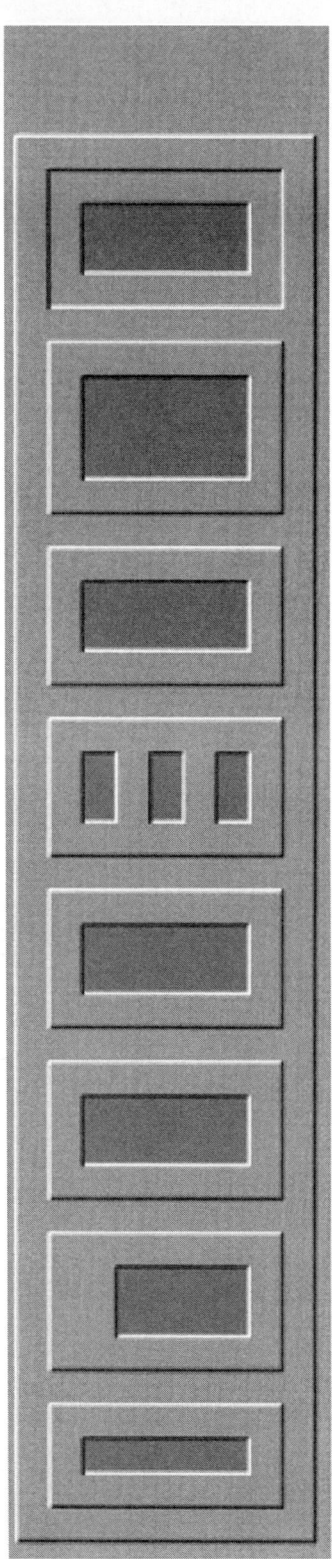

My plan was to be able to click the relevant button to determine what type of box to draw next. The only problem was that I was now using the mouse for two purposes – to select the box style, and for the actual drawing. If I clicked on a button as the code is right now, the onMouseDown function would still fire and begin drawing a box right at that point. That wouldn't do, so I needed some way of saying, "If I am clicking *here*, just read the button press, but if I'm clicking *over here*, then start drawing a box."

I decided to take an almost literal interpretation of that, using the position of where the mouse was clicked as the deciding factor. As you can see in the above screenshot, the buttons only extend out to 40 pixels from the left edge of the movie. So, if _xmouse is 40 or less when I press, then I am obviously going for a button. If it's more than 40, I must be drawing a box. Thus, the onMouseDown function should check this:

```
onMouseDown = function () {
    if (_xmouse>40) {
        x1 = Math.round(_xmouse/10)*10;
        y1 = Math.round(_ymouse/10)*10;
        onEnterFrame = rubberBand;
        drawing = true;
    }
};
```

Note the last line that sets a variable drawing to true. I'll use this shortly in the onMouseUp function.

Now that that business was sorted out, I could go about assigning my button handlers. For this, I simply had each one assign a value to the mode variable. Note that I first set mode to a default value of panel so we can start off drawing, without the need to hit a button:

```
mode = "panel";
panel_btn.onRelease = function() {
    mode = "panel";
};
inset_btn.onRelease = function() {
    mode = "inset";
};
screen_btn.onRelease = function() {
    mode = "screen";
};
textBox_btn.onRelease = function() {
    mode = "textBox";
};
```

Then when I'm ready to draw a box, I just need to check which mode I want and draw the appropriate type of box. This happens in the onMouseUp function:

```
onMouseUp = function () {
    if (drawing) {
        rb_mc.clear();
        delete onEnterFrame;
        xRound = Math.round(_xmouse/10)*10;
        yRound = Math.round(_ymouse/10)*10;
        x2 = xRound<x1 ? x1 : xRound;
        y2 = yRound<y1 ? y1 : yRound;
        if (x1 != x2 && y1 != y2) {
            switch (mode) {
            case "panel" :
                makePanel(x1, y1, x2-x1, y2-y1);
                break;
            case "screen" :
                makeScreen(x1, y1, x2-x1, y2-y1, 0x666666);
                break;
            case "inset" :
                makeInset(x1, y1, x2-x1, y2-y1);
                break;
            case "textBox" :
                myTextBox = makeTextBox(x1, y1, x2-x1, y2-y1,
            ➥ 0x666666, "_serif", 12, 0xffffff);
                myTextBox.display_txt.text = "Text goes in
            ➥ here.";
                break;
            }
            drawing = false;
        }
    }
};
```

See how first it checks to make sure the drawing variable is true. This will only be the case if you've clicked on the screen area to the right of the buttons. If so, it goes through the normal routine of calculating the points to draw to, and then uses a switch statement – switch is like an if/else statement made much simpler. The value you are testing goes inside the parentheses after the switch keyword:

```
switch (mode) {
case "panel" :
    makePanel(x1, y1, x2-x1, y2-y1);
    break;
```

3

Then you make a series of case statements inside the brackets. After case, you put the value you are testing, followed by a colon. If the value matches what's there, it will execute the statements that follow. You should remember to put a break statement after each case block to tell Flash that you want to stop executing code there. Here, we compare the variable mode against the four possible variables to discover what mode we are in, and then draw the appropriate box.

This function then sets drawing to false, ready for the next round of drawing. Here's the complete code for ui11.fla:

```
#include "interface.as"
mode = "panel";
panel_btn.onRelease = function() {
   mode = "panel";
};
inset_btn.onRelease = function() {
   mode = "inset";
};
screen_btn.onRelease = function() {
   mode = "screen";
};
textBox_btn.onRelease = function() {
   mode = "textBox";
};
createEmptyMovieClip("rb_mc", 10000);
onMouseDown = function () {
   if (_xmouse>40) {
      x1 = Math.round(_xmouse/10)*10;
      y1 = Math.round(_ymouse/10)*10;
      onEnterFrame = rubberBand;
      drawing = true;
   }
};
onMouseUp = function () {
   if (drawing) {
      rb_mc.clear();
      delete onEnterFrame;
      xRound = Math.round(_xmouse/10)*10;
      yRound = Math.round(_ymouse/10)*10;
      x2 = xRound<x1 ? x1 : xRound;
      y2 = yRound<y1 ? y1 : yRound;
      if (x1 != x2 && y1 != y2) {
         switch (mode) {
```

```
            case "panel" :
                makePanel(x1, y1, x2-x1, y2-y1);
                break;
            case "screen" :
                makeScreen(x1, y1, x2-x1, y2-y1, 0x666666);
                break;
            case "inset" :
                makeInset(x1, y1, x2-x1, y2-y1);
                break;
            case "textBox" :
                myTextBox = makeTextBox(x1, y1, x2-x1, y2-y1,
                ➥ 0x666666, "_serif", 12, 0xffffff);
                myTextBox.display_txt.text = "Text goes in
                ➥ here.";
                break;
            }
            drawing = false;
        }
    }
};
function rubberBand() {
    rb_mc.clear();
    rb_mc.lineStyle(1, 0, 30);
    rb_mc.moveTo(x1, y1);
    xRound = Math.round(_xmouse/10)*10;
    yRound = Math.round(_ymouse/10)*10;
    xtemp = xRound<x1 ? x1 : xRound;
    ytemp = yRound<y1 ? y1 : yRound;
    rb_mc.lineTo(xtemp, y1);
    rb_mc.lineTo(xtemp, ytemp);
    rb_mc.lineTo(x1, ytemp);
    rb_mc.lineto(x1, y1);
}
```

Test this FLA to see what kind of dynamic interfaces you can design:

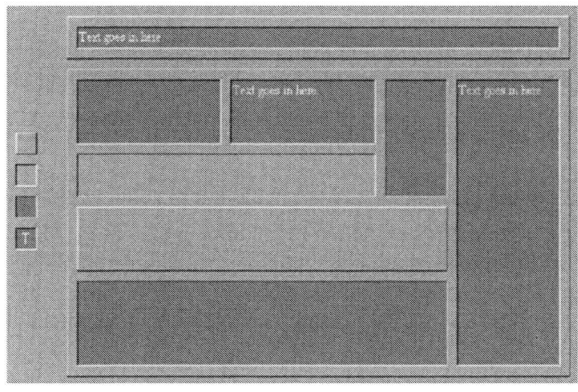

At this point, I was almost there – but there was still one more improvement I wanted to make. As things stand, if you make a mistake in drawing your boxes, you have to start over again from scratch. I figured the least I could do was to allow the user to delete a box if he made an error.

To do this required two things: firstly, in order to remove a movie clip from the stage, you need to tell Flash which one, so we need a reference to the movie clip that contained that last box drawn, so that it can be deleted. Luckily, I had constructed the box drawing functions so that they returned a reference. That came as a relief. Next, I needed some way to signal that deletion was desired. I figured the left cursor key would do just fine for that purpose.

As far as coding, I also needed to add a bit to the lines that draw the boxes in the onMouseUp function, so that they retain a unique reference to each new box created. By saving each box with a separate, numbered variable name, I could effectively have multiple levels of undo. Cool!

This new program is saved as ui12.fla, but don't worry - we'll discuss the modifications right now. Firstly, note that I need to set up the variable count to equal 0. This is done outside the function so that it only runs once. Then, whenever a box is made, it gets a dynamically assigned variable name. The first one would be _root["box"+0], which ends up being _root.box0; the next would be _root["box"+1], or _root.box1, and so on.

I've also added the code to make the left cursor button work as a delete function. Up at the top of the file, right after the #include line, I've got a line that allows the main time line (_root) to respond to key presses:

```
Key.addListener(_root);
```

Now that _root can *listen* to the keyboard, we set up a function at the end of the file to tell it what to do when one is pressed:

```
_root.onKeyDown = function() {
   if (Key.getCode() == Key.LEFT) {
      if (count>0) {
         count-;
         removeMovieClip(_root["box"+count]);
      }
   }
};
```

The first line of the function checks to see if it was in fact the left cursor key that was pressed. Then we check the value of the count variable to make sure it is at least 1. That keeps us from going into negative numbers, which might cause some very odd results. The next line subtracts 1 from count and deletes the movie clip associated with that value - this will be the last movie clip created. If you test out ui12.fla, you'll see that subsequent presses of the left cursor key go right back down the chain of boxes that have been created, deleting them. Perfect!

All right – the application was now pretty much what I had set out to do in the first place. Of course, this is only really the beginning. As with any interface, it merely serves to present content in a certain format. And remember, at the start of this chapter I mentioned that this example should be highly extensible – you can use it as a base to create some really interesting and low-cal dynamic Flash interfaces.

To start off, you'll most likely want to change the text in the text box. I'm sure you can think of something more interesting to say! Furthermore, you could easily use the `loadVars` method to load in an external text file, or even access a database for updated content.

For example, you'd first set up a text file on your server named something like `content.txt`. This could contain the following:

```
info=All work and no play makes Jonny a dull boy!
```

Now, in Flash, create a `loadVars` object named `textLoader` and create a function for it to run when it loads some text. Then tell it to load the text file:

```
#include "interface.as"
makePanel(60, 10, 510, 360);
makeInset(70, 20, 490, 340);
myTextBox = makeTextBox(80, 200, 470, 150);
makePanel(80, 30, 230, 160);
makePanel(320, 30, 230, 160);
makeInset(90, 40, 210, 140);
makeInset(330, 40, 210, 140);
textLoader = new loadVars();
textLoader.onLoad = function() {
    myTextBox.display_txt.text = this.info;
};
textLoader.load("content.txt");
```

3

Now, when the text file loads in, it will assign the text to that text box. Rather than updating the Flash file whenever you want to change the content, you just need to revise the text file. Try this out with ui13.fla:

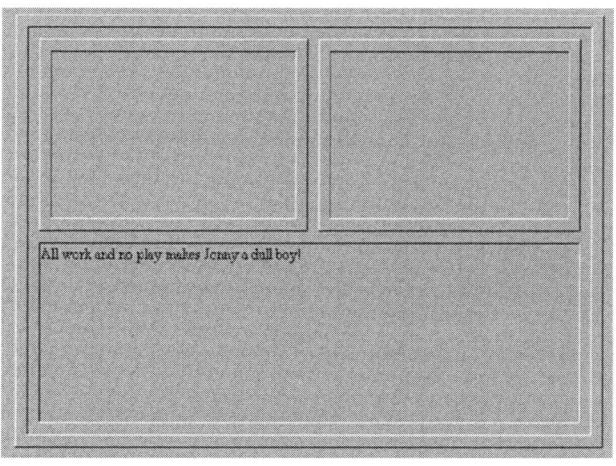

You can load other content into these boxes – for instance, if you're getting a little bored with the flat gray panels in our examples (OK, I admit it, they're not the most exciting things in the world!), you can load another whole Flash movie in with `loadMovie`, or you can even directly load in a picture. But remember, before loading anything into a box, it's worth first creating an empty movie clip within that box and then loading the content into that. For example, open up `ui14.fla` to see how this can be achieved:

```
#include "interface.as"
makePanel(60, 10, 510, 360);
makeInset(70, 20, 490, 340);
myTextBox = makeTextBox(80, 200, 470, 150);
myTextBox.display_txt.text = "Here is a picture of myself
➥ with a strange grin.";
makePanel(80, 30, 230, 160);
makePanel(320, 30, 230, 160);
pic = makeInset(90, 40, 210, 140);
pic.createEmptyMovieClip("picHolder", 0);
pic.picHolder.loadMovie("face.jpg");
makeInset(330, 40, 210, 140);
```

Here I saved a reference to one of the inset boxes I created, calling it `pic`. Then I created an empty movie clip inside `pic` called `picHolder` and loaded the picture into that. In this case, I had already sized my picture to fit in the box, but if the incoming picture was another size, you could even resize `picHolder` using its `_width` and `_height` properties to make it fit exactly. Note that when you prepare your JPEG files for loading, it's important that they are of a standard JPEG format, without progressive encoding. This is usually an option that can be turned on or off in a graphics program like Photoshop. Flash MX is unable to load and display a progressive JPEG file.

Here's what this ends up looking like:

Here is a picture of myself with a strange grin.

Don't forget that you can also change the size, color, and font of the text, and combine any of the techniques and effects that we've covered to create eye-catching interfaces. Just refer back to the functions we've looked at throughout this chapter. The examples we've studied have shown us how to create a dynamic Flash user interface with nothing but ActionScript.

More than anything, I hope that you've picked up some valuable tips on how to start using the drawing API to create cool interface elements and, ultimately, to minimize the file size of your Flash movies.

3

4 MATH-BASED ANIMATION AND DYNAMIC DRAWING

KEITH PETERS

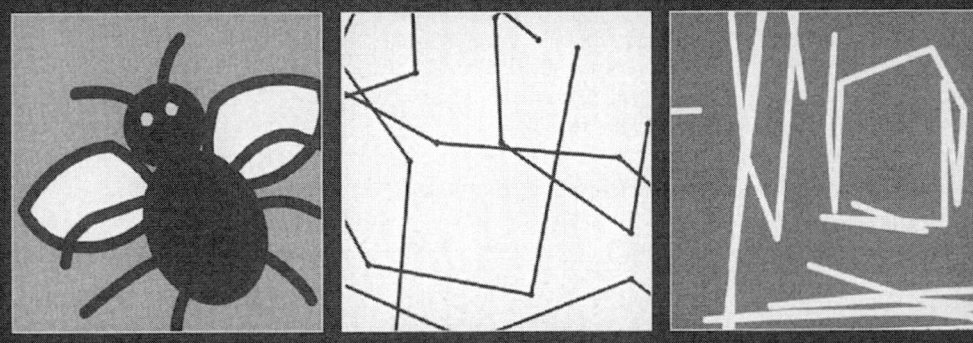

In this chapter I'll cover a few simple and compact ways to add a little punch to your Flash files through math-based animation and some dynamic drawing using the drawing API of Flash MX. It's time to start getting math and ActionScript to do the hard work for you!

Traditional timeline-based Flash animation works like this:

1. Create a keyframe and draw your object;

2. Create another keyframe and move your object to it's new position;

3. Finally, Flash creates the *in-between* frames to perform a smooth animation. This, as you'll know, is called tweening.

That's the way it's been done for many years, and there's nothing wrong with that. However, if you're willing to learn a bit of math and some ActionScript, you can do much much better. With just a few lines of code, you can create some seemingly complex and continually changing animation.

We'll extend upon what we learned about the drawing API in the last chapter to create not only a simple on-screen drawing program, but one that can save and play back our drawings in real time!

Math-based animation

In math-based **scripted animation**, we take a completely different approach to that of the tweened animation we've just described.

Typically, an animated object from such a movie will be static in the authoring environment - located on the stage, or maybe held in the Library. Flash will then perform some calculations, according to your ActionScript, to determine where the object will move to in the compiled SWF. With some calculations, we don't necessarily know exactly where it's going to end up, just where it is at any particular point. In this way, you can often get much more realistic and dynamic animations than are possible through tweening, where you are pretty much stuck with what you create in the first place.

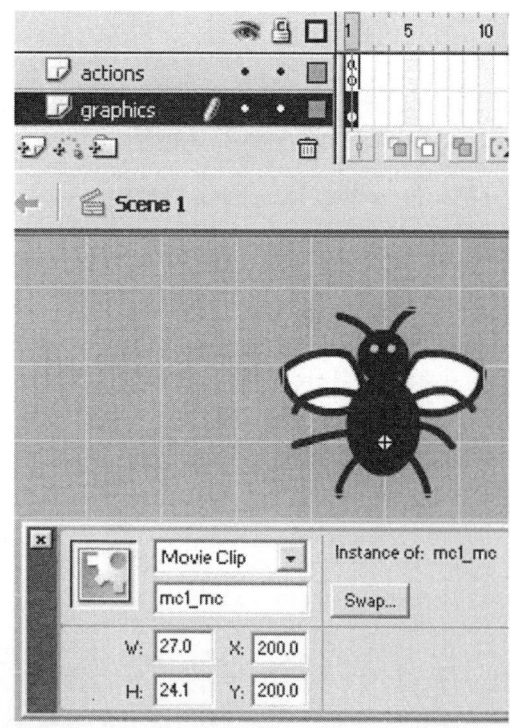

Another great thing about scripted animations is that their SWF file sizes are, in general, much smaller than pre-rendered tweens. We don't need dozens of frames of information about where the object is – we just need the object itself and a few lines of code containing a particular formula.

You just take the equation that you want to control your animation and put it inside a function that, for instance, might run the code on every new frame. Whatever code you put in an onEnterFrame block will be executed every time Flash begins a new frame, which can be many times per second. Let's look at a simple example to get started - open up fly1.fla from this chapter's code files.

Here I have a movie clip – a picture of a fly – on the stage and I've named this instance `mc1_mc`.

I've also placed the following code in a layer named actions on frame 1 of the main timeline:

```
mc1_mc.onEnterFrame = function() {
    this._x += 5;
};
```

Test the movie, and the movie clip should zip across the stage to the right. OK, simple enough! The expression `_x += 5` just adds 5 pixels to the x position of the movie clip on each new frame. Note that even if you only have one frame in the movie, Flash will still generate an `enterFrame` event twenty times a second, or whatever you set your frame rate to.

Introducing sine waves

Now, I happen to be a big fan of math when it comes to programming in Flash. It's not that I'm so fond of numbers, but by using math you can create some very compact functions that enable highly complex behavior. One of my all time favorite math functions is **Math.sin**. You probably noticed in the above example that the movement was pretty linear to say the least. It moved in one direction at one speed and will continue doing that until you end the program.

We could program a confusing series of `if` statements, so that when the clip got to the right edge, it would turn around and go the other way, and then when it got to the left edge, it would turn around again, and so on. But we'd still have the problem of speed. It's traveling at 5 pixels per frame and suddenly it's moving the same speed in the opposite direction. Not very realistic! But the `Math.sin` command can handle all of that!

Before you start getting nervous, I'm not going to teach you trigonometry, at least not any of that confusing triangle stuff. I'm simply going to show you how to utilize this very useful function, what you put into it, and what you can get out of it. All you really need to know about `Math.sin` is that you give it the value of an angle, and it gives you back a number between -1 and 1.

The following diagram shows how the sine value oscillates from 0 to 1, to 0 then -1, and back to 0 again – you can clearly see why it's referred to as a sine *wave*:

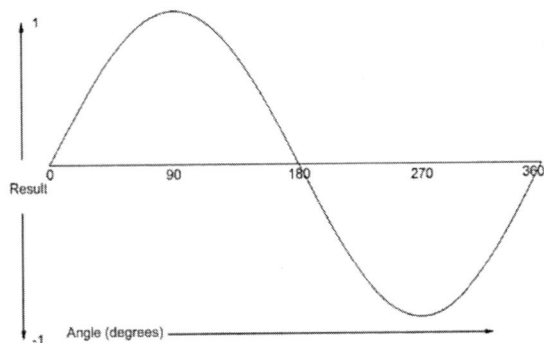

4

The way we use this is that on each frame we give the `Math.sin` function a slightly larger angle, so if we start at 0, the result will be 0. As we increase the angle on each frame, the result will be a small fraction, then a little bigger and bigger, until it finally reaches 1. As we continue increasing the angle, it will go back into fractions, eventually arriving at 0, then continuing down to -1. If we continue increasing the angle, this up and down cycle continues as the output, and we can use this to control whatever we want.

In case this has gotten you completely confused, let's see it in action.

First, however, there is one thing you should know about using `Math.sin` in Flash. Above, I've shown the angle as being between 0 and 360 degrees, which is usually how we think of angles. But for some reason, people who create computer languages with trig functions tend to like a different form of measurement: **radians** instead of degrees. A full circle (360 degrees) is about 6.28 radians. All this really boils down to for our purposes is that we need to use a much smaller number to increment our angle each frame. To simplify our example, instead of going from 0 to 360 in one circle, we're just going to go from 0 to 6.

OK, let's look at the relevant code - in fact, it's really simple, but the result is pretty cool. Open up `fly2.fla`. You'll see that I've used the `fly` movie clip from the previous example, `mc1_mc`, but I've changed the code inside the `onEnterFrame` loop:

```
mc1_mc.onEnterFrame = function() {
    result = Math.sin(angle)*50;
    this._y = 200+result;
    angle += .1;
};
```

If you test this movie, you should have a nice up and down bobbing motion going on with your movie clip. What I did was take the sine of angle, which is going to range from -1 to 1, and multiply it by 50, making the result go from -50 to 50. In the next line, I added that to 200, giving us a range of motion from 150 to 250. I applied that to the _y position of the clip, and finally, incremented the angle by just a little each time (0.1 radians, or about 6 degrees, each frame).

Try playing around with this `.1` number - the higher it is, the faster your clip will move. You'll probably want to keep it between .01 and 1.

Next, being a stickler for optimization, I squished all this code into one line, giving me the following function:

```
mc1_mc.onEnterFrame = function() {
    this._y = Math.sin(angle += .1)*50+200;
};
```

Believe it or not, this is the exact same thing - it increments the angle, gets the sine value of it, multiplies it by 50 and adds it to 200, finally assigning the result to the movie clip's _y property! Whew!

If you wanted to abstract this into terms you could think with, instead of just plain numbers, you could write it something like this:

```
this._y = Math.sin(angle += speed)*range + center
```

We already covered the `speed` parameter earlier; `range` determines how much it moves in each direction, and `center` is merely the point it moves around. In fact, it would normally be good programming practice to write it out just like that, and assign values to the variables `speed`, `range`, and `center` earlier. I was just shooting for the smallest, most compact and efficient code I could get, while retaining at least some legibility!

Flying in waves

Occasionally someone asks me how to get an object to fly around the screen randomly, like a housefly buzzing around the room. They usually go at it trying to create random numbers for velocity and so forth. I came up with a pretty good trick that's just one step away from what I just showed you.

In the previous example, the movie clip only moving on the y-axis; of course, I can do exactly the same thing for the x-axis too. The key for a seemingly random motion is to give them different angles to increment, effectively giving them different speeds. Take a look at the following code from `fly3.fla`:

```
mc1_mc.onEnterFrame = function() {
    this._x = Math.sin(angleX += .08)*200+275;
    this._y = Math.sin(angleY += .12)*200+200;
};
```

Here I've added another line for the x-axis, and changed `angle` to `angleX` and `angleY`. I also changed the range and center points and came up with some different speeds. When you test this FLA, you'll see a pretty smooth, fluid motion from only two lines of code!

You might ask where I came up with the 'speed' numbers of .08 and .12. To be honest, I just played around with them until the result was what I wanted. Feel free to do the same! For instance, I got an entirely different effect by upping the speeds and lowering the ranges like this:

```
mc1_mc.onEnterFrame = function() {
    this._x = Math.sin(angleX += .75)*20+275;
    this._y = Math.sin(angleY += .79)*20+200;
};
```

Clearly, these experiments are just the beginning - so far, we've only used two properties of a movie clip, _x and _y. So, realizing that there was a lot more that could be done, I decided to explore further.

4

Scale

How about scale? A movie clip has properties for _xscale and _yscale, and it took relatively minor changes to convert the code to deal with that (fly4.fla):

```
mc1_mc.onEnterFrame = function() {
    this._xscale = Math.sin(angleX += .08)*100+100;
    this._yscale = Math.sin(angleY += .12)*100+100;
};
```

I simply addressed the scale properties rather than the position, and went back to the earlier values for the trig functions to create a slower cycle. I then multiplied by 100 and added 100, to give me a result that scaled each axis of the movie clip from 0% to 200%. Test the FLA to see the result - the fact that the x- and y-axes scale independently gives it a very jello-like feel!

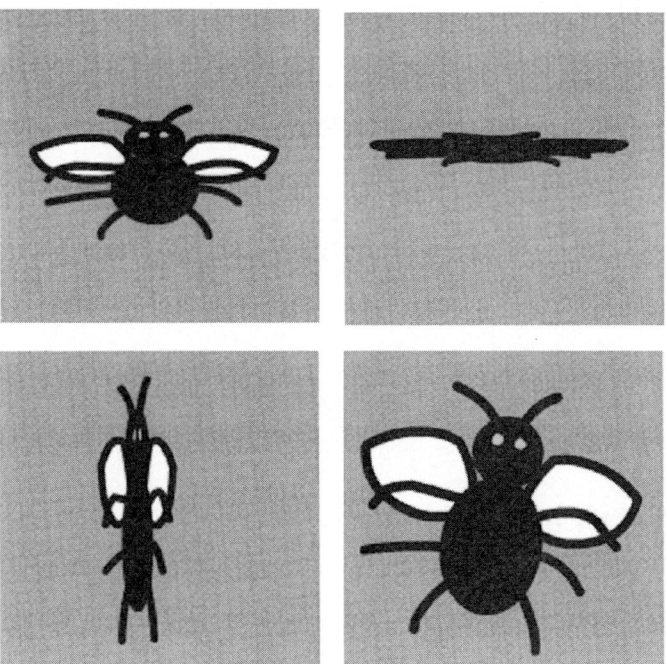

If you wanted a more solid, but throbbing kind of effect, keep them the same:

```
mc1_mc.onEnterFrame = function() {
    this._xscale = Math.sin(angleX += .08)*100+100;
    this._yscale = this._xscale;
};
```

This just sets the _xscale and tells the _yscale to be the same. You could even try leaving off one scale altogether.

Transparency

Hmmm... this is getting fun! Next up, I wanted to play around with the transparency using the _alpha property. Check out fly5.fla, in which I've centered the range around 50 in order to cycle the opacity from 0 to 100, producing a cool fading in and out effect. Here's the relevant code:

```
mc1_mc.onEnterFrame = function() {
    this._alpha = Math.sin(angleX += .08)*50+50;
};
```

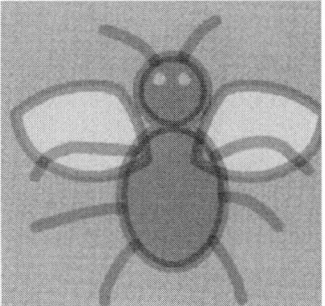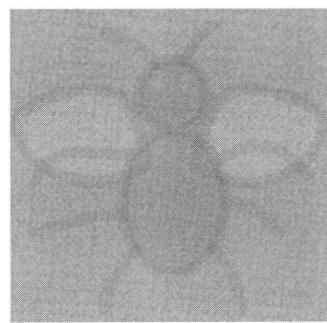

Rotation

Next up: rotation! To use this property, ensure that the movie clip you are using has some features that might indicate which direction it is rotated. Obviously, a plain circle will not look any different, no matter how you turn it! Check out this code - you'll find it inside fly6.fla:

```
mc1_mc.onEnterFrame = function() {
    this._rotation = Math.sin(angleX += .08)*180;
};
```

Note that in this case the _rotation property takes the rotation of the movie clip in degrees, rather than radians. Here, I've just set mine up to go from −180 to +180 degrees.

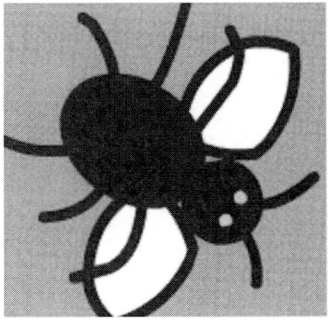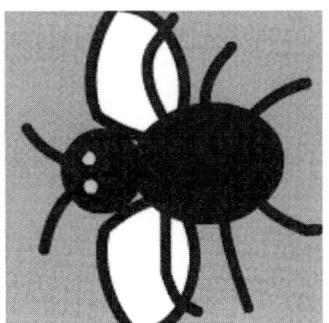

4

If you wanted something different, just remember the *range* and *center* that we discussed earlier. For instance to make it go from 0 to 180 degrees, specify the center as 90, so it goes 90 degrees either way:

```
mc1_mc.onEnterFrame = function() {
    this._rotation = Math.sin(angleX += .08)*90+90;
};
```

Well, there you have it - trigonometry can be a powerful tool to create smooth animation in a compact Flash file!

Run-time drawing applications

As we've just seen, ActionScript combined with a little math can be great for creating either very random seeming, or very regular, effects. But what about if you have some very specific shape or path you want to appear on screen, such as a little doodle or a hand-drawn message?

Well, in the last chapter we saw that the drawing API in Flash MX can be used to create specific shapes at run-time, but a commonly requested feature is to be able to draw a picture from a Flash movie, save it, and redraw it again later. So this was the next project I wanted to tackle - my end goal was to have the original drawing re-animate itself, as if drawn by an invisible hand.

In this case, you need to *record* and *play back* each position that has been drawn. After thinking it over long and hard, I came up with what I believe is some pretty compact code that will do just that. First though, I needed to get to grips with using arrays to store my drawing data.

Using arrays

I knew that any Flash drawing was going to generate a whole bunch of x and y coordinate values and I'd need a place to store all this information - **arrays** were my answer. An array is simply a list of values stored under one name (such as myArray). You can then access the individual values within an array numerically:

```
myArray[0]
myArray[1]
myArray[2]
  .
  .
  .
```

Or by string labels:

```
myArray["name"]
myArray["date"]
myArray["color"]
    .
    .
    .
```

The number or label used inside the brackets is called the **index**, and the information stored in the array under that index is called the **element**. To store a value in an array element, just type it as above and use it like any other variable. For example, consider these lines of script:

```
myArray = new Array();
myArray[0] = "Hello";
myArray[1] = " World!";
trace(myArray);
```

When tested, this would result in the following output:

Note that I've used the array constructor here, `new Array()`, to create the array before populating it with a couple of strings. On tracing the array to the Output window, we see that a comma delimits the two elements.

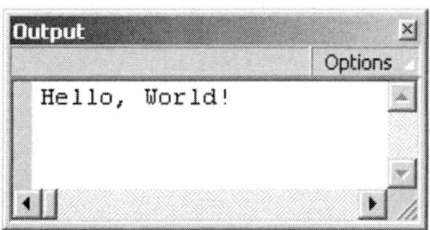

Even more useful is that the array in Flash MX is a fully-fledged object with several valuable methods and properties. These make possible powerful routines for moving through the array, accessing or changing data, or adding and removing elements. For more information, take a look at the ActionScript Reference window, accessible through the Actions panel - I used several of these in the next files.

Just to get the hang of using arrays, let's look at a little exercise I created that uses the drawing API to draw some lines based on the values contained in an array. Open up `array1.fla`, and take a look at the code on frame 1 of the main timeline - the result of this code is very similar to the simple dynamic interfaces we were constructing in the previous chapter, but the technique here is rather different.

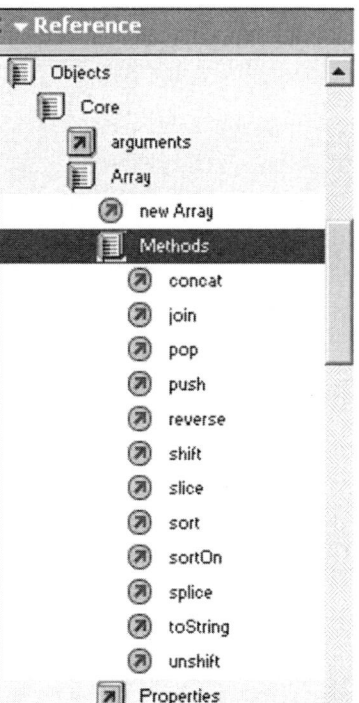

4

I start out by making an array called `points` and immediately filled it with a bunch of numbers.

```
points = [20, 20, 530, 20, 530, 360, 20, 360, 20, 20];
```

Although it isn't immediately obvious, these numbers are grouped together as (x, y) pairs. The first is (20, 20), then (530, 20), and so on. There are more elegant ways of setting up an array, as we saw with the constructor code earlier, but this will give us an extremely compact routine for retrieving (and later on storing) the data.

Next, I set the index (using the variable `i`) to 0. By using array elements `i` and `i+1`, I can access the first two elements from the array, which form an (x, y) point. Then I use this in a `moveTo` command and then set a `lineStyle`:

```
i = 0;
moveTo(points[i], points[i+1]);
lineStyle(1, 0, 100);
```

This moves the drawing tool to point (20, 20) and sets a black line one point thick. Next, I start to draw a line:

```
i += 2;
while (i<points.length) {
    lineTo(points[i], points[i+1]);
    i += 2;
}
```

I then need to jump to the next pair of (x, y) values, (530, 20). I do this by adding 2 to the value of `i`. This makes the array pointer jump forward two elements.

The next command is wrapped in a `while` loop – the basic structure is like this:

```
while (condition is true){
        do this
}
```

In other words, as long as the condition inside of the parentheses is true, the stuff inside the brackets will execute over and over and over. You have to be careful with `while` loops. If you set up a condition that never changes, or never evaluates to `true`, the program will hang right there, looping infinitely. In fact, Flash will eventually notice there's a problem and step in and ask you if you want to stop running the loop. But you shouldn't let it get that far!

The code in question looks like this:

```
while (i<points.length) {
    lineTo(points[i], points[i+1]);
    i += 2;
}
```

The condition we are checking for translates to this:

Is i less than the length of the points array? If it is less, then there is more data in the array and we should keep executing the lines that follow. If it is not, then we have hit the end of the array and should stop what we are doing.

The code within this while loop simply draws a line to the next point, and adds 2 to the index again to set it up for the next line.

One thing I didn't like about this was that I had one line, i += 2, in there twice. This was clearly inefficient, and in need of further optimization. After playing around with it a bit, I found a more elegant solution to create the box (array2.fla):

```
points = [20, 20, 530, 20, 530, 360, 20, 360, 20, 20];
i = 0;
moveTo(points[i], points[i+1]);
lineStyle(1, 0, 100);
while ((i += 2)<points.length) {
    lineTo(points[i], points[i+1]);
}
```

In this case, the optimized while statement adds 2 to the index just before it checks it against the length. This takes care of the first increment and each increment inside the loop.

OK, so now test the movie - it draws a simple rectangle on the screen. That's one line of ActionScript for the data, and half a dozen lines to draw it. The important thing to note is that you don't need to change those half dozen lines if you want to draw more lines - we've created a *reusable* chunk of code here. You can add as many pairs of numbers to the array as you want and those few lines will run through them all to draw the lines.

4

Next, I thought it would be nice if I could start drawing in a new place using the same array. Of course, this would be done with an additional moveTo, but I needed some way to indicate that the array contained a new drawing. I decided to use the value of null to be the signal. Check out the revised code in array3.fla:

```
points = [20, 20, 530, 20, 530, 380, 20, 380, 20, 20, null,
➥ 40, 40, 510, 40, 510, 360, 40, 360, 40, 40];
i = 0;
lineStyle(1, 0, 100);
moveTo(points[i], points[i+1]);
while ((i += 2)<points.length) {
   if (points[i] == null) {
      i++;
      moveTo(points[i], points[i+1]);
   } else {
      lineTo(points[i], points [i+1]);
   }
}
```

In the while loop, I just check to see if the current element is null. If so, I increment the value of i to jump to the next value pairs, and then moveTo that next point. This is what the result should look like when you test this code:

OK, not the most exciting of designs - but the important thing is that we've used an array of points containing the coordinates for both rectangles, and a null value element to separate the two sets of points. Obviously, this code is quite extensible - you can enter as many point pairs as you want, and use null each time you want to start a new shape. The code will handle it all quite happily!

Gathering data for your drawing

Now that we've learned how to pull data out of an array to draw with, let's see how to automatically collect it into an array. The idea here is to translate a visual representation into numerical data for later use.

I've saved this example as `draw_array.fla` – you'll find it in the code files that go with this chapter. First, I needed some visual element to show the points that I'd be entering. I made a simple movie clip containing a 2x2 pixel circle and named it `dot`. I usually use `attachMovie` to place movie clips on the screen, especially in cases like this where you don't know when or how many will be needed - `attachMovie` pulls a movie clip right out of the Library and puts it on stage while the movie is running.

However, in order to access movie clips in the Library at runtime, you have to remember to give them specific linkage names so that Flash can go in and grab it when needed. When you are converting a shape to a symbol, you have the option in the Advanced section to Export for ActionScript, so be sure to check that and give it an export name. I generally use the same name that I give the movie clip, to avoid confusion. Here, you can see I used `dot` for both the movie clip name *and* linkage name:

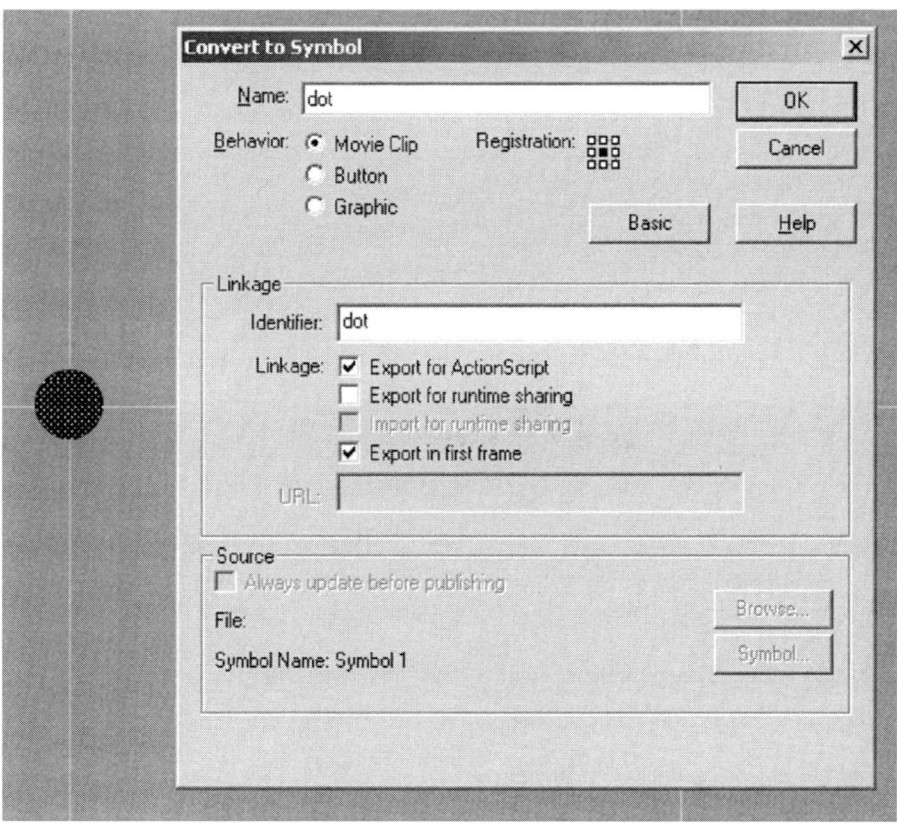

4

So now we don't need to leave any instances of dot on the stage because we can attach them dynamically as required.

Turning your attention to the ActionScript on frame 1 of the main timeline of draw_array.fla, after setting up an empty array, again called points, I've defined a function that enables me to create my drawing points. This will run each time I press the mouse button:

```
points = [];
onMouseDown = function () {
    attachMovie("dot", "dot"+dotCount, dotCount++,
    ➡ {_x:_xmouse, _y:_ymouse});
    points.push(_xmouse, _ymouse);
};
```

The first line of this function attaches a copy of the dot movie clip to the stage. The part of this line that you might not recognize is the optional fourth parameter for attachMovie, called the initialization object:

```
attachMovie("dot", "dot"+dotCount, dotCount++,
➡ {_x:_xmouse, X_y:_ymouse});
```

Flash will take any properties set up in that initialization object and transfer them over to the newly created clip after it is attached - it's a neat code-saving technique. Here, I've set up the _x and _y properties of the object to equal the mouse coordinates, so they will be instantly assigned to the new dot movie clip, placing it exactly where I click the mouse.

Next up, I use the push method of the points array to update the array:

```
points.push(_xmouse, _ymouse);
```

Any values put inside points.push will be tacked onto the end of the array as new elements. Pretty simple.

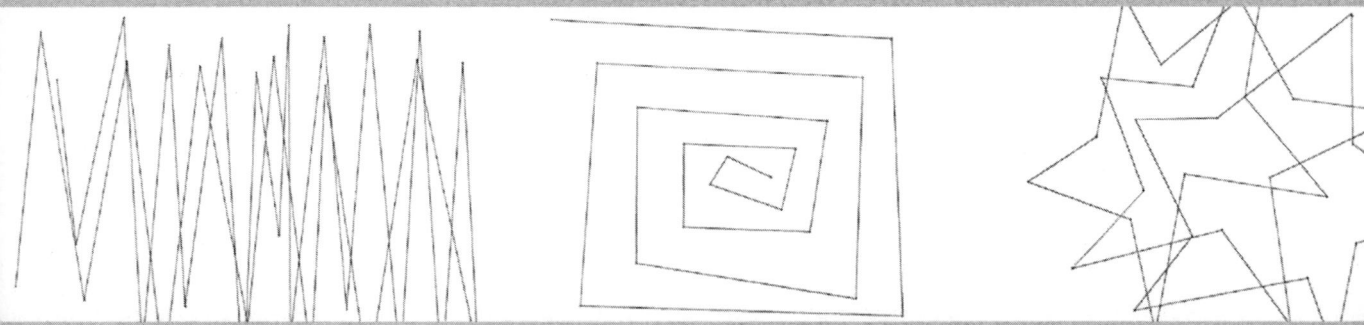

The next step was to take our reusable drawing code from the previous example and put it in its own function so I could easily call it at any time:

```
function draw() {
    clear();
    i = 0;
    lineStyle(1, 0, 100);
    moveTo(points[i], points[i+1]);
    while ((i += 2)<points.length) {
        if (points[i] == null) {
            i++;
            moveTo(points[i], points[i+1]);
        } else {
            lineTo(points[i], points[i+1]);
        }
    }
}
```

The only change I made here was to add the clear statement, making it possible to run this function several times and start with a fresh screen each time.

Finally, I wanted to use a key press to signal that I had finished drawing one line and wanted to start another. To do this, I had to make the root timeline be able to respond to key presses. I used a listener on the Key object, like this:

```
Key.addListener(_root);
```

Once that was done, I just had to set an onKeyDown handler function. This would execute when any key was pressed:

```
_root.onKeyDown = function() {
    points.push(null);
    draw();
};
```

Plainly enough, all this does is push a null value onto the points array and call the draw function, which you're no doubt familiar with by now. Now you can click away to add points to the screen and hit any key to draw the resulting shape and start a new one. Actually, *any* key is a bit misleading. Depending on the platform you are on and whether you are testing the movie, running it as a projector, or in a browser, certain keys such as ESC, TAB, DEL, and ENTER may or may not have an effect. For this reason, you might want to tell the user to press a key that you know will work, such as the SPACE bar.

4

For the sake of completeness, here's how the whole program looks so far:

```
points = [];
onMouseDown = function () {
    attachMovie("dot", "dot"+dotCount, dotCount++,
    ➡ {_x:_xmouse, _y:_ymouse});
    points.push(_xmouse, _ymouse);
};
function draw() {
    clear();
    i = 0;
    lineStyle(1, 0, 100);
    moveTo(points[i], points[i+1]);
    while ((i += 2)<points.length) {
        if (points[i] == null) {
            i++;
            moveTo(points[i], points[i+1]);
        } else {
            lineTo(points[i], points[i+1]);
        }
    }
}
Key.addListener(_root);
_root.onKeyDown = function() {
    points.push(null);
    draw();
};
```

Now, if you are thinking to yourself right now that it would have been a lot easier to just draw the lines directly on the screen itself and skip all this array stuff, you're absolutely right. But remember, what we are actually doing here is trying to convert graphics into raw data, which can then be stored, saved, and turned back into graphics - so we've got the makings of a pretty cool application here.

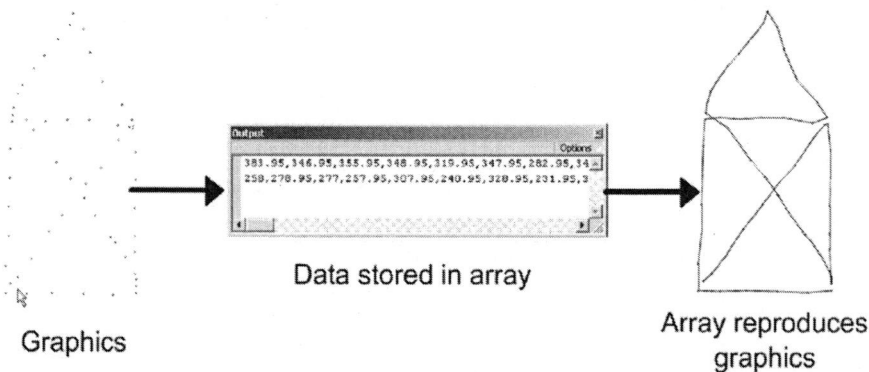

Graphics

Data stored in array

Array reproduces graphics

I attached dots and drew the lines *later* just to show that the data had been successfully stored, and that we could later use that data to draw lines to the exact points that had been clicked. In fact, you can use the trace command to show the exact values and prove to yourself that they were indeed stored.

Saving the data

OK, so we've managed to create some data, store it, and then use it. But so far, the data is born, lives, and dies within the program. Accordingly, we need to find some way of getting it out so we can store it somewhere and use it later. This was my next challenge.

Local shared objects

Unfortunately, for various security reasons, Flash cannot access external files on a user's hard drive. However, there is a neat little thing called a **shared object** which is a specialized file used for storing information locally. These are similar to the cookies that you probably come across on a day-to-day basis on the Web. But whereas cookies can typically store a relatively short, simple string, a shared object can hold any data type – including objects, arrays, and so on.

In my next permutation of the drawing application, I decided to store the `points` array as a shared object. So, let's go through the basics of how to create and use them. First you need to create the object, like this:

```
localData = SharedObject.getLocal("myData");
```

Here we've created a file called `myData` that will store our data, which we can find and check. The key part is the `SharedObject.getLocal` method - inside the parentheses you put the string that will be the name of the object stored on the local drive.

Now that we've defined our local data object, `localData`, we need to populate it with whatever data we want to send to the local file. So, to store something in the shared object, you create a variable and tag it onto the `data` property of the shared object. For example:

```
localData = SharedObject.getLocal("myData");
greeting = "Hello World!";
localData.data.message = greeting;
```

4

When you run this, Flash looks to see if a shared object exists with that name. If it finds one it returns a reference to it, which we store in the variable `localData`. If there is no object with that name, it will create one and then return the reference. Either way, `localData` is now our key to saving and retrieving data on the local drive.

If you ran a file containing those lines, you wouldn't see anything, but the string, `"Hello World!"` would be stored on your hard drive in the shared object. But where's this file located? A good tip is to look in your installation folder - open the `Configuration` folder and read `Configuration_readme`. For instance, on my Win2K system I have the file `myData.sol` within `C:\Documents and Settings\<username>\Application Data\Macromedia\Flash Player\localhost`.

You can then close down the Flash file, even shut down your PC and come back next week and test to see if it's still there with the following two lines:

```
localData = SharedObject.getLocal("myData");
trace(localData.data.message);
```

At this point you should make sure that your preferences are set up appropriately to allow us to store things. For example, if you're working on a PC you can test an empty FLA, right-click on the screen, and select Settings... In the Local Storage tab, make sure Never is not checked and set the size slider to 10KB (which should be enough).

Saving an array

Now that we've seen a simple example of storing a string, it's time to get back into the drawing project. For this, I wanted to store an entire array. Open up save_drawing1.fla from the code files to see the revised version of this example, featuring the use of local shared objects to save the data.

If you look at the code on the main timeline, you should notice a couple of additions to the previous version of this application.

First we create (or check for) a shared object called localPoints. Then we check if localPoints.data.points exists as an array. If it does, we copy it into the variable points and run the draw function:

```
localPoints = sharedobject.getLocal("pointData");
if (localPoints.data.points) {
   points = localPoints.data.points;
   draw();
} else {
   points = [];
}
```

In other words, if there is already a saved drawing, it will be displayed. If there is no shared object, it is then created and we will then create an empty array in the points variable.

The rest of the program is pretty much unchanged, except for the onKeyDown function at the end:

```
Key.addListener(_root);
_root.onKeyDown = function() {
   points.push(null);
   localPoints.data.points = points;
   draw();
};
```

Here, we save the current points array into the shared object. Now, any time you run the file, it will check for and draw any existing drawing, and allow you to add to it.

The only problem with this is that the array just keeps building up! I needed a clear function. I chose the left cursor key as a clear key, as this is generally available in any browser and platform combination. I then set the right cursor key to save the drawing. This time, any other key will have no effect.

Here's the full code for our new improved drawing app, saved as save_drawing2.fla:

```
localPoints = sharedobject.getLocal("pointData");
if (localPoints.data.points) {
   points = localPoints.data.points;
   draw();
} else {
   points = [];
}
dotCount = 0;
onMouseDown = function () {
   attachMovie("dot", "dot"+dotCount, dotCount++,
{_x:_xmouse, _y:_ymouse});
   points.push(_xmouse, _ymouse);
};
function draw() {
   clear();
   i = 0;
   lineStyle(1, 0, 100);
   moveTo(points[i], points[i+1]);
   while ((i += 2)<points.length) {
      if (points[i] == null) {
         i++;
         moveTo(points[i], points[i+1]);
      } else {
         lineTo(points[i], points[i+1]);
      }
   }
}
Key.addListener(_root);
_root.onKeyDown = function() {
   if (Key.isDown(Key.LEFT)) {
      for (i=0; i<points.length; i++) {
         removeMovieClip(_root["dot"+i]);
      }
      dotCount = 0;
      points = [];
      clear();
   } else if (Key.isDown(Key.RIGHT)) {
      points.push(null);
      draw();
      localPoints.data.points = points;
   }
};
```

4

Here, I just checked to see if the left cursor key was pressed. If so, I removed all the dots and set the dotCount back to 0. Then I reset the array and cleared the screen. If the right cursor key is pressed, it saves the data as before. Try it out for yourself by testing save_drawing2.fla.

Extending and enhancing the drawing application

Now that I was familiar with using arrays and shared objects, as well as a number of code optimization techniques, I was getting hungry to improve the drawing application further!

Enabling 'freehand' drawing

I wanted to incorporate a more standard drawing routine in the application. Ideally, I wanted to just press the mouse button to start drawing, and release it to stop - like how most drawing programs work.

Accordingly, I put together a new version of the drawing application - possibly the simplest freehand drawing code you can get - using some of the commands we've already looked at in this chapter. You can find this code in the file freedraw1.fla:

```
onMouseDown = function () {
    moveTo(_xmouse, _ymouse);
    lineStyle(1, 0, 100);
    onMouseMove = function () {
        lineTo(_xmouse, _ymouse);
    };
};
onMouseUp = function () {
    onMouseMove = undefined;
};
```

Basically, you press the mouse button down and it moves the drawing position to that point, and sets the lineStyle and onMouseMove handler. Now, whenever you move the mouse, a line is drawn to the new location. When you release the mouse button, the onMouseMove handler is set to undefined, so nothing happens anymore. Test the FLA, and play around to see how it works:

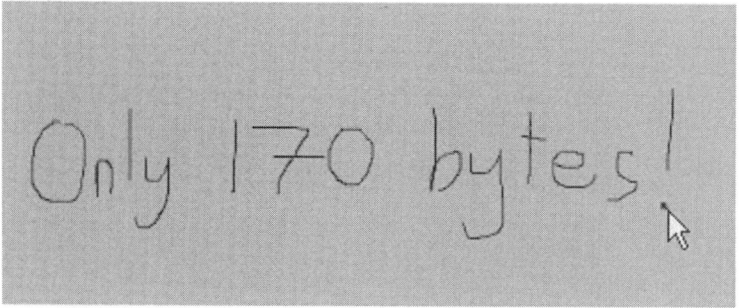

Next, I just needed to integrate that code into the earlier file so we could save and view the drawings. To see how the code looks after I did this, check out `freedraw2.fla`:

```
localPoints = sharedobject.getLocal("pointData");
if (localPoints.data.points) {
   points = localPoints.data.points;
   draw();
} else {
   points = [];
}
onMouseDown = function () {
   moveTo(_xmouse, _ymouse);
   lineStyle(1, 0, 100);
   points.push(_xmouse, _ymouse);
   onMouseMove = function () {
      lineTo(_xmouse, _ymouse);
      points.push(_xmouse, _ymouse);
   };
};
onMouseUp = function () {
   onMouseMove = undefined;
   points.push(null);
};
function draw() {
   clear();
   i = 0;
   lineStyle(1, 0, 100);
   moveTo(points[i], points[i+1]);
   while ((i += 2)<points.length) {
      if (points[i] == null) {
         i++;
         moveTo(points[i], points[i+1]);
      } else {
         lineTo(points[i], points[i+1]);
      }
   }
}
Key.addListener(_root);
_root.onKeyDown = function() {
   if (Key.isDown(Key.LEFT)) {
      points = [];
      clear();
   } else if (Key.isDown(Key.RIGHT)) {
      localPoints.data.points = points;
   }
};
```

4

The only changes here are in the onMouseDown and onMouseUp functions that implement the freehand drawing code - lines have been added to push the current coordinates (or null) onto the points array.

So far, so good - we can now draw 'freehand' with the mouse cursor, then either save the drawing (right cursor key) to our hard drive using the shared object, or just clear it (left cursor key). There were, however, still a couple of optimizations that I wanted to make to this - I was looking for perfection!

Optimizing the stored data array

First of all, if you were to trace the array at any point, with the line trace(points), what you would see is a long list of numbers such as 129.35, 194.45, 49.85, and so on. Those are the pixel measurements of each point being drawn to. When I saw this, my first reaction was, "Do I really need that much accuracy?" All those decimal places take up a lot of space on the user's hard drive, and if you someday wanted to expand the drawing application to download a list of points from a server, they would take extra time to transmit.

Since no one is going to notice the difference of a fraction of a pixel, why not round it off and save space? The next version of the program does just that! The only changes relative to the code listed above concerned the onMouseDown function (see also freedraw3.fla):

```
onMouseDown = function () {
    xm = Math.round(_xmouse);
    ym = Math.round(_ymouse);
    moveTo(xm, ym);
    lineStyle(1, 0, 100);
    points.push(xm, ym);
    onMouseMove = function () {
        xm = Math.round(_xmouse);
        ym = Math.round(_ymouse);
        lineTo(xm, ym);
        points.push(xm, ym);
    };
};
```

This just creates two new variables, xm and ym, which are the rounded off values of _xmouse and _ymouse. It uses these values, rather than the raw mouse coordinates, in drawing and in the array. If you now traced the array, you'd see a much cleaner, compact version.

Another similar idea for optimizing came to me when I looked at the resulting array of a very small drawing I had made. The array of points was huge! But my drawing was tiny. How could that be? Well, since we are using onMouseMove, a new point will be added every time the mouse moves. How far does it have to move in order for a new point to be added? Just a fraction of a pixel! So, if you move the mouse just a few pixels in one direction, particularly if you move it slowly, you could generate quite a few points. That would not do!

The answer is to measure how far the mouse has moved, and *only* draw a line if it has moved a certain distance. The next version of the program, freedraw4.fla, takes this into account. Again, the changes affect the onMouseDown function only:

```
onMouseDown = function () {
    xm = oldx = Math.round(_xmouse);
    ym = oldy = Math.round(_ymouse);
    moveTo(xm, ym);
    lineStyle(1, 0, 100);
    points.push(xm, ym);
    onMouseMove = function () {
        xm = Math.round(_xmouse);
        ym = Math.round(_ymouse);
        dx = xm-oldx;
        dy = ym-oldy;
        dist = Math.sqrt(dx*dx + dy*dy);
        if(dist>10){
            lineTo(xm, ym);
            points.push(xm, ym);
            oldx = xm;
            oldy = ym;
        }
    };
};
```

Here I needed two more variables, oldx and oldy. Obviously, to measure distance, you take where something is, and subtract where it was - for instance, if you are at point 10, and you were at point 8, then you moved 2 points.

When you first press the mouse button, xm and oldx will be set to the same thing (and likewise for the y position):

```
xm = oldx = Math.round(_xmouse);
ym = oldy = Math.round(_ymouse);
```

4

This is our starting point for any measurement. When we get to the mouse move block, we subtract `oldx` from `xm`, and `oldy` from `ym`, telling us how much the mouse has moved on each axis:

```
dx = xm-oldx;
dy = ym-oldy;
```

But we then need to figure out the actual distance between these two points. This is found using what is commonly known as the Pythagoras theorem - we square the two distances, add them, and then calculate the square root of the result:

```
dist = Math.sqrt(dx*dx + dy*dy);
```

Then we check to see that the distance is at least 10:

```
if(dist>10){
```

If so, we draw the line and `push` the point. At that point we also reset `oldx` and `oldy` ready for the next loop.

If you now go ahead and trace the `points` array, you'll see it is much smaller for an equivalent sized drawing. And small is good, right?

You may feel, however, that the drawing has become a bit 'choppy' - this might be more noticeable on lower resolutions. This is easy to handle — just change the value you are comparing the distance to. Instead of 10, make it 5:

```
if(dist>5){
```

This will result in more points being recorded, but a smoother drawing. You see you can easily adjust the quality versus the size of your drawing by changing this factor.

Standardizing the program with setInterval

Now that I had a few technical details ironed out, I decided to enhance the presentation again. My mind works that way – fix up one thing, then look around to see what else can be improved or enhanced. Anyway, as it stands, the draw function spits out the whole drawing in one shot, one frame. One second it's not there, then suddenly it's there! That's because it all happens in the while loop, which fully executes before updating the screen.

My original idea was to have the lines draw in real time. Luckily, the way I'd been building the file made it easy to convert to this behavior. I had all the coordinates, in the exact order they were originally drawn. I just needed to add in a time factor to space out the drawing commands.

My first thought was to do this via an onEnterFrame function: instead of drawing all the lines at once, just draw one line each frame, incrementing the index each time. Prior to Flash MX, that's exactly how I would have done it. The only minor problem with that method is that it's hard-wired to the frame rate. If you find that the drawing is going too fast, you have to reduce the frame rate, or vice versa, if it's too slow, increase the frame rate. Also, different computers and systems will play back at different speeds, so you'd have no real control over how the end presentation looked.

However, in Flash MX we've now got the setInterval command. This allows you to execute a function over and over at a ... well, at a *set interval*. All you have to do is give it the name of the function and how many milliseconds to wait between function calls. If, for example, you want to draw ten lines per second, put a tenth of a second between intervals (that is, 100 milliseconds). This will render the same on all computers. Of course, if you have more going on in that function than can be done in 100 milliseconds, it's going to bog down, but overall it'll be far more reliable than the frame rate. Here's how I used setInterval in the file:

```
setInterval(draw, 100);
```

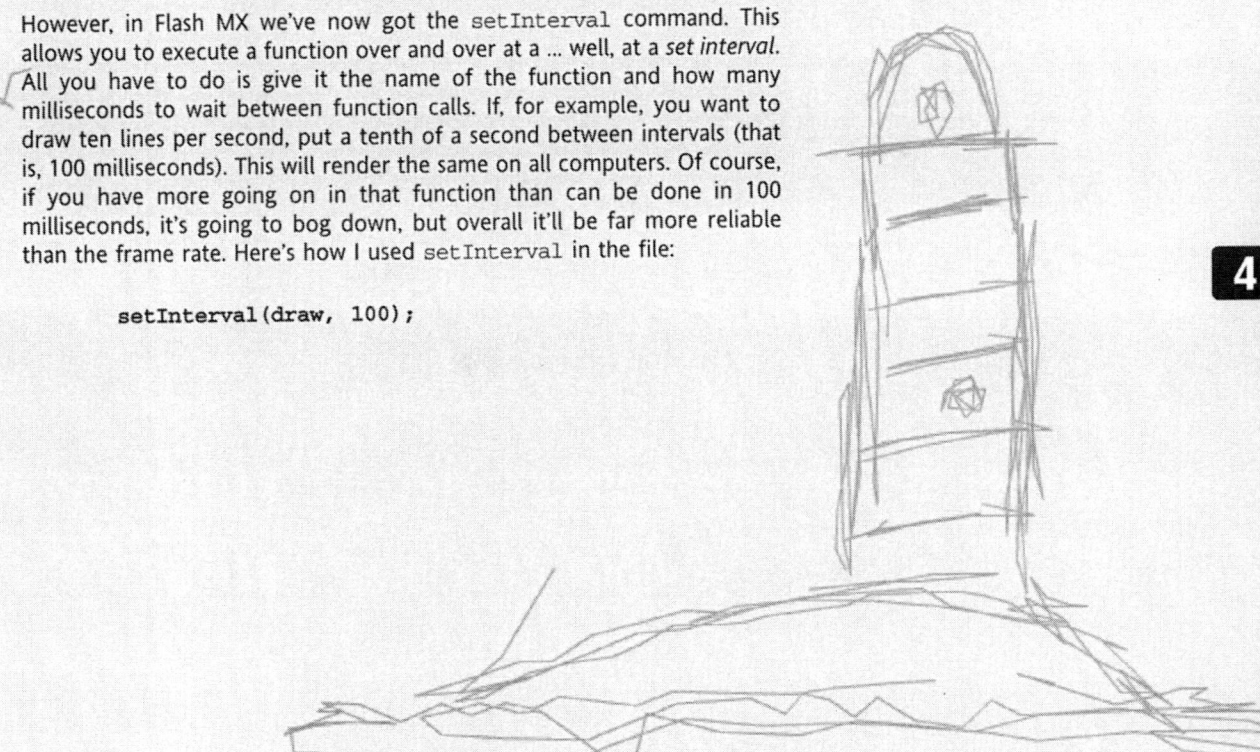

4

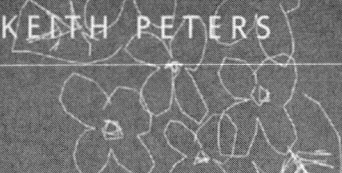

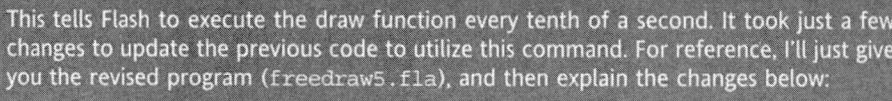

This tells Flash to execute the draw function every tenth of a second. It took just a few changes to update the previous code to utilize this command. For reference, I'll just give you the revised program (freedraw5.fla), and then explain the changes below:

```
localPoints = sharedobject.getLocal("pointData");
if(localPoints.data.points){
  points=localPoints.data.points;
  startDraw();
} else {
  points = [];
}
onMouseDown = function () {
  xm = oldx = Math.round(_xmouse);
  ym = oldy = Math.round(_ymouse);
  moveTo(xm, ym);
  lineStyle(1, 0, 100);
  points.push(xm, ym);
  onMouseMove = function () {
    xm = Math.round(_xmouse);
    ym = Math.round(_ymouse);
    dx = xm-oldx;
    dy = ym-oldy;
    dist = Math.sqrt(dx*dx + dy*dy);
    if(dist>10){
      lineTo(xm, ym);
      points.push(xm, ym);
      oldx = xm;
      oldy = ym;
    }
  };
};
onMouseUp = function () {
  onMouseMove = undefined;
  points.push(null);
};
function startDraw() {
  clear();
  i = 0;
  lineStyle(1, 0, 100);
  moveTo(points[i], points[i+1]);
  drawInt = setInterval(draw, 100);
}
function draw() {
```

```
        if ((i += 2)<points.length) {
            if (points[i] == null) {
                i++;
                moveTo(points[i], points[i+1]);
            } else {
                lineTo(points[i], points[i+1]);
            }
        } else {
            clearInterval(drawInt);
        }
    }
    Key.addListener(_root);
    _root.onKeyDown = function(){
        if(Key.isDown(Key.LEFT)){
            points = [];
            clear();
        } else if(Key.isDown(Key.RIGHT)){
            localPoints.data.points = points;
        }
    };
```

First, way up at the top, I've called a new function startDraw rather than draw. Then, I've taken the first four lines out of the draw function and moved them into the startDraw function:

```
        clear();
        i = 0;
        lineStyle(1, 0, 100);
        moveTo(points[i], points[i+1]);
```

This is because draw will now be executed repeatedly, and these actions only need to occur once. If I left them in the function, it would continually clear the drawing and not much would happen since the index would keep being set to 0!

Next, I set up the setInterval:

```
        drawInt = setInterval(draw, 100);
```

When you set an interval, the command returns an ID to that interval. We want to store that in a variable, drawInt. Then we can use it later to cancel the interval when we are done drawing. Otherwise it would go on trying to draw forever. You can change the value of 100 to cause the drawing to happen faster or slower.

4

In the draw function itself, I simply changed the while statement (which would have run repeatedly until it ran out of data) to an if statement (which will run exactly once). Now all the function does is increment the i variable, check if there is still data to be drawn, and if so, draws one line. The next time the function is called, a tenth of a second later, it draws the next line, and so on. When it runs out of data, it executes the else portion of the if statement, which clears the interval, ending the automatic execution of this function.

This is getting pretty fun! You can draw shapes, even intricate drawings, and hit the right cursor key to save them in the shared object localPoints. The next time you run the file, whatever drawing was last saved will be pulled up and redrawn in real time.

Creating a picture gallery

I realized that it wouldn't be too difficult to save a whole gallery of drawings, so I set out to add the necessary code that would enable me to store several separate drawings. My idea was that each one would be accessible by pressing one of the number keys, and the left and right keys would continue to serve as clear and save.

After removing all the shared object code from the top of the program, the only changes I needed to make related to the onKeyDown function - so here's what I came up with (the full code can be seen in freedraw6.fla):

```
Key.addListener(_root);
_root.onKeyDown = function() {
  clearInterval(drawInt);
  if (Key.isDown(Key.LEFT)) {
    points = [];
    clear();
  } else if (Key.isDown(Key.RIGHT)) {
    localPoints.data.points = points;
  } else {
    num = Key.getAscii();
    if (num>48 && num<58) {
      numDisplay.text = "Drawing "+(num-48);
      localPoints = sharedobject.getLocal("pointData"+num);
      if (localPoints.data.points) {
        points = localPoints.data.points;
        startDraw();
      } else {
        clear();
        points = [];
      }
    }
  }
};
```

So, when the user presses a key, I clear the interval, in case a drawing happens to be in progress. I then check if clear or save was hit and do the usual actions there.

Next, I check if a number key was hit. You might be wondering about the 47 and 58 in this part of the code. Here's the important line:

```
num = Key.getAscii();
```

This gives us the ASCII code for the key was pressed. It so happens that the number 1 has an ASCII code of 49, 2 has a code of 50, 3 is 51, and so on, up to 9, which has a code of 57 (hey, I didn't make up the code!). So I check to see if num is between 47 and 58. If so, I display the number (after subtracting 48 from it to bring it back to a logical range) in a dynamic text field that I've created on the stage, and given the instance name numDisplay. This gives us a visual indication of which drawing we are showing or making, between 1 and 9 in this case.

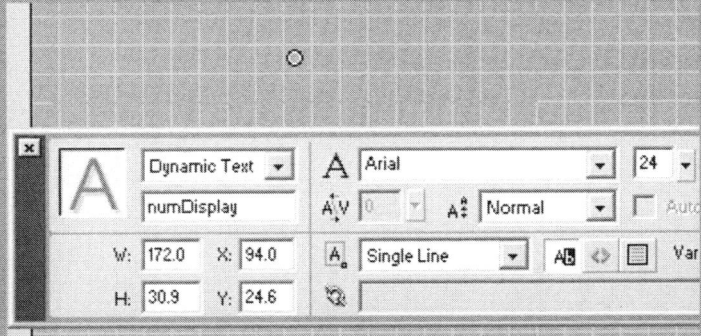

Only then do I make the shared object. Note that the name I give the object itself is dynamically created using num:

```
localPoints = sharedobject.getLocal("pointData"+num);
```

This lets us create a distinct shared object for each drawing. The rest of the code is unchanged. We either load the drawing and display it, or clear the screen and reset the array.

4

Now test the movie. It's worth remembering that the testing of any application is a crucial stage in its development cycle, so for testing this application I've enlisted the help of a friend's 2-year-old daughter...

Great! Now you can draw a picture, save it to your local hard drive using the right cursor key, then 'turn the page' of this virtual drawing pad by pressing the relevant number key. After using every page of `freedraw6.swf`, take a look in your `Application Data` folder to see that each drawing has been stored locally as a shared object - note that the file names reflect the ASCII code of the relevant number keys.

Name	Size	Type	Modified
pointData49.sol	1 KB	SOL File	25/10/2002 09:15
pointData50.sol	1 KB	SOL File	25/10/2002 09:15
pointData51.sol	1 KB	SOL File	25/10/2002 09:16
pointData52.sol	1 KB	SOL File	25/10/2002 09:16
pointData53.sol	1 KB	SOL File	25/10/2002 09:16
pointData54.sol	1 KB	SOL File	25/10/2002 09:16
pointData55.sol	2 KB	SOL File	25/10/2002 09:16
pointData56.sol	2 KB	SOL File	25/10/2002 09:16
pointData57.sol	2 KB	SOL File	25/10/2002 09:16

This is a pretty workable little application – no doubt you can customize it further from here. Other areas you might want to look into are sending the points data to be stored on a server, so that others could view it online. For that, you'd need to know a bit about a server scripting language, such as PHP. For those interested, it might be worth checking out either *Foundation PHP for Flash* (ISBN 1-903450-16-0) or *Advanced PHP for Flash* (ISBN 1-904344-03-8), both available from friends of ED.

In this chapter we've looked at a number of different ways to use ActionScript to create small, efficient animations and some cool dynamic drawing effects. Hopefully these examples will serve to convince you of the almost limitless possibilities with ActionScript, and inspire you to take your programs further.

4

5 SOUND TOYS

KIP PARKER

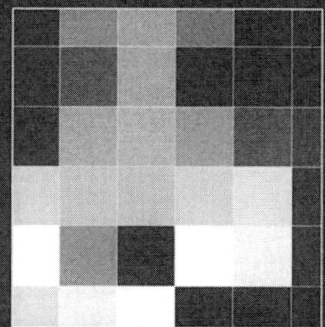  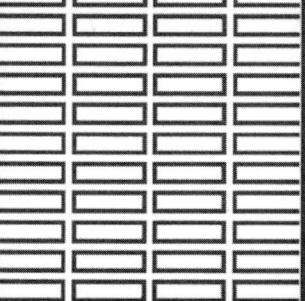

Trying to squeeze sound into low bandwidth sites creates a lot of problems. Sound files are extremely bandwidth heavy, and although sound compression in Flash is excellent, there is only so far a sound can be compressed before it starts to become unusable. This means you can only use a maximum of about two seconds of sound, and even less if you use a large number of small sounds.

However, Flash MX has a number of sound handling features that help us to deal with these problems. Samples can be looped and volume effects can be added to change a sound. Different segments of one sound can be played. And these things can be controlled with ActionScript, which allows fairly complex effects to be built up.

Stylophone

The stylophone was one of the first widely available electronic instruments in the UK, popularized by top Australian entertainer Rolf Harris. It's a little plastic box with printed metal keys that you play using the stylus attached to the box, a simple design that makes it ideal for conversion to a digital toy. Let's do just that – it'll be a great way to show you the power of sound optimization in Flash.

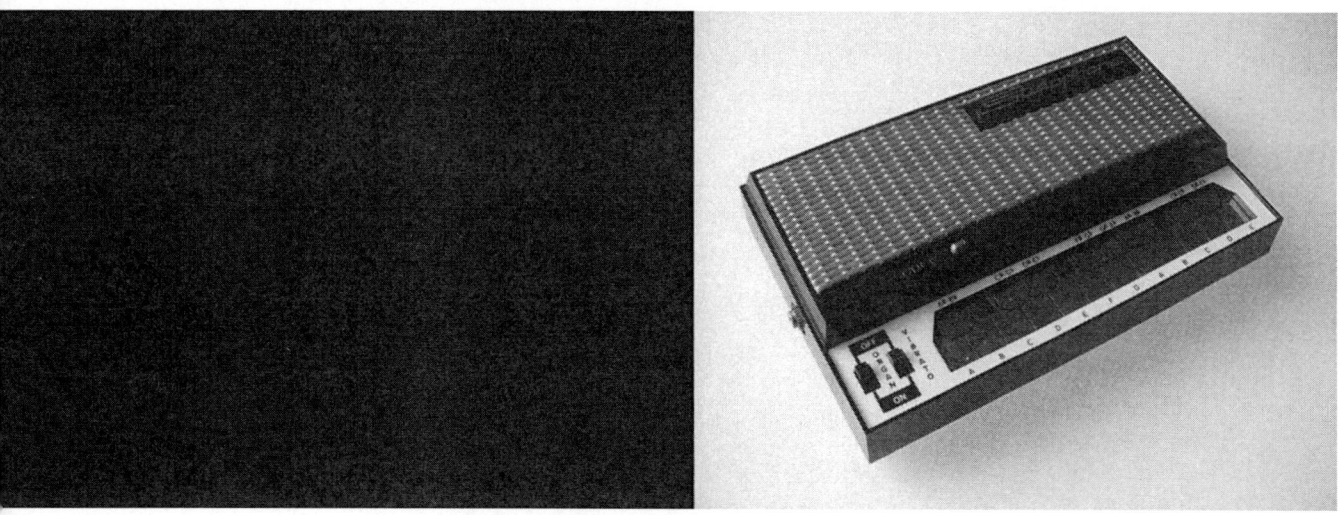

First, I made my stylophone. I imported the image as a GIF, and used Trace Bitmap to break it up into elements. To give you a head start here, I have included a file called `stylophone_start.fla` in the download files.

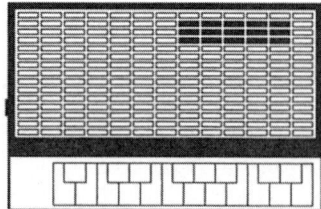

I tried to keep the file size as low as possible, but even with duplicating as many elements as I could, and stripping out extraneous details of the original, the graphics took up 3 KB. I needed 20 sounds, so there was only a tiny amount of bandwidth available for each file. However, in this case it isn't too much of a problem. As the sounds needed to emulate the stylophone's tones are very simple waveforms, with no changes in shape throughout the length of the note, they can be cut down to a tiny size and looped in Flash.

Synthesizing the sounds

I first of all synthesized the sounds in Sound Forge (a fairly elderly version 4.0 from 1997). Whilst the following instructions are specific to the program, most sound editors will handle sound synthesis in more or less the same way.

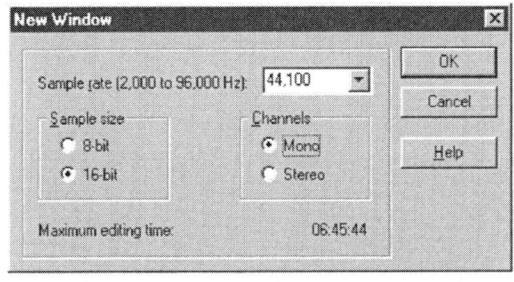

The sound of the stylophone is very similar to a basic saw-shaped wave, so I created 20 sounds in Sound Forge using the simple synthesis feature under Tools > Synthesis > Simple.

For each note I made a new sound, keeping the sample rate and size fairly high, as it's best to do the compression in Flash, rather than before.

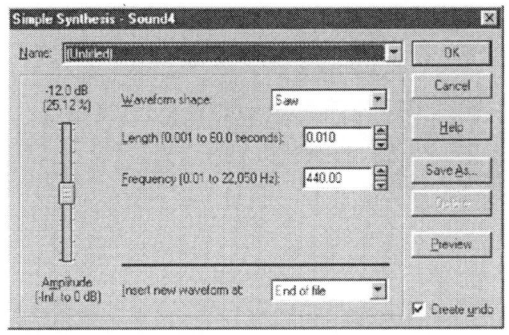

I created very short sounds (0.01 seconds) for each of the 20 notes I wanted. The frequency determines the pitch of the note (440 Hz is A). You'll need to consult a table to get the frequencies. The following table shows the frequencies I used for the stylophone, starting with the lowest first – which will go on the leftmost key.

5

Note	Frequency	Note	Frequency	Note	Frequency
A_3	220.00	E_4	329.63	B_4	493.88
$A^{\#}_3/B^b_3$	233.08	F_4	349.23	C_5	523.25
B_3	246.94	$F^{\#}_4/G^b_4$	369.99	$C^{\#}_5/D^b_5$	554.37
C_4	261.63	G_4	392.00	D_5	587.33
$C^{\#}_4/D^b_4$	277.18	$G^{\#}_4/A^b_4$	415.30	$D^{\#}_5/E^b_5$	622.25
D_4	293.66	A_4	440.00	E_5	659.26
$D^{\#}_4/E^b_4$	311.13	$A^{\#}_4/B^b_4$	466.16		

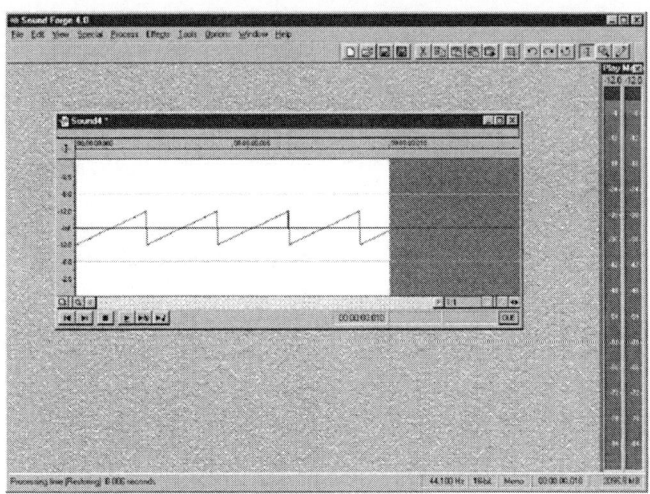

The problem remains that if this sound is looped in Flash, which is necessary in order to recreate the stylophone's endlessly sustained notes, there will be lots of distortion, as the note's frequency at the end of the loop does not match with that at the beginning. I had to crop each note to fix this.

Now the loops will appear seamless and completely unnoticeable.

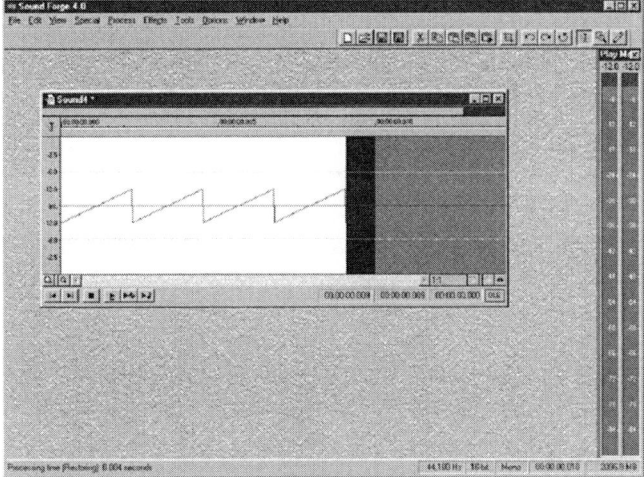

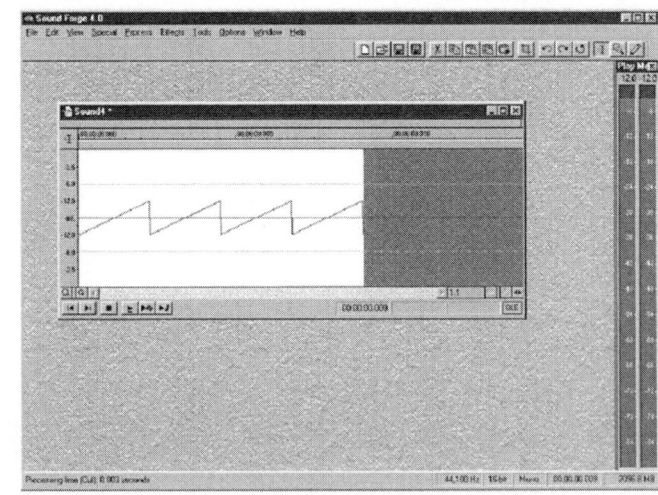

Building the stylophone in Flash

I imported all the files into my movie (you can import them from the sound files folder in the download files). Unlike with graphics, you won't see anything on the stage, but they are all available in the Library after importing, and I put them all into a folder called sounds.

Going through each key of the stylophone in turn, I turned each one into a button, giving it the same name as the sound that would be attached to it. For example, the first key on the board is called a3. To show which note is being played, I colored the keys gray in the Over frame by adjusting the Tint.

Each button then needs an endlessly sustained note on the over state, so I dragged the correct sound from the Library into the Over frame, and set it to loop for as long as possible.

To loop a sound more or less forever, you type in a very big number (say 999999999) into the Loop field. Flash will automatically reduce this number to whatever number of loops it can manage.

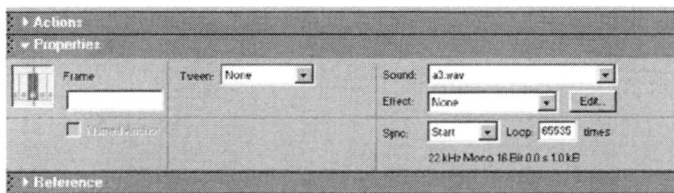

For my a3.wav, Flash has come up with 65535 loops as the maximum it's prepared to deal with. I've never really figured out what the basis is for the figures Flash puts in – it'll set anything up to a couple of thousand million loops. Nonetheless it always seems to make the sound last for a long, long time. Here for example, 65535 loops of a WAV file of length 0.01 seconds gives you about ten minutes of constant sound, enough for even the biggest fan of endless droning.

Synching

You also need to set synching for the sound. The default setting Start is fine here, but it's worth looking at what each setting does.

- Event – synchronizes the sound to the occurrence of an event. An event sound plays when its starting keyframe is first displayed and plays in its entirety, independently of the timeline, even if the movie stops. You have to be careful when using this with a longer sound, as you can end up with dozens of instances of the sound running at the same time.

- Start – the same as Event, except that if the sound is already playing, no new instance of the sound is played, avoiding the multiple instances problem. I've used this setting here, but Event would have worked the same way.

5

■ Stream – With this setting, Flash forces the sound to run at the same pace as the frame rate. It's useful if you have a long animation with a synched sound track. It also allows the sound to be played in segments. You need to make sure that the sound occupies enough frames to complete, as it will stop when the clip it is inside stops.

■ Stop – this stops the sound selected.

I've got endlessly sustaining notes, but as they'll last for the full ten minutes once triggered, even if the button returns to its off state, I need a way of turning them off. In what I think is a very counter-intuitive manner (although it might just be me) the way to do this is to add the sound to the Up frame of the button, but instead of setting Sync to Start or Event, set it to Stop, which has the effect of switching off the sound when your mouse isn't *over* the button.

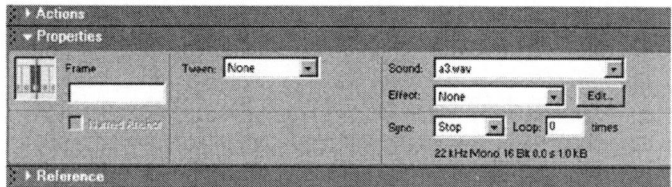

Finally, I needed to tweak the sound compression so that the file sizes were low enough to fit into my bandwidth limit. Sound compression settings are under the Flash tab in Publish Settings. Event sounds and streamed sounds can have different settings, but in this case I've only used event sounds.

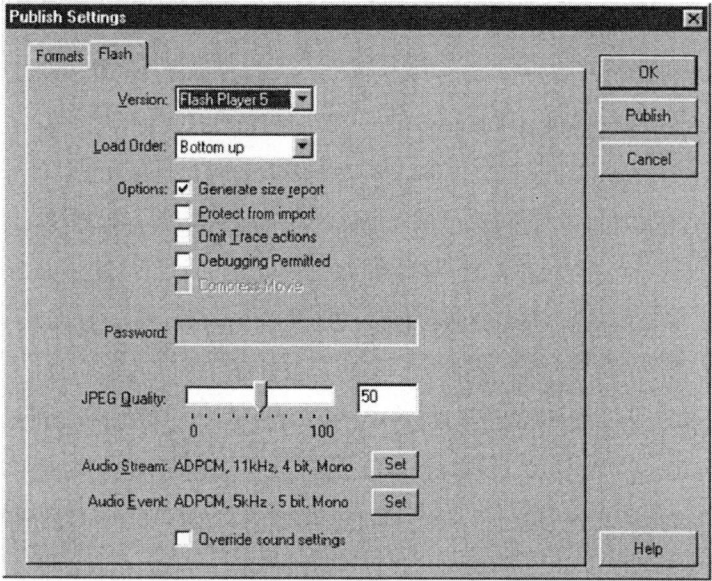

Note that the techniques in this toy are simple enough for it to work with the very first version of the Flash player.

Clicking on Set next to Audio Event brings up the window to decide on compression settings. The two options to consider are MP3, and ADPCM, a wave file format compression. ADPCM tends to give better results and lower file sizes for short sounds, which is what I've chosen here.

Getting the sample rate right is a matter of trial and error, I just keep changing them and going to Test > Movie until I reach the acceptable balance between quality and size. Flash Help lists a 5 KHz sample rate as being "barely acceptable for speech", but it works OK with this sound.

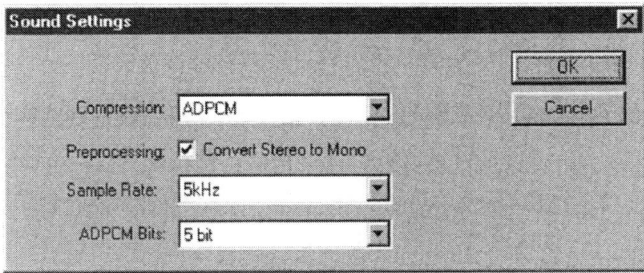

Clicking Publish, it's now a fully functioning digital stylophone, ready to play *Oh When The Saints*, *Super Trouper*, and other classics. My finished version can be found in the download files, called `stylophone.fla`.

A couple of problems emerged when I was building this 5 KB stylophone. Although I carefully cut the waveforms to size, dealing with such tiny loops means that some distortion is inevitable, particularly after the sounds have been through compression in Flash.

Fortunately, the original stylophone had a distinctly crappy sound, so I can claim the distortion in the name of authenticity!

I also noticed that on some of the sounds, there appears to be another sound playing, which is due to slight clipping of the wave forms creating harmonics. (These are the complementary sounds that are heard echoing around the primary note). In some places the harmonic sound almost overwhelms the main note, which isn't ideal, but it's worth remembering these unexpected effects for future use. I often find that some strange glitch creeps in and makes better sounds than those intended. In this case, I got two sounds for the price of one!

Grid

Buttons are quite limited, and for most of my sites I tend to use ActionScripted movie clips to get the effects I want.

For this experiment, I wanted to explore making interesting sound effects with the very simplest of elements.

Grid1

I chose to use a filled rectangle, and the short beeps from the stylophone. This completed experiment is included in the download files as `grid1.fla`.

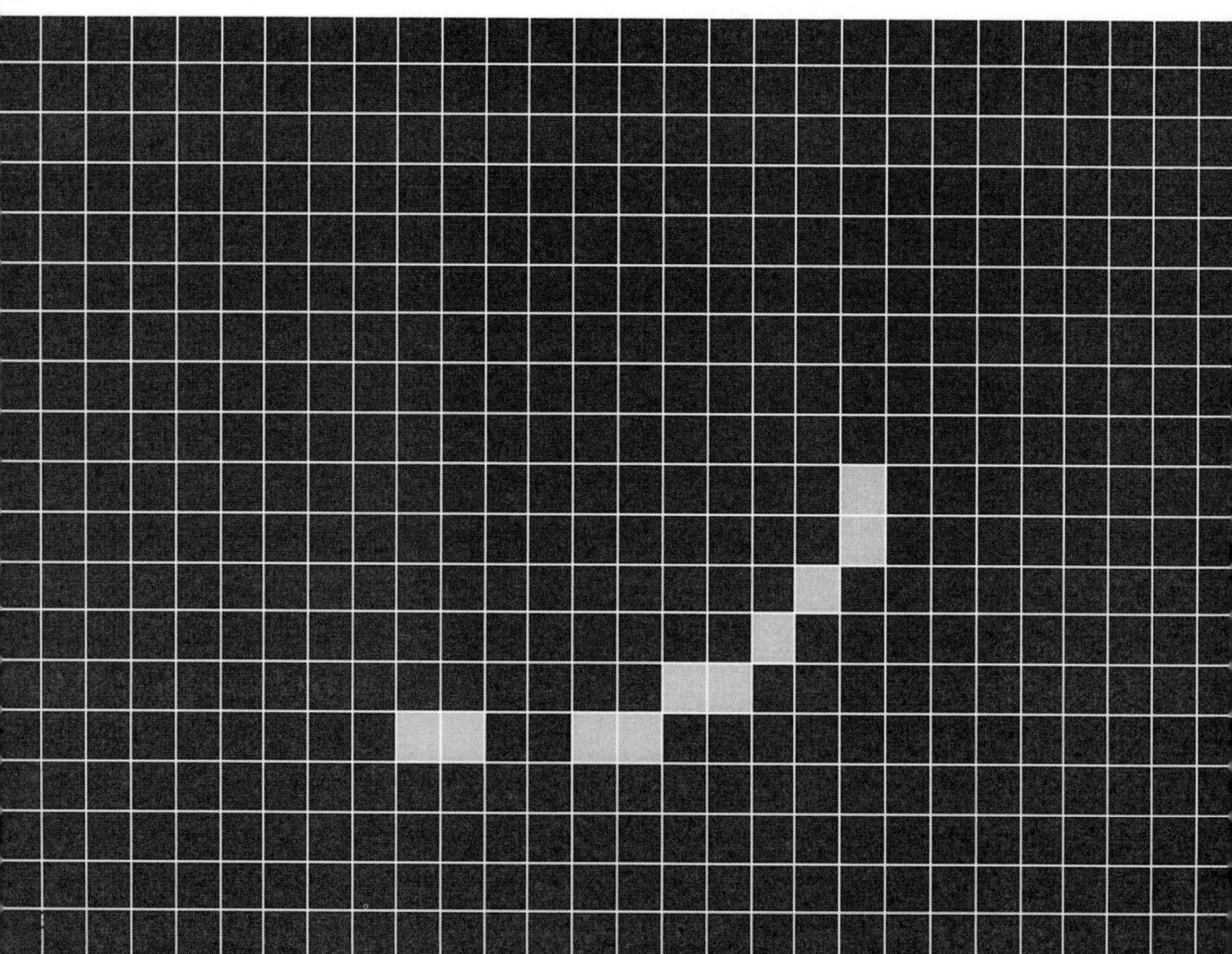

Opening a new document (600x400 px, with a black background), I made a 20x20 px square with a white stroke and black fill, and converted it to a movie clip, called sound_trigger. Editing the clip, I selected the fill of the square and put it onto a new layer called fill below a layer called outline that now contained only the white outline.

I put in a keyframe at frame 10 of the fill layer, and changed the color to gray to give a visual clue for which sound is playing. The sound, a3.wav, which I imported, is also added to this frame, set to Start.

I decided that the tiny a3.wav clip would be too short, so I looped the sound 4 times to make it longer. I also wanted each sound to have an obvious start and finish, so I needed to give it an effect. By going to the Edit button next to Effect, you can alter the decay over the length of the looping:

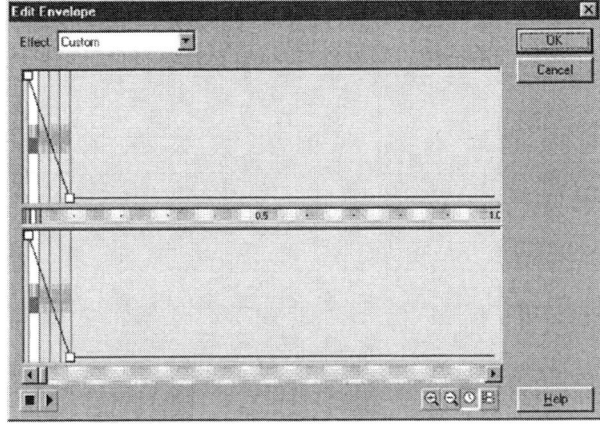

The sound will now start loudly and finish quietly.

Finally, I labelled the first frame off, and the tenth frame on, on a new layer called Labels, to make scripting easier, and added a stop(); action to the first frame to stop it playing before there has been any user interaction. I also had it in mind that I would like the on state to be visible for a little while, so I added an action in a keyframe at frame 15 for the movie to return to the off state:

```
gotoAndStop("off");
```

The final timeline for the sound_trigger movie clip looks like this:

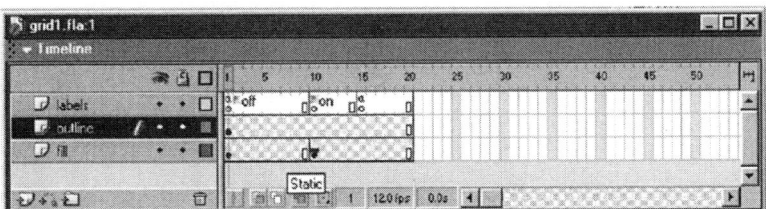

Going back to the main movie, delete the instance from the stage, and then right-click on the movie clip in the Library and give it a Linkage name of sound_trigger.

With everything in place, I can now use some ActionScript to create the grid. The following code goes into the first frame of the main timeline.

```
w = 20;
h = 20;
across = 600/w;
down = 400/h;

for(i=0;i<down;i++){
    for(j=0;j<across;j++){
        counter = ((i*across)+j);
        attachMovie("sound_trigger",
        ➥"trigger"+counter,counter);
        mv = _root["trigger"+counter];
        mv.onRollOver = function(){
            this.gotoAndPlay("on");
        }
        mv._x = j*w;
        mv._y = i*h;
    }
}
```

The code both creates the grid and gives each clip an onRollOver action.

Here's how it all works, line by line. I started off by setting a few variables:

```
w = 20;
h = 20;
across = 600/w;
down = 400/h;
```

w and h are respectively width and height, both dimensions of the clip being 20 pixels. across and down store the number of columns and rows that will be needed to fill the stage with squares.

With those in place, I added the code to duplicate the clip:

```
for(i=0;i<down;i++){
    for(j=0;j<across;j++){
        counter = ((i*across)+j);
```

The i loop represents the number of rows, and goes from 0 to down (which here is 400/h, or 20). For each step of the i loop, or in other words for each row, the j loop goes from 0 to the number of columns (600/w, or 30).

The two loops between them now go through every position of the grid, from (0,0) to (20,30).

Each duplicated clip will need to have a unique name, and be placed in a different level to the others. The `counter` variable is used for this, and its value is set to go from 0 to the number of squares in the grid (600).

The movie can then be attached.

```
attachMovie("sound_trigger", "trigger"+counter,counter);
```

`sound_trigger` is the movie to be attached. `"trigger"+counter` is its name, so the newly attached movie clips will be called `trigger0` to `trigger600`, and put into their corresponding level, `counter`.

I use `mv` to store a reference for each clip duplicated:

```
mv = _root["trigger"+counter];
```

That reference can then be used to move the clip to its correct position on the grid, which is easily calculated by setting `_x` to width (`w`) *times* position in the `rows` loop, and `_y` to height (`h`) *times* position in the `columns` loop:

```
mv._x = j*w;
mv._y = i*h;
```

Finally, I used `mv` to add an `onRollOver` to each clip:

```
mv.onRollOver = function(){
this.gotoAndPlay("on");
}
```

The action on frame 15 of the clip itself deals with sending the clip back to the off state.

5

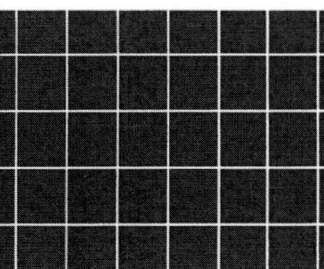 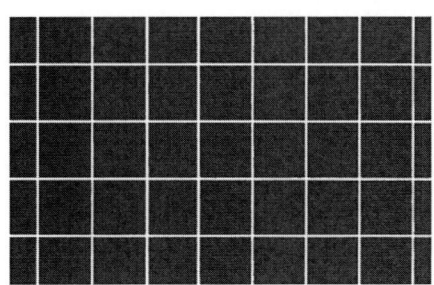 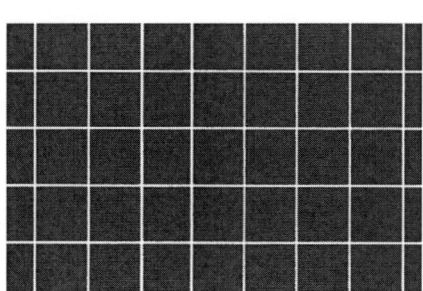

Although the grid makes a satisfying crackling sound and displays a trail when you roll over it, unless you're a really big fan of the minimal the joys of it will fade quickly.

Scale

We are going to build on `grid1.fla` to produce a slightly more interesting effect. Save your document again under a different name. You can find the finished version of this stage in the download files, saved as `scale.fla`.

I wanted to add different sounds to each row to brighten things up a little. As it happens, I've got 20 sounds that I used for the stylophone, so I decided to reuse those.

It would be possible to duplicate the movie clip 20 times, change the sound in the on frame, and then use some simple ActionScript to duplicate it over the stage, for example:

```
for(i=0;i<20;i++){
    for(j=0;j<30;j++){
    attachMovie("clip"+i, "clip"+i+j, (i*20)+j;
    }
}
```

You would then get 20 rows with different sounds in each row. However, this is very inefficient, as if I want to set the amount of time the clip is in its on state for, for example, I'd have to go through and change each of the 20 clips.

Instead, I put all the sounds in one movie, with the sounds from frame 2 to 21, in order of pitch. I didn't put any sounds in frame 1, as you'll then get a clonk when your movie first loads. I set each of the sounds to loop four times and set the effect as before. There is a `stop();` action in frame 1.

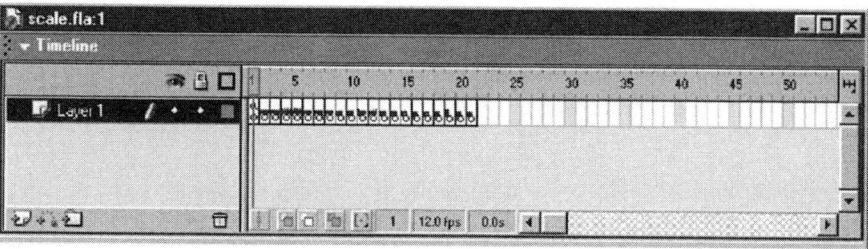

The clip was then dragged from the Library into the sound_trigger clip, on its own layer, and given an instance name of scale. I also removed the sound from the on frame, as the scale clip will now provide sounds.

A problem with using a clip made up only of sounds is that having no graphical content, it's almost invisible on the stage. It is just about possible to select it but very awkward. Sometimes I put some text into the movie to make it visible and hide it off stage, but in this case I avoided that as it would affect the width of the sound_trigger clip and therefore my layout code, so I just made sure that I named the instance when I first dragged it to the stage and it was automatically selected.

I added some code to the duplication loops in frame 1 of the main timeline, so that when each clip is attached, it is given a number representing the frame in the scale clip that it should play. Here is the complete altered code, with changes in bold:

```
w = 20;
h = 20;
across = 600/w;
down = 400/h;

for(i=0;i<down;i++){
    for(j=0;j<across;j++){
        counter = ((i*across)+j);
        attachMovie("sound_trigger",
        ➥"trigger"+counter,counter);
        mv = _root["trigger"+counter];
        mv.onRollOver = function(){
          this.gotoAndPlay("on");
          this.scale.gotoAndStop(this.soundToPlay);
          this.scale.gotoAndStop(1);
        }
        mv.soundToPlay = i+2;
        mv._x = j*w;
        mv._y = i*h;
    }
}
```

There are just three additions to the code for grid1.fla. Each movie clip has a variable soundToPlay, which tells it which frame of the scale clip contains the sound for its row.

The onRollOver action still goes to the on frame, but it also tells the scale clip to go to and stop at the correct frame.

It also helps to add a line to tell Flash to return to frame 1 of scale, as Flash gets a bit buggy when asked to move from one sound frame to another very quickly, and this gets around that.

Playing the grid now gives the effect of running your finger up and down a Bontempi organ.

5

Horizontal movement

Instead of just having each square play a sound when rolled over, I wanted to have a look at ways I could modify the FLA so that clicking a square would trigger off trails of sound.

In order to produce these trails, I added some ActionScript in the on frame of sound_trigger:

```
scale.gotoAndStop(soundToPlay);
scale.gotoAndStop(1);
```

Adding this means that the scale movie is not just targeted when the mouse button is clicked on a movie clip, but each time a movie clip plays. This is important as I planned to get each clicked-on movie clip to trigger another one.

To do this I needed to get each clip to work out another clip to play once it has finished playing its own sound. I did that by adding an action on frame 11 of a new layer in the sound_trigger movie clip, which calls a function, getNext, and sends itself as an argument.

```
_root.getNext(this);
```

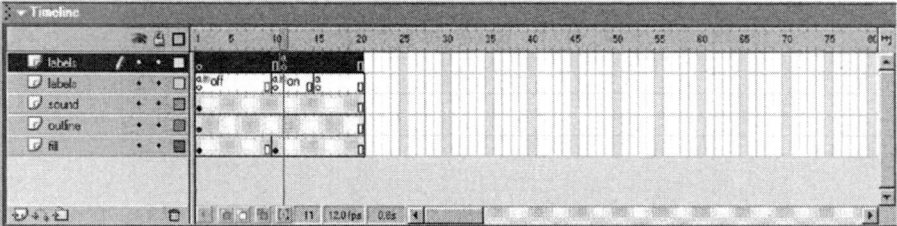

In the main timeline, I added in the function that would allow each movie clip to trigger another:

```
function getNext(obj){
    num = obj._name.substring(7);
    num++;
    if(num<across*down){
        with(_root["trigger"+num]){
            gotoAndPlay("on");
        }
    }
}
```

To get the squares playing from left to right through the whole grid we just need to get each movie clip to target the next numbered clip – if `trigger23` calls `getNext`, it needs to get `trigger24` to play next. To achieve this, I first had to get the number element from the clip's name. I used the variable `num` to hold the part of the name from the character after `trigger` (which is 7 characters long – remember counting starts from 0, so the first seven characters are 0-6) to the end of the name.

I then incremented `num`, checked this isn't the very last clip in the grid, and finally, got a clip reference to the next movie clip, and told it to play.

We also need to change the event handler within the layout code to `onRelease`:

```
mv.onRelease = function(){
```

Testing this out, I found the graphic side of things was a bit ugly, as because each clip stays on for five frames several of them are in the same on state at any one time. I decided to add a fade to the sound_trigger clip by setting frame 10 to a white fill, adding a shape tween, and putting a keyframe in frame 25 of the fill layer, where I changed the fill to black.

To let the whole of the new fade play, I moved the `gotoAndStop(off)` action from frame 15 to 25.

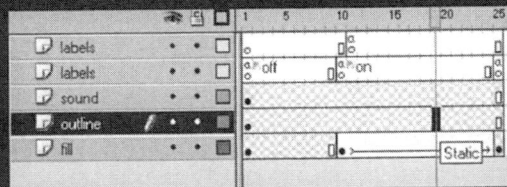

It gives a much more interesting visual effect as the movie clips play.

5

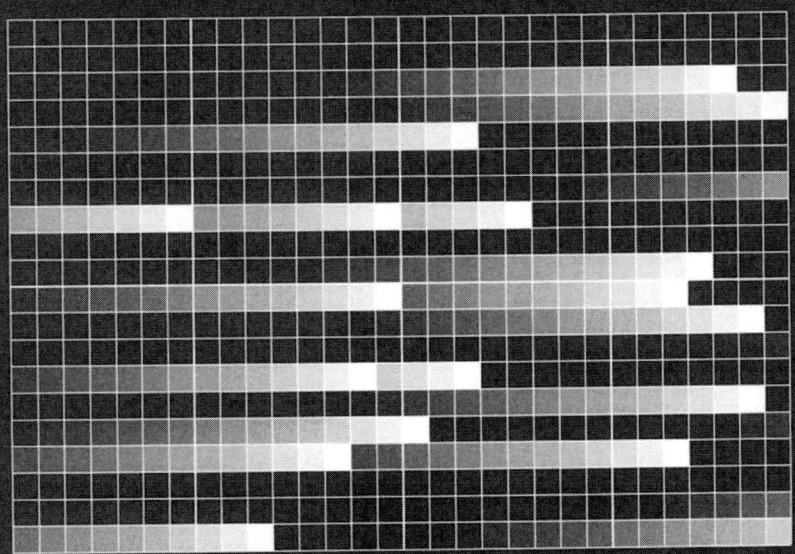

Vertical movement

A simple adjustment to the getNext function makes the movement go from bottom to top, instead of from left to right:

```
function getNext(obj) {
    num = obj._name.substring(7);
    num = num-across;
    if (num>=0) {
        with (_root["trigger"+num]) {
            gotoAndPlay("on");
        }
    }
}
```

Instead of num being incremented, it skips to the row before. The if condition also has to be changed. It now checks to make sure it hasn't already hit the last row. You can see the finished effect in the download files, saved as vertical_movement.fla.

Adding sound effects

As well as using the effects selectable from the frame, it's possible to apply effects to sounds using the Sound object. The completed file is included in the download files, named `vertical_movement_sound_object.fla`.

A Sound object is created with:

```
new Sound(target);
```

The target is the movie clip that this Sound object will control. If there's no target, the Sound object will control sound for the entire movie.

Once a Sound object has been created, various methods are available to alter the sounds it controls.

One method of the Sound object is `setVolume`. At the moment each line of my vertical trailing grid sounds the same. I decided to change the layout code to make the volume of each column rise from left to right:

```
for(i=0;i<down;i++){
    for(j=0;j<across;j++){
        counter = ((i*across)+j);
        attachMovie("sound_trigger",
        ➡"trigger"+counter,counter);
        mv = _root["trigger"+counter];
        mv.onRelease = function(){
            this.gotoAndPlay("on");
            this.scale.gotoAndStop(this.soundToPlay);
            this.scale.gotoAndStop(1);
        }
        mv.soundToPlay = i+2;
        mv._x = j*w;
        mv._y = i*h;
        mv.snd = new Sound(mv);
        mv.snd.setVolume(parseInt((j/across)*100)+1);
    }
}
```

I've added a variable to each movie clip, and set it to a Sound object. It might just be me, but I always get this bit wrong, and confuse myself trying to work it out. `snd` is a variable held by the `mv` movie clip. Even though it is within `mv`, it has to target itself, otherwise it will control the entire movie, hence `new Sound(mv)`.

Then for each Sound object I've set the volume to reflect its column position. Volume ranges from 1 to 100, and I've added 1 to the amount to make sure that the leftmost column isn't silent.

Right to left panning

Another method of the Sound object is setPan. Pan values range from -100 to 100. -100 means entirely in the right-hand speaker, +100 entirely in the left. Similarly, a value of -20 would give a balance of 120 right to 80 left, or 60/40.

I changed the setVolume lines from the last example to:

```
mv.soundToPlay = i+2;
mv._x = j*w;
mv._y = i*h;
mv.snd = new Sound(mv);
mv.snd.setPan(pan);
pan = ((j/30)*200)-100;
```

I also wanted the movement to reflect the right to left movement of the panning, so I changed the getNext function to:

```
function getNext(obj) {
  num = obj._name.substring(7);
  num--;
  if (num%30<>29 && num>=0) {
    with (_root["trigger"+num]) {
      gotoAndPlay("on");
    }
  }
}
```

In this case, I wanted the movement to stop once it got to the left-hand edge, rather than wrapping around, so I used the modulus (%) operator to check for column position. Mod returns the remainder after division, so a remainder of 29 means that the next movie is on the next row. Also, as checking the next row after trigger0 would cause an error, num must not be a negative number.

The sound now moves from speaker to speaker as the squares move across the screen. Move your speakers far apart for best effect, or alternatively clamp a speaker to each ear. It may not be surround sound, but if you close your eyes you may just fool yourself that there's a musical mosquito flying across the room. You can look at my version, right_to_left.fla, in the download files.

20 steps

For a final variation, I wanted to get something a bit more random going on. I kept the duplicate code the same as in right_to_left.fla so that the pan effect was still there. My completed file is saved as 20step.fla.

The getNext function was changed to:

```
function getNext(obj) {
    num = parseInt(obj._name.substring(7));
    decider = random(4);
    switch (decider) {
    case 0 :
        num = num-across;
        break;
    case 1 :
        num = num+across;
        break;
    case 2 :
        num++;
        break;
    case 3 :
        num--;
        break;
    }
    if (num>0 && num<across*down) {
        with (_root["trigger"+num]) {
            gotoAndPlay("on");
        }
    }
}
```

In this case, the next trail can move in any of four directions, up (-across), down (+across), left(-1), and right(+1). In one of these cases (num + across), Flash will treat + as a string operator, rather than an arithmetic operator, so I needed to explicitly make num a number by wrapping it in parseInt().

To decide which of the four routes to take, I set a variable to a random number between 0 and 3. Then I used a **switch** statement to set a different movement for each of the 4 possible values of decider. The if condition now just checks to make sure the trail isn't trying to go off the grid altogether.

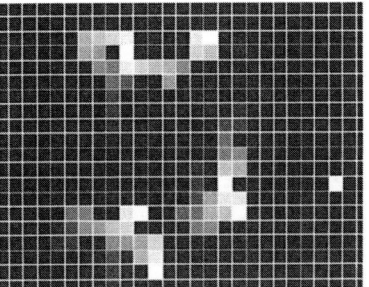

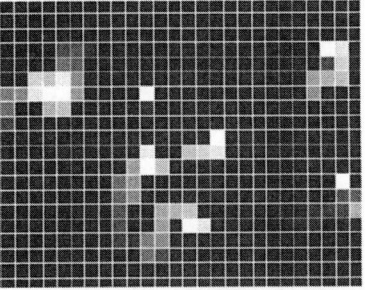

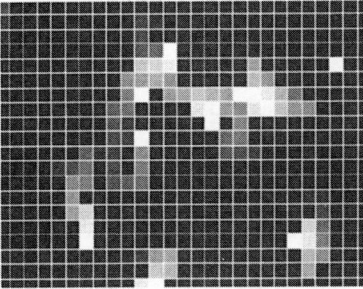

5

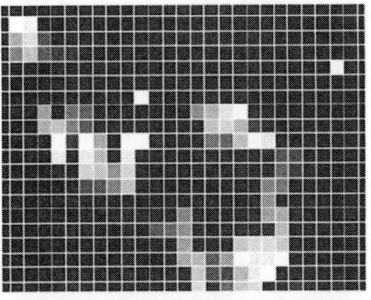

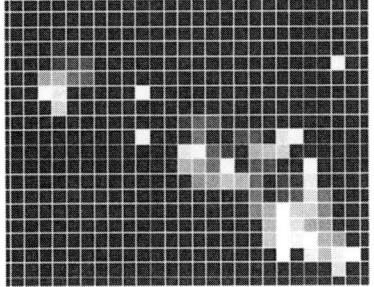

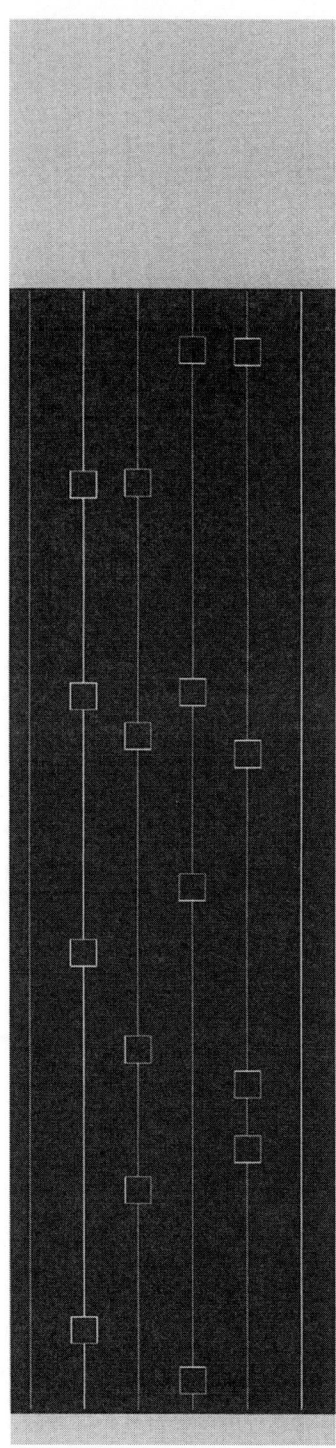

Scripting streaming sounds

A technique I've used a lot of times that works fairly well is to take a longer sound (about 2 seconds is the most that's likely to fit into 5k – the filesize I've been aiming for) which rises in pitch, then use ActionScript to play different parts of the note. It gives an effect a bit like a digital swanee whistle with lots of whoops and slides, and only a vague approximation of a tune. I called this experiment `sliders.fla`.

I made a simple sine wave sound with the synthesis feature in Sound Forge, setting its pitch pretty low (100 MHz). I used the Pitch Bend feature to make the sound start very low and rise very high. I saved it as `whoop.wav`.

After importing the sound into Flash, into a new document, 350x400 px, with a black background, I put it into a new movie clip, called whoop_sound, setting the Sync option to Stream. This allowed me to play the sound in segments, something that can't be done with Event sounds.

It's important that there are enough frames for the entire sound to be played. Flash displays a wave form that makes this easy to work out. Here we need 29 frames. I added a `stop` action in the first frame.

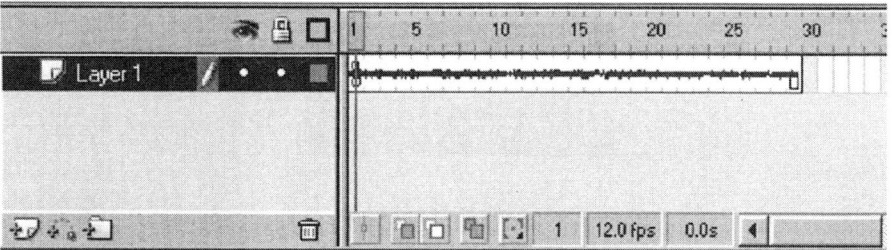

To control the sound, I wanted to use a set of sliders where the position of the slider will determine which part of `whoop.wav` plays. I made a square, and turned it into a movie clip named display. I also dragged the clip containing the sound into display, and gave it an instance name of whooper.

Frame 1 sets up the dragging behavior of the clip:

```
limitY = (400-this._height)+1;
this.onPress = function() {
   startDrag(this, false, this._x, 0, this._x, limitY);
   play();
};
this.onRelease = function() {
   stopDrag();
};
```

The dragging is constrained so that the clip only moves straight up and down, and cannot go off the edge of the stage. limitY is set in the first frame of the movie to the height of the movie, minus the height of the whooper clip itself to stop it being able to move outside of the bounding box, with a final adjustment of one to make it sit perfectly on the bounding box.

Next, at the third frame, which I labeled loop, the clip works out the appropriate bit of the sliding sound to play:

```
translated =
parseInt((this._y/limitY)*29);
```

This sets a variable, translated, with a value of a number from 1-29 (the number of frames in the whoop_sound clip) based on the y position of the display clip. Then I tell the clip to play the whoop_sound clip from there:

```
whooper.gotoAndPlay(translated);
```

Four frames later, in frame 7, I tell the clip to go back to frame loop to do it all again:

```
gotoAndPlay("loop");
```

With all this in place, I dragged four of my display movie clips into place at the bottom of the stage and added four lines on a lower layer to show the sliders' path, and a bounding box the same size as the stage on another layer.

All four sliders can now be controlled individually – a kind of inharmonic four-part harmony.

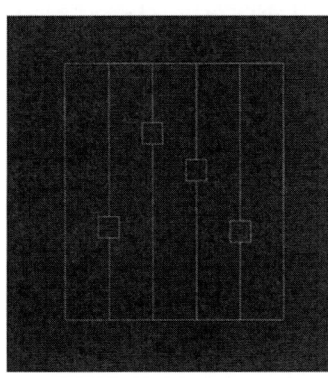

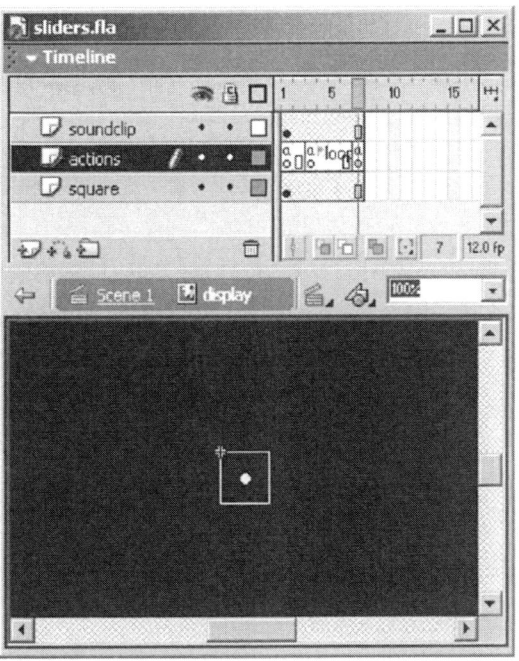

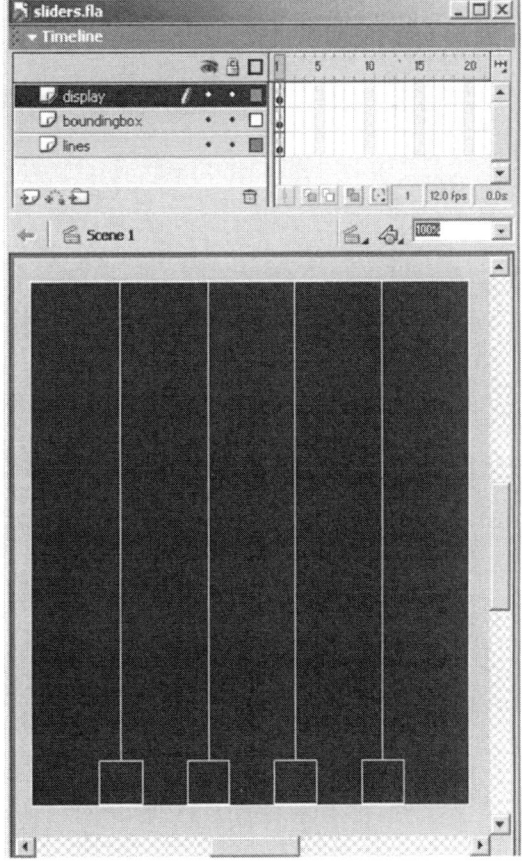

5

Bouncer

This little game is based on the classic digital motif of *Pong*. A ball bounces around inside a bounding box, playing a different note as it hits each wall.

As with the grid, a good way of getting interesting effects out of limited sounds is to use duplication, as using the same sound more than once doesn't add to file size. With this toy, I wanted to make the duplication interactive, rather than set.

A new feature in Flash MX allows a **class** (just an object really) to be associated with a movie clip, so that each time a clip is added to the stage, it automatically takes on the methods and properties you have set for it.

The basic process is to construct an object using an empty function:

```
function aClass(){}
```

Setting the prototype of the class to MovieClip allows it to inherit all of the MovieClip object's methods and properties:

```
aClass.prototype = new MovieClip();
```

Finally, you have to associate the class with the correct movie clip, using the name you have given it under Linkage in the Library:

```
Object.registerClass("movie clip to register", aClass);
```

You can then go on and add methods to your new object.

```
ball.prototype.doSomething = function(arguments){
    make the clip do something
}
```

As I wanted to duplicate lots of balls here, and I knew I'd have to track their co-ordinates individually, this approach is ideal.

First of all, I drew the ball, made it into a movie clip, and linked it as ball from the Library, removing the instance from the stage, as we'll call it with ActionScript later.

The boundaries of the box will be static and shared by all the movie clips, so I put these outside the class itself, along with a counter variable to test how many duplications had been performed:

```
right = 510;
left = 10;
top = 10;
bottom = 360;
counter = 0;
```

Next, I added the empty constructor for my `ball` object, made it inherit the `MovieClip` class, and registered my `ball` movie clip to that class:

```
function ball(){}
ball.prototype = new MovieClip();
Object.registerClass("ball", ball);
```

The first function I added sets the position of the clip, the amount it will move along the x and y axis, and gives it a Sound object to use:

```
ball.prototype.init = function(x,y){
    this._x = x;
    this._y = y;
    this.moveX = 10;
    this.moveY = this.moveX;
    this.snd = new Sound(this);
}
```

Each time the ball hits a wall, it will need to play a different sound.

```
ball.prototype.playSound = function(wav){
    this.snd.attachSound(wav);
    this.snd.start(0,5);
}
```

This function needs to take the name of a linked sound file, so I imported four sounds, and linked them as one, two, three and four.

Then I needed a function to perform the animation – to move the ball along the x and y axes, and reverse its movement when it hits an edge. As the `animate` function needs to be triggered from somewhere, I put a second frame into my ball clip, with an action to:

```
this.animate();
```

Here's the `animate` function:

```
ball.prototype.animate = function(){
    if(this._x>right||this._x<left){
        this.moveX = this.moveX*-1;
        if(this._x>right){
            this.playSound("one");
        }else{
            this.playSound("three");
        }
    }
```

5

```
if(this._y>bottom||this._y<top){
  this.moveY = this.moveY*-1;
  if(this._y>bottom){
    this.playSound("two");
  }else{
    this.playSound("four");
  }
}
this._x = this._x + this.moveX;
this._y = this._y + this.moveY;
}
```

Before moving the ball, it checks to see if the ball has hit the vertical or horizontal edges, with the two outer if statements:

```
if(this._x>right||this._x<left){
```

...and...

```
if(this._y>bottom||this._y<top){
```

...if either is true, the relevant direction needs to be reversed.

Secondly, the inner if statements then look to see which border has been hit (top or bottom, left or right) and play an appropriate sound, using the playSound function.

The ball object now does everything it needs to, and I just needed an easy way of putting it on the stage:

```
function makeBall(){
  counter++;
  attachMovie("ball", "ball"+counter, counter);
  return(_root["ball"+counter]);
}
```

This just increments the counter so that all clips are given a unique name and put into different levels, attaches the movie, and returns the ball object.

The ball can now be tested by getting the ball object from makeBall and initializing it with init:

```
aBall = makeBall();
aBall.init(100,100);
```

These two lines will create an animated ball at (x, y) co-ordinates of (100,100), as in one_ball.fla.

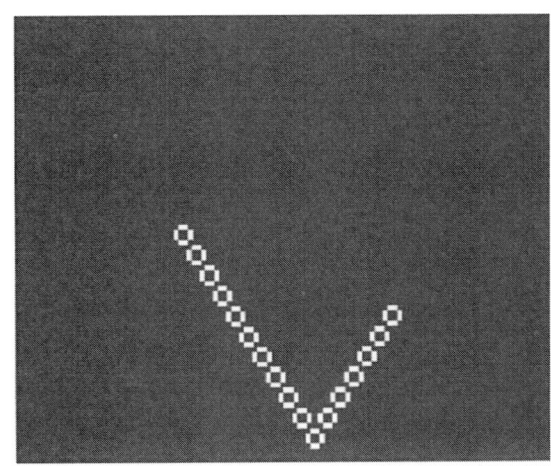

Diagonal balls

But the whole point of using this technique is to allow easy duplication. I replaced the two lines which make the ball in one_ball.fla with a loop which places balls across the diagonal, and saved the file as diagonal_balls.fla.

```
for(i=20;i<bottom;i+=20){
    aBall = makeBall();
    aBall.init(i/1.5,i);
}
```

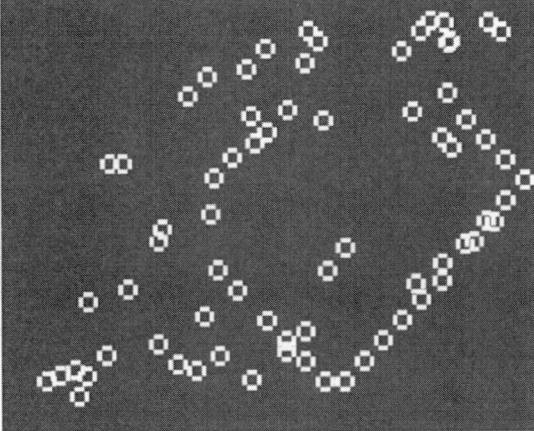

Many balls

To make a ball appear wherever the user clicks, I added an invisible button laid over the entire movie, gave it an instance name of trigger, and replaced the loop above with a bit of ActionScript to the main timeline to make the button initialize new balls:

```
trigger.onRelease = function(){
    b = makeBall();
    b.init(_xmouse, _ymouse);
}
```

I saved this as many_balls.fla.

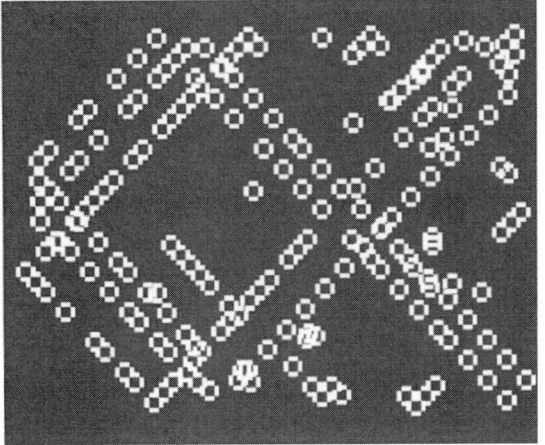

5

Draggable balls

To give another layer of interactivity, I wanted to be able to drag over the movie and create a direction for the balls to move in.

I changed the trigger code to:

```
trigger.onRelease = function(){
    if(startX!=_xmouse){
        ball = makeBall();
        ball.init(_xmouse,_ymouse,_xmouse-startX,_ymouse-
          ➡ startY);
    }
    startX = 0;
    startY = 0;
}


trigger.onPress = function(){
    startX = _xmouse;
    startY = _ymouse;
}
```

When the user presses the mouse, the x and y co-ordinates at that point are stored. When the mouse is then released, as well as sending the current co-ordinates to init, the difference between the *press* and *release* co-ordinates are sent, which are used by init to set the angle the ball moves along.

I changed the init function to:

```
ball.prototype.init = function(x,y,moveX,moveY){
    this._x = x;
    this._y = y;
    this.moveX = moveX/5;
    this.moveY = moveY/5;
    this.snd = new Sound(this);
}
```

Pachinko

The original version of this was created for www.13amp.tv.

It's inspired both by Pong (which you'd be right to guess is a strong influence) and Pachinko, the Japanese pinball game.

Instead of the balls just bouncing around the box, I wanted to add paddles to control them, so that the user can change the direction of the balls, creating little tunes in the process.

I began by adding a few global variables to the code:

```
right = 600;
left = 0;
top = 0;
bottom = 400;
counter = 0;
movement = 10;
```

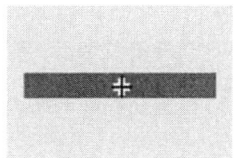

For the paddles used to control the balls' movement, I made a black bar into a clip called bar, put it into a clip called paddles, and laid a blank button over the top, calling it trigger.

The bars need to be able to rotate so that the balls will bounce off them in different directions. Moving in 45° steps, there are four unique positions that the bar can be in:

The positions correspond to 0°, 45°, 90° and 135°, so I added an onRelease function into a new layer in the paddles timeline for the trigger button to move it through these four positions when clicked:

```
trigger.onRelease = function () {
    if(this._parent._rotation == 135){
        next = 0;
    }else{
        next = this._parent._rotation+45;
    }
    this._parent._rotation = next;
}
```

In other words, if the paddle is currently rotated 135, go back to 0, otherwise add 45 to the current position.

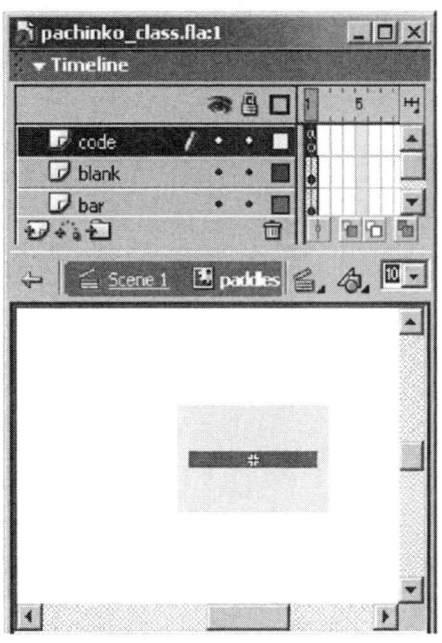

5

Going back to the main timeline, I decided on a set of nine paddles laid out across the stage, so I wrote two arrays to give their y and x positions:

```
yArr = new Array(100,200,300);
xArr = new Array(130,300,470);
```

I then attached them to the stage accordingly:

```
for(i=0;i<xArr.length;i++){
    for(j=0;j<yArr.length;j++){
        attachMovie("paddle", i+","+j, (3*i)+j+1000);
        with(_root[i+","+j]){
            _x = xArr[i];
            _y = yArr[j];
        }
    }
}
```

Their names correspond to their position with columns and rows named from 0 to 2, so that top row in the middle would be x=0, y=1 or (0,1).

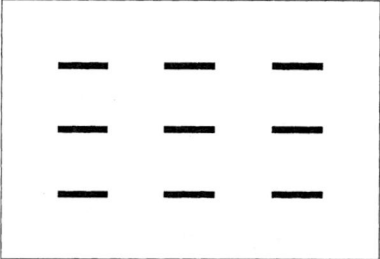

I used the class technique for this toy as well. I made a small black square to use as the ball, converted it to a movie clip, and linked it as ball.

On the main timeline once again, I added the initialization code:

```
function ball(){}

ball.prototype = new MovieClip();

Object.registerClass("ball", ball);

ball.prototype.init = function(x,wav){
    //starts off moving straight down
    this.moveX = 0;
    this.moveY = movement;
```

```
      this._x = x;
      this._y = 50;
      this.snd = new Sound(this);
      this.snd.attachSound(wav);
  }
```

This is very similar to the code we used to do this job before. In this case, each ball only ever plays its own sound, so I attached the sound in the init function. All the balls start moving off in the same direction (down), and start at the same point on the y axis. As before, the ball clip has an action in frame 2:

```
  this.animate();
```

Then we need the animate function:

```
  ball.prototype.animate = function(){
```

When the ball hits an edge, I wanted it to wrap round the screen rather than rebounding:

```
if(this._x>right){
    this._x = 0;
  }else if(this._x<=0){
    this._x = right;
  }
  if(this._y>bottom){
    this._y = 0;
  }else if(this._y<=0){
    this._y = bottom;
  }
```

The function also needs to check if any of the paddles have been hit:

```
  paddle = false;
  for(i=0;i<xArr.length;i++){
    for(j=0;j<yArr.length;j++){
      if((this._y == yArr[j])&&(this._x == xArr[i])){
        paddle = _root[i+","+j];
        //break;
      }
    }
  }
```

paddle is set to false, so that later it's easy to check if a collision has been detected. A nested loop then goes through each of the possible center points of the bars, and sets paddle to hold the MovieClip object that the ball hits if there is a collision.

Having worked out which paddle has been hit, the tricky bit is working out all the variations of how balls react when they hit the paddle. Going through the change in direction I wanted to happen each time a ball hit a paddle, I ended up with this frankly ugly piece of code, which I added to the animation routine:

```
if(paddle!=false){
    switch(paddle._rotation){
      case 135:
        if(this.moveX == 0){
          if(this.moveY>0){
            this.moveX = -movement;
          }else{
            this.moveX = movement;
          }
          this.moveY = 0;
        }else{
          if(this.moveX>0){
            this.moveY = -movement;
          }else{
            this.moveY = movement;
          }
          this.moveX = 0;
        }
        break;
      case  45:
        if(this.moveX == 0){
          if(this.moveY>0){
            this.moveX = movement;
          }else{
            this.moveX = -movement;
          }
          this.moveY = 0;
        }else{
          if(this.moveX>0){
            this.moveY = movement;
          }else{
            this.moveY = -movement;
          }
          this.moveX = 0;
        }
        break;
      case 90:
        this.moveX = -this.moveX;
        break;
      case 0:
        this.moveY = -this.moveY
        break;
    }
```

As an example, if the paddle is rotated 135°, and the ball hitting it is moving top to bottom, it will change direction to move right to left:

```
case 135:
        if(this.moveX == 0){
          this.moveY = 0;
          if(this.moveY>0){
            this.moveX = -movement;
          }
```

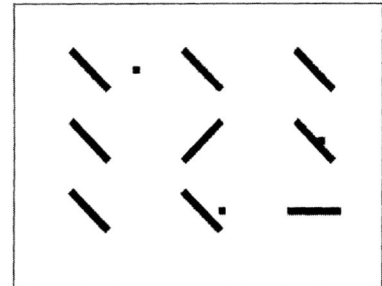

Each change in direction corresponds to how a ball might naturally bounce off the paddle.

Also, whichever way the ball hits a paddle, it plays its own sound:

```
      this.snd.start();
      }
```

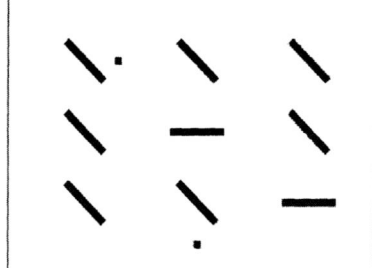

Adding the moveX and moveY to the current x and y positions starts off the animation:

```
    this._x = this._x + this.moveX;
    this._y = this._y + this.moveY;
    }
```

Next I wrote a function to make each instance of the ball:

```
function ballMaker(){
    counter++;
    attachMovie("ball", "ball"+counter, counter);
    clip = _root["ball"+counter];
    return clip;
}
```

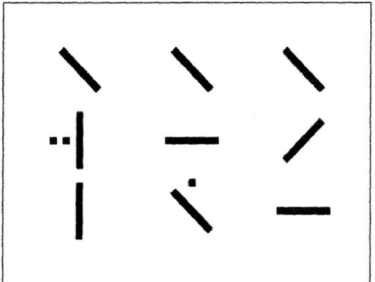

I used it to create three instances of the ball object, one over each column of paddles:

```
ball_1 = ballMaker();
ball_1.init(130,"one");
ball_2 = ballMaker();
ball_2.init(300,"two");
ball_3 = ballMaker();
ball_3.init(470,"three");
```

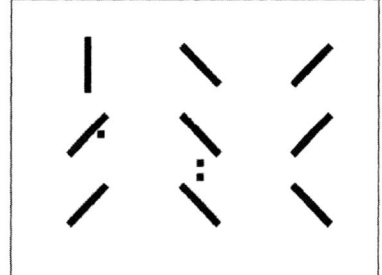

5

Each ball is given a different sound to play on collision. These sounds were imported into Flash and given linkage names of one, two and three.

And that's it. The balls now happily bounce around the box, rebounding off paddles, and playing a pretty little tune in the process.

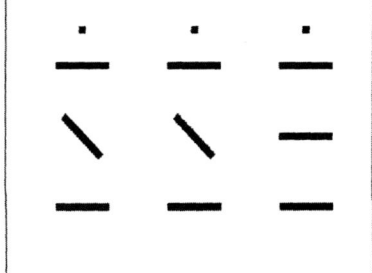

Sampling the VL-Tone

The *Casio VL-Tone* keyboard has a fine selection of tones that are ripe for sampling. Being a simple digital instrument, the sounds it produces compress down to low sizes with ease. On most instruments, you can get hold of a lead that will allow you to plug it into your sound card and record directly.

I recorded one of the drum-tracks from the VL-Tone, and cut it up into separate instruments, which gave me a high and low ping and a cymbal sound.

I also wanted another bassy tone, so I pitch shifted the low tone down a few octaves. I wanted two separate percussive noises, so I merge pasted a low ping and a high ping with the cymbal sound.

Hey Mickey

Two seconds of sound is not enough to play a whole tune, so I had to think of ways of using ActionScript to play a tune.

I decided to choose *Hey Mickey* by eighties one-hit wonder and performance artist Toni Basil. The choice was inspired by Anthony, my partner at www.friendchip.com, and his habit of drumming rhythms on the desk which he claims are the very latest tunes, but which always sound like the intro to *Hey Mickey*.

Fortunately, the intro to *Hey Mickey* is very simple, only having six separate notes, so it works with my self-imposed 5 KB limit. To fit with the eighties themes, I used the sounds I sampled from the Casio VL-Tone, shifted in pitch to match the tune, and imported them into a new Flash document, 640x400 px.

However, I still needed a way of reusing the notes and triggering them at the right point. I decided to use a similar technique to a player piano. The player piano has a roll of paper which slowly moves through on which the notes are marked out by holes. Each key has its own position on the roll, and when the piano encounters a hole in the position it will play that note.

My digital solution uses a timer to move through the score, and arrays instead of a roll of paper. Notes are marked with 1s, silence with a 0.

For example, if I had a four-beat bar, and I wanted to play a note on the first and fourth beats, I'd put:

```
bar = new Array(1,0,0,1);
```

So I now had to break down the tune into all its component parts.

The vocal line takes the longest to move through an entire loop, four bars. Splitting that up into its component beats gives 32 beats, which meant that my tune had to be 32 beats long.

In all I ended up with six parts:

- The two notes in the vocal

- The two notes in the bass

- The high and low percussion beats

Here's my score in table format:

Key

1. Lower bass
2. higher bass
3. Low percussion
4. High Percussion
5. Low voice
6. High voice

1									X	X	X	X	X	X	X	X	Repeat							
2	X	X	X	X	X	X	X	X									Repeat							
3		X		X		Repeat					Repeat					Repeat								
4	X		X			Repeat					Repeat					Repeat								
5	X		X	X	X	X	X		X	X	X	X	X	X	X	X								
6														X	X	X				X	X	X		

Which I expressed as an array:

```
score = new Array();
voices = new Array("bass_seventh", "bass_tonic", "cymbal",
"low_drum","lo_voice", "hi_voice");
beats = 32;
score[0] = new Array(0,0,0,0,0,0,0,0,1,1,1,1,1,1,1,1);
score[1] = new Array(1,1,1,1,1,1,1,1,0,0,0,0,0,0,0,0);
score[2] = new Array(0,0,1,0,0,0,1,0);
score[3] = new Array(1,0,0,1,0,1,0,0);
score[4] = new
➥ Array(1,0,1,1,1,1,1,0,1,1,1,1,1,1,1,0,0,0,0,0,0,0,0,0,0,0,
➥ 0,0,0 ,0,0,0);
score[5] = new
➥ Array(0,0,0,0,0,0,0,0,0,0,0,0,0,0,0,1,1,1,0,0,0,0,0,1,1,1,
➥ 0,0,0, 0,0,0);
```

`voices` lists the names of the WAV files for each part. I then put the appropriate beats into arrays within the `score` array, with positions matching the positions of the voices, so for example the `"cymbal"` part is at `score[2]`.

Just to make it a bit tidier, I didn't want to copy and paste the repeated parts of the score, so I wrote an extension to the array prototype, to go before the array code:

```
array.prototype.double = function(arr){
   //store length to avoid infinite loop
   len = this.length;
   for(i=0;i<len;i++){
      this.push(this[i]);
   }
}
```

This allows an array to duplicate its contents to the end of itself.

I then changed the score to:

```
score[0]  = new Array(0,0,0,0,0,0,0,0,1,1,1,1,1,1,1,1);
score[0].double();
score[1]  = new Array(1,1,1,1,1,1,1,1,0,0,0,0,0,0,0,0);
score[1].double();
score[2]  = new Array(0,0,1,0,0,0,1,0);
score[2].double();
score[2].double();
score[3]  = new Array(1,0,0,1,0,1,0,0);
```

```
score[3].double();
score[3].double();
score[4] = new
➡ Array(1,0,1,1,1,1,1,0,1,1,1,1,1,1,1,0,0,0,0,0,0,0,0,0,0,0,
➡ 0,0,0,0,0,0);
score[5] = new
➡ Array(0,0,0,0,0,0,0,0,0,0,0,0,0,0,0,0,1,1,1,0,0,0,0,0,1,1,1,
➡ 0,0,0,0,0,0);
```

All the arrays are now the correct 32 beats in length.

Each part in the score needs a Sound object to be played in.

```
sounds = new Array();
for(i=0;i<voices.length;i++){
    sounds[i] = new Sound();
    sounds[i].attachSound(voices[i]+".wav");
}
```

The sounds array is now filled with Sound objects with the correct sound attached.

To move through the score, I needed to create a timer that would move through the score on each beat. However, frame rate in Flash is surprisingly flexible. Whilst the frame rate seems to have become more stable over successive versions, I still find that it is affected by the amount of memory available to Flash, so if a memory hungry background program is running, I find the rhythm becomes extremely erratic. Dancing to anything made in this fashion is out of the question.

The new setInterval function in Flash MX filled me with excitement (no, really) as it seemed to offer a way of dealing with this, but unfortunately setInterval uses the frame rate to get its timings, so behaves just as badly when you use it for rhythms.

Luckily, in Flash MX there is a new sound feature which, with a bit of programming, allows me to construct an accurate timer, which seems less susceptible to changes due to memory use, and is completely independent of the frame rate. Unlike previous versions of Flash, you can now trigger an event at the end of a sound playing. By importing a silent sound (a WAV file full of nothing) the length of the time interval I want to check for, I can get an accurate beat. Plus being able to create the whole thing in ActionScript without having to mess around with all that visual timeline stuff appeals to the geek in me.

5

I imported and linked as `silence.wav` a completely silent WAV file at the length I wanted each beat to be, 0.2 seconds. Each time the sound is played, it triggers the function that checks the score and moves along to the next note.

```
timer = new Sound();
timer.attachSound("silence.wav");
timer.start();
counter = 0;
timer.onSoundComplete = function () {
      for(i=0;i<voices.length;i++){
        if(score[i][counter]==1){
           sounds[i].start();
        }
      }
      timer.start();
      if(counter<beats-1){
      counter++;
      }else{
        counter = 0;
      }
};
```

`counter` keeps track of the current position in the score. For each of the voices, the script checks if it has 1 in the `counter` position, and if it does, tells the sound to play with `start`. `timer` also has to tell itself to play again. Finally, if the `counter` has got to the end of the score, `beats-1`, it's reset to 0.

If you want to check that all the sounds are playing, amend the `timer.onSoundComplete` function by adding a line of code as shown:

```
timer.onSoundComplete = function () {
      for(i=0;i<voices.length;i++){
        if(score[i][counter]==1){
                    trace(voices[i]);
          sounds[i].start();
        }
      }
```

This will show the voices in the output window as they play.

Graphical Hey Mickey

Though the movie now works, and the happy sounds of *Hey Mickey* are playing, visually it's rather dull, being just a white screen.

To get a visual representation, I created a new movie clip, containing a black-bordered white rectangle, 15 x 30 px, in the first frame, along with a `stop` action. I added a black to white fade over nine frames to show when it's playing. I gave it a Linkage name of `square`.

I then wrote some code to attach the clip to the stage, with a row of 32 rectangles for each part:

```
levels = 0;
h = 30;
w =15;
startX = (640-(beats*w))/2;
startY = (400-(voices.length*h))/2;
y = startY;
for(i=0;i<voices.length;i++){
  x = startX;
  for(j=0;j<beats;j++){
    _root.attachMovie("square",voices[i]+j,levels);
    mv = _root[voices[i]+j];
    mv._x = x;
    mv._y = y;
    x+=w;
    levels++;
  }
  y+=h;
}
```

I made some changes to the `timer.onSoundComplete` function, removing the `trace` line and adding two lines to make the movie clip play:

```
timer.onSoundComplete = function() {
  for (i=0; i<voices.length; i++) {
    if (score[i][counter] == 1) {
      sounds[i].start();
      mv = _root[voices[i]+counter];
      mv.play();
    }
  }
}
```

5

I also created a movie clip with a dynamic text field called label to allow the name of each clip to be shown. I added code to duplicate that as well inside the i loop.

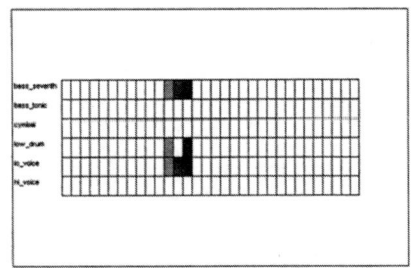

```
for(i=0;i<voices.length;i++){
    x = startX;
    _root.attachMovie("label", "label"+i, levels+1000);
    lb = _root["label"+I];
    lb.txt = voices[i];
    lb._x = 2;
    lb._y = y;
```

This file was saved as hey_mickey_graphical_labelled.fla.

Finally, I thought it'd be good to allow the different parts to be turned on and off so I added a new array, called switched, where the sounds array is set up:

```
sounds = new Array();
switched = new Array();
for(i=0;i<voices.length;i++){
    sounds[i] = new Sound();
    sounds[i].attachSound(voices[i]+".wav");
    switched[i] = 0;
}
```

switched holds the on/off state. All sounds are off at the beginning, so the switched array is filled with 0s.

I created a new movie clip, with a Linkage name of trigger, containing the square clip, given an instance name of marker, and an invisible button covering it. I added code to position the triggers to the right of each line:

```
levels = 0;
h = 30;
w =15;
startX = (640-(beats*w))/2;
startY = (400-(voices.length*h))/2;
y = startY;
for(i=0;i<voices.length;i++){
    x = startX;
    _root.attachMovie("label", "label"+i, levels+1000);
    lb = _root["label"+i];
    lb.txt = voices[i];
    lb._x = 2;
    lb._y = y;
```

```
        for(j=0;j<beats;j++){
            _root.attachMovie("square",voices[i]+j,levels);
            mv = _root[voices[i]+j];
            mv._x = x;
            mv._y = y;
            x+=w;
            levels++;
        }
    _root.attachMovie("trigger", "trigger"+i, levels+2000);
        mv = _root["trigger"+i];
        mv.voice = i;
        mv.onRelease = function(){
            if(this.isOn==true){
                _root.switched[this.voice]=0;
                this.isOn=false;
                this.marker.gotoAndStop(1);
            }else{
                _root.switched [this.voice]=1;
                this.isOn=true;
                this.marker.gotoAndStop(4);
            }
        }
        mv._y = y;
        mv._x = 590;
//move down a level
        y+=h;
    }
```

The onRelease function tells the clip to flip between on and off states for the line of the score it represents. Three things need doing to achieve this – set the switched array to the right value, store a variable isOn to hold the state, and send marker to the correct frame for this state.

Finally, add a condition to the timer function to check that each sound is on before it's played:

```
if(score[i][counter]==1&&switched[i]==1){
        sounds[i].start();
        mv = _root[voices[i]+counter];
        mv.play();
    }
```

I saved this file as
hey_mickey_graphical_labelled_switched.fla.

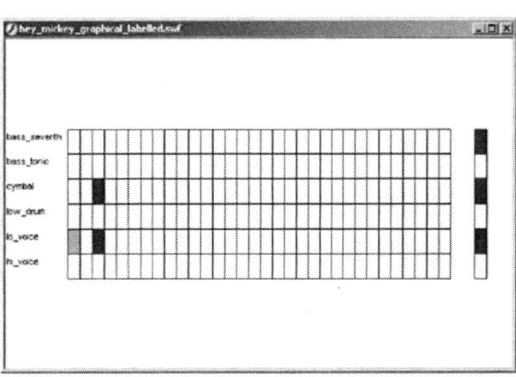

Score

Having made this work, it struck me that it wouldn't be too hard to change it so that the score could be set by the user, instead of being read from the arrays. Instead of putting 1s and 0s into the score array, I just set them to be 32 in length:

```
beats = 32;
score[0] = new Array(beats);
score[1] = new Array(beats);
score[2] = new Array(beats);
score[3] = new Array(beats);
score[4] = new Array(beats);
score[5] = new Array(beats);
```

Instead of duplicating the square clip across the stage, I used trigger instead, so that each square could be selected and deselected to change the score:

```
for(i=0;i<voices.length;i++){
    x = startX;
    _root.attachMovie("label", "label"+i, levels+1000);
    lb = _root["label"+i];
    lb.txt = voices[i];
    lb._x = 2;
    lb._y = y;
    for(j=0;j<beats;j++){
        _root.attachMovie("trigger",voices[i]+j,levels);
        mv = _root[voices[i]+j];
        mv.row = i;
        mv.column = j;
        mv._x = x;
        mv._y = y;
        mv.onRelease = function(){
            flick(this);
        }
        x+=w;
        levels++;
    }
}
```

Each of the triggers when clicked calls the flick function, passing itself to the function. I added this function to the beginning of the code:

```
function flick(obj){

if(score[obj.row][obj.column]==0||score[obj.row][obj.column]=
Â =null){
```

```
        obj.marker.gotoAndStop(2);
        score[obj.row][obj.column]=1;
    }else{
        obj.marker.gotoAndStop(1);
        score[obj.row][obj.column]=0;
    }
}
```

`flick` then checks if the button is currently on or off, and puts it to the opposite state. It will also change a 1 to a 0 and a 0 to a 1 in the score.

I also wanted to have an indicator for which beat was currently being played, so I attached a row of half-height sized squares along the top:

```
for(i=0;i<voices.length;i++){
    x = startX;
    _root.attachMovie("label", "label"+i, levels+1000);
    lb = _root["label"+i];
    lb.txt = voices[i];
    lb._x = 2;
    lb._y = y;
    for(j=0;j<beats;j++){
if(i==0){
            attachMovie("square", "beat"+j, levels+10000);
            bt = _root["beat"+j];
            bt._height = bt._height/4;
            bt._y = y-25;
            bt._x = x;
        }

    _root.attachMovie("trigger",voices[i]+j,levels);
        mv = _root[voices[i]+j];
        mv.row = i;
        mv.column = j;
        mv._x = x;
        mv._y = y;
        mv.onRelease = function(){
          flick(this);
        }
        x+=w;
        levels++;
    }
```

I then needed to amend the `timer.onSoundComplete` function, removing references to the `switched` array, and adding code so that on each beat the correct `beat` clip is told to play:

```
timer.onSoundComplete = function () {
    for(i=0;i<voices.length;i++){
        if(score[i][counter]==1){
            sounds[i].start();
            mv = _root[voices[i]+counter];
            mv.play();
        }
    }
    with(_root["beat"+counter]){
        play();
    }
    timer.start();
    if(counter<beats-1){
    counter++;
    }else{
        counter = 0;
    }
};
```

Now your score should be fully adjustable when you test it – a bit like a very basic version of Cubase really.

Here's what the score for *Hey Mickey* looks like when drawn:

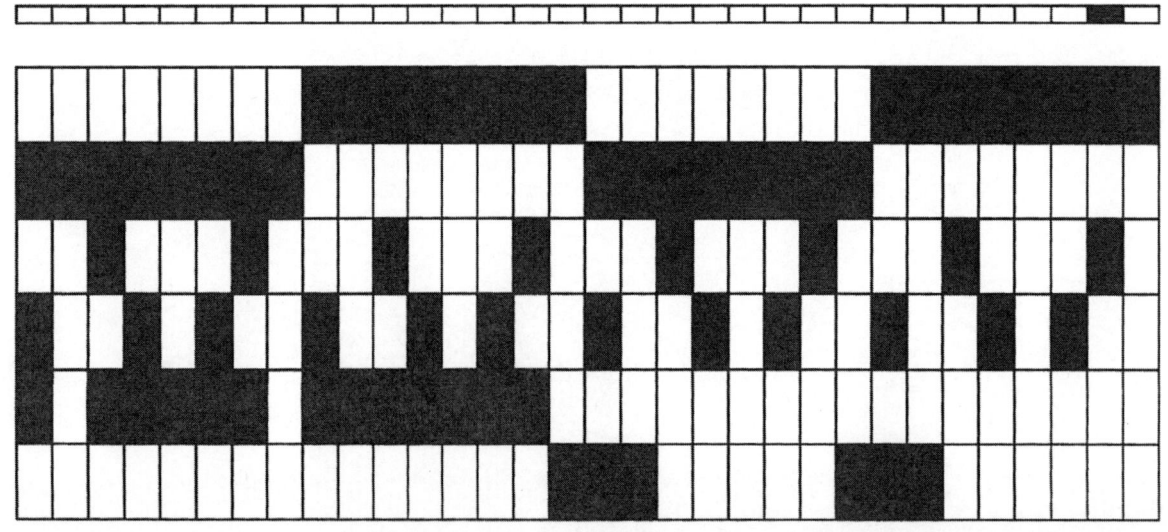

Or just draw a picture and see what it sounds like.

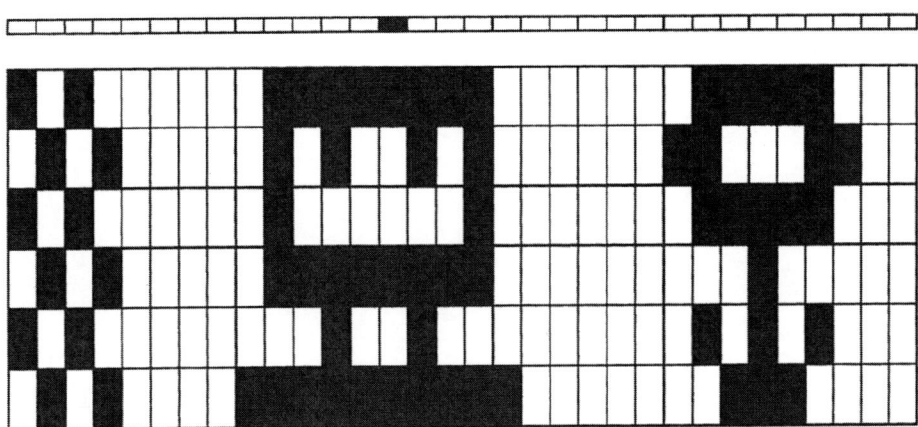

Not very good is probably the answer!

The end and beyond

I hope this chapter has shown you that it is entirely possible to get good sound effects with Flash using very small file sizes. You do need to be flexible, as you'll probably find that the effect Flash produces is not quite the same as the effect you were after, but work with Flash's slightly quirky sound handling rather than trying to beat it into submission and you'll find there are hundreds of possibilities, even with the handful of sound features Flash offers. As always, creativity is the key.

5

6 CITY BLOSSOM

DAVID HIRMES

The challenge was to make it small. How small? Well, the contest rules said no more than 5 kilobytes in which to create the most compelling program I could imagine. The winner would take home the big bucks – $51.20 to be precise! Well, OK, the 5K contest at www.the5k.org isn't really about the cash. It's about the challenge! How much could I get Flash to do in less than 5 KB?

Optimization and efficiency, typically thought of as rather 'geeky' words to many designers, were to become my motto for this project. Indeed, in the words of the contest organizers themselves, the reason for the contest was that "the rigid constraints of designing for the web are what force us to get truly creative." What would give me the most bang for my buck in Flash? In this chapter I'll explain how I created and minimized my design.

For the record, I'm very happy to say that my piece ended up as an editor's pick (www.the5k.org/2002editors.asp) in the *Most Original* category.

A city in under 5K

I called my piece **City Blossom**, and you can play around with it by opening city_blossom.swf from the source files (available from www.friendsofed.com).

I describe this SWF as a *tile–based random oscillating cityscape generator and interactive creation system viewed as a scrolling isometric projection*.

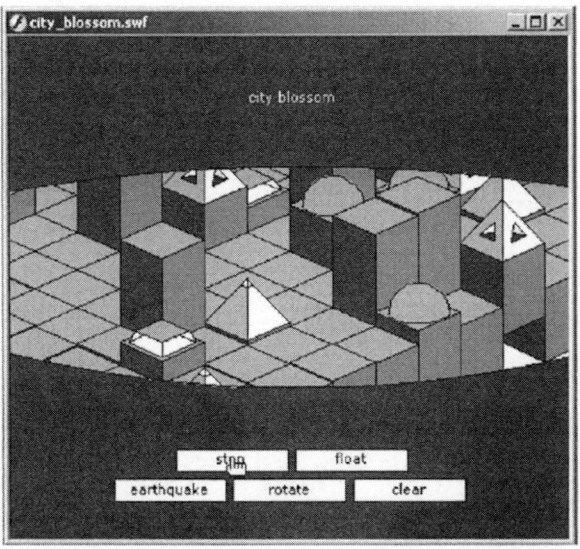

That description isn't as needlessly pretentious as it might sound. Each element of it is an explanation of something that Flash does well – in a small amount of space. Let's break it down...

Tile-based

Not many people know that it was a video games developer who first coined the phrase, *"reduce, reuse, and recycle"*. OK, not really, but I'm sure that it could have been! Starting way back with *Breakout*, and down the video game continuum to today, programmers have been reusing simple elements to improve the efficiency of their programs. Utilizing a small set of pre–defined tiles allows us to reuse graphical and code elements, reduce our file size, and recycle the work we've already done – in Flash of course we call these basic elements **movie clips**.

Random cityscape generator

Randomization is the ugly sister of complexity. If you don't have the time or space to code an algorithm that can realistically produce a stylized city with buildings distributed in some logical manner, randomization is a decent stand–in. And every once in a while it can even produce something beautiful!

Oscillations

City Blossom uses the same few lines of code to create numerous effects throughout the program. This code emulates the oscillating motion of a spring when it has been pulled and let go, and it's a pretty good example of optimizing your ActionScript. You'll see later on in the chapter how this tiny algorithm can produce a variety of different effects.

Interactivity

It's one thing to passively watch a program move pixels around the screen, and another to let the user actively create something themselves. In City Blossom, the user can create their own cityscape with a few clicks and drags. You'll soon learn that a tiny bit of code and a single invisible button was all it took to add this functionality.

Scrolling

Scrolling screens full of graphics in Flash is easy enough to code, but it can get pretty tough to make it efficient and retain a decent frame–rate. However, with enough optimization, it *is* possible.

Isometric projection

Most of the first generation of video games were 2D – that is, all of the action took place on a single plane, often looking down from above, like in *Asteroids*. These early games used this technique because that was all older computers could handle. Later, as PCs got much faster, games like *Quake* were able to create truly three–dimensional spaces in which players could view rooms and objects from almost any angle. **Isometric projection** lies somewhere in between these two extremes – it's a kind of psuedo–3D view, but the angle in which you see the objects never changes. The term *isometric* simply *refers to* the fact that the angles of the 3D axis are all equal. Here's a diagram to clarify the differences between 2D, 3D, and isometric views:

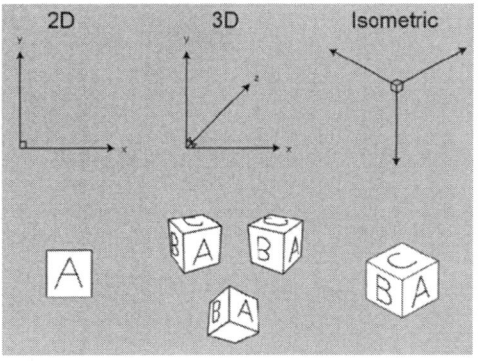

6

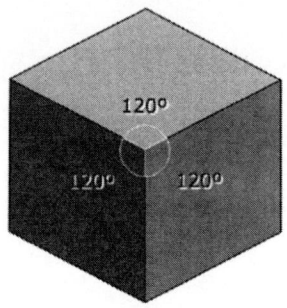

Isometric Projection

In a typical 2D projection, you will only ever see a single side of an object, whereas in a 3D projection you can view an object from any angle. While 3D can be impressive, it generally takes a lot of computing power to produce. With an isometric projection, objects will appear to have depth, but the angle in which they are viewed will always be the same – in this case the angles between each axis are all 120°. This can give you the illusion of a 3D view with a rendering speed approaching that of a 2D view – so it's a pretty fundamental optimization.

Recognizing the limitations of Flash allowed me to focus in on the many things that Flash does well. Rather than try to build a poor version of *Quake*, I searched for a set of features that could create the biggest impact in the smallest possible package. Now it's time to go into the finer details about how I implemented the program. If you're a relative newbie, you'll probably benefit by reading the chapter straight through – if you're confident in your ActionScript skills feel free to skip around to areas that interest you. Also, if you haven't actually tried City Blossom yet, play around with it for a few minutes to familiarize yourself with the functionality of the program.

Creating the tiles

To create the basic tiles for City Blossom, I started with a simple procedure:

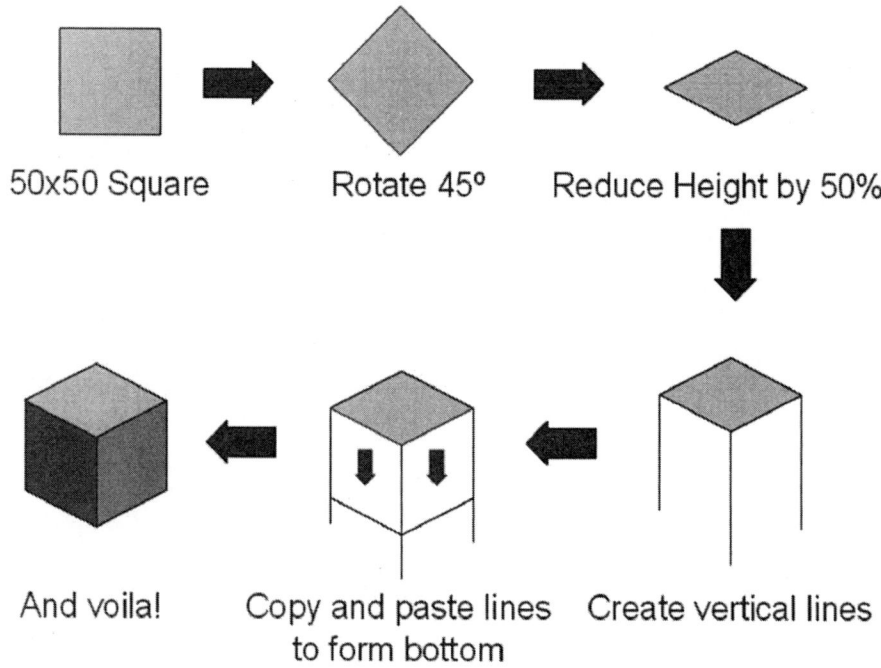

50x50 Square   Rotate 45°   Reduce Height by 50%

And voila!   Copy and paste lines to form bottom   Create vertical lines

Note that after reducing the height in the third stage, I selected everything and used the Info panel (Window > Info) to accurately change the width and height. For an isometric view, you'd want to make the tile exactly twice as wide as it is tall. However, in City Blossom I actually modified the ratio further, giving a width of 70 pixels and a height of 30 pixels. This was really just an aesthetic choice, but it actually means that the projection isn't truly isometric, since the angles of each axis are no longer all 120°.

The resulting cube is a mere 89 bytes. Next I constructed 5 more tiles within the same movie clip (I compiled them separately to determine their size):

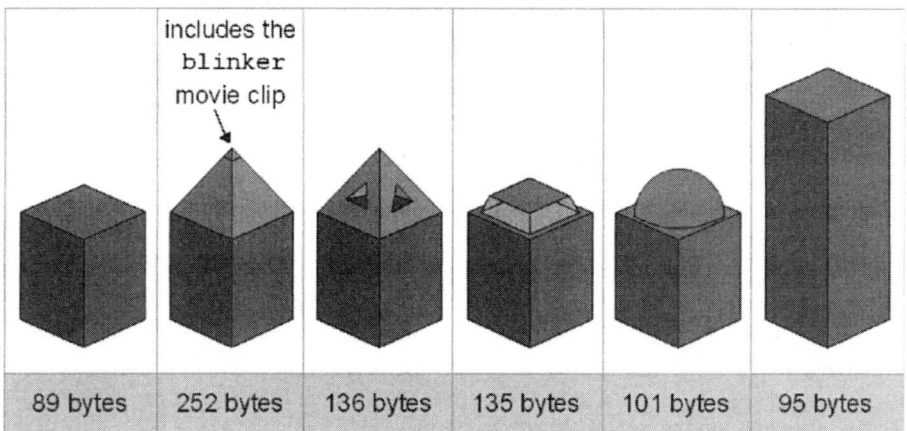

| 89 bytes | 252 bytes | 136 bytes | 135 bytes | 101 bytes | 95 bytes |

If you open up the Library (F11) in city_blossom.fla, you'll notice that I've included all these tiles inside a movie clip called tiles.

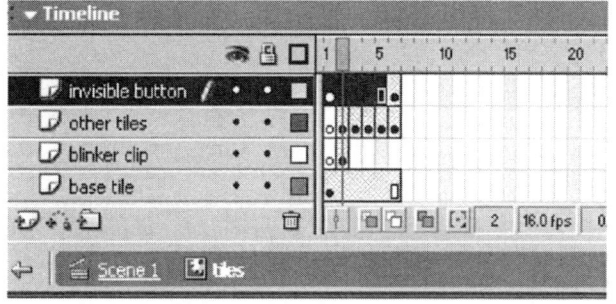

It's worth noting that virtually the entire set of graphics needed for the City Blossom movie come in at a total of 808 bytes. One basic method for reducing file size when dealing with a tile–based system is to separate reusable elements into new layers like this. The base tile layer contains that first tile which weighs in at 89 bytes, as I mentioned earlier. To determine the size of a particular graphic, just open an empty FLA and paste your graphic in. Publish the file and check the file size. Be sure to subtract 30 bytes (the size of an empty SWF), and this will give you the exact size of your graphic.

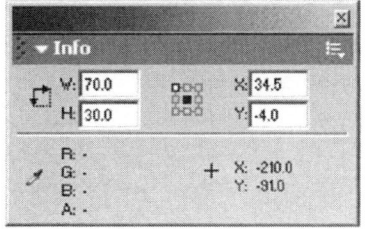

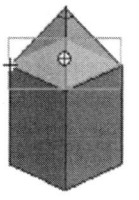

All of the other five tiles use that first tile to build upon, but since the base tile has its own layer and only consists of a single keyframe, it's used in the other frames without any additional file size cost. In the end I saved about 17% of the total graphics weight using this method. I often find similar percentage savings in larger projects. On the other hand, if you are more concerned with speed than with reducing your file size, flattening your tiles so that all the graphics are on a single layer can give a slight improvement to your frame rate.

Finally, I've given this movie clip the Linkage name of `tiles` so that it is available for run–time access via ActionScript:

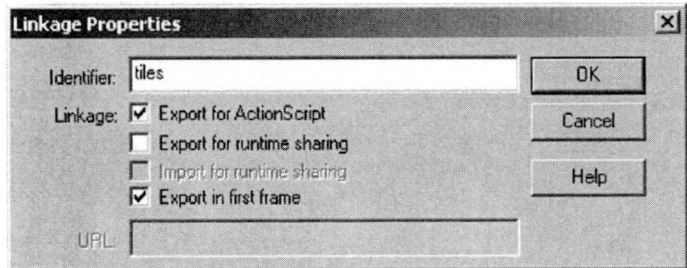

The advantages of having all of your tiles in a single movie clip don't end with optimization though. As you'll soon see, almost all of the code that controls and modifies these tiles takes advantage of this system.

There is much debate within the Flash community about what kind of graphics to use to get the fastest frame rate, but in truth it really depends on the type of project you're developing. In my experience, I've found that for tile–based scrolling games, using imported bitmaps for almost every element works best, whereas a program like City Blossom works well with natively drawn vectors.

As an aside, it seems to take Flash less effort to display vector shapes than lines. In fact, if you want to see City Blossom *really* fly, check out the test version in which I removed all the black lines from the tiles (`city_blossom_no_lines.fla`) – the increase is quite dramatic!

Creating the tile grid

Once I had my tiles clip created and optimized, I was ready to write the code to display the tiles as a grid plane. Before getting into the City Blossom code, I'd like to back up a little and explain how to create both 2D and isometric grids using some smaller examples.

A 2D grid

First, take a look at the file 2D_grid.fla. Note that there's no content on the stage of this movie, but if you run it (Control > Test Movie), it produces a 2D grid like this one shown here.

1	2	3	4
5	6	7	8
9	10	11	12
13	14	15	16

The file has a single clip in the Library that is simply a square and a dynamic text field, with instance name myName. All of the code can be found on the first frame of the root timeline:

```
this.createEmptyMovieClip("grid",1);
for (var y = 0; y<4; y++) {
    for (var x = 0; x<4; x++) {
        tiles++;
        grid.attachMovie("2DtileClip", tiles, tiles);
        grid[tiles]._x = x*grid[tiles]._width;
        grid[tiles]._y = y*grid[tiles]._height;
        grid[tiles].myName.text = tiles;
    }
}
```

If that chunk of code makes perfect sense to you, you can skip down to the next section where I describe creating a grid with an isometric projection. If not, stay with me as I go through it briefly line by line.

I start off by creating an empty movie clip on the root level, calling the clip grid, and setting its depth to 1:

```
this.createEmptyMovieClip("grid",1);
```

Next up, I set up a for loop to cycle through the columns of the grid, and then another that will loop through the tiles for each row of the grid:

```
for (var y=0; y<4; y++) {
    for (var x=0; x<4; x++) {
```

The tiles variable that follows is used as a unique name and depth for the movie clips that we're about to create:

```
tiles++;
```

6

In case you're not familiar with this syntax, `tiles++` is just a compact way of writing `tiles = tiles + 1;`.

The next line creates a new instance of the movie clip `2DtileClip`:

```
grid.attachMovie("2DtileClip", tiles, tiles);
```

Remember that you always need to set the appropriate Linkage properties of any movie clips that you want to export with the `attachMovie` method, as detailed earlier. You can set the Linkage name either in the dialog that appears when you first create a movie clip (after clicking on the Advanced button), or from the Linkage... option in the Library panel.

The next two lines put the new instance of `2DtileClip` into the proper grid position:

```
grid[tiles]._x = x*grid[tiles]._width;
grid[tiles]._y = y*grid[tiles]._height;
```

The syntax `grid[tiles]` is used here because the name of your new object is a number (the variables `tiles`, declared earlier). This may look a little different to what you've seen in other code. For instance, if you wanted to change the `_x` value of a clip called `myTile`, you might write this:

```
grid.myTile._x = 10;
```

...or this:

```
grid["myTile"]._x = 10;
```

Both lines are equivalent to each other, but in my code in `2D_grid.fla`, I'm using a number instead of a string, so I need to use the bracket syntax. If I tried the line:

```
grid.tiles._x = 10;
```

Flash would look for a movie clip called `tiles` instead of the *value* of the variable `tiles`. So why make things complicated by using numbers? Optimization, my friend! It's both faster and more compact to increment the `tiles` variable each time I iterate through the loop rather than create a name like `myTile1`, `myTile2`, `myTile3`, and so on each time. Not only does this technique decrease the file size a bit, but also the code runs a little faster because it doesn't have to do the processor–intensive string concatenation. Equally useful is the fact that variable name doubles as the specific depth of each movie clip instance.

One last note about the positioning code – notice how I multiplied the x and y values with the width and height of the clip I've just created. Now, if I knew that my tiles were 10 pixels by 10 pixels, I could have written the lines as:

```
grid[tiles]._x = x*10;
grid[tiles]._y = y*10;
```

This would have made the code run ever so slightly faster because Flash wouldn't have to go look up the _width and _height properties of the clip before multiplying that value with x and y. The advantage with the former method is that I can go in at any time and change the size of the tile clip and the code will still produce a perfect grid. You'll see that in some of the examples in this chapter I tend to use the former method because it better illustrates how various elements related to one another, but in the City Blossom code I use the actual numbers as much as possible to reduce file size and increase playback speed.

One last line of code to go over is this:

```
        grid[tiles].myName.text = tiles;
    }
}
```

This line simply places the name (which is also the depth) of the current tile into a dynamic text field called myName that lives in each tile clip. Displaying the numbers is simply a way to show you the order in which the tiles are being created.

An isometric grid

OK, so creating a standard grid of square tiles wasn't such a big deal, was it? How about an isometric grid? Well, it turns out that it's not that much more difficult! Take a look at what an isometric grid might look like:

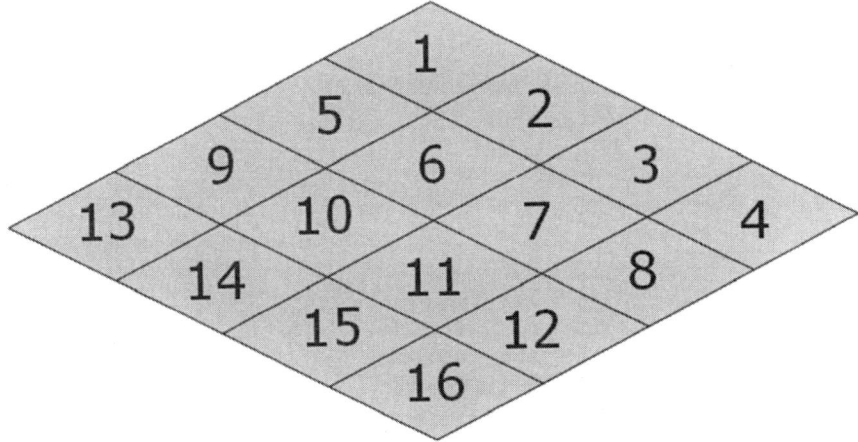

The thing to notice here is the ordering of the tiles – if you tilt your head to the right a bit it might be easier to recognize our old friend the 2D square grid. In fact, rather than thinking about an isometric grid as a completely different entity, it's helpful to think of it as just a square grid whose tiles are just positioned differently.

6

Now seems like the perfect time for an example – open up `isometric_grid.fla`. Before we look at the relevant ActionScript, open up the Library to see the isometric tile movie clip that will form this example – notice where the registration point of `tilesClip` is located:

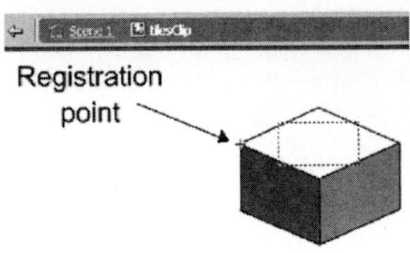

Registration point

As usual, the code for this example can be found on frame 1 of the root timeline:

```
this.createEmptyMovieClip("grid", 1);
grid._x = 225;
grid._y = 60;
gridWidth = 6;
gridHeight = 6;
tileFaceHeight = 30;
for (y=0; y<gridWidth; y++) {
    for (x=0; x<gridHeight; x++) {
        tiles++;
        grid.attachMovie("tilesClip", tiles, tiles);
        grid[tiles]._x = (x*(grid[tiles]._width/2))+left;
        grid[tiles]._y = yPos++*(tileFaceHeight/2);
        grid[tiles].myName.text = tiles;
    }
    left -= (grid[tiles]._width/2);
    yPos -= (gridHeight-1);
}
```

This code works in much the same manner as the square grid code, except that it has a little more work to do to position the tiles correctly. What follows is a line–by–line breakdown of the new ActionScript – if you're an expert you might want to skip ahead to the City Blossom stuff in the next section.

First off, after creating the grid movie clip to hold the content, we need to set its x and y position:

```
grid._x = 225;
grid._y = 60;
```

Next, I've used a few variables to store the number of tiles that will make up the width and height of the grid, and the height of the top, or face, of the tiles because, unlike the 2D grid, these values are referred to within the code:

```
gridWidth = 6;
gridHeight = 6;
tileFaceHeight = 30
```

In the square grid, each tile on a given row was one tile width to the right of the previous tile, and each row was one tile height below the previous one. This new code adds two variables, `left` and `yPos` to help position the tiles in the isometric configuration:

```
grid[tiles]._x = (x*(grid[tiles]._width/2))+left;
grid[tiles]._y = yPos++*(tileFaceHeight/2);
```

Every tile is to the right of the previous tile by one half of the tile width and down by one half of the tile height. Each row (represented in the output image below as tiles 1 to 6, 7 to 12, and so on) needs to start half a tile width to the left and half a tile height down from the first tile of the previous row. This is accomplished by reducing the variable `left` by half the width of a tile after each row is created, and subtracting one less than the row width from `yPos`:

```
left -= (grid[tiles]._width/2);
yPos -= (gridHeight-1);
```

Test the FLA, and you should see that the results look like this:

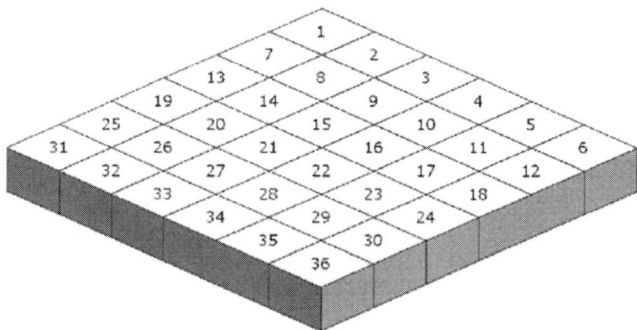

Once last important point about the grid creation: in the `attachMovie` line, the depth value of each clip is again equal to the name of the clip. As you can see from the illustration above, the clips are created from back to front, so that the depth value of any given clip is higher than the clips behind it and lower than the clips in front of it. This is a crucial aspect of the grid creation because it ensures that when the tiles begin to overlap each other, the illusion of three dimensions remains.

6

Correct depth ordering, 3D illusion preserved.

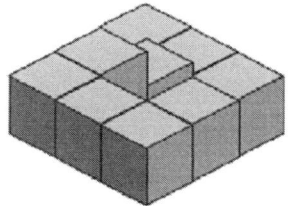

Depth ordering that only M.C. Escher could love...

The making of City Blossom

Now that you know how to create an isometric grid plane, let's move onto the code and structure of the City Blossom movie itself – open up `city_blossom.fla`, and spend some time familiarizing yourself with its layout. You'll immediately notice that there's nothing on the stage in the authoring environment – all of the content is dynamically generated at runtime from the ActionScript and the symbols in the Library. Indeed, select Window > Library to open it up, and you'll see how the content has been broken down into the reusable elements.

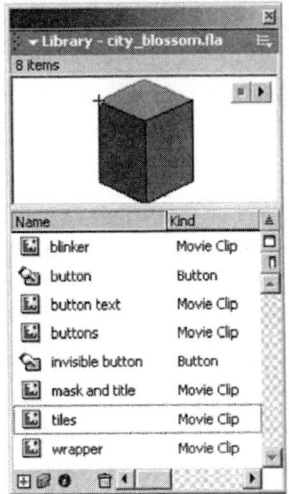

The core ActionScript resides in the first frame of the main timeline of `city_blossom.fla`, and within the structure of the tiles (more specifically, within the `wrapper` and `tiles` movie clips, as will soon become evident). For the sake of completeness, and for reference, I'll list these three chunks of code in the following subsections, before starting to deconstruct the City Blossom movie.

Main code

The main code is located on frame 1 of the root timeline in `city_blossom.fla`:

```
_highquality = false;
// setup clips
this.createEmptyMovieClip("main", 1);
this.attachMovie("maskAndTitle", "maskAndTitle", 2);
this.attachMovie("buttons", "buttons", 3);
// build initial grid
main._x = 200;
//
for (y=0; y<13; y++) {
   for (x=0; x<10; x++) {
      createTile();
   }
   left -= 35;
   yPos -= 9;
}
// functions
function createTile() {
   main.attachMovie("wrapper", ++tileCount, tileCount);
   m = main[tileCount];
   m._x = (x*35)+left;
```

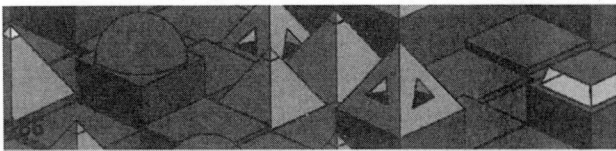

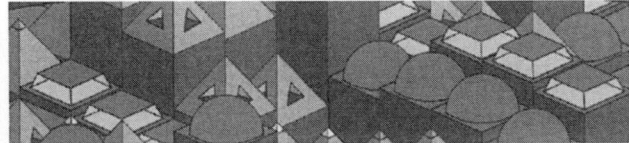

```
        m._y = yPos++*15;
        m._rotation = r;
        m.yHome = m._y;
        m.tiles.floatVelocity = random(6)-3;
    }
    //
    main.scroller = function() {
        this._y--;
        this._x += 2.335;
        if (++aNewLine == 15) {
            aNewLine = 0;
            for (x=0; x<10; x++) {
                createTile();
                this[++deleteCount].removeMovieClip();
            }
            left -= 35;
            yPos -= 9;
        }
    };
    //
    main.clearGrid = function() {
        var t = deleteCount+131;
        while (--t>deleteCount) {
            tellTarget (this[t]) {
                tiles.gotoAndStop(1);
                if (_y != yHome) {
                    tiles._y = _y-yHome;
                }
                tiles.yHome = 0;
                _y = yHome;
            }
        }
    };
    //
    main.spin = function() {
        r += 15;
        var t = deleteCount+131;
        while (--t>deleteCount) {
            this[t]._rotation = r;
        }
    };
    // event handler
    main.onEnterFrame = main.scroller;
```

6

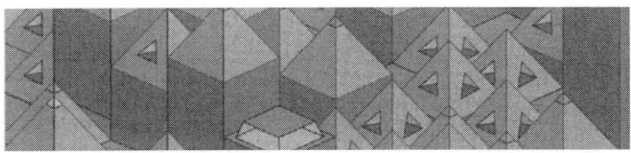

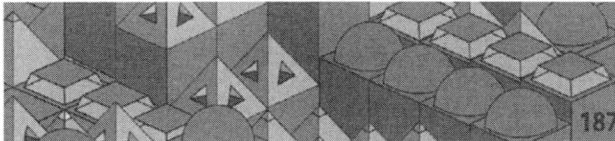

187

```
// button code
buttons._x = 200;
buttons._y = 350;
buttons.b0.t = "stop";
buttons.b1.t = "float";
buttons.b2.t = "earthquake";
buttons.b3.t = "rotate";
buttons.b4.t = "clear";
//
buttons.but1.onRelease = function() {
   if (buttons.b0.t == "stop") {
      buttons.b0.t = "go";
      main.onEnterFrame = null;
   } else {
      buttons.b0.t = "stop";
      main.onEnterFrame = main.scroller;
   }
};
buttons.but2.onRelease = function() {
   fl = !fl;
   if (fl) {
      buttons.b1.t = "stop float";
   } else {
      buttons.b1.t = "float";
   }
};
buttons.but3.onPress = function() {
   quake = true;
};
buttons.but3.onRelease = function() {
   quake = false;
};
buttons.but4.onRelease = function() {
   main.spin();
};
buttons.but5.onRelease = function() {
   main.clearGrid();
};
```

Tile code

The code found on the tiles clip inside the wrapper movie clip is this:

```
onClipEvent (load) {
    if (random(5) == 1) {
        gotoAndStop(random(6)+1);
        _y -= random(40);
    } else {
        gotoAndStop(1);
    }
    yHome = _y;
    spr = .2;
    decay = .8;
    _y = random(100)-50;
}
onClipEvent (enterFrame) {
    if (_root.quake) {
        _y = random(100)-50;
    }
    if (_root.fl) {
        _y += floatVelocity;
    } else {
        y = ((yHome-_y)*spr)+(y*decay);
        _y += y;
    }
}
```

Invisible button code

The code attached to the invisible button inside the tiles movie clip is as follows:

```
on (press) {
    tempY = _parent._y;
    startDrag(_parent, false, _parent._x, _parent._y-225,
➥_parent._x, _parent._y+225);
}
on (release, releaseOutside) {
    stopDrag();
    if (_parent._y == tempY) {
        if (_currentframe == _totalframes) {
            gotoAndStop(1);
        } else {
            nextFrame();
        }
    }
}
```

6

Deconstructing the City Blossom program

At this point, you could be forgiven for thinking that this project is a little daunting, and not altogether simple. But don't panic just yet! Now that we've looked at all of the code involved in this Flash movie, however briefly, and we're aware of the major elements contained within the Library, however vaguely, we're in a fine position to try to understand how it all fits together.

Let's start, rather obviously, with the main code for City Blossom. It's here we'll learn that this movie is essentially composed of three central clips: **main**, **maskAndTitle**, and **buttons**. But before that, you've probably noticed that I've specified for the quality not to be high using the global property _highquality:

```
_highquality = false;
```

This turns off Flash's built–in anti–aliasing, and it's the single easiest way to get a dramatic speed increase in your movies. The downside of course is that unless you've optimized your graphics to look good without anti–aliasing, your movies will look lousy. If you're creating a movie in which almost all of the elements look fine without anti–aliasing, a useful tip is to convert the few that don't into GIFs, since images retain their quality regardless.

Next up comes the part that I've just hinted at – I created an empty clip called main where all of the tiles will live, and then I placed the mask and title and buttons on the screen at higher depths than the main clip so that the tile grid will be underneath the rest of the interface:

```
this.createEmptyMovieClip("main",1);
this.attachMovie("maskAndTitle","maskAndTitle",2);
this.attachMovie("buttons","buttons",3);
```

Now I can position and create the initial grid, as I demonstrated earlier in the chapter. Notice that I'm using numbers instead of variables for the grid sizes, and the amounts subtracted from left and yPos to speed things up:

```
main._x = 200;
for (y=0; y<13; y++) {
   for (x=0; x<10; x++) {
      createTile();
   }
   left -= 35;
   yPos -= 9;
}
```

Let's look more closely at the `createTile` function:

```
function createTile() {
    main.attachMovie("wrapper", ++tileCount, tileCount);
```

Another difference with the generic isometric grid example and the City Blossom code is that each tile clip lives inside of another clip called `wrapper`. We'll see later on why this was useful.

```
    m = main[tileCount];
```

Here I've set a new variable `m` to point to the current tile clip. Not only will this make the code below more compact, but you'll get a small speed increase since Flash doesn't need to look up the movie clip name each time I use `m` below. Again, I've used numbers here instead of variables to speed things up a bit (35 is half the width of tiles and 15 is half the height):

```
    m._x = (x*35)+left;
    m._y = yPos++*15;
```

These final three lines set variables that will be used later.

```
    m._rotation = r;
    m.yHome = m._y;
    m.tiles.floatVelocity = random(6)-3;
}
```

Skipping the aptly named `scroller`, `clearGrid`, and `spin` functions that follow `createTile` in the main code for now (we'll cover these in the following sections), that leaves this line:

```
    main.onEnterFrame = main.scroller;
```

This sets the `enterFrame` event handler of the newly created `main` movie clip to point to the `scroller` function. This means that every time the `enterFrame` is triggered in `main`, the `scroller` function will run, allowing me to easily turn the scrolling of the grid on and off, as you'll see later.

6

Going for a scroll through the city

We can think of scrolling the grid plane as three separate tasks:

1. Scrolling the `main` clip.
2. Adding a new row of tiles to the bottom of the grid.
3. Removing the tiles that go off the top of the screen.

Flash is actually quite good at not spending too much computing power on graphics that are off the visible canvas, but if I just let the tiles keep piling off screen, eventually Flash will slow down (not to mention the wasted memory for all those tiles that will never be seen again). Here's a reminder of what the `scroller` function from the main code looks like:

```
main.scroller = function() {
this._y--;
this._x += 2.335;
if (++aNewLine == 15) {
   aNewLine = 0;
   for (x=0; x<10; x++) {
     createTile();
     this[++deleteCount].removeMovieClip();
   }
   left -= 35;
   yPos -= 9;
  }
};
```

The first thing this function does is move the `main` movie clip up by 1 and to the right by 2.335. These numbers represent the ratio necessary to keep the grid moving in the desired diagonal direction. The ratio was determined using some basic trigonometry (and some trial and error!). The process basically involved using the angle at which I wanted the grid to move along – in this case, that's approximately 23° from the horizontal.

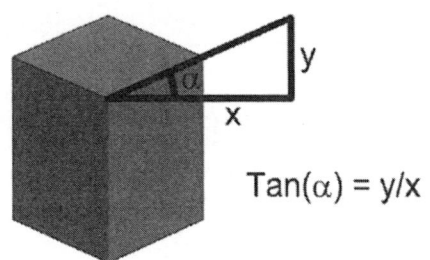

$$Tan(\alpha) = y/x$$

Then I relied on some high school math to calculate that for every 1 unit the grid moves upwards, the `Math.tan` value (in ActionScript terms) of 23° shows that the grid should move 2.335 units horizontally to create this nice slope. OK, and since the angle is not precise, I had to fiddle with this number a little bit as well until I was happy!

Anyway, being able to scroll all those individual tiles with just two statements is one of the advantages of keeping all of your clips within a parent clip (in this case `main`). The individual clips don't really move – just their parent.

Since the height of the tiles is 30, I need to create a new row after the grid has traveled half that distance (if you don't remember why it's half the height, it's probably worth reviewing the section on building isometric grids). To this end, I created a variable called aNewLine which increments by 1 and checks to see if it has reached 15 each time the scroller function is called. This was also why I was using vertical increments of 1 for the scrolling – so that it would be easier to keep track of when it was time to create a new row. Once 15 is reached, I create a new row by calling createTile within a for loop. The createTile function uses the same variables, left and yPos, that were used in the code that created the initial grid because, as the initial grid was finished, the values of left and yPos are set to exactly where the new row should begin. The last two lines of the scroller function perform this same task.

In order to remove tiles that have scrolled up and off the screen, I first needed to figure out a simple way to keep track of the names of the tiles to delete. Remember that when the tiles are first created, their name is represented by a number (for instance, the tiles in the very first row are named 1 through 10). So the solution was to create a variable called deleteCount. Each time a new tile is created, deleteCount is incremented by 1, and used as the name of the next tile to be deleted.

To get a better view of how the adding and removing of rows works, turn to the city_blossom.fla file again, and comment out the lines that attach the mask and buttons, like this:

```
this.createEmptyMovieClip("main", 1);
//this.attachMovie("maskAndTitle", "maskAndTitle", 2);
//this.attachMovie("buttons", "buttons", 3);
```

Then test the movie to run the SWF, and maximize the window – make sure that the movie is playing at 100% magnification. This will allow you to see the far edges of the grid that are normally off screen, and how the new and old rows at either side are continually generated and removed.

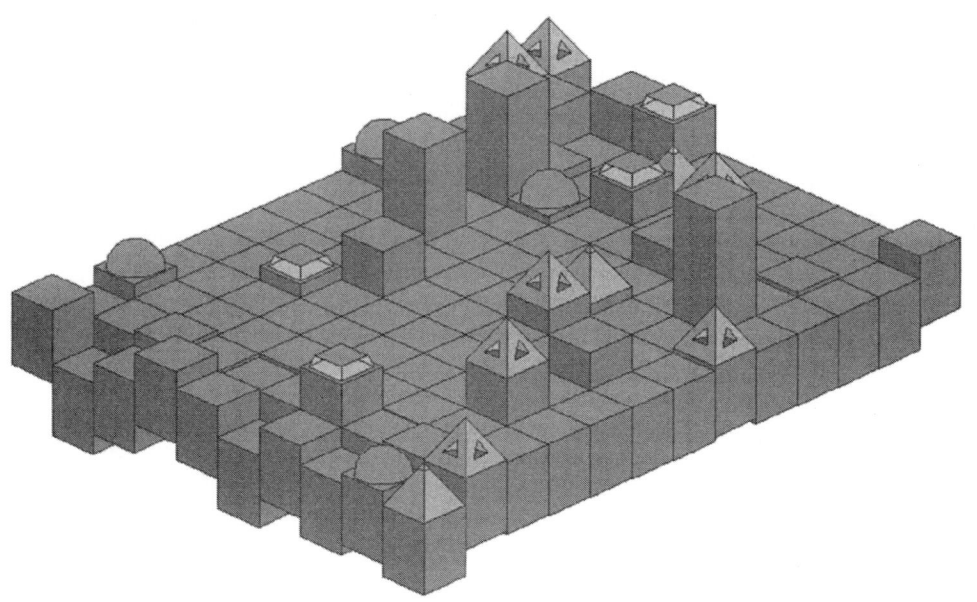

6

Making the tiles 'blossom'

When I was describing the `createTile` function, I mentioned that each actual `tiles` movie clip lives inside its own parent clip called `wrapper`. It is the wrapper clips that are created with `attachMovie` in the `createTile` function and named by number. This is useful for two reasons:

1. I can change the `_y` value of the `wrapper` clip when creating the grid, while independently changing the `_y` value of the actual `tiles` clip for other purposes.

2. I can place the clip event code onto the `tiles` clip itself, to construct a reusable element for the movie.

So, let's look at the code attached to the `tiles` movie clip again. Firstly, whenever a new clip is created, the `load onClipEvent` is triggered and two things happen– a tile type is selected, and some variables are set in preparation for the tile's spring–like motion:

```
onClipEvent (load) {
    if (random(5) == 1) {
        gotoAndStop(random(6)+1);
        _y -= random(40);
    } else {
        gotoAndStop(1);
    }
    yHome = _y;
    spr = .2;
    decay = .8;
    _y = random(100)-50;
}
```

The method for selecting a tile type is pretty basic– a random number between 0 and 4 is generated. If the number is a 1, then the clip is told to go to a random frame between 1 and 5 and rise up from the grid a random amount between 0 and 39, otherwise the clip will go to frame 1, which is the blank tile. This ensures that most of the time blank tiles will be chosen, but other tile types will be picked often enough to create buildings scattered around the grid.

Setting up the spring–like motion requires three variables:

- `yHome` is the `_y` value that the tile always wants to return to.

- `spr` is the amount of 'springiness' in the motion.

- `decay` determines how quickly the motion will slow down to 0.

To initiate the motion, the _y value of the clip is now set to a random value. Once the _y value of the clip is changed, it will always try to 'spring back' to yHome, thanks to the piece of code inside the following enterFrame clip event. Feel free to play around with the values of spr and decay (but perhaps limit the fooling to between 0 and 1!) to see the different kind of spring effects you can achieve.

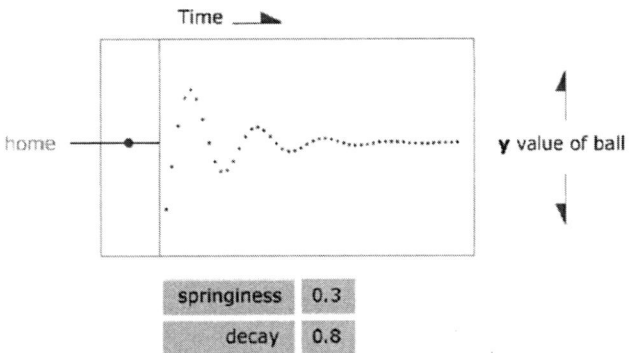

The enterFrame code actually contains instructions for three types of clip movement, but the spring–like motion all takes place in the last two lines, which do all the work to create this spring motion:

```
onClipEvent (enterFrame) {
    if (_root.quake) {
        _y = random(100)-50;
    }
    if (_root.fl) {
        _y += floatVelocity;
    } else {
        y = ((yHome-_y)*spr)+(y*decay);
        _y += y;
    }
}
```

Don't confuse the variable y (which determines the amount of change to apply to _y) with _y itself (the actual value of the movie clip's y position).

For a more visual explanation of this algorithm, check out spring_graph.swf, and for further reading take a look at the section on springs in my chapter in *Flash Math Creativity*, from friends of ED (ISBN 1–903450–50–0).

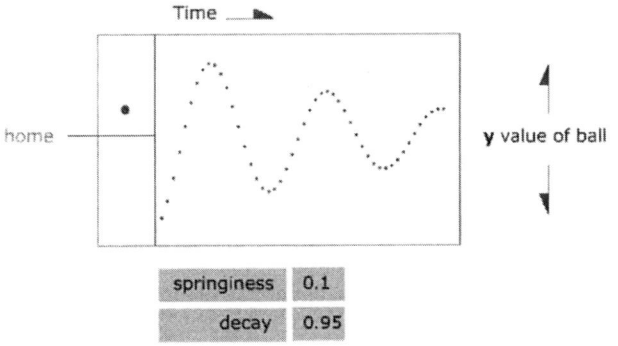

6

UI on a tight budget

I knew that all of the buttons in City Blossom were going to have the same look and feel, so I just made one – a single button with three states:

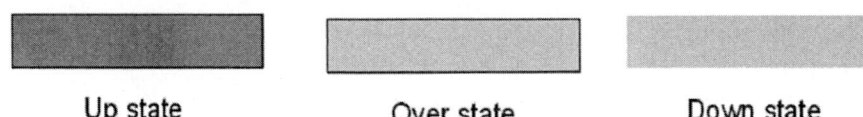

Up state   Over state   Down state

Notice what's missing– there's no text. That's because the text for each button is actually held in separately named movie clips that are laid on over the buttons, consisting solely of a dynamic text field (with variable name t). These clips, named b0 through b4, are placed on a layer right above the layer holding the buttons. This way I can create five buttons using a single button type and a single movie clip, copied five times. The text is generated in code in the first frame of the main timeline, with their event handlers (we'll go into the finer details of this script shortly):

```
buttons._x = 200;
buttons._y = 350;
buttons.b0.t = "stop";
buttons.b1.t = "float";
buttons.b2.t = "earthquake";
buttons.b3.t = "rotate";
buttons.b4.t = "clear";
//
buttons.but1.onRelease = function() {
    if (buttons.b0.t == "stop") {
        buttons.b0.t = "go";
        main.onEnterFrame = null;
    } else {
        buttons.b0.t = "stop";
        main.onEnterFrame = main.scroller;
    }
};
buttons.but2.onRelease = function() {
    fl = !fl;
    if (fl) {
        buttons.b1.t = "stop float";
    } else {
        buttons.b1.t = "float";
    }
};
buttons.but3.onPress = function() {
    quake = true;
};
```

```
buttons.but3.onRelease = function() {
   quake = false;
};
buttons.but4.onRelease = function() {
   main.spin();
};
buttons.but5.onRelease = function() {
   main.clearGrid();
};
```

This is, in fact, one of those cases where the more intricate your single button is, and the more times you use it, the more optimized for size your project will become, because you're taking advantage of one of the great strengths of Flash – repeated use of the same symbols barely increases your file size at all. This is the same technique I employed when reusing the tiles clip over and over to form the grid plane. And, as you'll see, the buttons are now flexible enough to easily have multiple text states; for instance, the Go button turns into a Stop button when it is first clicked.

The text fields themselves are set to 12 point Verdana, but what's important to realize is that the font outlines are *not* included in the movie. Including the font outline information in a Flash movie has the distinct advantage of near complete control over the display of the font. At larger point sizes this makes all the difference in the fact that Flash uses vector information to draw the font – the letters can therefore be anti–aliased (smoothed) and manipulated like other native graphics. There are, however, two downsides:

- Often at small point sizes you actually don't want to have the text anti–aliased because it appears blurry (although this problem can often be solved by using so–called **pixel fonts** created specifically for this purpose).

- Font outlines are like other vector information – they take up space in your file to store the information.

If outlines are not included in the Flash file, the Flash plug–in relies on the user's operating system to provide the font information. The main disadvantage to this technique is that by relying on the operating system, you're never quite sure what you're going to get. If the font you specified in your Flash file does not exist on the user's system, there's no guarantee what the text in your movie will end up looking like. On the other hand, if you pick a ubiquitous font like Verdana, the chances are it will look very close to what it looks like on your development machine and won't increase your file size at all. In the end, the trade off is really between file size and greater control over what your fonts will look like.

Once the buttons were built, it was time to actually make something happen when the user clicked on them. Accordingly, let's go through each button's functionality one at a time.

6

Go/stop button

All that needs to happen here is to check for which state the button is in. If the button says stop, then I change the text to go and set main's onEnterFrame handler to null:

```
buttons.but1.onRelease = function() {
    if (buttons.b0.t == "stop") {
        buttons.b0.t = "go";
        main.onEnterFrame = null;
    } else {
        buttons.b0.t = "stop";
        main.onEnterFrame = main.scroller;
    }
};
```

By setting it to null, Flash essentially does nothing when the onEnterFrame is triggered – exactly what you'd expect to happen when you click on a stop button. Conversely, when the button is set to go, the event handler gets set back to the scroller function and the grid starts to scroll across the screen again. This system could become even more useful if I had several functions – say, scrollUp, scrollDown, scrollLeft, scrollRight. I could set up four buttons for each direction and all they could have to do is set the event handler to a particular function for that function to get triggered every enterFrame of the main clip.

Float/stop float button

This two–state button is even simpler than the go/stop button:

```
buttons.but2.onRelease = function() {
    fl = !fl;
    if (fl) {
        buttons.b1.t = "stop float";
    } else {
        buttons.b1.t = "float";
    }
};
```

The first line after the function declaration, in a very compact way, says this:

make the variable fl the opposite of whatever it currently is. If fl = 1, then make fl = 0. If fl = 0, then make fl = 1.

Then the code goes on to say that if the variable fl is true (that is, 1 rather than 0), then change the button text to stop float, otherwise, set it to float. Now, before we go any further, we've got to review some code from a few other spots in the program.

This line appears in the `createTile` function:

```
this[tileCount].tiles.floatVelocity = random(6)-3;
```

What it does is assign a random number between –3 and 2 to a variable called `floatVelocity`. OK, so what? Well, now recall a bit of code from the `enterFrame` clip event attached to the `tiles` clip (remember that each `tiles` clip lives inside a wrapper clip):

```
if (_root.fl) {
   _y += floatVelocity;
} else {
   // do the spring code
   y = ((yHome-_y)*spr)+(y*decay);
   _y += y;
}
```

A–ha! So if the variable `fl`, located at the root level of the movie (which happens to be where the buttons are located too) is `true` (that is, `1`, not `0`), then add the number associated with the variable `floatVelocity` (a number between –3 and 2) to the current `_y` position of the clip.

The result? If `fl` is indeed `true`, the program won't calculate the spring algorithm anymore, and instead will have each clip start heading up (if `floatVelocity` is negative) or down (if `floatVelocity` is positive), or it might stay still (if `floatVelocity` is 0). And here's the beauty of it – when you click on the stop float button, `_root.fl` is set to `false` (0) and the spring algorithm starts getting called again. Since all this algorithm wants to do is to spring back to `yHome`, all of the clips spring back into their original places in the grid. End result – a really flashy seeming feature in only few lines of code.

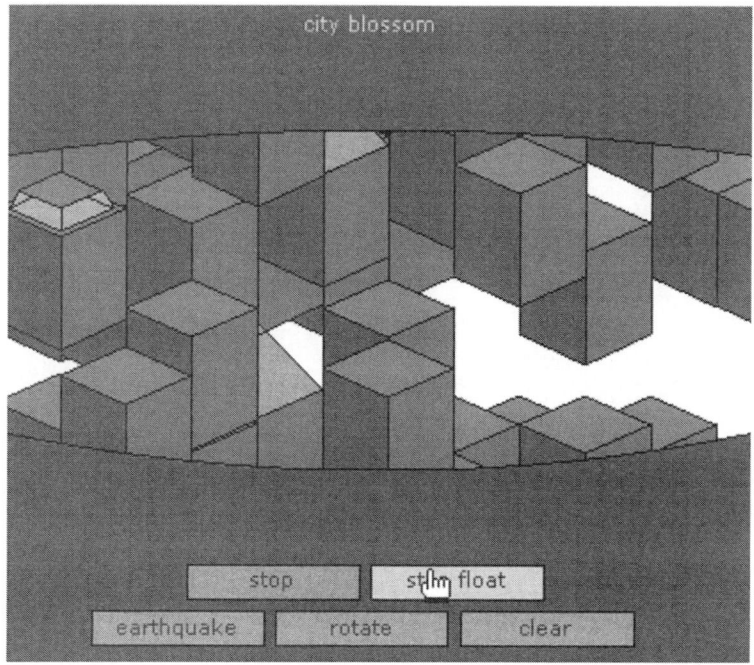

6

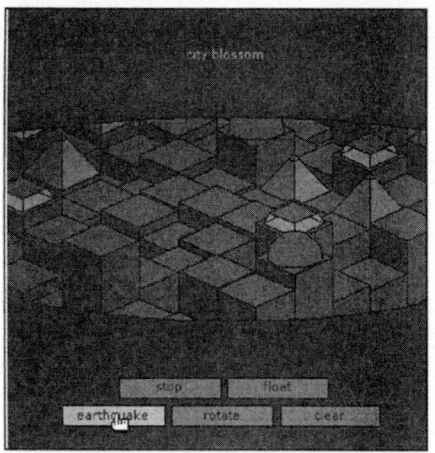

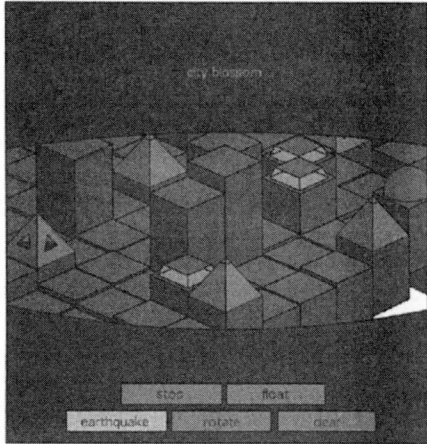

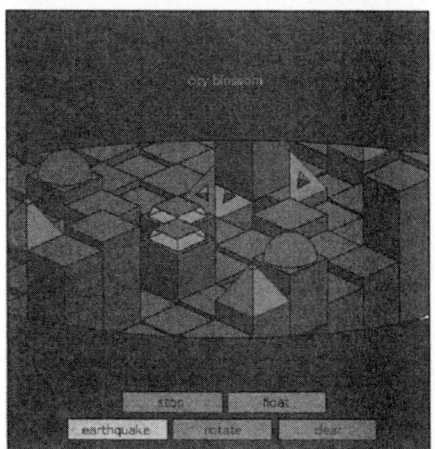

Earthquake button

By now you can probably guess how this button works. It sets a variable called quake to true when you press down on the button, and sets it back to false as soon as you let go:

```
buttons.but3.onPress = function() {
    quake = true;
};
buttons.but3.onRelease = function() {
    quake - false;
};
```

If we now take a peek at the enterFrame code of the tiles clip again, we'll notice this little snippet:

```
if (_root.quake) {
    _y = random(100)-50;
}
```

All this does is set the y position of the clip to a random number between –50 and 49. Of course, this is happening to all the clips at once, each getting a different random number. Result? As soon as the spring algorithm gets a chance (which is as soon as you let go of the earthquake button) all of the tiles start to spring back to their pre–assigned places (remembered in the yHome variable) and the whole grid appears to have been shaken by its roots.

Rotate button

This button calls the spin function from the main code:

```
buttons.but4.onRelease = function() {
    main.spin();
};
```

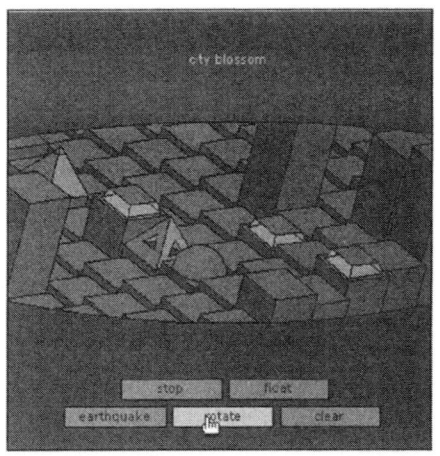

The spin function looks like this:

```
main.spin = function() {
    r += 15;
    var t = deleteCount+131;
    while (--t>deleteCount) {
        this[t]._rotation = r;
    }
};
```

Because I wanted all of the clips to rotate a certain amount equally, I have a variable called r inside this function that increments by 15 each time the rotate button is pressed. Then I find the last tiles clip that was created – there are 130 tiles in a full screen, so I start with the last deleted clip (which would be the clip that just went off the top of the screen) and add 131. Then I cycle through every tile between the last one created and the one before the last clip deleted (which is, in fact, all of the tiles clips) and tell each one to rotate to the value of r. Can you guess how many times you need to click on the rotate button to get back to the original position? Well, since a full rotation is 360°, divide that by the amount r is incremented by, 15, and you get 24.

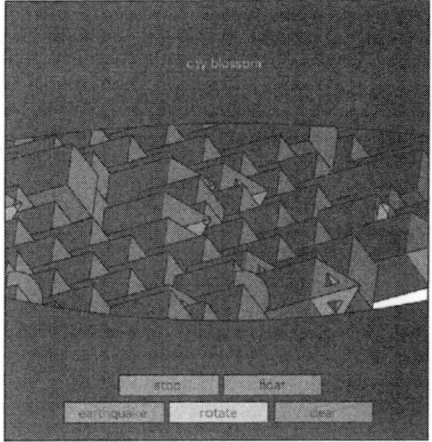

In case the while statement looks a little weird to you, here it is in plain English:

while the variable t, which is decreased by 1 each time around the loop, is greater than the value of deleteCount, execute the following line.

Pretty simple, right?

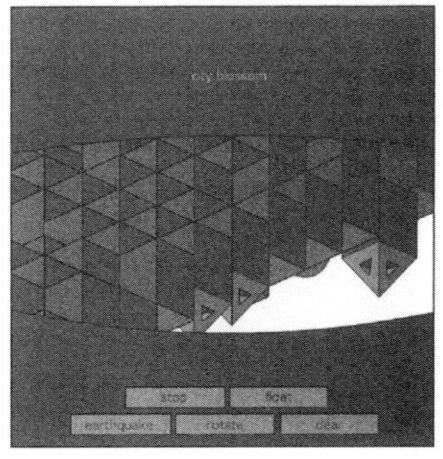

6

Clear button

Clicking on the clear button triggers the `clearGrid` function from the main code:

```
buttons.but5.onRelease = function() {
    main.clearGrid();
};
```

...which, in turn, looks like this:

```
main.clearGrid = function() {
    var t = deleteCount+131;
    while (--t>deleteCount) {
        tellTarget (this[t]) {
            tiles.gotoAndStop(1);
            if (_y != yHome) {
                tiles._y = _y-yHome;
            }
            tiles.yHome = 0;
            _y = yHome;
        }
    }
};
```

This starts off with the same technique as the rotate button: determining the range of clips to alter and looping through them. But there's a little more work to do done within the loop this time.

In this loop, I have to access and change several variables in each of the 130 tiles clips – a perfect use of the (deprecated) `tellTarget` command. So, why am I using a command that Macromedia specifically, albeit gently, suggests we shouldn't use? Speed! In this case, using `tellTarget` is actually faster than the dot syntax! There are certain situations in which the older ActionScript syntax is just plain faster than newer methods – so it's great that we've still got the option to use some of the older commands.

Within the `tellTarget`, I first set the tiles clip back to frame 1 (the *generic* tile), then prepare the clip, regardless of where it is, to head back to the original grid position. The `if` statement checks for tiles that have been changed by the tiles' `load` clip event code when they were first created (that is, the height of a 'building'), while the `tiles.yHome = 0` line resets any change to the y position that was made by the user (more on this below).

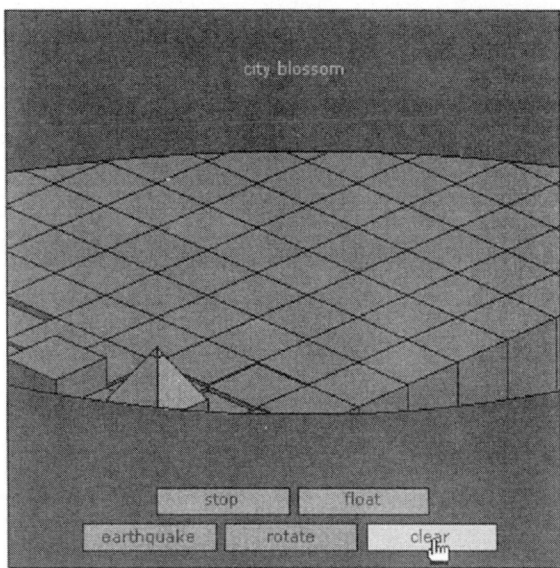

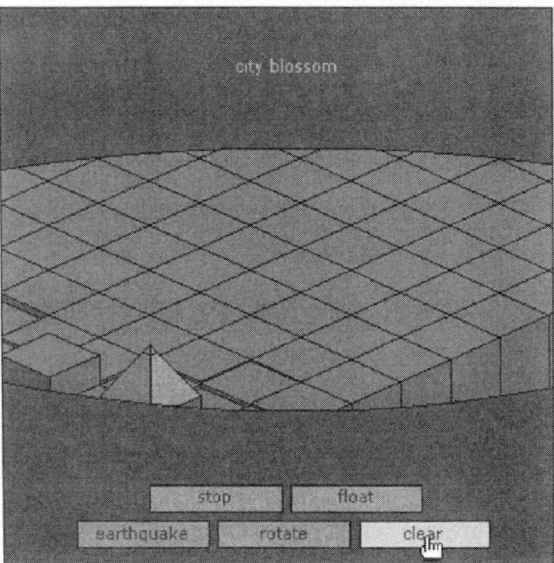

Cities created by the user

The final element of City Blossom is the ability for users to interactively create their own cityscapes. I wanted to let users change any tile on the screen into any of the six building types (see the earlier section on *Creating the tiles*), as well as choose a height value (y position). I decided the easiest way to implement this would be to have the user click on a tile to change its building type and click and drag the tile to change its height. As you'll see, the way the program had been structured up to this point made this task pretty easy.

Let's look at the physical structure of the tiles movie clip again:

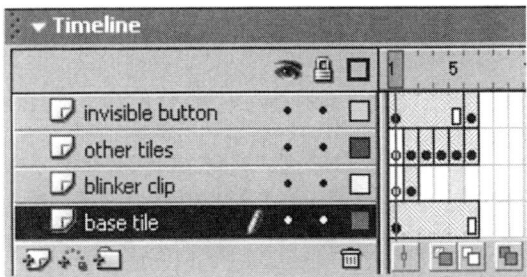

We've already discussed how when the program creates a new row of tiles, it randomly sets each tiles clip to a frame between 1 and 6 in order to place new tile types on the grid. Now take a look at the first layer. It is an invisible button than covers the tops of each tile. We briefly saw the code attached to this button earlier:

```
on (press) {
    tempY = _parent._y;
    startDrag(_parent, false, _parent._x, _parent._y-225,
➡ _parent._x, _parent._y+225);
}
on (release, releaseOutside) {
    stopDrag();
    if (_parent._y == tempY) {
        if (_currentframe == _totalframes) {
            gotoAndStop(1);
        } else {
            nextFrame();
        }
    }
}
```

6

When the user presses the invisible button, the variable `tempY` remembers the value of the y position of the wrapper clip (which is the `_parent` movie clip to this invisible button) and gives the user the ability to drag it. The drag is constrained so that the user cannot move the clip left or right by making the allowable horizontal movement consist only of the current x position, and vertically constrained by 225 pixels up or down from where the tile started.

When the user lets go of the button, I first check to see if the drag has actually gone anywhere (`_parent._y == tempY`). If it hasn't, then I can assume the user meant to click, not drag, and therefore, they wanted to change the tile type.

The way the tile type changes is that every time the user clicks, I advance to the `nextFrame` in the tiles clip. If the current frame of the clip is at the last frame, then it knows to go back to the beginning.

And that's it! 14 lines of code and the user can create their own isometric cityscape.

Who knew it would take about 30 pages to describe a program that weighs in at only two and a half kilobytes?!

What I hope you've gotten out of this chapter, besides a bunch of optimization tips and tricks, is some insight into the things that Flash excels at, and how you as a designer can work with these advantages to create mind–blowing programs.

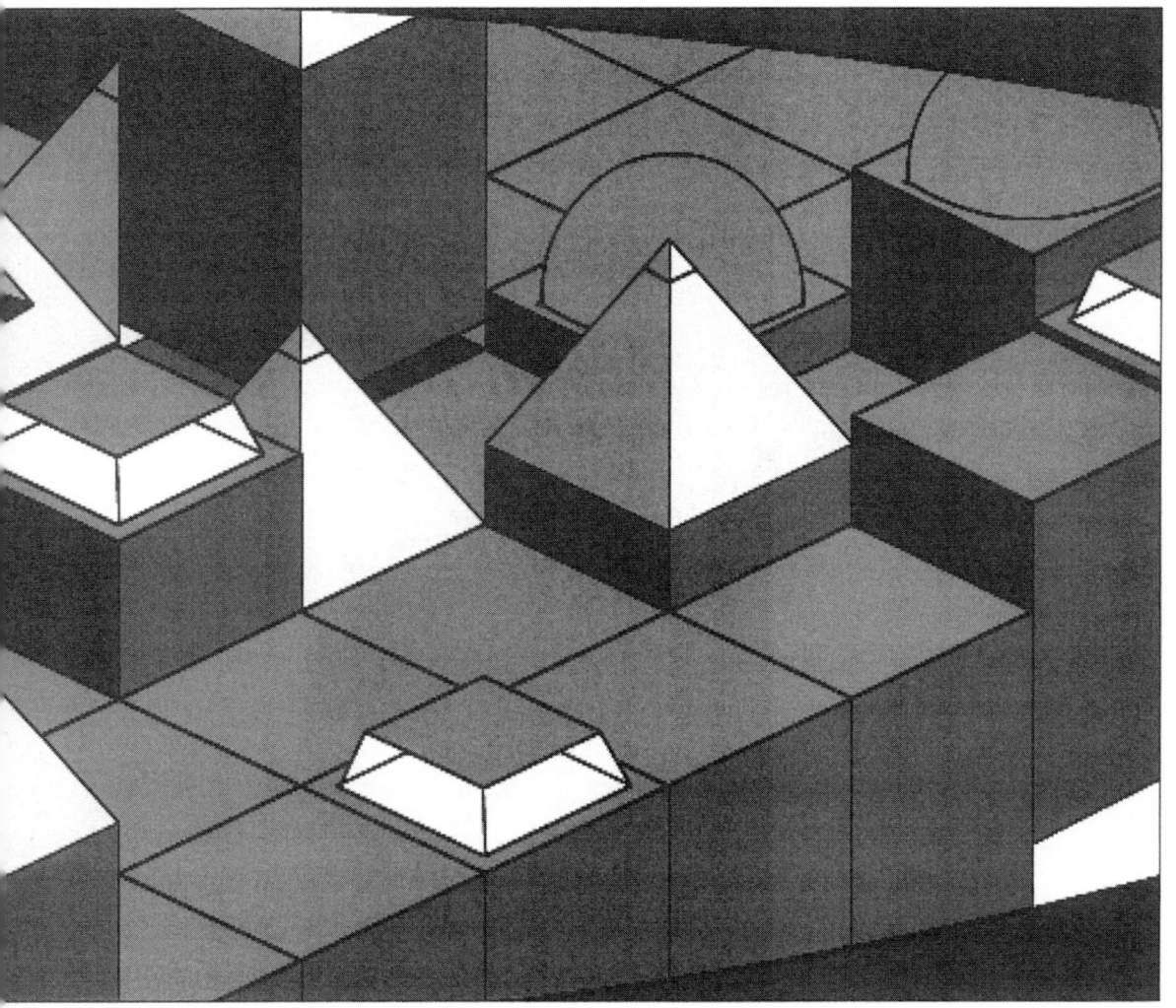

6

7 BEYOND THE CITY LIMITS

DAVID HIRMES

If you've read the first City Blossom chapter, you're probably well acquainted with every aspect of the internal workings of the City Blossom design. So where can we go from here? Well, in this chapter I've taken the City Blossom idea in a new direction, in that it can now save your creations, and load them back as you wish. On top of this example, I've constructed three more Flash designs that are all based, in some way, on the original City Blossom code. As you'll see, each of the new projects either adds some new functionality to the original scrolling isometric grid engine, or takes the basic concept in another direction altogether.

Beginning and intermediate readers may benefit from reading the chapter straight through, as certain concepts are introduced in the earlier pieces and then utilized in later examples. The more experienced ActionScripters should feel free to dip in and out of these examples.

City Blossom II: saving, storing, and replaying your designs

The first step towards creating more sophisticated tile-based programs is to have the ability to create, edit, and save layouts and designs. In this first project, which is based on the City Blossom isometric display engine that we examined in the last chapter, I've added the basic functionality to save, load, and play back any cityscape you design. As a teaser of what we're going to learn about, take a look at `city_blossom2.swf`:

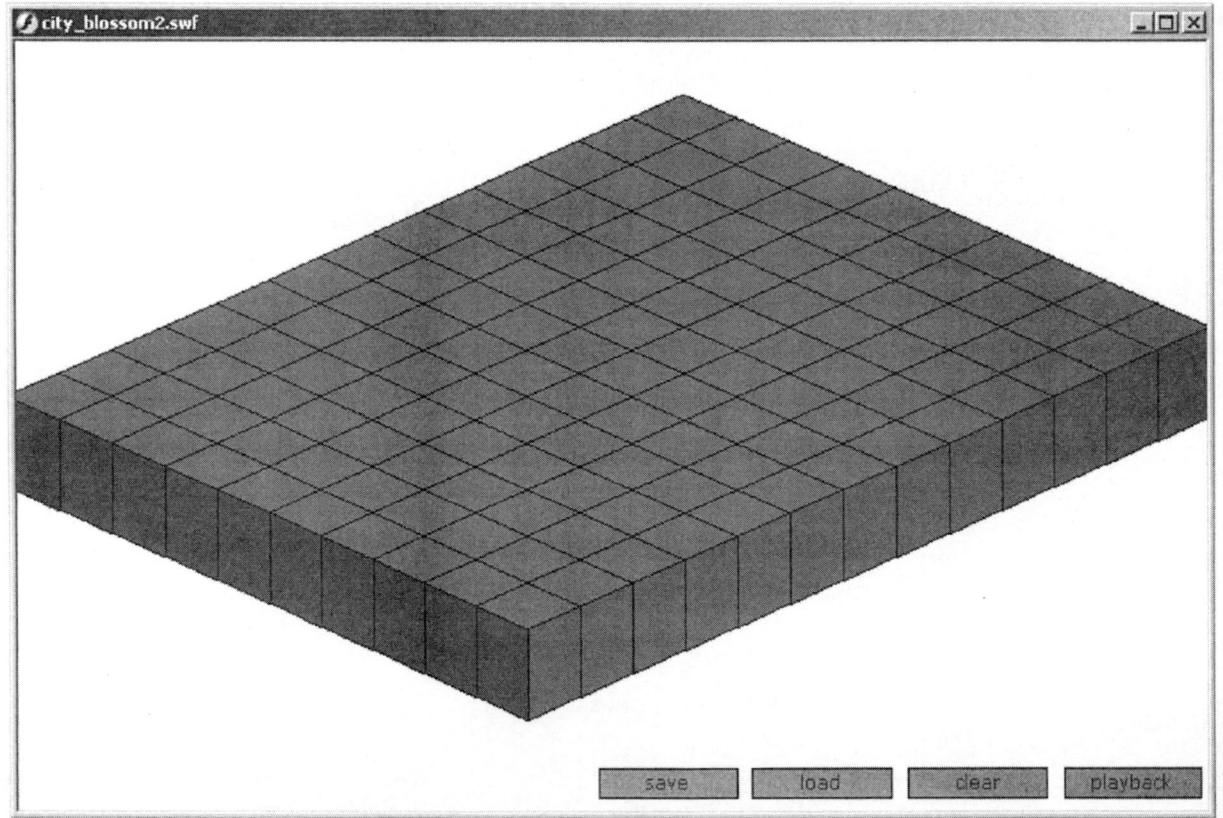

After creating a cityscape design, or 'map', for the first time, a user can either click on the playback button to watch the map blossom, press the save button to store the map on the local hard drive, or hit clear to start over again.

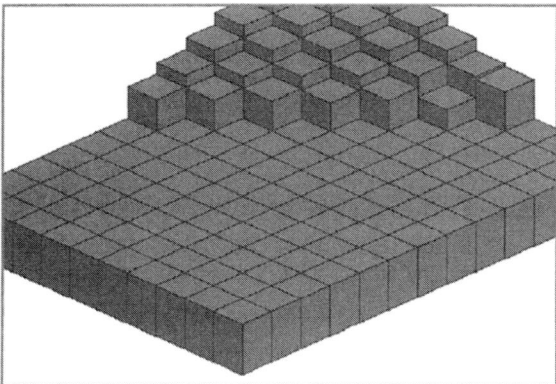 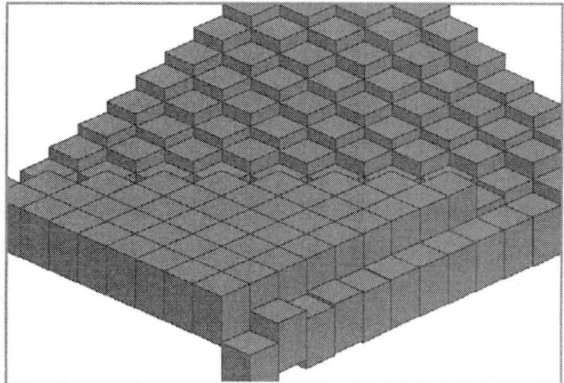

After quitting the Flash movie, and then re-launching it, clicking on the load button will load any previously saved map back into memory. To redisplay the map, the user can click playback and then continue to modify the map. The program is designed in such a way that any modifications to the map are saved. This produces a cool effect during playback, where the map is dynamically created and appears to be modified on its own.

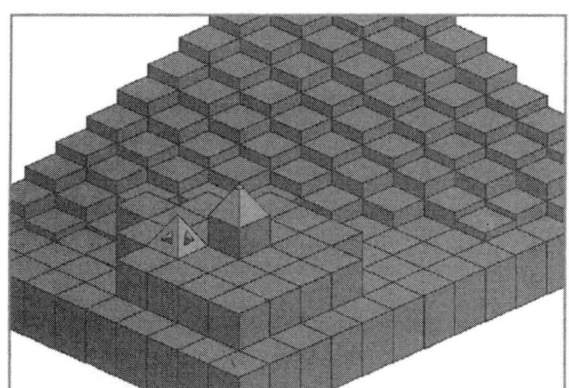 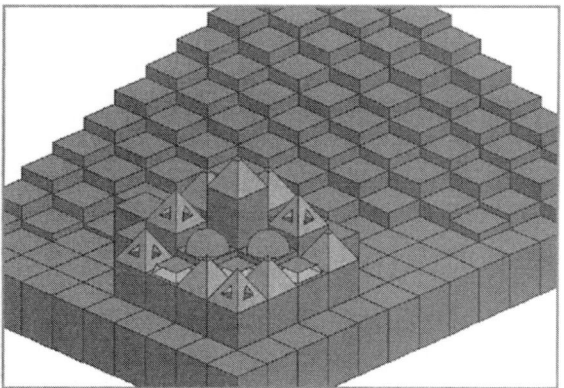

Let's now investigate the ActionScript that makes this project possible – open up city_blossom2.fla. Much like the City Blossom movie that we studied in the last chapter, all of the code in this piece lives on the first frame of the root timeline and inside the wrapper and tiles movie clips. We'll start by looking at the code on the root timeline:

```
_highquality = false;
this.createEmptyMovieClip("main",1);
main._x = 415;
main._y = 50;
```

7

After turning anti-aliasing off, I created and positioned a clip called `main` where all of the tiles will live.

In order to save data to the user's hard drive, I've utilized a feature of Flash MX called **shared objects**. The concept is very similar to that of browser cookies – a small file on the user's hard drive used to store persistent data. An obvious example of cookies in action is the way in which Amazon.com magically *remembers* who you are. The following line of code sets the variable `mazeSO` to point to a shared object file called `citycookie`:

```
main.mazeSO = SharedObject.getLocal("citycookie");
```

It doesn't matter if the shared object exists yet or not – if it doesn't exist, Flash just creates it! If it does exist, Flash can either read *from* it or write *to* it. If you'd like to find out more about shared objects, they are used extensively in the chapter 'Math-based Animation and Dynamic Drawing'.

Next up, we create an array called `recorder` in which the user's map data will be stored:

```
main.recorder = [];
```

Note that this is just a slightly faster way of typing the `Array` object constructor like this:

```
recorder = new Array();
```

The first real action that takes place when this movie runs is the creation of a standard grid plane – I discussed this early on in the previous chapter:

```
for (y=0; y<13; y++) {
   for (x=0; x<10; x++) {
      createTile();
   }
   left -= 35;
   yPos -= 9;
}
```

Here, the `createTile` function is pretty much identical to that found in the original City Blossom, but the code pertaining to the `float` function has been removed since that feature isn't used in this design:

```
function createTile() {
   main.attachMovie("wrapper", ++tileCount, tileCount);
   m = main[tileCount];
   m._x = (x*35)+left;
   m._y = yPos++*15;
   m.yHome = m._y;
}
```

The clearGrid function is the next chunk of code:

```
main.clearGrid = function() {
   var t = deleteCount+131;
   while (-t>deleteCount) {
      this[t].tiles.onEnterFrame = this[t].tiles.spring;
      tellTarget (this[t]) {
         tiles.gotoAndStop(1);
         if (_y != yHome) {
            tiles._y = _y-yHome;
         }
         tiles.yHome = 0;
         _y = yHome;
      }
   }
   if (this.playIt) {
      playbackCounter = 0;
      _global.playbackInterval =
      ➡ setInterval(_root.main.playbackStart, 1000);
   }
};
```

The first half of this function retains all of the elements found in City Blossom with a few additions. This line 'turns on' the spring functionality for each tile:

```
this[t].tiles.onEnterFrame = this[t].tiles.spring;
```

This wasn't necessary in City Blossom because the spring function was always running in each tile's enterFrame clip event. Remember that the spring function itself is attached to the tiles movie clip:

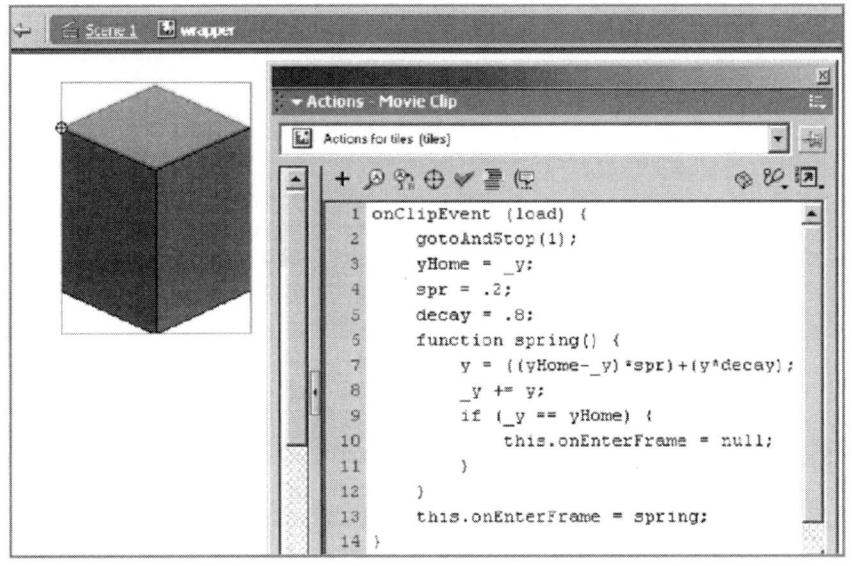

7

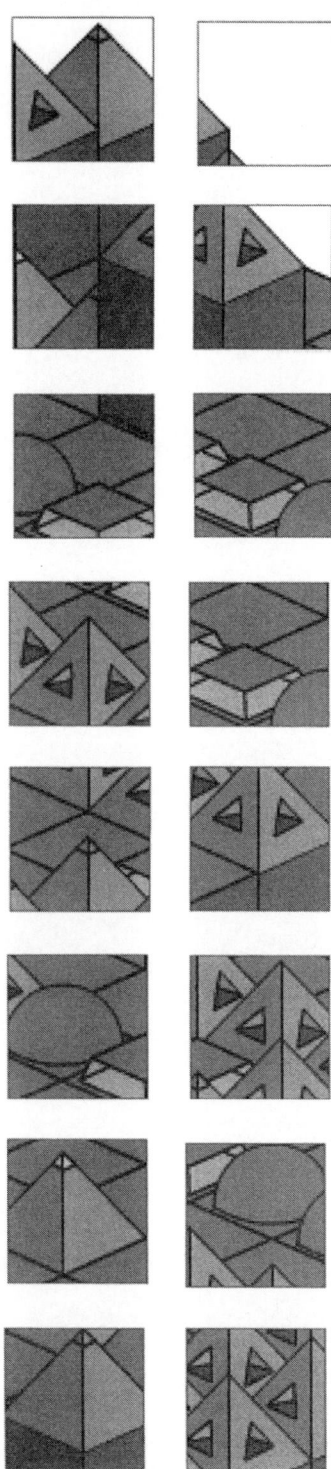

Returning our attention to the root timeline of `city_blossom2.fla`, the second part of the `clearGrid` function starts the playback of the user's map using a Flash MX feature called `setInterval`:

```
if (playIt) {
    playbackCounter = 0;
    _global.playbackInterval =
    ➥ setInterval(_root.main.playbackStart, 1000);
}
}
```

The `setInterval` command simply tells Flash to repeatedly call a particular function (in this case `playbackStart`) at a particular time interval measured in milliseconds – in this case, every 1000 milliseconds, that is, every 1 second. Using this feature can allow a programmer to create accurate time-based actions without having to deal with a timeline.

In this code, `setInterval` is only called if the `playIt` variable has been set to `true`. If you look at the code for the clear and playback buttons, you'll see that they both call the `clearGrid` function, but only the playback button sets `playIt` to true. This is because both options clear the grid, but obviously only the playback option would want to initiate the playback of the user's map. Also note that `setInterval` returns a value that I'm putting into the global variable `_global.playbackInterval`. I'll use that variable in a moment to 'shut off' the `setInterval` command.

Let's now look at the `playbackStart` function:

```
main.playbackStart = function() {
    clearInterval(_global.playbackInterval);
    _global.playbackInterval =
    ➥ setInterval(_root.main.playback, 200);
};
```

As promised, the first thing that this function does is call `clearInterval`. When you tell `setInterval` to repeatedly call a function like I did in the `clearGrid` function, it will do it forever – or until you tell it to stop. And `clearInterval` is what you use to do this.

Once the original `setInterval` is cleared, I go ahead and start a new one, but this time it calls the `playback` function, which is what actually does all of the playback work. Why did I first call the `playbackStart` function only to then call the `playback` function? I just wanted a 1 second delay before beginning the actual playback. If I hadn't done this, the grid would still be springing back to a flat plane and I preferred the visual effect this way. Maybe I went a little overboard!

Before I describe the playback function, I need to take a slight detour and look at the code that lives on the invisible button inside each tile:

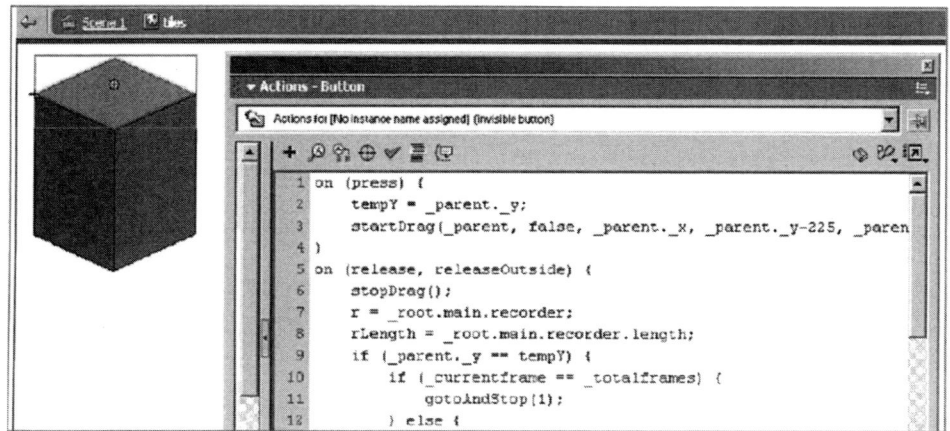

You've already seen a simplified version in City Blossom – it dealt with what happens when the user clicks or drags a tile. In this program, there's a little more work to be done since I have to record each of those clicks and drags. Here's how the code starts – the on (press) code is just the same as in the original City Blossom:

```
on (press) {
    tempY = _parent._y;
    startDrag(_parent, false, _parent._x, _parent._y-225,
    ➥ _parent._x, _parent._y+225);
}
```

The on (release, releaseOutside) code that follows has some additional lines that save the user's changes into the recorder array:

```
on (release, releaseOutside) {
    stopDrag();
    r = _root.main.recorder;
    rLength = _root.main.recorder.length;
    if (_parent._y == tempY) {
        if (_currentframe == _totalframes) {
            gotoAndStop(1);
        } else {
            nextFrame();
        }
        if (rLength>0) {
            if (r[rLength-1].tile == Number(_parent._name)) {
                r[rLength-1].frame = _currentframe;
```

7

```
        } else {
          r[rLength] = {tile:Number(_parent._name),
          ➥ frame:_currentframe, startY:tempY,
          ➥ endY:_parent._y};
        }
      } else {
        r[0] = {tile:Number(_parent._name),
        ➥ frame:_currentframe, startY:tempY,
        ➥ endY:_parent._y};
      }
    } else {
      r[rLength] = {tile:Number(_parent._name),
      ➥ frame:_currentframe, startY:tempY, endY:_parent._y};
    }
  }
```

Each time the user makes a change to a tile, I save a number of pieces of data into recorder:

- The name of the tile that was changed.

- The tile type (that is, the style of 'building') recorded by saving the current frame that the tiles movie clip is on.

- The y position of where the tile started before the user dragged it, and the y position after the drag has stopped.

The way I store this data in the recorder array is by creating a new object, placing all those values into that object, and placing the object itself into a new element at the end of the recorder array. Now, the traditional way to create a new object might look something like this:

```
someObject = new Object();
someObject.a = 1;
someObject.b = "hello ";
```

But these three statements can be condensed into one using this syntax:

```
someObject = { a: 1, b: "hello " };
```

OK, with that syntax in mind, let's look at how this code would read in plain English:

```
if (_parent._y == tempY) {
    if (_currentframe == _totalframes) {
        gotoAndStop(1);
    } else {
        nextFrame();
    }
    if (rLength>0) {
        if (r[rLength-1].tile == Number(_parent._name)) {
            r[rLength-1].frame = _currentframe;
        } else {
            r[rLength] = {tile:Number(_parent._name),
    ➥ frame:_currentframe, startY:tempY,
    ➥ endY:_parent._y};
        }
```

"If the tile has not been dragged then that means the user meant to click in order to change the tile type, so change the tile type. If the length of the `recorder` array is larger than 0, meaning that I've already recorded at least one user action, then, if the last action recorded was the same tile as the current one, then just update the tile type, because we know the position hasn't changed, otherwise add a new element to the array and save the name of the tile, its type, and its start and end positions into that new element."

```
    } else {
        r[0] = {tile:Number(_parent._name),
    ➥ frame:_currentframe, startY:tempY,
    ➥ endY:_parent._y};
    }
```

"If the length of the `recorder` array is not more than 0, then assume this is the user's first action, and record the relevant data in the first element of the `recorder` array."

```
} else {
    r[rLength] = {tile:Number(_parent._name),
    ➥ frame:_currentframe, startY:tempY, endY:_parent._y};
}
```

"If the tile *has* been dragged, record all of the relevant data in a new element."

This may seem a bit complex, but each `if` statement handles one of the many situations which could arise from a user action. For those wondering how a new array element could be created by using the length of the array itself, remember that the value of *someArray.length* is always one larger than the number used to access the last element of that array:

```
a[0] = "first element ";
a[1] = "second element ";
trace(a.length)    // would display 2, because there are
                   // two elements in the array
a[a.length] = "third element ";
trace(a.length)    // would now display 3
```

Well, I hope you've made it this far without getting a migraine! Now that we've seen how the movie actually saves information, let's look at the `playback` function, which is back on the root timeline:

```
main.playback = function() {
    tempObj = _root.main.recorder[playbackCounter++];
    m = _root.main[tempObj.tile];
    m.tiles.onEnterFrame = m.tiles.spring;
    m.tiles.yHome += (tempObj.endY-tempObj.startY);
    m.tiles.gotoAndStop(tempObj.frame);
    if (playbackCounter>=_root.main.recorder.length) {
        clearInterval(_global.playbackInterval);
    }
};
```

As you saw in `playbackStart`, this function gets called every 200 milliseconds. The function itself is actually pretty simple – for the current tile, I turn the `spring` action on by setting the `onEnterFrame` event handler to point to the `spring` function which will begin the spring effect. I then change the `home` value (the place where the tile ends up when the springing is done) to the difference between where it started and ended up, and change the tile to its new type. Then I check to see if the `playback` function has gone through all of the elements in the `recorder` array, and if so, stop the `setInterval` from calling `playback` again.

The last bits of code in this piece are short and sweet, to set up the buttons:

```
this.attachMovie("buttons", "buttons", 2);
buttons._x = 390;
buttons._y = 470;
buttons.b0.t = "playback";
buttons.b1.t = "clear";
buttons.b2.t = "load";
```

```
buttons.b3.t = "save";
buttons.but3.onRelease = function() {
   main.mazeSO.data.recorder = main.recorder;
};
buttons.but2.onRelease = function() {
   main.recorder = main.mazeSO.data.recorder;
};
buttons.but1.onRelease = function() {
   main.recorder = [];
   main.playIt = false;
   main.clearGrid();
};
buttons.but0.onRelease = function() {
   main.playIt = true;
   main.clearGrid();
};
```

Here, after setting up the position and names of the buttons, saving the user's map to disk takes only a single line of code:

```
buttons.but3.onRelease = function() {
   main.mazeSO.data.recorder = main.recorder;
};
```

All Flash needs to do, is to copy all of the data in the recorder array and store it in the shared object. Note that using this technique will overwrite any previously saved map data in the shared object.

Loading a previously saved map relies on another single line:

```
buttons.but2.onRelease = function() {
   main.recorder = main.mazeSO.data.recorder;
};
```

It couldn't be any easier!

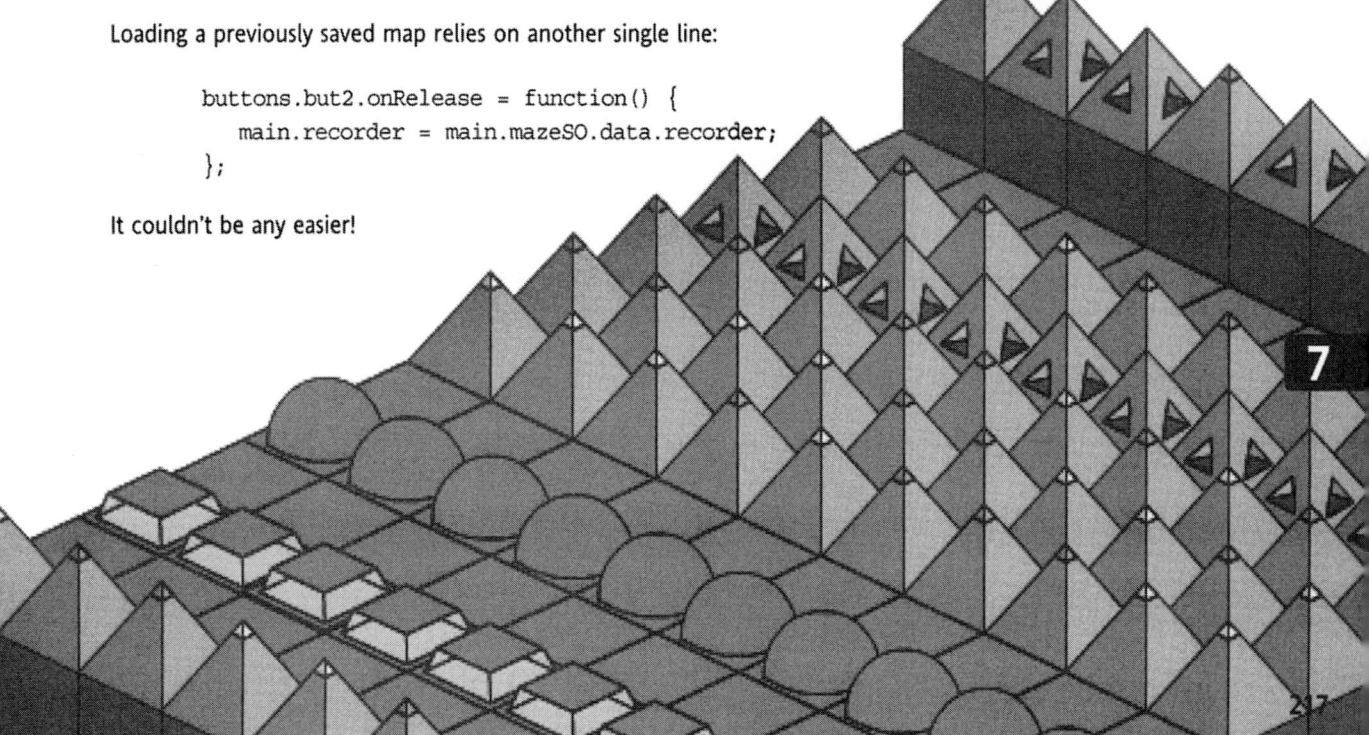

3D text scroller

In this movie, when a user types, 3D letters are dynamically generated using a simple, code-based font. A slider at the bottom of the screen can alter the speed of the scrolling. The program introduces a number of changes to the original isometric scroller that I used in the City Blossom movie, and I'll go over them one at a time. Open up and test `text_scroller.fla`:

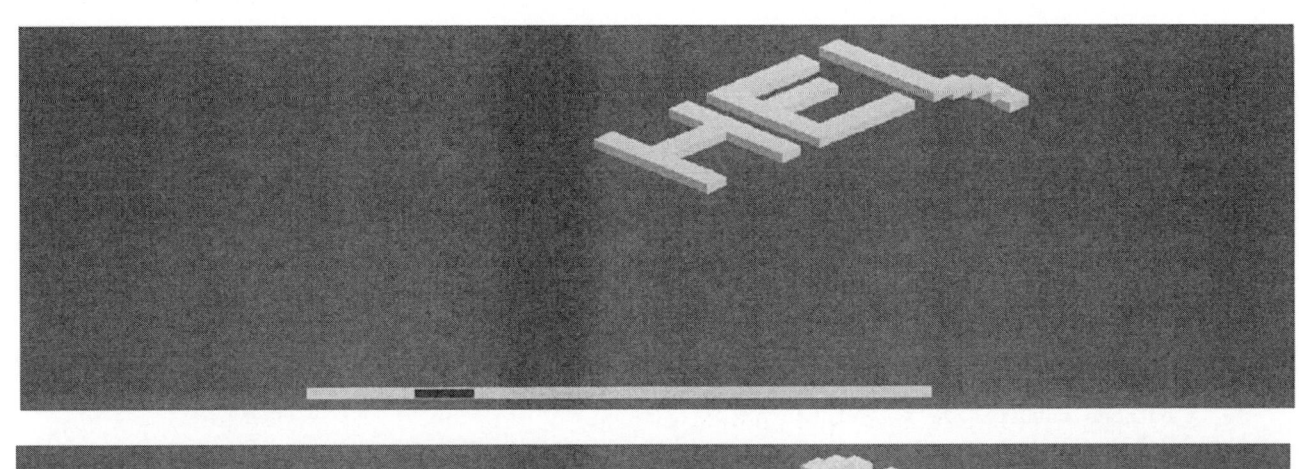

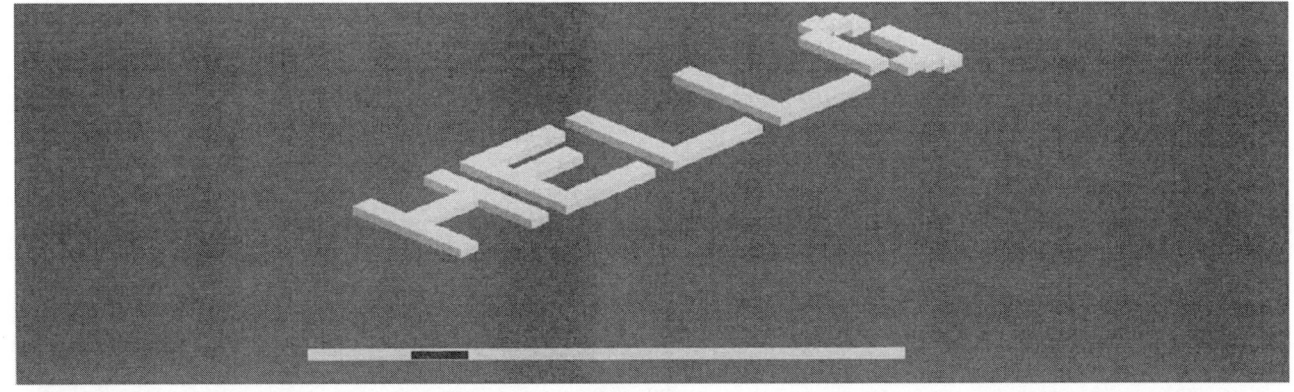

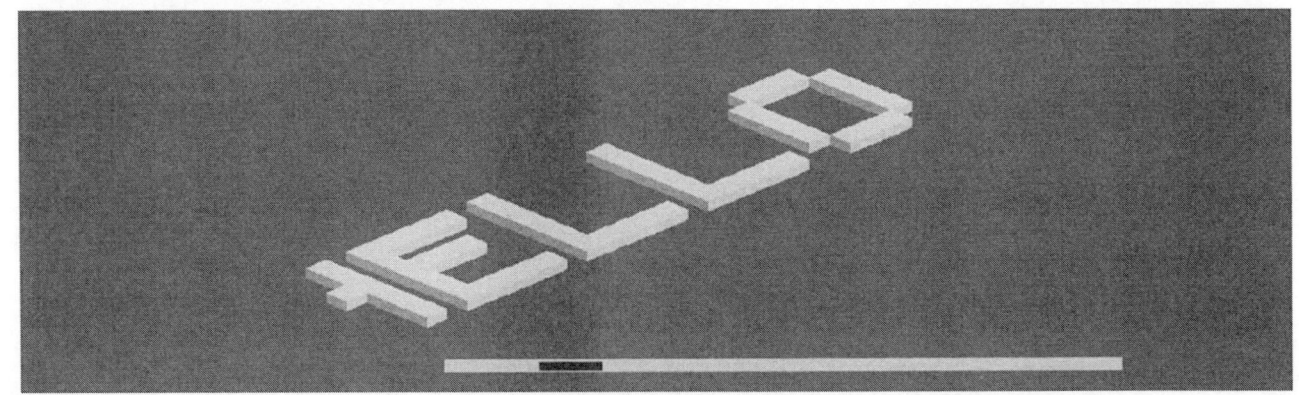

Let's start with the generation of the 'font'. I put that word in quotes because the font is not a real font in the traditional sense – it's not made up of vectors. Instead, I've developed a kind of home-brewed version that consists of discrete points stored in ActionScript as an array of binary numbers. To create the font, I first decided that each letter would be five units wide by six units tall. Then I sketched out each letter on a piece of graph paper, resulting in something like this:

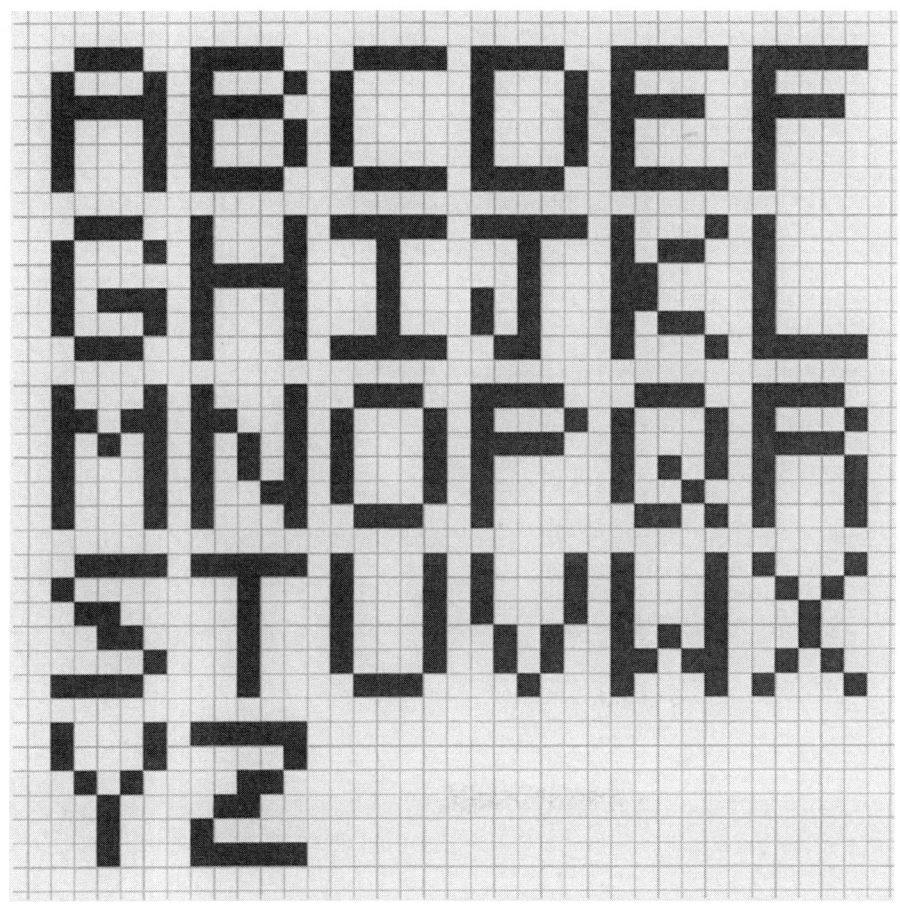

Now you'll notice that each square in the grid above is either black or white, that is, *on* or *off*. The simplest way to store this kind of data is with an array of zeros and ones. But the order in which the array is stored is important. Since the piece creates the letters one vertical line at a time, the letter data needs to be stored in that same order, so if I just had the letter A stored in an array, the ordering would look like this:

0	6	12	18	24
1	7	13	19	25
2	8	14	20	26
3	9	15	21	27
4	10	16	22	28
5	11	17	23	29

So, if the gray squares are ones and the white ones are zeros, the array sequence would look like this:

```
theLetterA = "0, 1, 1, 1, 1, 1, 1, 0, 1, 0, 0, 0, 1, 0, 1,
➡ 0, 0, 0, 1, 0, 1, 0, 0, 0, 0, 1, 1, 1, 1, 1";
```

Now, since every letter consists of a series of 30 ones and zeros, we know that the array will have a length of 780 (30x26 letters). Additionally, I've included a *spacer* at the beginning that adds an extra 30 elements at the front of the array. Thus, to get to the beginning of the data sequence of any particular letter, simply multiply the position of the letter in the alphabet (A=1, B=2, C=3, and so on) by 30. Therefore, the letter H would begin at position 240 of the array, while the letter L would begin at 360. Let's look at an extract of the first bit of code (for the full code, take a look at the code on the root timeline of text_scroller.fla):

```
_highquality = false;
this.createEmptyMovieClip("main",1);
main.initialize = function() {
    this._x = 600;
```

```
    fontArray = [0, 0, 0, 0, 0, 0, 0, 0, 0, 0, 0, 0, 0, 0, 0,
➡ 0, 0, 0, 0, 0, 0, 0, 0, 0, 0, 0, 0, 0, 0, 0, 0, 1, 1,
➡ 1, 1, 1, 1, 0, 1, 0, 0, 0, 1, 0, 1, 0, 0, 0, 1, 0, 1,
➡ 0, 0, 0, 0, 1, 1, 1, 1, 1, 1, 1, 1, 1, 1, 1, 1, 0...
// this goes on for a while...
    letterBuffer = [240, 150, 360, 360, 450];
    letter = letterBuffer.shift();
    letterColumnCount = 0;
```

After the familiar creation of the main clip, I create a function called `initialize`. The array `fontArray` holds the entire font as 1s and 0s. The array `letterBuffer` contains the starting values for the letters that will be displayed on startup. When the program first runs, the word HELLO scrolls across the screen because `letterBuffer` is initialized here with the start values for those letters. The variable `letter` holds the current letter being created, and `letterColumnCount` keeps track of which of the five columns of the letter is being created (remember that each letter is five units wide and six high).

Next, in order to receive input from the user, I need to *listen* to the keyboard for keystrokes. To do this I first create an object called `keyListener` and attach a function to it. That function will be used to handle the keystrokes (more on the function in a moment):

```
keyListener = new Object();
keyListener.onKeyUp = function() {
    letterCount++;
    letterBuffer.push((Key.getAscii()-96)*30);
};
```

I also need to *register* the `keyListener` object to the global `Key` object:

```
Key.addListener(keyListener);
```

`Key` works as a 'broadcaster' in that every time a key is pressed, it sends a message to any object that has registered to listen. In this case, I only have a single object listening, but the notion of certain objects broadcasting to others can be very powerful in more sophisticated programs.

So, what does the function do when a key is pressed and let go? Two small tasks – first, it increments the variable `letterCount` by 1, since when the user hit a key, the amount of letters just went up by one. Next, it adds a new element to the end of the `letterBuffer` array using the `push` command. ActionScript arrays have a number of built-in methods to add and remove elements, and `push` simply adds an element to the end of the array.

The number is determined by taking the ASCII value (a number between 0 and 255) of the key that was pressed, subtracting 96 from it, and then multiplying it by 30. Why subtract 96? Well, this is because the ASCII value of the letter 'a' is 97, and the rest of

7

the letters run sequentially from there (so 'z' = 122).

Next, I set some variables that I'll be using later on:

```
yJump = .915;
xJump = -2.331;
clipCount = 20000;
deleteCount = 20240;
this._y = oldy=-75;
```

Finally, I set the `onEnterFrame` event handler of the `main` movie clip to run the `mainLoop` function, which is defined next:

```
main.onEnterFrame = main.mainLoop;
};
```

That's it for the initialization function, now let's look at the `mainLoop` function:

```
main.mainLoop = function() {
  this._y += (yJump*(_root.slider._x*.01));
  this._x += (xJump*(_root.slider._x*.01));
  yDelta = this._y-oldy;
  c += yDelta;
  if (c>=7) {
    loopNum = Math.floor(c/7);
    c = c%7;
    while (loopNum-) {
      currentLetterLine = letter+(6*letterColumnCount);
      yPos += 5;
      x = 6;
      while (x-) {
        clipCount-;
        if (fontArray[currentLetterLine+x] == 1 && space
➡       != true) {
          this.attachMovie("tile", clipCount, clipCount);
          this[clipCount]._x = (x*18)+left;
          this[clipCount]._y = (yPos*7);
        }
        if (this[-deleteCount]) {
          this[deleteCount].removeMovieClip();
        }
        yPos-;
      }
      letterColumnCount++;
```

```
if (letterColumnCount>4) {
    if (space != true) {
        letterColumnCount-;
        space = true;
    } else {
        space = false;
        letterColumnCount = 0;
        letter = letterBuffer.shift();
    }
  }
 }
 left += 18;
    }
  }
 oldy = this._y;
};
```

The first thing I do is scroll main down and to the left (instead of the way City Blossom does, which is up and to the right):

```
this._y += (yJump*(_root.slider._x*.01));
this._x += (xJump*(_root.slider._x*.01));
```

I take the x position of the slider clip and multiply it by 0.01 in order to scale it down to a smaller value. Scaling the value down is necessary because the maximum x value of the slider position is approximately that of the width of the Flash window, but I only want the scrolling to change by about 1% of that amount. Then I multiply that value with the amount in yJump and xJump, as defined earlier, so that the diagonal scrolling works properly.

The speed of the grid scrolling in City Blossom was a constant rate. In making the speed user controlled in this piece, I had to write some extra code to compensate for this added unknown:

```
yDelta = this._y-oldy;
c += yDelta;
if (c>=7) {
    loopNum = Math.floor(c/7);
    c = c%7;
    while (loopNum-) {
```

The code above starts off by finding out how far the main clip has traveled since the last eventFrame. If it has traveled half of the tile height (7) or more (remember that in an isometric projection, each row is placed half of the tile height down from the last one), then I first have to determine how many new rows I need to create.

The Math.floor method will take a number with a decimal value (say 1.2 or 34.8) and return its integer value – it simply rounds the number down (so 1.2 would become 1 and

7

34.8 would become 34). So, `loopNum` will tell me how many extra new rows need to be created.

Finally, I use the modulo operator (`%`) to get the remainder of what would be left if divided by the distance traveled by 7, so that the next time we cycle through, that left over amount will be added to the distance traveled.

Now I'm ready to start building the new row. Each row is actually a single column of a letter from the font stored in `fontArray`. To find the correct starting point of the column within `fontArray`, I take the current column count and multiply it by 6 (the number of rows) and add that value to the first position in `fontArray` of the current letter:

$$currentLetterLine = letter+(6*letterColumnCount);$$

Perhaps an illustrated example would be appropriate right about now. Say I want to display the third column of the letter H. We already know how to get to its starting point – H is the eighth letter of the alphabet, so preceded by seven letters plus the spacer, and each letter in this font consists of 30 elements (6 rows and 5 columns), so 8 x 30 = 240. This means there are 240 elements before the start of the letter H, and as the array starts with 0, the 241st element, the first in the letter H is 240. Once we're at 240, to get to the third column I simply multiply 6 by the column number of 2, so 2 x 6 = 12 (remember that the first column is 0, so the third column is 2). Finally, I add that to the starting value of H to get the start position of the third column: 240 + 12 = 252.

240	246	252	258	264
241	247	253	259	265
242	248	254	260	266
243	249	255	261	267
244	250	256	262	268
245	251	257	263	269

It is important to note that the *columns* of the letter array get mapped onto the *rows* of the isometric grid.

So now that I've got the starting position of the current column of the current letter stored in currentLetterLine, we are ready to do a number of things...

We set the position of the row of tiles:

```
yPos += 5;
x = 6;
```

Loop through the column of the letter (if that was the third column of the letter H again, that would be the 252nd through the 257th element of the fontArray):

```
while (x—) {
  clipCount—;
```

See if that cell is turned on (that is, check if the value of the current fontArray element is 1):

```
if (fontArray[currentLetterLine+x] == 1 && space !=
➥ true) {
```

If it is, create and position the tile:

```
this.attachMovie("tile", clipCount, clipCount);
this[clipCount]._x = (x*18)+left;
this[clipCount]._y = (yPos*7);
}
```

Note that the depth value for each tile created gets smaller (the clipCount variable, defined at the start of the code, is decremented). This is due to the fact that new rows are being placed *behind* previous rows rather than in front of them as in City Blossom, and in order for the new clips to actually appear behind the previous row, their depth value must be lower.

Next, we get rid of tiles that have gone off screen:

```
if (this[—deleteCount]) {
  this[deleteCount].removeMovieClip();
}
yPos—;
}
```

Now it might be clear why the original value for the deleteCount variable was set a few hundred higher than clipCount:

```
clipCount = 20000;
deleteCount = 20240;
```

7

I only want to start deleting tiles once they've gone off the screen, so by the time deleteCount *catches up* to the value of the first tile created, that tile is off the screen. Once that is taken care of, it's time to go on to the next column:

```
letterColumnCount++;
```

But if the letter is done (if I've gone through all of its columns), I need to make sure that the next row created is blank so that there are spaces in between each letter:

```
if (letterColumnCount>4) {
  if (space != true) {
    letterColumnCount--;
    space = true;
  } else {
```

Otherwise, I grab the next letter to display:

```
      space = false;
      letterColumnCount = 0;
      letter = letterBuffer.shift();
    }
  }
  left += 18;
  }
 }
 oldy = this._y;
};
```

Next up in the main code, we've got the script that controls our slider movie clip, which in turn controls the speed of the text scrolling via its x position:

```
slider.gotoAndStop(1);
slider.onPress = function() {
  this.startDrag(false, 0, this._y, Stage.width-this._width,
  ➡ this._y);
};
slider.onRelease = function() {
  stopDrag();
};
slider.onReleaseOutside = function() {
  stopDrag();
};
```

```
    };
    slider.onRollOut = function() {
        this.gotoAndStop(1);
    };
```

This code is fairly self-explanatory – we set up how the `slider` movie clip reacts to the mouse cursor, and give it draggable properties.

The last line of code for the piece is:

```
    main.onEnterFrame = main.initialize;
```

This is actually the line that sets everything in motion by setting the `enterFrame` event handler to the `initialize` function. The `initialize` function runs, and at the end of that function, `main`'s `enterFrame` event handler is set to the `mainLoop` function. This method is a workaround since I couldn't use `main`'s `onLoad` event handler because the `onLoad` event is triggered as soon as `main` is created, which is before any `onLoad` handler exists.

That does it for the code! The final aspect of this piece I need to talk about is the tile clip itself. If you look at the clip, you'll notice that it consists of a motion tween (note that the tile tween movie clip held in the Library has been given the linkage name of `tile` so that it can be accessed by the code).

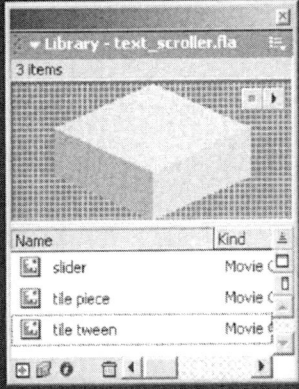

This is a great example of the usefulness of combining a movie that is mostly code with a bit of traditional Flash animation. The tween simply moves the tile into its grid position, but the overall effect during playback creates a kind of curving motion for all of the letters. As long as the final frame of this clip ends where it does now, you can create an endless number of funky effects. Try moving the clip in the first frame to different positions, or playing with tint and alpha values.

Now you can go ahead and try inputting different words and phrases by changing the `letterBuffer` array as you wish:

```
    letterBuffer = [30, 390, 30, 780, 270, 420, 210];
```

Maze generator

In this next piece, I've implemented a classic maze algorithm that is visualized by our old friend the isometric grid, and given some dynamic placement using our trusty spring-motion function. I use three programming techniques that beginning programmers may not be familiar with, so if *binary numbers*, *bitwise operators*, and *LIFO stacks* don't mean anything to you, you'll want to read this section carefully. For more advanced users, you can skip straight to the explanation of the code.

As a teaser of what's to come, open up `maze.swf`:

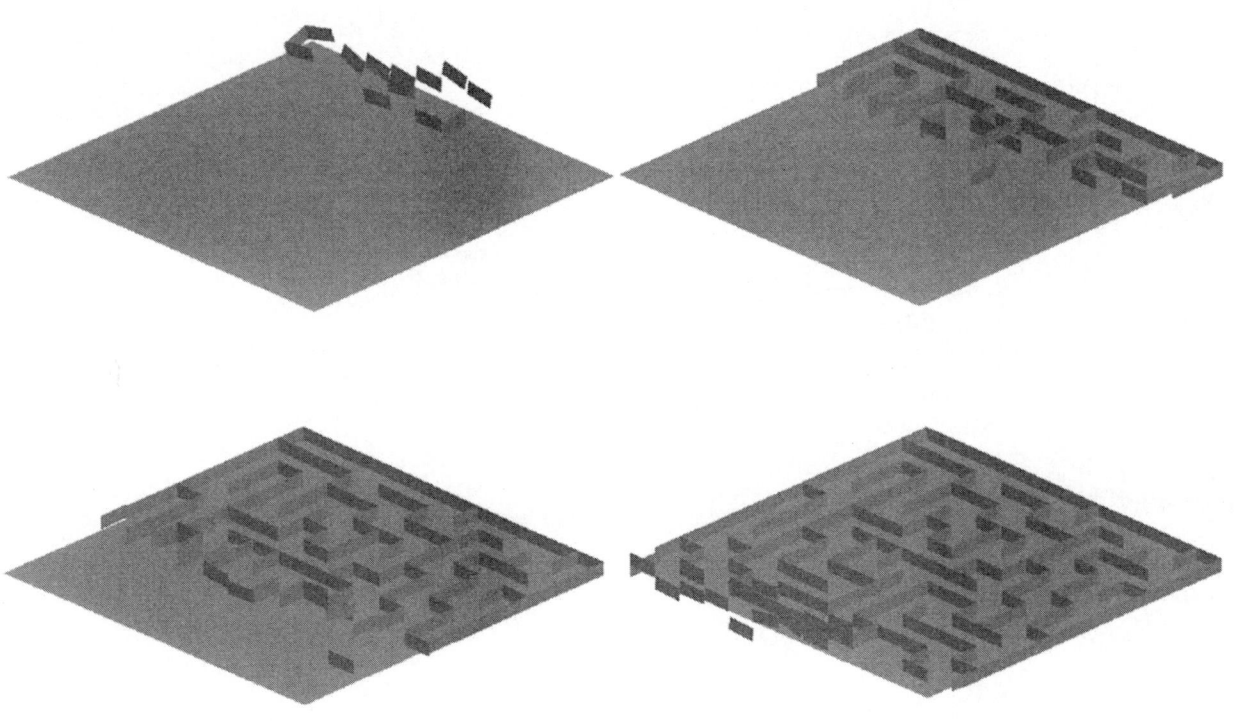

Let's start by talking about bits. You might already know that a **bit** is the smallest possible chunk of data that your computer can recognize – it can either be a 1 or a 0. Flash developers don't often write code to manipulate individual bits in their programs, but if you've got a situation where you need to store a bunch of data as either *on* or *off*, like say, the walls in a maze, it can become a fast and efficient means to do so.

When numbers are represented in binary, they just consist of a series of 1s and 0s (for example, 1101001), but there is a method to this madness! The trick to figuring out the decimal value is knowing that each bit represents its own number. Take a look at this chart:

All binary numbers are read from right to left, and each bit represents a value twice as much as the previous bit. Add up all of the values that are *on* (those that are 1 instead of 0) to determine the decimal value of this binary number. In this case, the binary number 1101 corresponds to 1 + 4 + 8 = 13 in decimal.

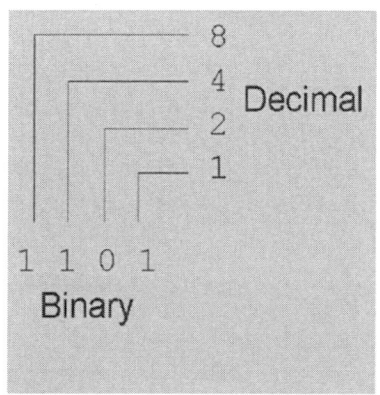

Here are all the possible values for a 4-bit binary number:

Binary	Decimal
0000	0
0001	1
0010	2
0011	3
0100	4
0101	5
0110	6
0111	7
1000	8
1001	9
1010	10
1011	11
1100	12
1101	13
1110	14
1111	15

7

Now there's a reason I've been showing you 4-bit numbers – as I hinted at earlier, 4-bits can equate to four walls! So, by storing four discrete values within a single decimal number, I can use less memory and compare values faster. Think of a 4-bit number now as this:

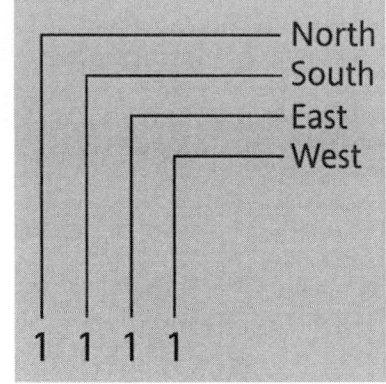

So for example, if I've got a cell in the maze with all four walls intact, I can represent it as decimal 15, because the binary equivalent is 1111. Now say I want to remove just the South wall. Well, I know that the third column from the right of a binary series when turned on (1) equals 4. So, in code I could write:

```
cell = 15;
newCell = cell - 4;
```

Now the new decimal value of cell is 11, while the binary representation is 1011. We'll see all of these concepts in action when we go over the code.

The second programming concept I need to introduce for this movie relates to the use of **bitwise operators**. Such operators work in a similar fashion to standard math functions like +, -, or * in your code. In simple terms, they take two numbers and return a result.

The bitwise operator I use in this maze project is called **logical AND** – it's represented by the & character. The logical AND operator stacks up two numbers in binary format and goes column by column with a simple rule – if both columns contain ones, then put a 1 in the result column, otherwise, put a 0. Here's a simple example:

```
a = 5;
b = 12;
c = a & b;
```

Variable	Decimal	Binary	Why
a	5	0101	1+4 = 5
b	12	1100	4+8 = 12
c	4	0100	The 4 column is the only one turned on for both a and b.

This will become useful in the maze display code when I want to quickly determine which walls in a cell are still up.

The last general programming technique I want to cover before hitting the code is the notion of a **LIFO stack**. As you know, an array is just a series of ordered data, so that if you initialize an array like this:

```
websiteArray = ["praystation", "levitated", "bit-101"];
```

websiteArray[0] will equal praystation, websiteArray[1] will equal levitated, and websiteArray[2] will equal bit-101. Simple enough!

Remember that we talked about the push method of an array earlier – so if I did websiteArray.push("presstube"), then websiteArray[3] would equal presstube. Conversely, there is a method called pop which works like this:

```
newVar = websiteArray.pop()
```

What this does is simultaneously remove the last element of the array and put the value of that element into the variable newVar. By utilizing the push and pop methods, you can use an array as a *Last In First Out* (LIFO), stack.

The maze algorithm I use in this piece is often called a *Depth-First Search* and produces what is known as a *perfect* maze, that is, a maze in which every cell is accessible via some path to any other cell. The basic way the algorithm works is as follows:

1. Create a grid of cells, with each cell containing four walls.
2. Choose a random cell as your *current* cell.
3. Determine if any of the current cell's neighbors (those cells to the north, south, east, and west) have all of their walls still intact.
4. If so, choose one of the neighbors at random, remove the walls between the current cell and the neighbor, and make the neighbor the current cell. If not, go back to the previous current cell and choose a different neighbor.
5. Continue steps 3 and 4 until all of the cells in the grid have been accessed.

OK, on to the ActionScript – all of the code for this piece can be found in the first frame of the root timeline of maze.fla. First, after the setting the quality property, I write the function that will create the maze array:

```
_highquality = false;
this.makeMaze = function() {
    // set up variables and maze array
    xlength = 12;
    ylength = 12;
    totalcells = xlength*ylength;
```

7

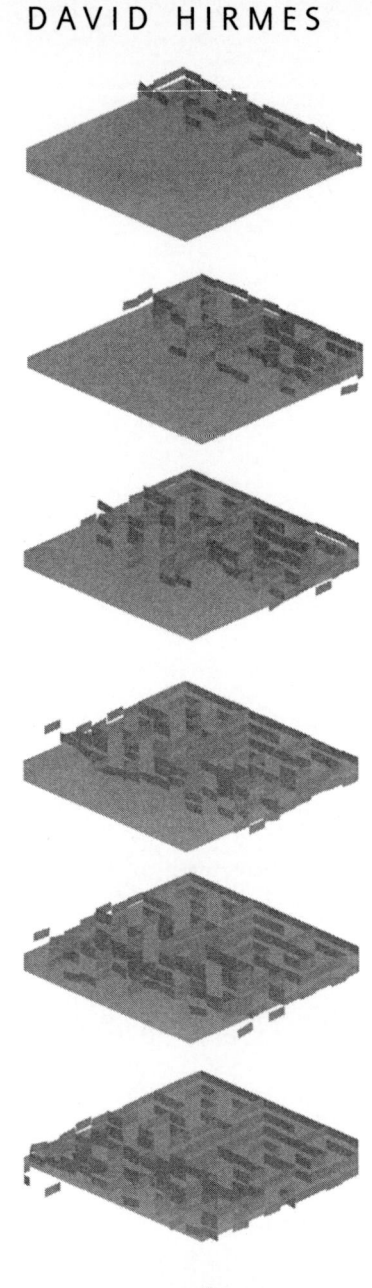

Here, `xlength` and `ylength` determine how many cells are in each row and column of the maze. Note that the algorithm is smart enough to deal with non-square mazes, so you can set `xlength` and `ylength` to different values.

Next, a nested loop fills each cell in the two dimensional maze array `m` with the number 15 (binary: 1111) meaning that each cell begins with all four walls up:

```
m = [];
for (rows=0; rows<xlength; rows++) {
  m[rows] = [];
  for (cols=0; cols<ylength; cols++) {
    m[rows][cols] = 15;
  }
}
```

The starting cell is then picked at random:

```
visitedcells = 0;
currentx = random(xlength-3)+3;
currenty = random(ylength-3)+3;
stack = [];
```

Here, the `stack` array is the LIFO stack that will keep track of the route in which the code moves through the maze array while removing random walls.

Next up is the main loop that creates the maze – it will run until every cell has been visited, at which point the maze is complete:

```
while (visitedcells<totalcells) {
  // get info on the current cell's neighbors
  livecells = 0;
  // 1 = n, 2 = s, 3 = e, 4 = w
  liveNeighbors = [];
  if (currenty>0) {
    if (m[currentx][currenty-1] == 15) {
      liveNeighbors[livecells++] = 1; // 1 = North
    }
  }
  if (currenty<ylength) {
    if (m[currentx][currenty+1] == 15) {
      liveNeighbors[livecells++] = 2; // 2 = South
    }
  }
  if (currentx<xlength) {
    if (m[currentx+1][currenty] == 15) {
```

```
        liveNeighbors[livecells++] = 3; // 3 = East
      }
    }
    if (currentx>0) {
      if (m[currentx-1][currenty] == 15) {
        liveNeighbors[livecells++] = 4; // 4 = West
      }
    }
```

The code above checks each of the current cell's four neighbors (within the bounds of the maze size). Each time it finds a neighbor with all four walls intact, it adds it to the liveNeighbors array. Remember that decimal 15 equals 1111 in binary, so 15 here refers to all four walls being intact.

If none of the current cell's neighbors have all their walls up, go back to the previous current cell by removing the previous cell from the stack array:

```
    if (livecells == 0) {
      currentx = stack.pop();
      currenty = stack.pop();
      if (stack.length<=0) {
        visitedcells = totalcells;
      }
```

Otherwise randomly pick one of the neighbor cells that has all four walls and remove the walls between the current cell and the picked cell:

```
    } else {
      // knock down the wall between current cell and
      // picked cell
      pick = random(livecells);
      if (liveNeighbors[pick] == 1) {
        pickedx = currentx;
        pickedy = currenty-1;
        m[currentx][currenty] -= 1;
        m[pickedx][pickedy] -= 2;
      } else if (liveNeighbors[pick] == 2) {
        pickedx = currentx;
        pickedy = currenty+1;
        m[currentx][currenty] -= 2;
        m[pickedx][pickedy] -= 1;
      } else if (liveNeighbors[pick] == 3) {
        pickedx = currentx+1;
        pickedy = currenty;
```

7

```
            m[currentx][currenty] -= 4;
            m[pickedx][pickedy] -= 8;
        } else if (liveNeighbors[pick] == 4) {
            pickedx = currentx-1;
            pickedy = currenty;
            m[currentx][currenty] -= 8;
            m[pickedx][pickedy] -= 4;
        }
```

Finally, push the current cell onto the LIFO stack, turn the `current` cell into the `picked` cell, and increment by 1 the variable keeping track of all the cells that have been visited:

```
            stack.push(currenty);
            stack.push(currentx);
            currentx = pickedx;
            currenty = pickedy;
            visitedcells++;
        }
    }
    _global.mazeDisplayer = setInterval(builder, 50);
};
```

That almost does it for the `makeMaze` function. In terms of optimization, I tried to find a balance between file size, speed, memory usage, and readability. The algorithm can certainly be improved in any of those directions – but at the likely cost of the other three.

Once the maze array is complete, I use `setInterval` to begin the process of displaying the maze one wall at a time:

```
    _global.mazeDisplayer = setInterval(builder, 50);
};
```

Before I get into the details of how that is done, let's discuss the modifications to the isometric engine I made in order to display the maze. First off, the tiles movie clip has now been reduced to a single layer with four frames, and given the linkage name `tiles`. This is placed within the movie clip `wrapper` (which has a linkage name `wrapper`):

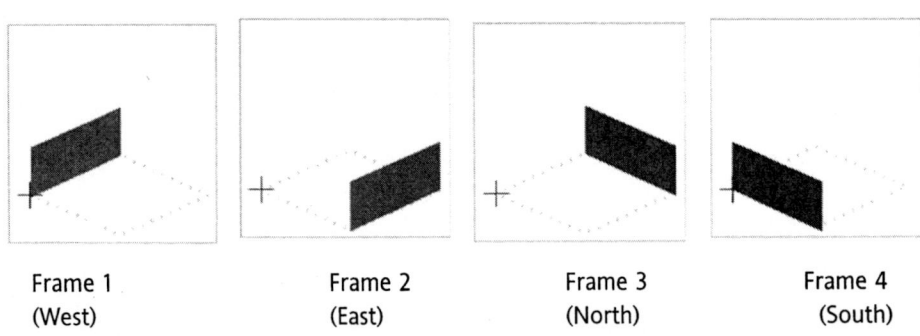

| Frame 1 | Frame 2 | Frame 3 | Frame 4 |
| (West) | (East) | (North) | (South) |

Next up in the code I set two variables that will keep track of the location of the current tile being displayed, and then I define a function called `builder`:

```
x = 0;
y = 0;
this.builder = function() {
    if (x>(xlength-1)) {
        x = 0;
        y++;
        left -= 35;
        yPos -= (xlength-1);
    }
    if (y>(ylength-1)) {
        clearInterval(_global.mazeDisplayer);
    }
    createTile();
    x++;
};
```

This function goes through the two-dimensional array in the same way the City Blossom engine creates the initial grid plane. The difference here is that rather than build the whole thing at once with `for` loops, I've created a function so that each tile is created one at a time. As you saw earlier, the `builder` function is called using `setInterval` in the last line of the `makeMaze` function.

Next, I define a function called `createTile`:

```
this.createTile = function() {
    i = m[x][y];
    tempx = ((x*35)+left)+366;
    tempy = (yPos*15)+62;
    if (i & 1) {
        this.attachMovie("wrapper", ++tileCount, tileCount);
        this[tileCount]._x = tempx;
        this[tileCount]._y = tempy;
        this[tileCount].tiles.gotoAndStop(3);
    }
    if (i & 8) {
        this.attachMovie("wrapper", ++tileCount, tileCount);
        this[tileCount]._x = tempx;
        this[tileCount]._y = tempy;
        this[tileCount].tiles.gotoAndStop(1);
    }
```

7

```
if (i & 4) {
    this.attachMovie("wrapper", ++tileCount, tileCount);
    this[tileCount]._x = tempx;
    this[tileCount]._y = tempy;
    this[tileCount].tiles.gotoAndStop(2);
}
if (i & 2) {
    this.attachMovie("wrapper", ++tileCount, tileCount);
    this[tileCount]._x = tempx;
    this[tileCount]._y = tempy;
    this[tileCount].tiles.gotoAndStop(4);
}
yPos++;
};
```

This function uses that & bitwise operator I talked about earlier – it checks the current cell for the existence of each of the walls that could exist and creates a new wall tile for each.

After this, I define the clearMaze function:

```
this.clearMaze = function() {
    tileCount++;
    while (tileCount--) {
        this[tileCount].removeMovieClip();
    }
    y = x = yPos = left = 0;
    makeMaze();
};
```

As its name suggests, this simply removes all of the existing tiles, sets the position variables to 0 and creates a new maze. It is triggered by the new maze button on the root timeline (see below).

Finally, I set up code to control the new maze button – its release calls the clearMaze function – and then call the makeMaze function to run the movie:

```
newMaze_btn.onRelease = function() {
    clearMaze();
};
makeMaze();
```

The last bit of code to consider lives on top of the tile clip inside wrapper. It looks a lot like the code found in City Blossom, with a few exceptions.

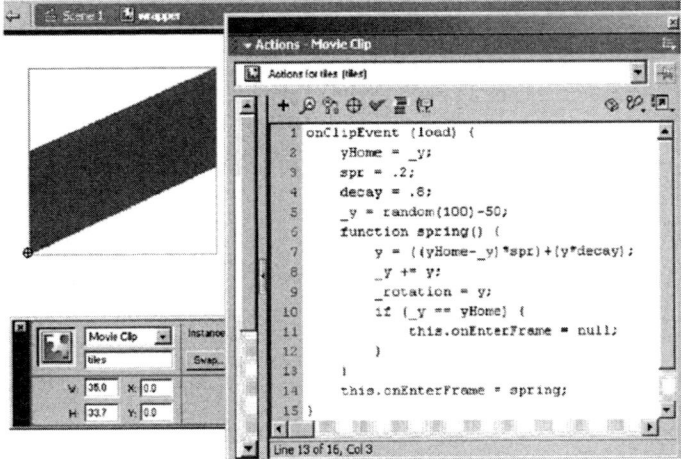

By now you're familiar with the concept of assigning functions to clip events. So when the tile is first created, the clip's onEnterFrame is set to the spring function. Each time the spring function is called, it checks to see if it has reached its home, and if it has, it sets the onEnterFrame to null. This way, the spring function only runs when it has to, improving the speed at which the program runs since it isn't doing anything unnecessary.

The other change I've added is setting the rotation value of the tile to the spring motion. This creates that wind-like effect. Since y will eventually equal 0, I know that when the spring function is done, the _rotation value of the tile will return to 0 as well. To get even funkier effects, you can use the y variable to change other aspects of the tile like:

```
_xscale = 100 + (y * 10);
```

or:

```
_alpha = 100 - (y * 10);
```

But you'll need to remember to set the values back to 100 when you turn off the spring function to ensure the tiles are perfectly placed:

```
if (_y == yHome) {
    f = null;
    _xscale = 100;
    _alpha = 100;
}
```

For more information on mazes, check out www.mazeworks.com. It was this fun and informative site that reminded me of the *Depth-First Search* algorithm that this Flash movie relies on.

7

Isometric terrains using the drawing API

In this final design, I wanted to start with the familiar isometric projection, but this time show what could be done using the drawing API of Flash MX. Rather than use the movie clip based tile method of the other movies in this chapter, this program uses ActionScript alone to draw all of the graphics. I use the `Math.cos` command to oscillate the grid, creating a wave-like effect. Note that both the drawing API and the `Math.cos` command are utilized and discussed in the chapters 'Dynamic Interfaces' and 'Math-based Animation and Dynamic Drawing'.

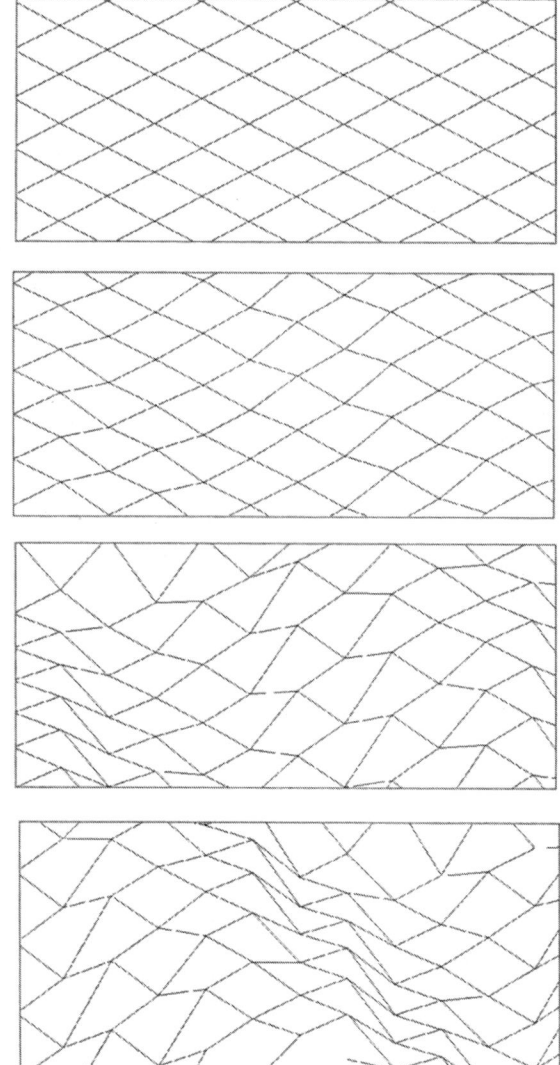

Check out `terrains.swf` to see the finished design in action – moving the mouse from left to right increases the amplitude of the cosine wave:

The first thing you might notice when opening up this file (`terrains.fla`) is that the Library is completely empty! All of the code for this Flash movie resides in the first frame of the root timeline. Here's how it begins:

```
_highquality = false;
this._x = -84;
py = [];
size = 6;
doubleSize = size*2;
for (j=1; j<=doubleSize; j++) {
   py[j] = [];
   for (i=0; i<=size; i++) {
      py[j][i] = 0;
   }
}
```

First off, I create a two-dimensional array to store the height values of each point in the grid. This technique differs from the tile-based grid we've become used to, in that rather than keeping track of entire tile clips, I'm keeping track of the individual points where the tiles (or rather, polygons) intersect.

The `counter` variable is used to cycle through the cosine wave (which is used shortly):

```
this.onEnterFrame = function() {
   counter += 0.2;
```

The first `while` loop simply takes the values of the points of each row and places them in the row below them:

```
d = doubleSize+1;
while (d−) {
    s = size+1;
    while (s−) {
        py[d][s] = py[d-1][s];
    }
}
```

This makes the wave move through the grid.

This second `while` loop introduces the waveform into the first row:

```
s = size+1;
    while (s−) {
        py[1][s] = (Math.cos(s+counter))*(_root._xmouse*0.08);
    }
```

As I mentioned earlier, the _x value of the mouse is used to alter the amplitude (or 'height') of the wave.

Next, `clear` removes all graphics from the screen and `lineStyle` defines the type of lines that will be drawn:

```
this.clear();
this.lineStyle(0, 0);
```

In this case, the width will be hairline (0), and the color will be black (0).

The large segment of code below is the main loop where I determine how much each of the points of a given tile need to be raised or lowered along the y axis. The code is a little confusing because I have to deal with four cases: odd rows, even rows, the first row, and the second row. However, the basic concept can be summarized as finding the values that each end of line point needs to be altered by to form the wave. Here's the relevant code:

```
y = 0;
for (j=1; j<=doubleSize; j++) {
    for (i=1; i<=size; i++) {
        if (j%2 == 0) {
            // row is even
            x = i*56+28;
            left = py[j-1][i];
            right = py[j-1][i+1];
```

7

```
      top = py[j-2][i];
      bottom = py[j][i];
    } else if (j == 1) {
      // first row
      x = i*56;
      left = py[j][i-1];
      right = py[j][i];
      top = py[j-1][i];
      bottom = py[j][i];
    } else {
      // row is odd
      x = i*56;
      left = py[j-1][i-1];
      right = py[j-1][i];
      top = py[j-2][i];
      bottom = py[j][i];
    }
    if (j == 2) {
      // second row
      x = i*56+28;
      left = py[j-1][i];
      right = py[j-1][i+1];
      top = py[j-1][i];
      bottom = py[j][i];
    }
```

Finally, each tile is drawn:

```
        this.moveTo(x, y+left);
        this.lineTo(x+28, -14+top+y); // line 'A'
        this.lineTo(x+56, right+y); // line 'B'
        this.lineTo(x+28, 14+bottom+y); // line 'C'
    }
    y += 14;
  }
};
```

So, this is what a basic tile looks like when no cosine wave is applied:

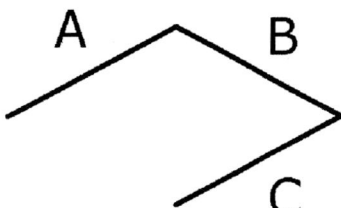

The variables `left`, `right`, `top`, and `bottom` determine how the basic tile will be altered – simple or what?

I hope these pieces have shown you some worthwhile tips and techniques that you can integrate within your own projects. Remember, small is beautiful!

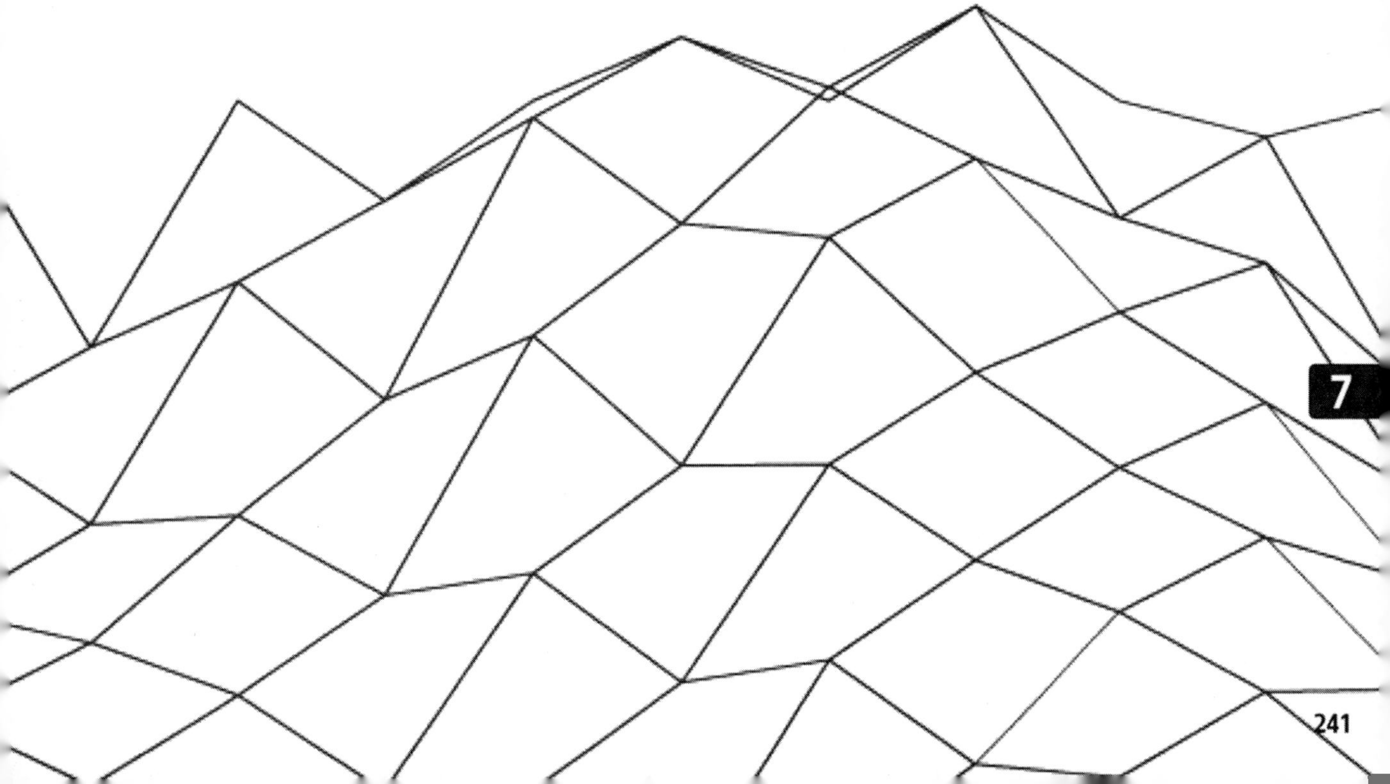

7

8 USING JAVASCRIPT WITH FLASH MX

GENEVIÈVE GARAND

This chapter is about interface design, and looks at the possibilities available to us when it comes to designing a user interface with optimally small file sizes that is both interactive and highly original. I've packed this chapter with experiments that can be used to create high-impact websites at a minimal size. The files used in the following exercises are made with Flash MX, combined with a special ingredient... JavaScript! I know some of you will probably be a bit scared about this, but really there's no need to be -you don't need to be a master of JavaScript or ActionScript to understand and to play with these simple experiments. The scripts aren't very complicated, but they do open up a whole new vista of possibilities when it comes to exciting interface design.

JavaScript enables us to create surprising interfaces without huge Flash files. Incorporating these design ideas will permit you to create beautiful interfaces that can be fun for the user. You just have to take the ones that interest you, play with them, shape them, and blend them with your own ideas, and you'll be able to achieve highly innovative sites.

Playing with your browser

When creating minimal-sized websites, my favorite trick is to play with the limits of the browser. I'm always looking for new ways of presenting the information I want to display, and redefining the role that the browser itself can play in this.

I always wait until I have a definite idea about what exactly I want the user to understand about my project before I begin constructing my interface. When I begin designing, I try to put myself in the user's position. As designers, we shouldn't forget that we are creating an experience for the user. The way I construct my interface defines how the user will perceive and understand the information that I am trying to communicate.

The user interface and the content are intimately linked, and influence each other. If one aspect of the interface changes, the whole vision of the project will be affected. Accordingly, it's important that my interface represents and enriches my concept.

When trying to do this as well as create a website that is small in size, we need to think in simple terms; and no, simple doesn't necessarily mean easy! We need to refine our ideas so that we pare the interface down to a minimum, without diluting our carefully thought out concept. Learn economy – we can do a lot with less. With care, we can ensure that our work can be minimal without giving the impression that something is missing from it. All the elements that compose the website need to be balanced.

When we look at the software we use everyday, Photoshop or Flash for example, the interfaces are composed of several windows linked together. However, usually when we design we only think of using one browser window. Why is that? Juxtaposing windows with several movies can enrich the design without creating huge Flash files.

However, the interfaces I develop here would not be suitable for every kind of website. When I create an interface with multiple windows, it needs to be in harmony with my concept. What I like about the kind of interface we will look at in this chapter is that it is extremely interactive - the user can manipulate the windows and exploit their own creativity to modify the interface. Hopefully, this introduces an element of interactivity that will hold the users' attention on my design.

The creation of an interface for a website has to involve the browser – we don't have a choice about that. Why don't we play with its possibilities and use them to our own advantage? The browser's capabilities can be integrated in the design process so that we utilize them to explore new ideas. We should let the browser do the work - and in this chapter we'll learn how to achieve this using JavaScript with our Flash designs.

Communication between Flash and JavaScript

The method I use to get Flash and JavaScript to interact is to put a JavaScript function in an HTML page that also contains our Flash file. The ability to activate JavaScript from your SWF files opens up many new possibilities for creating highly interactive web pages. However, it is important to realize that sometimes with JavaScript things may not go as smoothly as they should - you need to script your HTML pages very carefully, and test them on every browser you have available.

There are several different methods that can be used to make Flash communicate with JavaScript. The `fscommand` action in Flash is the most commonly used function, but I prefer to use the `getURL` function because I've found it to be more stable and reliable across various platforms and browsers. I use it to call a JavaScript function in the HTML so that it can control browser-specific objects.

The best piece of advice I received when I started working with browser scripting was that I should always test the JavaScript on my HTML page before trying to make it work with my Flash movie. At first, this might seem like a waste of time, but, believe me, it will prevent a lot of frustration in the long run. The worst thing that can happen is to waste hours tearing your hair out trying to find a bug somewhere in one of your linked files, when most of the time the cause of the problem is a minor detail.

For those of you who might not have a lot of familiarity with HTML, its structure is very simple. Here's an example HTML file:

```
<html>
<head>
<title>
My website
</title>
</head>
<body>
Content that is displayed on the page goes here. This can be
in the form of text or images, or an embedded Flash file.
</body>
</html>
```

8

When you publish your Flash files, via File > Publish, Flash puts them into an HTML file like this, with the SWF embedded into the body section of the file. It's beyond the scope of this chapter to go any deeper into the HTML itself, but for our purposes, all you really need to know is that you can place JavaScript functions within the `head` tags of the document - these functions can be called upon by the content of the page in the `body` section.

I recommend you test your JavaScript function inside the HTML using an event handler. Most of the time, I use the `onload` event handler within the body tag of my HTML:

```
<body onload = your_function()>
```

This means that as soon as the browser loads the page, the function will run. Once you are happy that everything is OK with your JavaScript, you can bring in the Flash element. Let's take a look at the basics...

Opening a window

Before constructing a full site, we need to make sure we have our basic structure in place. First of all, let's see how I play with the launching of a pop-up browser window, and how I insert the `getURL` function into my Flash movie.

For this experiment, we are going to create three files:

- A Flash file, called `open.fla`, containing a `getURL` action attached to a button, which will call the JavaScript function responsible for the launching of the window.

- An HTML document named `index.html`, which contains the JavaScript function that the Flash calls. This HTML file will have `open.swf` embedded in it.

- A second HTML file, `menu.html`, which will open in the pop-up window when the function is called.

To make a window launcher function work, as with any other JavaScript function, two things are really important – the function itself, inserted in the `head` section of the HTML, and an event handler to call the function, which we are going to attach to a button within the Flash file.

Let's start by creating the main HTML document, index.html. First, we need to look at the openwin function that will launch our window:

```
<head>
<script language="JavaScript">
function openwin() {
   properties = 'menubar=0, toolbar=0,location=0,
➥directories=0, Xstatus=0, scrollbars=no, resizable=0,
➥width=500, height=400, top=150, Xleft=150'
   win_1 = window.open ('menu.html', 'menu', properties);
}
</script>
</head>
```

As you can see, the JavaScript is placed in the head of the HTML file. A window launching function should include three pieces of information:

```
win_1 = window.open ('menu.html', 'menu', properties);
```

- The URL of the page to load (menu.html)

- The name of the window you are about to create - you can choose the name you want, here I've named my window menu

- The attributes that will shape your pop-up window - in the openwin function, the variable properties contains all the features I want to pass to my new window

I set the width of my window to 500 pixels and the height to 400 pixels. The dimensions given to the pop-up are very important, because if you are designing for a page containing an embedded Flash document to be displayed within the pop-up, you need to make sure that these match the dimensions of your Flash file.

With the attributes top and left, I can control where on the screen I want my window to appear. The measurements I have specified mean that it will pop up 150 pixels from the top and from the left hand side. I have also added several other attributes, which we can look at in a bit more detail, along with some others that are useful and are supported by the window.open method.

8

Here is a list of the most useful supported attributes:

- **directories** – value of yes, no, 1, or 0, specifies whether to create the standard browser directory buttons.

- **height** – numeric value, specifies the height of the window in pixels.

- **left** (**screenX** in Navigator 4.0 and earlier) – numeric value, specifies the distance the new window is placed from the left side of the screen.

- **location** – value of yes, no, 1 or 0, specifies whether to display the location field, the input field for entering URLs directly into the browser window.

- **menubar** – value of yes, no, 1 or 0, specifies whether to create the menu at the top of the window.

- **resizable** – value of yes, no, 1 or 0, specifies whether to display resize handles at the corners of the window, to allow the user to change its dimensions.

- **scrollbars** – value of yes, no, 1, or 0, specifies whether to display horizontal and vertical scroll bars, when the content exceeds the dimensions of the window.

- **status** – value of yes, no, 1 or 0, specifies whether to create a status bar at the bottom of the window.

- **top** (**screenY** in Navigator 4.0 and earlier) – numeric value, specifies the distance the new window is placed from the top of the screen.

- **toolbar** – value of yes, no, 1, or 0, specifies whether to display the browser toolbar.

- **width** – numeric value, specifies the width of the window in pixels. The minimum value should be 100.

For the moment we won't include the Flash movie in index.html, as it is better to test the function first. Open a simple text-editing program, such as Notepad if you're in Windows, or SimpleText on a Mac, and save the following as index.html:

```
<html>
<head>
<title>
:: OPENING A WINDOW ::
</title>
<script language="JavaScript">
function openwin() {
    properties = 'menubar=0, toolbar=0,location=0,
    ➥ directories=0, status=0, scrollbars=no, resizable=0,
    ➥ width=500, height=400, top=150, left=150'
    win_1 = window.open ('menu.html', 'menu', properties);
}
</script>
</head>
<body onload=openwin()>
</body>
</html>
```

Here, the onload event handler within the body tag will call the openwin function when the page loads in the browser window.

Now that we have the recipe to open a new window, we need to create the page that goes in the pop-up we're about to launch. Open a new text file. We need to make sure that this new file is saved as a name identical to the URL in the function, and is in the same directory as the first HTML file. (If it's not in the same directory, you can specify the path.) Save it as menu.html. We don't need to bother giving it any content, as nothing is needed from this page to make the function work. Just include the following in menu.html:

```
<html>
<head>
<title>
menu
</title>
</head>
<body>
</body>
</html>
```

8

It's now time to test the launching function - open `index.html` in your browser and as soon as the page loads...surprise! A small pop-up window launches in the left hand corner of the screen. So now that we know that our JavaScript function works, it's time to open Flash.

We're going to create a movie that will be embedded in our `index.html` file. Create a new Flash document, 200 x 200 pixels in size. My version is saved as `open.fla`.

In ActionScript, the `getURL` action can communicate with JavaScript (as well as server-side scripts) and returns any information to the browser window. When using `getURL` you can refer to a JavaScript by using this general syntax:

getURL("JavaScript: yourFunction (yourArgument)");

Although I've assigned the `getURL` action to a button in this case, it can similarly be attributed to an event attached to a frame or a movie clip. For this example, I created a button with the word OPEN on it, and dragged an instance of it onto the stage. I've given my button an instance name of `open` in the Property inspector:

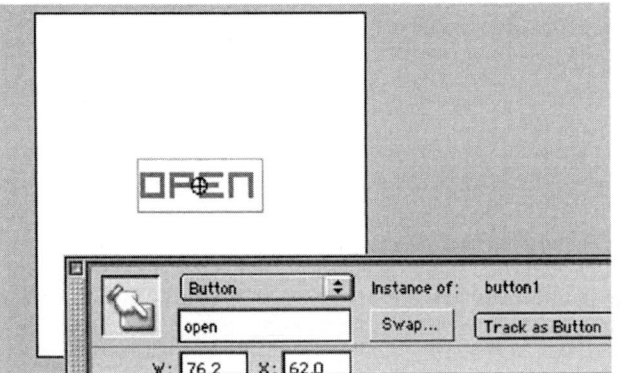

Then I've created a new layer and called it `actions`. In the first frame, I've typed the following code into the Actions panel:

```
open.onRelease = function() {
   getURL("javascript: openwin()");
};
```

This defines a function for the `onRelease` event handler attached to the `open` instance of our button – so the buttons triggers a `getURL` action. I just add my `getURL` action inside the function in order to call my JavaScript function, `openwin`.

You can now embed your file in the index.html page. The easiest way to do this is to publish your FLA so that an HTML file is generated by Flash, and then open the open.html file in a text editor (this is why I usually name my FLA and my HTML file differently - otherwise I'd overwrite the original HTML file when I published my FLA). So, I just need to select everything between the body tags in open.html and copy and paste it between the body tags of the index.html document (making sure to remove the old body tag containing the onload event handler from the testing stage). It is also worth copying over the body tag itself, as this will contain the HTML specifying the background color of the document to match your FLA. Finally, remember to save this updated HTML file.

Now let's test index.html again with our FLA embedded in the page. The window will open when you press the button.

Launching a full-screen window

Launching a full-screen window is like opening a big pop-up! The SWF file that I embed in this window is not necessarily a full-screen size - especially if I'm looking to minimize the file size, but the use of the full-screen window serves to enhance my movie and immerse the user in my project.

The script comes from www.loopmanifesto.ca/squaremeter, a project I did using a full-screen window. To achieve our purpose I use the same process that I use to launch a normal pop-up window, although of course the JavaScript function will be different.

Once again, we need three files for this experiment:

- index.html will be our first window, the one that contains the SWF to launch the window and also the JavaScript function that is called upon by the SWF.

- squaremeter.swf is the Flash movie embedded in index.html. This is the file that will call the full-screen launching function.

- fullscreen.html is the page that will be opened in the pop-up window.

8

The function that will be responsible for the launching of the full-screen window is called `fullsizewin`. This function works exactly like the `openwin` function that we saw in the previous example, and it needs the same kind of information (the URL to pop up, the name of the window, and the features you want to pass to your window). The difference here is that we will add a special piece of code that will automatically calculate the resolution of the user's screen.

Let's have a look at the JavaScript in my `index.html` document:

```
<script language="JavaScript">
function fullsizewin() {
  if (window.screen) {
    w = window.screen.availWidth;
    h = window.screen.availHeight;
  }
window.open('fullscreen.html','fullwin','width='+w+',height='
➡ +h+',top=0,left=0');
}
</script>
```

The variables `w` and `h` represent the values that we will give to the width and height of the window; `availwidth` and `availHeight` return the amount of horizontal and vertical space on the screen, in pixels, available to the windows.

We use the `window.open` method as we did for the `openwin` function earlier, where `fullscreen.html` is the file that will be opened in the full-screen window and `fullwin` is the name of this window. The new window's width and height parameters are defined using the variables `w` and `h`, so the window size will adapt to the user's screen resolution. The window will appear at the extreme top left of the screen (0,0).

Let's test this function as we did before. Here is the code of index.html in full:

```
<html>
<head>
<script language="JavaScript">

function fullsizewin() {
  if (window.screen) {
    w = window.screen.availWidth;
    h = window.screen.availHeight;
  }

window.open('fullscreen.html','fullwin','width='+w+',height='
➡ +h+', top=0,left=0');
}
</script>
</head>
<body onload=fullsizewin()>
</body>
</html>
```

Now we need another file, `fullscreen.html` - we'll put some more content in it later, but for now, it just needs to be a basic file to test:

```
<html>
<head>
<title>
fullwin
</title>
</head>
<body>
</body>
</html>
```

If you open `index.html` in a web browser, you'll see the full-screen window launch. OK, now we can bring in the Flash stuff!

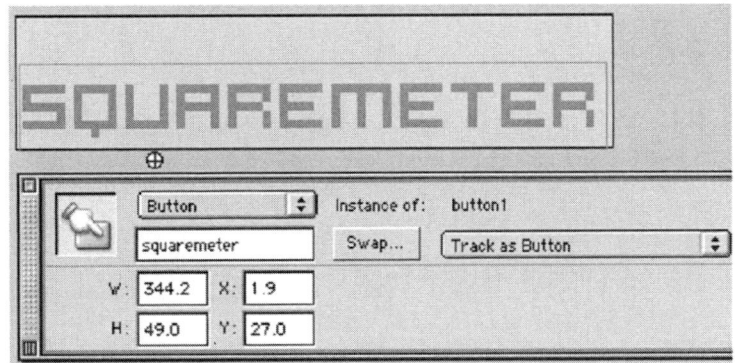

In `index.html` we will insert a Flash movie containing a `getURL` action attached to a button. This will call the `fullsizewin` function in `index.html`. This movie is very simple again, as it's only one button representing the name of the project. With the Property inspector, I named the instance of my button `squaremeter`. In the first frame of my timeline, I inserted the following ActionScript:

```
squaremeter.onRelease = function() {
    getURL("javascript: fullsizewin()");
};
```

I just added my `getURL` action inside the function in order to call my JavaScript function, `fullsizewin`. We can now embed this file into `index.html`. As before, the easiest way to do this is to publish your Flash file, open the HTML file that is generated, and copy everything between the body tags into `index.html`. Make sure that your SWF is published into the same folder that `index.html` is saved in. Even easier, you can open up `squaremeter.fla` from this chapter's download files and take a look at the code.

Now, if you open `index.html` in a web browser, the Flash file will be displayed. When you click on the button, `fullscreen.html` will open and completely fill the available space on your screen. This is a nice and simple technique to focus the attention on a particular web page.

8

Changing the background color of an HTML document

The next step in the experiment is to insert a file into fullscreen.html, and add a JavaScript function into the head of the document that will be called by this embedded SWF. This new file, which I've called menu.swf, is 740 by 325 pixels, and I placed it at the bottom right of the user's screen, using HTML table formatting. There are four items in my SWF file that randomly fade in and out. Open fullscreen.html from the download files, and click the buttons to see the effect we are going to create.

Now as I said, the Flash file in my window is not full-screen size, but the user will think it is. How did I do that? The answer is very simple. When the user presses the button in my Flash movie, the background color of my movie will change, as will the background of my HTML. Soon we'll see how I created simple Flash buttons that can change the background color of the HTML in which my Flash movie is embedded.

First, let's take a look at the JavaScript function that is called from the Flash movie to change the background color of the HTML document. As always, this has been inserted into the head of the fullscreen.html document:

```
<head>
<script language="JavaScript">
function changeBgColor (newBgColor) {
  if (window.document && window.document.bgColor) {
    document.bgColor = newBgColor;
  }
}
</script>
</head>
```

This function needs one argument, newbgcolor, in order to work. This argument will be passed in from the ActionScript, and will tell JavaScript which color we want our HTML document to become.

When we call this function using ActionScript, it is important to know the hexadecimal definition of the color we want to give to the browser window. RR, GG, and BB each consist of two hexadecimal digits specifying the offset of each color component. This hex value will be the argument (newbgcolor) to pass with our function, so for example:

- #000066 is the hex value for blue, so to change the background color to blue we call the function like this:

  changeBgColor('#000066')

- #FFFFFF is the hex value for white, so to change the background color to white we call the function like this:

  changeBgColor('#FFFFFF')

Now let's have a look at menu.fla, which will be inserted into the HTML document. It contains four buttons - when the user presses one of them the background color of the web page will change to the given value. Each of the buttons uses the same techniques, the only difference being the hex values.

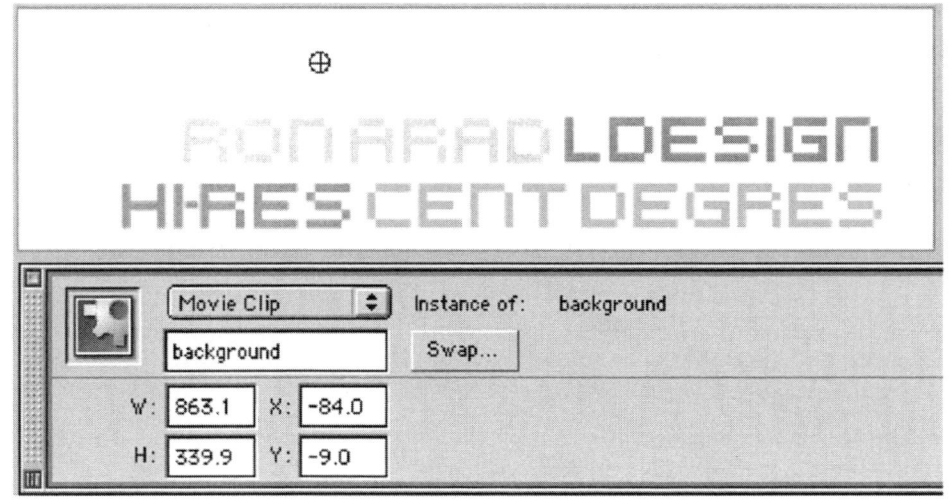

When the user clicks on the button, both the background color of the HTML and the color of the Flash movie are changed.

The background color of the Flash movie is changed by creating a movie clip, and then changing its color using ActionScript attached to a button. I created a large white rectangle to cover the stage, with no stroke, and converted it to a movie clip symbol, giving it an instance name of background:

Let's see how I created my buttons in Flash. Each of them has a getURL action attached that will call the changeBgColor(newBgColor) function in fullscreen.html. I gave a different name to each instance of my four buttons. As the code is basically the same for all four buttons, we'll just examine the HI-RES button, which I gave an instance name of hi.

8

In the first frame in my timeline, I inserted this code:

```
hi.onRelease = function() {
    couleur = "ECE8FF";
    hexCouleur = "0x"+couleur;
    getURL("javascript: changeBgColor('#"+couleur+"')");
    new Color(_root.background).setRGB(hexCouleur);
};
```

First I assign the `onRelease` event handler to the object `hi`. The variable `couleur` represents the color that I want to assign to my files. I just change the value to the color I want - here I give the value `ECE8FF` to `couleur` (this is the hex value for light purple). The second variable, `hexCouleur`, has the value `0x+couleur`. We need to add `0x` as this tells the ActionScript compiler that the number is a hexadecimal value.

Next up, `changeBgColor(newBgColor)` is called. To make sure JavaScript understands that the argument we use is a hexadecimal value, we need to put # in front of the variable `couleur`. This line will pass the value of `newBGColor` into the JavaScript function when it calls it.

The last line of code dynamically sets the RGB color value of the movie clip instance `background` using the `hexCouleur` variable.

For the other three buttons, we just have to change the value of the `couleur` variable. For completeness, here's the full ActionScript from `menu.fla`:

```
ron.onRelease = function() {
    couleur = "FFC40E";
    getURL("javascript: changeBgColor('#"+couleur+"')");
    hexCouleur = "0x"+couleur;
    new Color(_root.background).setRGB(hexCouleur);
};
ldesign.onRelease = function() {
    couleur = "050545";
    hexCouleur = "0x"+couleur;
    getURL("javascript: changeBgColor('#"+couleur+"')");
    new Color(_root.background).setRGB(hexCouleur);
};
hi.onRelease = function() {
    couleur = "ECE8FF";
    hexCouleur = "0x"+couleur;
    getURL("javascript: changeBgColor('#"+couleur+"')");
    new Color(_root.background).setRGB(hexCouleur);
};
cent.onRelease = function() {
    couleur = "8EAA00";
    hexCouleur = "0x"+couleur;
```

```
    getURL("javascript: changeBgColor('#"+couleur+"')");
    new Color(_root.background).setRGB(hexCouleur);
};
stop();
```

Test the code by opening up `index.html` in your browser, and clicking through each button - pretty neat, and the total file size is minimized because we're utilizing JavaScript functions as well as using ActionScript.

Opening multiple windows

Now let's look at opening more than one window. This time, when the user clicks on a certain link in my Flash movie, two things will happen – the background color of my HTML page changes, and then two pop-up windows are launched. At first sight, my Flash looks relatively boring, but when the user starts to play, the interface takes form and the fun starts.

We already know how to open one window, so opening two shouldn't be too complicated. There's just the small step of getting the JavaScript to perform two actions at the same time.

In addition to `fullscreen.html` and the Flash movie, `menu.swf`, contained in this web page, we will have to create two more files that will go in the two new windows we will open. The JavaScript code inserted in `fullscreen.html` needs to be updated, and we will add two new functions, `hires` and `pop_hires`.

First, open up `fullscreen.html` from the `multiple_windows` folder of this chapter's code files, and take a look at the `hires` function - this will call the `changeBgColor` and `pop_hiRes` functions:

```
function hiRes(){
    changeBgColor ('#ECE8FF')
    setTimeout('pop_hiRes()',1000)
}
```

This function will be called from our Flash movie. It passes the hex value that I want to assign to my HTML document into the `changeBgColor` function, and calls it. It then calls the `setTimeout` function, which will call the `pop_hiRes` function after 1000 milliseconds.

The `setTimeout` function works like this:

```
setTimeout(the function you want to call, the milliseconds
to wait)
```

I use this because JavaScript has trouble dealing with two functions at the same time, so I call the first function, wait one second, and then call the second one.

8

Now let's look at the pop-hiRes function, which will launch our two pop-up windows at the same time:

```
function pop_hiRes(){
    features = 'menubar=0, toolbar=0, location=0,
    ➥ directories=0, status=0, scrollbars=0, resizable=0,
    ➥ width=400, height=250'
    win_1 = window.open ('pop_hr.html','win_1',features)
    win_2 = window.open ('pop_hr_movie.html','win_2',features)
}
```

To open multiple windows I use the same function that we used before – I repeat the window.open function to correspond to the number of windows I want to pop up. We shouldn't forget to change the URL to access the file we want to put in each of our windows, and to use a different string for each window's name.

As I want the windows to be the same size, with the same attributes, I've used the same variable, features, to hold the attributes for each of our windows. However, if you wanted them to be different sizes, for example, you could easily create a new variable, features2, and pass it into the window.open function for win_2.

We also have to go back in Flash to update the ActionScript attached to the hi button that's contained in the first frame of the timeline. Open up the amended version of menu.fla, found in the multiple_windows\fla folder - the change is highlighted below:

```
hi.onRelease = function() {
    couleur = "ECE8FF";
    hexCouleur = "0x"+couleur;
    getURL("JavaScript:hiRes()");
    new Color(_root.background).setRGB(hexCouleur);
};
```

We only have to change the name of the function called by the getURL action. The Hi-Res button no longer calls the changeBgColor(bgColor) function directly, but rather the hiRes function, which will in turn call changeBgColor(bgColor).

Now we need to create the new pages, pop_hr.html and pop_hr_movie.html. Although they are identical in size, we don't want them to appear on top of each other, so we're going to use a shift function to reposition them on the screen.

First, here is the code for `pop_hr.html`:

```
<HTML>
<HEAD>
<TITLE>
Hi-Res
</TITLE>
<script language="JavaScript">
function shift() {
  self.moveTo(65,150)
}
</script>
</head>
<BODY onload=shift()>
</BODY>
</HTML>
```

The `shift` function uses the `self.moveTo` method to move the window to where we want it to be on the screen. We pass it the `x` and `y` pixel positions relative to the top left corner.

The code for `pop_hr_movie.html` works in exactly the same way:

```
<HTML>
<HEAD>
   <TITLE>Hi-Res</TITLE>
   <script language="JavaScript">
function shift() {
  self.moveTo(477,150)
}
</script>
</head>
<BODY onload=shift()>
</BODY>
</HTML>
```

The only difference is that the values passed to the `self.moveTo` method are different, so that the windows will move to positions next to each other on the screen.

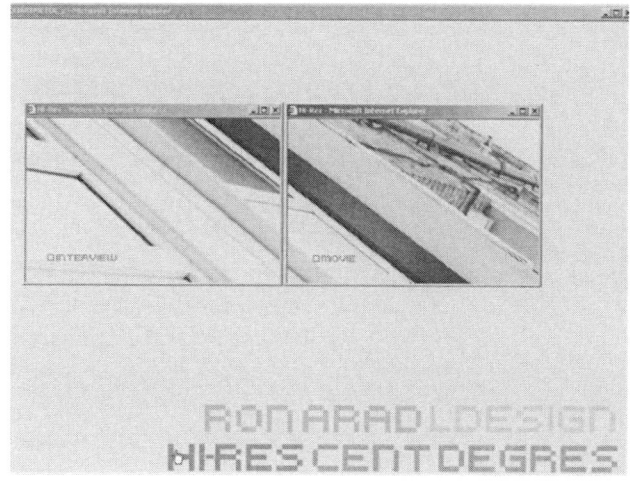

Finally, I've embedded a couple of Flash movies into these windows: `hires1.swf` and `hires2.swf`. Now, when you press the HI-RES button on the screen, the two windows will launch and move next to each other. Note that you may have to fiddle with the pixel values to get them where you want them, and that this may vary across platforms and screen resolutions.

8

Turning a window into a remote control

Creating a full site with several files linked to each other could be an excellent idea if you don't want to use huge Flash files. A trick that I often use is to create an interface composed of several windows. One of them is my menu window and completely controls all the others. This window works like a remote control and can change the content, the position, and the size of the other windows.

This experiment, and the next, were devised for my website www.3weeksinApril.com. This project is based around the concept of three weeks in the life of Catherine, a young, active woman whose mood changes all the time. By browsing through this website you will discover chosen moments of her life within a period of three weeks. Her everyday life is labeled and divided into a multitude of clips listed by themes. As the user explores the different categories, her life is revealed, the narrative develops and relations are created among dissimilar moments.

I conceived the interface of the *3 weeks in April* site with multiple windows in order to represent the many facets of my character's personality. Each window represents a different angle, another way to represent the same action.

For this experiment, all the interactions will take place in the menu window. The content will be displayed in the other pop-ups. In the following examples, many windows will be launched and I will use several files. Pay attention, otherwise you'll be completely lost! By the end of this experiment we will have a total of ten HTML files, and each of these will also contain a Flash movie. But don't worry, most of them will be almost identical, so it will be possible to cut and paste the coding and just change a few vital elements. OK, let's look at how I constructed this interface.

As always, we will have an `index.html` page that will open the first pop-up, which will become our menu window. From this window, four others will be launched. The opening of our menu window is very easy, as we will use the same function that we saw in the previous example. Let's start by looking at the JavaScript in `index.html` (this is found within the `window_remote` folder):

```
<script language="JavaScript">
function openwin() {
    properties = 'menubar=0, toolbar=0, location=0,
    ➥ directories=0,status=0, scrollbars=no, resizable=0,
    ➥ width=180, height=175, top=90, left=730'
    menu = window.open ('menu.html', 'menu', properties)
}
</script>
```

The size of my menu window is 180 x 175 pixels - it's important to note the size of the window when creating the Flash movie that goes in it. This pop-up menu will be our main item, where all the communications will converge.

In `index.html`, I embedded the Flash movie `3weeks.swf`. What is new in this example is that the `openwin` function won't actually be called from the SWF. Instead, it will be called directly from the HTML with the `onload` event handler in the body section of my HTML. Here's how I call the `openwin` function with the `onload` event handler:

```
<body onload=openwin>
```

As soon as our first page loads, the document `menu.html` will pop up. This file, and the JavaScript inserted in it, is essential as it is used to control all the other windows that I will launch. For this website, I decided to open four windows that will display the content. Any interactions will take place in the menu window.

Before thinking about how we will control our four windows, we should start by opening them. The first JavaScript function inserted in `menu.html` is the `popwin` function:

```
function popwin() {
    features = 'menubar=0,toolbar=0,location=0,directories=0,
    ➡ status=0,scrollbars=no, resizable=0,width=310,height=210'
    win_1 = window.open('intro_1.html','win_1',features)
    win_2 = window.open('intro_2.html','win_2',features)
    win_3 = window.open('intro_3.html','win_3',features)
    win_4 = window.open('intro_4.html','win_4',features)
    self.focus()
}
```

As I want to open four pop-ups, I repeat the `window.open` method four times. `intro_1.html`, `intro_2.html`, `intro_3.html`, and `intro_4.html` will be the four documents to be launched and they will all have the same attributes, stored in the variable `features`. I use `self.focus` so that our menu window remains active even after the others have opened. If we didn't do this, the user would have to click on the menu first to make it active, and then a second time to select an option.

To launch this function I again used the `onload` event handler in the body section of `menu.html` rather than in the Flash movie (be patient...Flash will soon be involved!):

```
<body onload=popwin() >
```

Now I needed to create the four files that go inside the pop-up windows. Once again, I didn't want my four windows to pop up at the same place on the user's screen, so each HTML document that goes in the pop-ups has a script that will automatically move the windows to the given position. The four windows will launch in the left corner of the screen and move when the pages load, and we will achieve this, as we saw before, by using the `shift` function.

8

When placing the content in the HTML file, I simply insert this generic script:

```
<script language="JavaScript">
function shift() {
self.moveTo(x,y)
}
</script>
```

The x and y pixel positions of the top left corners need to be as follows:

```
intro_1.html — 257, 438
intro_2.html — 571, 378
intro_3.html — 96, 239
intro_4.html — 413, 277
```

I then use the `onload` event handler to call my function:

```
<body onload=shift()>
```

As soon as the page is loaded, the window moves to the position given.

Next, in each of the windows I embedded a Flash movie. Each showed a piece of a picture, and the windows were then arranged so that the picture fitted together like a jigsaw, to give the appearance of viewing a single design. Have a look at my `intro.html` files, which embed the Flash movies `intro1.swf`, `intro2.swf`, `intro3.swf`, and `intro4.swf`. There's also a Flash movie, `menu.swf`, embedded in the `menu.html` file. So to recap, we now have six HTML documents:

- A basic browser window (`index.html`) that will launch the menu.html pop-up.

- The menu window (`menu.html`), that is responsible for the launching of my four content windows.

- Four HTML documents that go into my pop-up windows (`intro_1.html`, `intro_2.html`, `intro_3.html`, `intro_4.html`).

When we are dealing with an interface composed of several windows, it is important to understand how the communication takes place between them.

To perform actions on windows we have to respect a certain hierarchy. A group of windows is like a family. The parent window, the opener, is the one that has the power over the child windows. It is easier to open a window than to close it. If you deal with multiple windows, it is important to manage them properly. When you open a window, you always should plan how you will close it! A lot of people find pop-ups annoying, as they can present usability problems, so we want our interface to be able to sidestep these gripes by being well-designed and usable.

For example, if the window named win1 opens win2 and win3, only win1 will have the power to close them automatically or to send functions to the other windows, so this should be kept in mind when you are designing your interface.

So now that the interface is constructed, let's look more closely at the interactions that take place between the menu window and the pop-up windows. I have only constructed the files for the SHOW button here – but all the options could be constructed in exactly the same way.

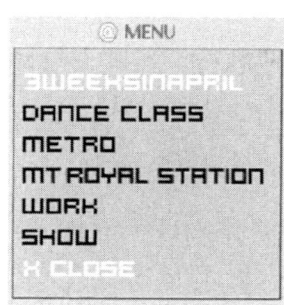

In my menu, I have five different possible choices. Depending which themes the user selects, the content and the position of the window will change. As we saw before, I use my content windows to display a picture. Each pop-up lays out a detail of a larger photo, and each window is positioned on the screen so that the details in every pop-up fit together, making it appear to be a continuous image.

I created four files, one for each window. Each file contains a Flash movie, which looks like it reveals part of a larger image. These are called show_1.html, show_2.html, show_3.html and show_4.html. Each of these has a Flash file embedded in it – these files can be found in the download files, called show1.swf, show2.swf, show3.swf and show4.swf.

When the user selects an item in my menu, the content of every window changes and reveals another picture. Let's have a look at the script inserted in my menu.html window that permits this action:

```
function show() {
    win_1.location = 'show_1.html'
    win_2.location = 'show_2.html'
    win_3.location = 'show_3.html'
    win_4.location = 'show_4.html'
}
```

8

This function will be launched when the user clicks on the SHOW option in the menu. Here, win_1, win_2, win_3, and win_4 correspond to the names I gave my windows when I opened them earlier. For each of these, I set the location, or URL, of the new file to be loaded. So when the option is clicked, the contents of each of the pop-ups will be updated.

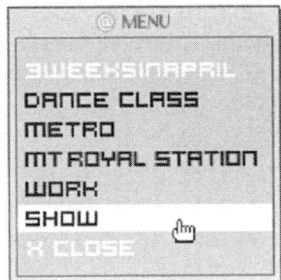

I was very careful when I named my files - because of the number of the files involved in this experiment, I used the same process for every file that went in a pop-up window. All the files in the same category have the same ending, 1 to 4. When the new pages load, each window will change position on the desktop. Each of these newly loaded files also contains the JavaScript function shift that we saw earlier:

```
<script language="JavaScript">
  function shift() {
  self.moveTo(x, y)
}
</script>
```

This is then called from an `onload` event handler within the `body` tag - `onload=shift()`. The x and y values for each of these show files are as follows:

    show_1.html – 140, 315
    show_2.html – 461, 315
    show_3.html – 461, 95
    show_4.html – 140, 95

It's now time to open Flash to see how I called the JavaScript function from my SWF. I named the instance of my button `show` and I called the JavaScript function `show` via the `onRelease` event handler. Here is the script attached to this button in the first frame of the timeline of `menu.fla`:

```
show.onRelease = function() {
    getURL("javascript: show()");
};
```

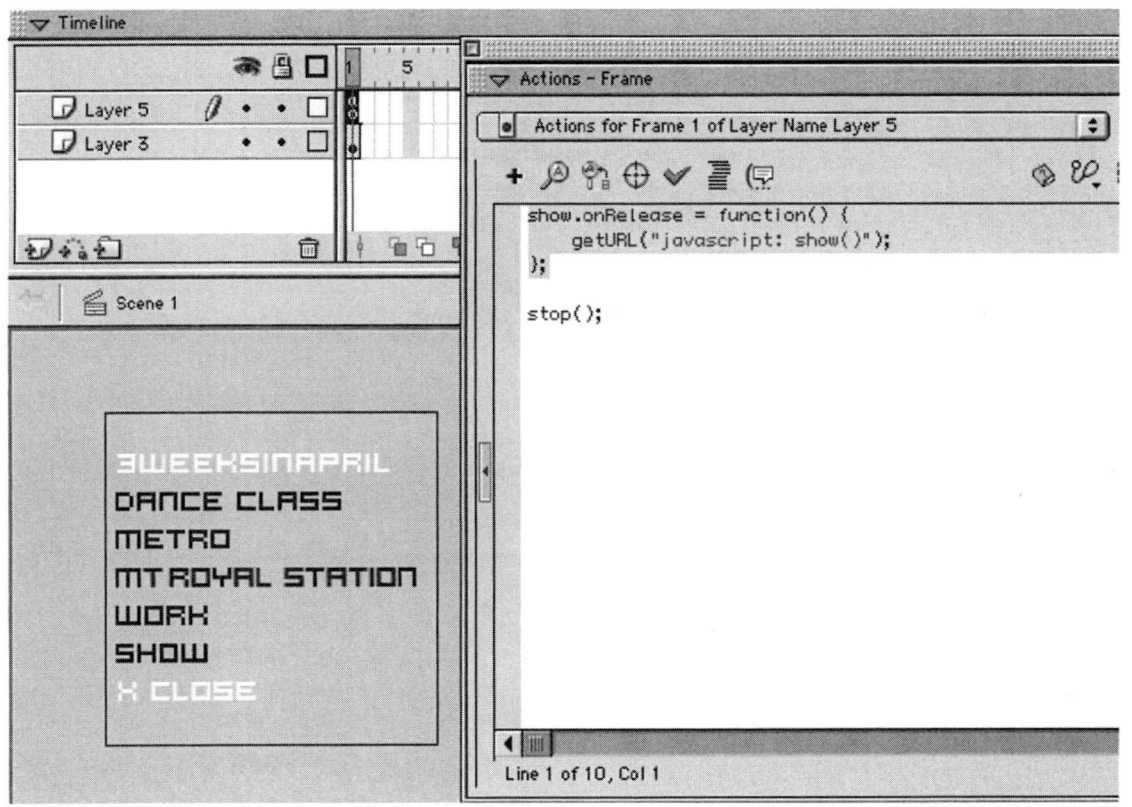

If you're good at math, you've probably already realized that if I have five different items in my menu, and each one changes the content of four windows, that means for this small project I used 20 HTML files! That's a lot of files, but it permits me to create a highly interactive website without huge Flash files. The menu window is now your most important window, the centre of our communication.

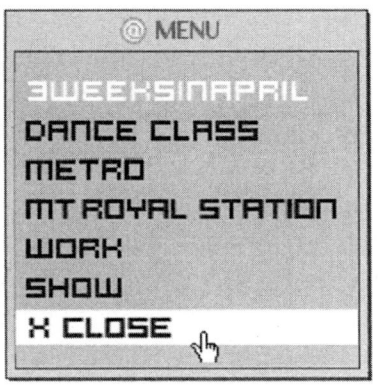

Before we finish, it's very important to remember to place a CLOSE option in the menu. Seeing so many windows open could be worrying for the users if they don't know how to get rid of them. I inserted a CLOSE button in order to let the users know that they could close all the windows without having to do it manually.

If we go back again to the JavaScript inserted in menu.html, notice this last function, shut, that will close all the windows:

```
function shut() {
    win_1.close()
    win_2.close()
    win_3.close()
    win_4.close()
    self.close()
}
```

This function will be called when the user presses the CLOSE button on the Flash movie embedded in menu.html. After having named the instance of my button closewin, I added this code in the first frame of my timeline:

```
closewin.onRelease = function() {
    getURL("javascript: shut()");
};
```

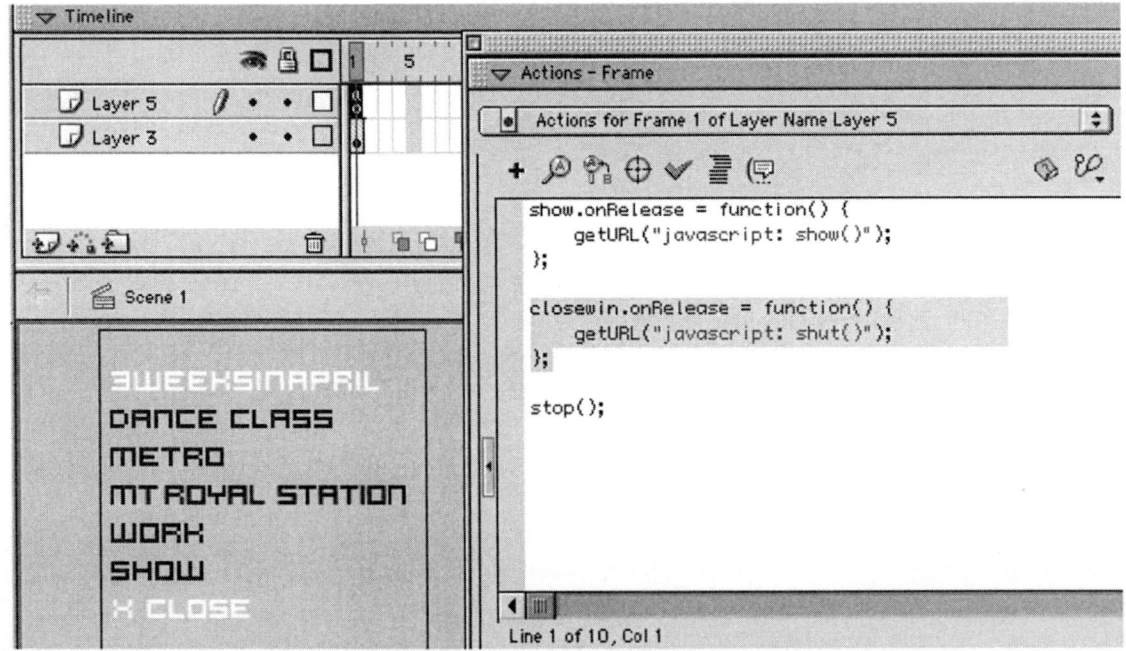

Now all the windows will close at the same time when the user clicks the CLOSE button.

Controlling Flash with JavaScript

As well as sending data from a Flash movie to an HTML page, you can also do the reverse - it's a two-way communication.

Browser scripting is not a feature on all browsers. In order to communicate with the Flash player the browser must have built in hooks that the Flash player can *listen* to. This is especially a problem for Internet Explorer on the Macintosh, so as always, be aware of your audience and provide recommendations for optimal usage on your front page. To achieve this communication we have to be careful. There are several things to keep in mind, and often, if you forget one seemingly minor detail, nothing will work! Let's take a look at an example.

Synchronizing one movie in several windows

In the following exercise, I'll describe another part of the *3 weeks in April* site where I wanted to show the user a moment in the life of Catherine, the site's character, where she is late. I divided the action between three windows. Each of them contains a detail of a still image. The windows will pop up randomly on the user's screen, with one containing a button. When this button is clicked, the pop-ups are aligned, and a play? button appears. On clicking the play? button, a video loads and the user sees the action. Here again, each window contains a part of the video so when the windows are lined up, we see Catherine running from one window to another.

Until now, I've only played with minimal-size files. However, in this exercise I used small videos that I embed in my Flash movies. The videos are very short, about five seconds, and I set the frame rate to ten frames per second, so their sizes work out at around 40-50 kB. OK, it's not quite byte-size, but everyone wants to use video these days, and this is a great way of incorporating the moving image into your work without crippling it with bandwidth issues. You can use a simple movie clip and divide your animations into different files embedded in several windows, and you'll achieve the same results. Now, let's see how the files were put together!

This experiment is similar to the previous example, where my MENU window acted as a remote control for the other windows. However, now each window will communicate and my Flash movies will be synchronized, even if they are in different browser windows.

To create this interface I used simple JavaScript functions. However, there are several steps to follow, in order to make Flash and JavaScript communicate. In total, we will work with four HTML documents, each containing a Flash movie:

- `index.html` – the main page that will launch our first window

- `lateness0.html` – the most important pop-up, which will launch the other two

- `lateness1.html` and `lateness2.html`

8

To begin, I follow the same process as used previously in the remote control exercise. My first HTML document, index.html, has the Flash movie 3weeks.swf embedded in it, which you can find in the download files. It will launch the first pop-up with the openwin function using the onload=openwin() event handler in the body section of the HTML code:

```
<head>
<script language="JavaScript">
function openwin() {
    features = 'menubar=0,toolbar=0,location=0,directories=0,
    ➥ status=0,scrollbars=0, resizable=0,width=100,height=160,
    ➥ left=50,top=210'
    late0 = window.open('lateness0.html','late0',features)
}
</script>
</head>
```

This script will activate my first pop-up window that will become the centre of all communications. This openwin function launches the document lateness0.html, in a pop-up window 100 x 160 pixels in size. This window will become the controller of my other windows.

3 weeks in April

As you can see from the image, it also has a Flash movie embedded in it, but we'll get on to that in a minute. First, let's look at how this window controls the opening of the others, because, as you will have seen if you've taken a peek at the completed project from the download files, this pop-up won't stay alone on the desktop for very long. From lateness0.html, two others will appear in random places on the user's screen, and when the windows are aligned by hitting the pink button, the movie in each pop-up can start playing.

The first JavaScript function inserted in lateness0.html opens two 'buddy' windows:

```
function puzzle(){
    features = 'menubar=0,toolbar=0,location=0,
    ➥ directories=0,status=0,scrollbars=0, resizable=0,
    ➥ width=100,height=160'
    late1 = window.open('lateness1.html', 'late1', features)
    late2 = window.open('lateness2.html', 'late2', features)
    self.focus()
}
```

As we need to open two windows, we use the window.open method twice, and as they are the same size and have the same attributes, we only need a single features variable to hold the attributes. I've then used self.focus to ensure that lateness0.html will be my active window and remain in front of the other windows. To launch this function, I chose to use the onload = puzzle() event handler within the <body> tag.

As you can see here, the features of my three windows are exactly the same – the sizes are still 100 x 160 pixels. So if I have three windows that have exactly the same features, why haven't I opened them all at the same time with my index.html window? The first window that opens is the one that controls the others. My first pop-up, lateness0.html, will be the one that will give the signal to the other windows to start their movie.

To position these two new windows on the user's desktop, I use a special JavaScript function that will place the pop-ups randomly. In lateness1.html and lateness2.html, I inserted the lets_move function, which will decide the window's position:

```
function lets_move() {
    var x = parseInt(Math.random()*400)
    var y = parseInt(Math.random()*400)
    self.moveTo(x,y)
}
```

Here, the x and y variables represent the horizontal and vertical positions of the windows on the desktop. The values of x and y will be chosen randomly, and could be anything from 1 to 400. When the random value is assigned to x and y, the windows move themselves to the given position via the self.moveTo method. Again, I use the onload = lets_move() event handler within the <body> tag to launch the function. So, every time the page loads, a different position will be assigned to the windows.

Now that our three pop-ups are opened, let's talk about the Flash files that they contain. In this exercise, the Flash embedded in my three pop-ups windows will be totally controlled by JavaScript. In order to make this work, we have to follow certain steps. We will need three JavaScript functions to be able to communicate with Flash. For each of these pop-ups - lateness0.html, lateness1.html, lateness2.html - we'll go back into the JavaScript and insert these.

First we need to set a variable to refer to the instance of our Flash movie:

```
var movieName = "myFlash";
```

The variable moviename refers to the instance of our Flash movie. When we embed our movies, we use the embed and object tags, and within these we use the name attribute set to myFlash. Here's the first of our three new functions:

```
function thisMovie(movieName) {
    if (navigator.appName.indexOf ("Microsoft") !=-1) {
        return window[movieName]
    } else {
        return document[movieName]
    }
}
```

Unfortunately, Netscape and Explorer don't refer to Flash movies in the same way - so this function finds out which browser is being used and gives the appropriate syntax for each browser, to ensure that it recognizes the syntax I use to refer to my movie name.

We want to control the Flash movie through JavaScript, but this can only happen once it is fully loaded in the browser, as otherwise it will generate an error message. So we need to make sure that our JavaScript can tell when the movie has loaded:

```
function movieIsLoaded (theMovie) {
   if (typeof(theMovie) != "undefined") {
      return theMovie.PercentLoaded() == 100;
   } else {
      return false;
   }
}
```

In this function, the PercentLoaded command returns the percentage of the Flash Player movie that has streamed into the browser so far. This ensures that the JavaScript will not try to control the movie before it is fully loaded.

Now for the function that will control the playhead of our Flash movie:

```
function go(theFrame) {
   if (movieIsLoaded(thisMovie(movieName))) {
      thisMovie(movieName).GotoFrame(theFrame);
   }
}
```

The argument theFrame refers to the frame I want my movie to play. It is zero-based – that is, theFrame is 0 in the first frame of the movie, 1 for the second frame, and so on. The function activates the frame number specified by theFrame in the current movie. If the data for a requested frame is not yet available, the player goes to the last frame available and stops, causing unexpected results during playback. That's why we use the PercentLoaded method to determine if enough of the movie is available to execute the go function.

The method I use to embed my Flash in my HTML is very important, as there are some unusual parameters we have to set. In total, we have three pop-ups, lateness0.html, lateness1.html, and lateness2.html, and for all of them, we have to follow a special process for embedding the Flash movies: late1.swf, late2.swf and late3.swf.

First, when you're working on your own files, you need to adjust the publish settings before you publish the FLA. Go to File > Publish Settings…, and on the HTML tab under the Playback options, make sure Paused At Start is checked, and Loop is unchecked:

8

271

Then, after you have published, taken the embed information from between the body tags of the resultant HTML file, and then pasted it into your final HTML file, you will need to alter some of the code. Here is how I embedded the Flash in my `lateness0.html` file - notice the subtle changes made to the Flash generated code shown in bold:

```
<object
    classid= "clsid:D27CDB6E-AE6D-11cf-96B8-444553540000"
    width= "100"
    height= "160"
    codebase="http://download.macromedia.com/pub/shockwave
    ➥ /cabs/flash/ swflash.cab"
    id= "myFlash">
        <param name="MOVIE" value="media/late1.swf">
        <param name="PLAY" value="false">
        <param name="LOOP" value="false">
        <param name="QUALITY" value="high">
        <param name="SCALE" value="SHOWALL">
        <embed
        name= "myFlash"
        src= "media/late1.swf"
        width= "100"
        height= "160"
        play= "false"
        loop= "false"
        quality= "high"
        scale= "SHOWALL"
        swliveconnect="true"
        pluginspage="http://www.macromedia.com/go
        ➥ /flashplayer/">
        </embed>
</object>
```

It is crucial to name the Flash movie exactly as we told JavaScript to recognize it earlier. In this example, I called my movie `myFlash` using `id` in the `object` tag and the `name` for the `embed` tag. It is extremely important for cross-browser compatibility that the names be identical for both. The variable `myFlash` in these examples refers to an instance of the Flash movie.

The `swliveconnect="true"` has to be included in the Flash movie's properties - this enables communication between JavaScript and a plug-in in Netscape. It can accept a value of `true` or `false`. But how does this communication help us in the creation of the interface?

We have three pop-ups, therefore three different HTML documents. In every file, we need to correctly insert the SWF and add the script for the communication between JavaScript and Flash - it's worth spending some time examining my HTML files supplied with this section's downloaded code.

Now we need to go back to the first pop-up, `lateness0.html`, and add two more functions necessary for the synchronization of Flash movies. This first function dictates to the other two windows to move to the given position:

```
function on_place(){
    late1.moveTo(274,210)
    late2.moveTo(162,210)
}
```

In the Flash movie embedded in `lateness0.html` there is a pink square button.

When the user clicks on this button, the `on_place` function is called from the ActionScript code on the main timeline of `late1.fla` - this FLA is embedded in the document `lateness0.html`, and it contains three frames. Open up `late1.fla` to have a look.

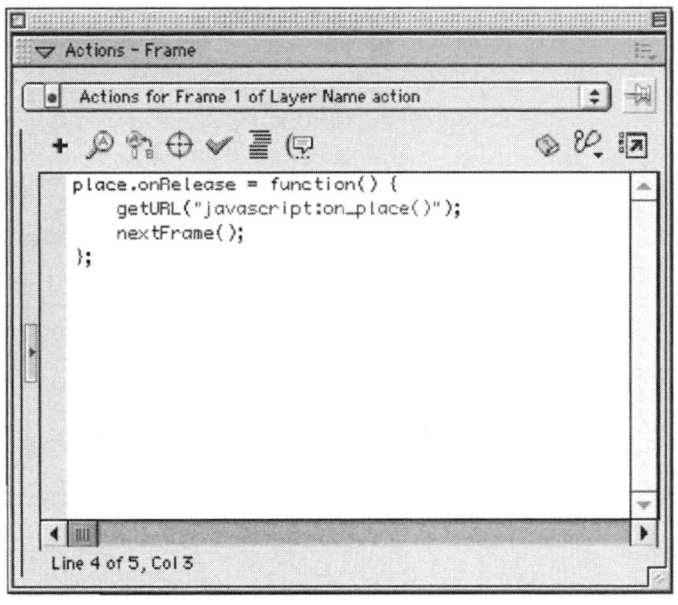

On frame 1, I've placed two symbols – a picture (a small JPG, quality 50%), and a pink square with an instance name of `place` that acts as a button. Also on frame 1 you'll find the relevant code that links this `place` button to the JavaScript function:

```
place.onRelease = function() {
    getURL("javascript:on_place()");
    nextFrame();
};
```

The `on_place` function then causes the two other windows to align next to the first one and form a complete image:

As well as calling the `on_place` function to align the windows, the previous code moves the Flash movie onto the next frame, where the pink square is replaced by a play? button - we'll consider this after looking at the associated JavaScript.

So, the next JavaScript function in `lateness0.html` is the one that will actually play our movie:

```
function play_movie(){
    late1.go(2)
    late2.go(2)
    go(2)
}
```

This calls the `go(theFrame)` function to move the playhead in the Flash movie forward to frame 3 of our SWFs, where the ActionScript imports a movie clip. It gives this instruction to `late1`, `late2`, and itself, `late0`.

Returning to late1.fla, the play_button on frame 2 is the one that starts the synchronization between the movie clips linked to frame 3 of my Flash movies embedded in my three windows:

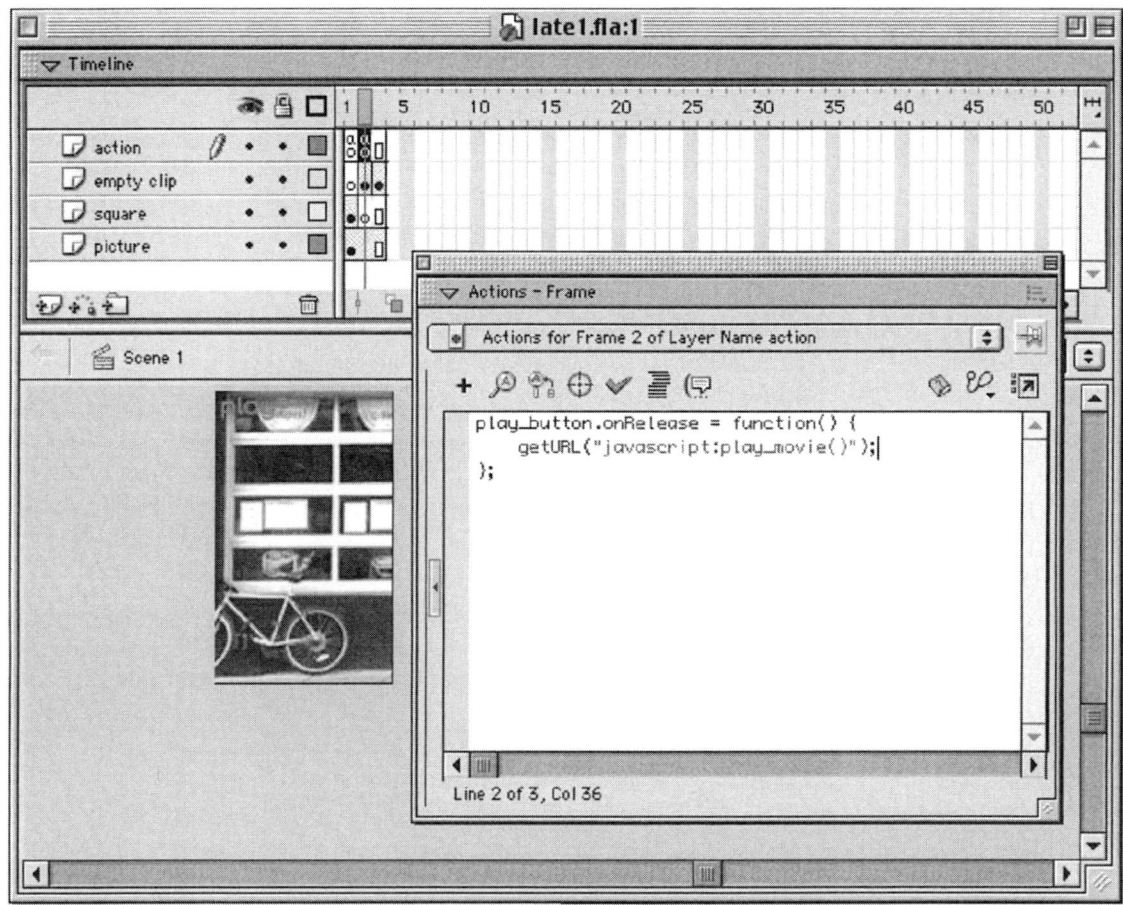

The ActionScript attached to this button will call the play_movie JavaScript function that we've just looked at:

```
play_button.onRelease = function() {
   getURL("javascript:play_movie()");
};
```

8

As we saw, this function calls each window and launches the function go(2), meaning that the playheads of each Flash movie in my three windows will simultaneously go to frame 3. In frame 3, an instance of my picture is still present on the timeline along with an empty movie clip. I gave the movie clip an instance name of vidload, and assigned a simple action to it using the onLoad method:

```
vidload.onLoad = function() {
    loadMovieNum("media/late_zyng1.swf", 1);
};
```

Note that if you are using this technique in your own files, you need to make sure that you copy the movie clips into the same directory that the main FLAs are located, and alter the path to reflect your own directory structure.

As soon as the playhead reaches frame 3, the file late_zyng1.swf is loaded into level one of my movie and will start playing. This file is composed of a movie clip that will loop.

What about the other two windows? The Flash movies embedded in these HTML documents are exactly like the SWF in lateness0.html, but they don't have any buttons - all the interactions take place in my first pop-up. So I just saved late1.fla under two different names, late2.fla and late3.fla, updated the picture, deleted the buttons, and changed the name of the file to be loaded when the empty movie clip on frame 3 loads. Pretty straightforward!

If you've managed to follow all this, you're now worthy of the honorary title of *Pop-up Master*! So I hope this chapter has given you an understanding of how JavaScript, in combination with Flash designs, can help you to create minimal interfaces and produce new kinds of interactivity.

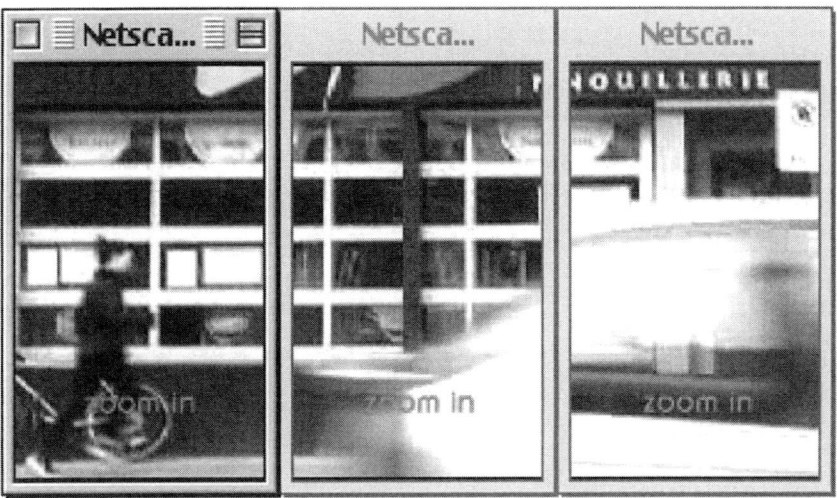

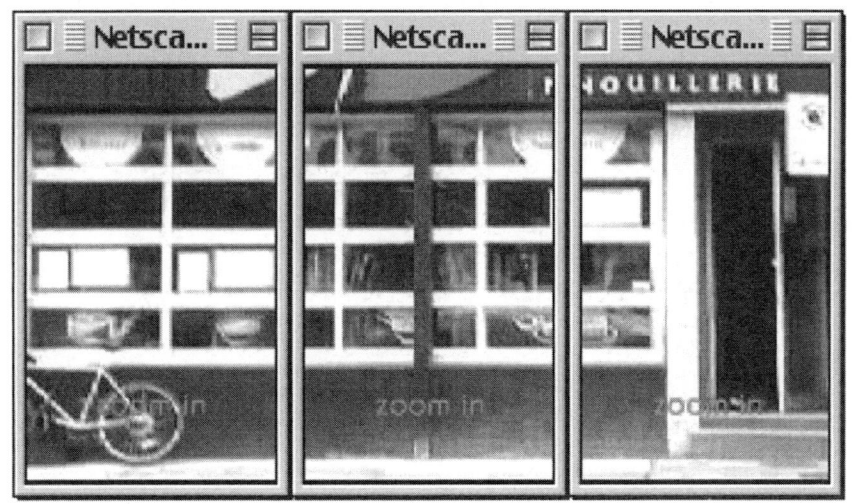

8

9 SEPARATING FORM AND FUNCTION: FLASH AND XML

ROBERT REICH

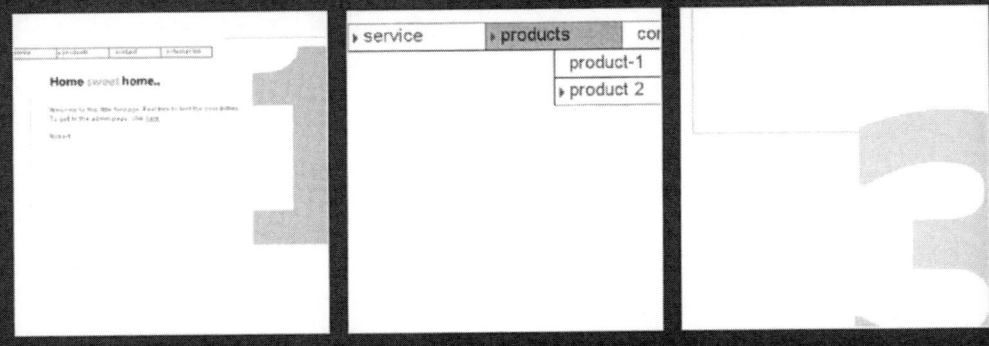

Once upon a time, there was a stressed Flash designer who constantly found himself asking "Am I always inventing the wheel, over and over again?", until one day his fairy godmother took pity on him and replied, "Only if you don't separate form and function, content and design."

This is a fairytale about making the next step in managing your design in Flash MX. This chapter will give you an insight into what a **Content Management System** can be, how it can guard you against hassle, save you time and money, and last but not least, increase the satisfaction of your site's visitors.

The focus here is to provide you with a fully dynamic system that allows maximum functionality with fewest design restrictions. In the end, you will have an easy to manage dynamic navigation system coded in ActionScript, and driven by two XML files – one for the navigation itself, and another for the style and behavior of the whole website.

I use this process because Flash has been able to easily read and manipulate XML since version 5. For those of you unfamiliar with **eXtensible Markup Language**, think of it as a simple text file very much like HTML. The only difference is that you store only data in it – it is a vehicle for *content* rather than *appearance*. Think of an XML file as a database you can build and edit with Notepad, SimpleText, or any other text-editing program!

One of the advantages of XML is that it supports the **object oriented** method of programming. Through its structure, you are able to create and store blocks of data nested inside another 'object' or tag, giving your data logical structure. This is perfect for building a navigational system.

The goal we're aiming towards is to invent a simple system which gives you the ability to alter every piece of text in your website, without the need for your Flash MX authoring environment. So now, when a client says to you "that's great, but can we just change the titles on the buttons, and add an extra section?", you will be able to say "Yes" and do it, just like that. No more painstaking hours of redesigning buttons and adding extra scenes to your movie. Simply make a few quick alterations to the XML file, and your site will rebuild itself for you!

And best of all, the site we create will be very tiny. My actual size for the `navigation.swf` is 3820 bytes. Add 1 KB each for the two XML files and you are still under 6 KB. You'll be hard-pushed to find many sites out there smaller than that.

Object oriented programming

Before we embark on this exercise, it is helpful to have some familiarity with the basics of object oriented programming. If you don't feel you have this, don't be afraid. This chapter is about content management, rather than an in-depth study in OOP. But you should understand what it means when there is a construct like this:

```
MovieClip.prototype.moveTo = function (x,y) {

    this._x = x;
    this._y = y;

}


someMovieClip.moveTo(20,20);
```

This isn't a function as we would usually understand it. The *MovieClip.prototype* makes this **method** (a more accurate name) accessible for all objects that are of the type *MovieClip*. In this case you can attach *moveTo* to nearly all objects where *_x* and *_y* makes sense. So you can assign this method globally without the need to give a path to its original destination. It can be used to move objects throughout your movie.

The next thing to understand is the small but very important word *this*. It's a placeholder. It covers the place for the object or movie clip that the method *moveTo* is assigned to. So the above code is the same as:

```
someMovieClip._x = x;
someMovieClip._y = y;
```

The difference, of course, is that you don't have to keep writing this out again for every new movie clip you want to control.

So in the following sections, keep in mind that you don't jump to or call these functions. You don't go over to these functions, rather you let them come to you. We'll store them neatly in a layer of their own, and when they are needed they get assigned to the object like a virtual copy.

OK, let's begin. Don't be intimidated by what may be new concepts to you. The way through the first part may be a little bit stony, but when you have completed it you will have a much better idea of what this is all about. And when you've finished the second part, I promise you will do the rest with a smile, thinking of all the hard work and headaches you can avoid in the future!

9

Dynamic navigation

Navigation is a crucial issue for web design no matter what tools you use. The navigation is the heart of every website. It controls when, how, and where something will change, and new text or graphics will show up. As this is the case, we're going to begin by inventing a dynamic navigation system creation tool, which only has one aspect that is fixed. If you press a button, something happens. But all the design aspects of that button will be held in a separate file. This XML file, `navigation.xml`, will cover the buttons' labels, colors, the text content, and all the other things that we want to be changeable.

In the second section of this chapter, we'll go on to separate every possible design-relevant object from the content and navigation in a style construct. This will take the form of another XML file, called `style.xml`. Finally, when we have all this working, the last stage will be to create templates, which will display our actual content, controlled by `navigation.xml` and formatted and styled by `style.xml`.

But for now, let's crack on with the first part, designing our engine, which will set up our site.

Navigation

First we need a new blank file, containing two layers. Name the top one functions, and the other one actions. Our finished movie will be four frames long. Insert key frames at frames 1, 3 and 4 of the actions layer, and at frame 1 of the functions layer.

As a general point, all text beginning with // is – as you probably know – a comment. These aren't necessary for the functionality of your code, so you don't need to include them if you don't want to. For this reason, I haven't added comments into the code in this chapter, but the download files are fully commented. And I have always found that adding sensible comments helps a lot if you ever need to review your code later. So if you finish building a new section of your ActionScript, comment it. A month or two on, you'll be very glad that you did, especially if it's a huge project.

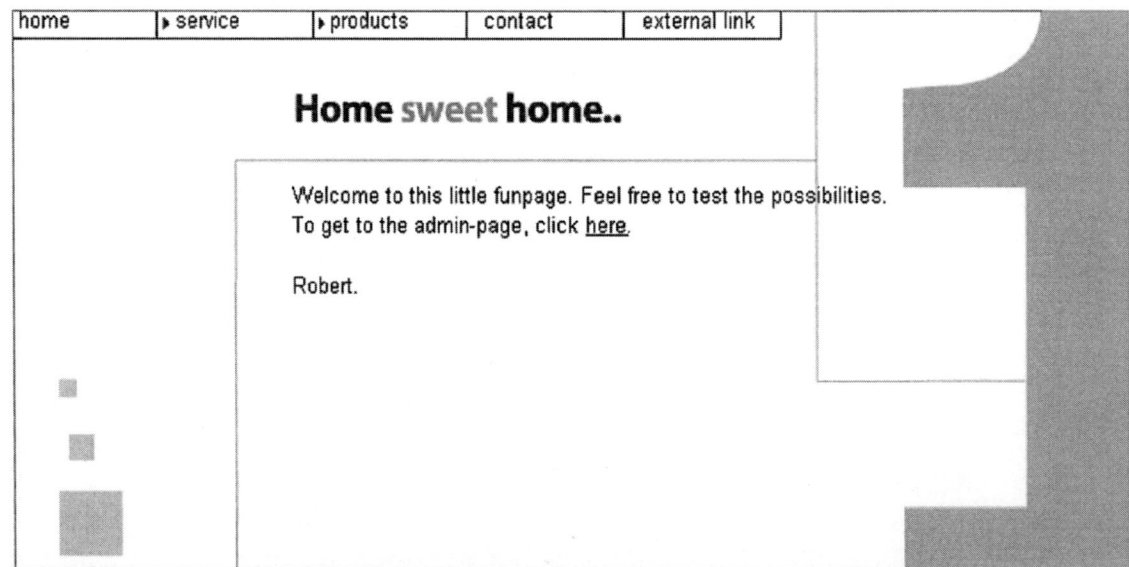

Actions

Begin by placing this ActionScript in the first frame of the actions layer:

```
navi_xml = new XML();
navi_xml.ignoreWhite = true;
navi_xml.load("navigation.xml");
```

This simply loads the XML file that handles the navigation. As an XML file is only a text file, when we write it we use formatting so that we can read it easily, such as blank lines and carriage returns. As we want to make sure that this is ignored, we use ignoreWhite to make sure that all the whitespace created by this formatting is disregarded.

Then place this in the third frame:

```
if (navi_xml.loaded) {

gotoAndPlay(4);
} else {
gotoAndPlay(2);
}
```

This code tells the movie to wait until the XML file is loaded before displaying its contents, to avoid any error messages that might occur if the ActionScript is looking for the XML file before its loaded. Although officially in Flash MX we could have used the onLoad method, there have been some problems associated with it, so I prefer to use a tried and tested method.

Then at frame 4, we simply need to add the initialization code:

```
stop();

this.initMenu(navi_xml);
```

This calls the initMenu function that we will write later, which, surprise surprise, initializes the menu. We use a stop action so that the movie will not loop.

9

Buttons

To place and manage the buttons of the navigation we are going to create with ActionScript, we need a generic button. So create a new layer for this – in my file I called it temp. This layer is temporary, because when we have finished making our button movie, we will delete the instance on the stage and attach it dynamically from the library, using the attachMovie command.

Select the Rectangle tool and draw a box on the screen, in white, with a thin black stroke. Then in the Properties box make the dimensions 80x16 px. These numbers are chosen to fit the distance definitions in the XML files. Now select the box, convert it into a movie clip (F8) and call it menu. Click the Advanced button, check Export for ActionScript and give it a Linkage name of menu as well.

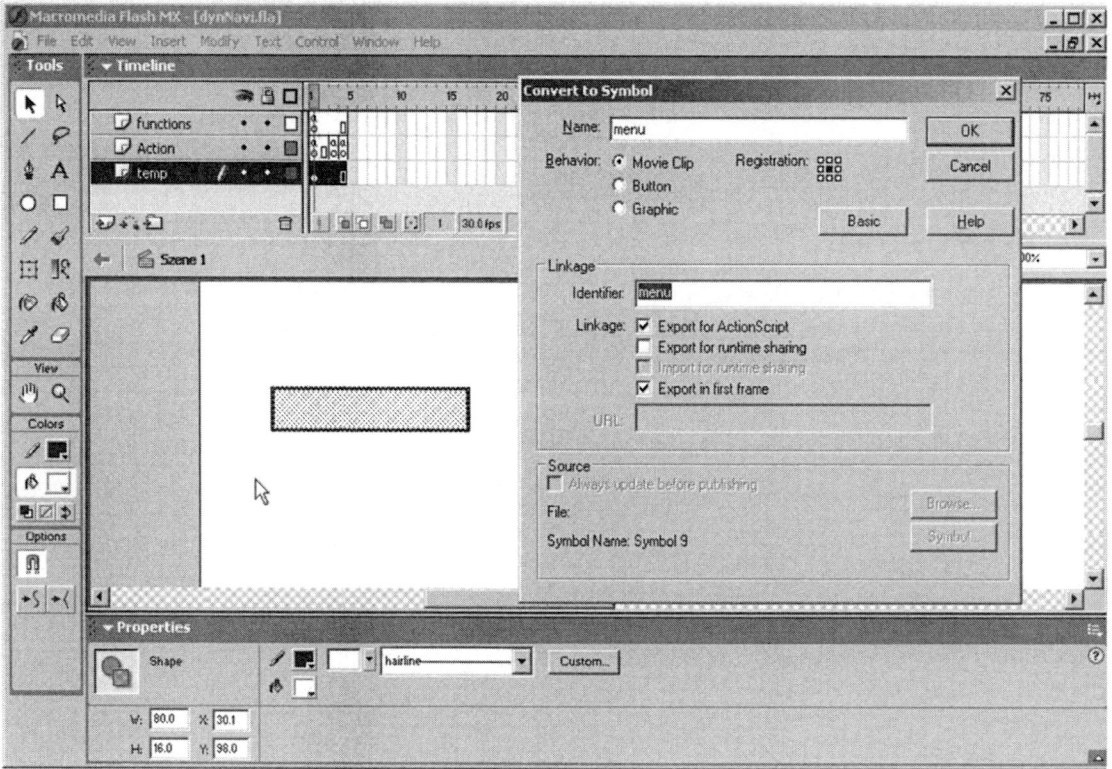

Go into Edit in Place mode, and add two extra layers to our movie clip. The top one should be called text, the second button, and the original one bg.

Place a text box in the text layer, above your box shape. Make the text type dynamic, give it an instance name of textbox, and a variable name title. Make sure that the text box is not selectable as this will interfere with the button that we are going to place under the text layer. Use a system font like Arial or Verdana, and set the text color to black.

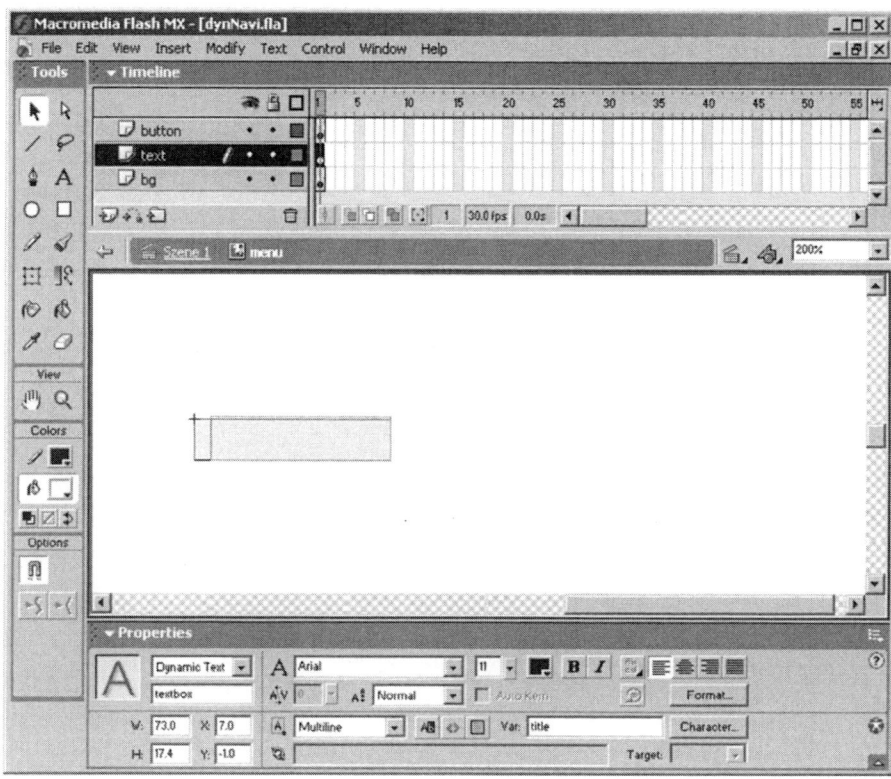

Still inside the menu movie clip, select the rectangle again, copy it with CTRL+ALT+C, place it on the button layer with CTRL+ALT+V, and convert it into a button. Call it button, check Export for ActionScript, and give it a Linkage identifier of button. Also make sure you give it an instance name of button.

Now, just to double check, open your Library, and right-click on the movie clip menu you have created. Check if your linkage is selected and that the movie clip has a Linkage identifier of menu. Also make sure that Export in first frame is checked, to avoid any problems with the script trying to find the movie clip when it hasn't yet loaded.

The last step is to simply delete the instance of menu from the stage.

Now we have constructed the building blocks of our interface, let's move onto the XML.

9

XML – a brief introduction

First, let's have a little introduction to the way XML works.

If you haven't already worked with XML, then I hope you have a little experience with arrays. There are a few small differences, but it helps to look at some arrays as examples to better understand XML.

A simple array could look like this:

```
myArray = new Array ("John", "Anne", "Hamburg", "4711");
```

Inside Flash, if you go to Debug > List Variables in the Preview window, it looks like this:

```
_level0.myArray = [
    0:"John",
    1:"Anne",
    2:"Hamburg",
    3:"4711"
  ]
```

This is a one-dimensional array, and instead of *New Array* you can also write *myArray = []*, which creates a new, empty array. To retrieve these strings, you can simply write *myArray[0]*, which will return *John*, or *myArray[2]* will return *Hamburg*.

But as you probably know, you can also put an array inside another array, to form a **nested array**:

```
myArray = new Array (   "John" , "Anne" , "Hamburg" , "4711"
);
my2ndArray = new Array ( myArray , "Joe" , "Peter" );
```

Inside Flash, this will look like this:

```
_level0.my2ndArray = [
    0:
[
0:"John",
1:"Anne",
2:"Hamburg",
3:"4711"
],
    1:"Joe",
    2:"Peter"
  ]
```

So if you want to get *John* returned from *my2ndArray*, you have to use *my2ndArray[0][0]*. Or *my2ndArray[0][2]* for *Hamburg*.

Now let's switch over to our XML example:

```
<NAVIGATION>
    <MENU title='home' _x='0' _y='0' />
    <MENU title='service' _x='0' _y='20' />
    <MENU title='products' _x='0' _y='40' />
</NAVIGATION>
```

In an abstract way, viewed as an array, this would pretty much look like this:

```
myXML = [
    NAVIGATION:[
        MENU:[ title:"home" ,
_x:"0" ,
_y:"0"
] ,
        MENU:[ title:"service" ,
_x:"0" ,
_y:"20"
],
        MENU:[ title:"products" ,
_x:"0" ,
_y:"40"
]
        ]
]
```

If you get *John* by asking for *my2ndArray[0][0]*, how do you get *home*, for example?

While an array has simply one type of compartment for data, XML has more than one. You can have:

- **Attributes** – *<NodeName Attribute1="value" Attribute2="value" ... ></NodeName>*
- **TextNodes** – *<NodeName>value</NodeName>*, where *value* is usually normal text.

So to get an answer for the initial question, you could ask:

```
myXML.childNodes[0].childNodes[0].Attributes.title
```

9

This will return *home*. One of the great advantages of using attributes is that you can ask explicitly for *title* by name.

But you can also use numbers:

MyXML.childNodes[0].childNodes[0].Attributes[0]

This will also return *home*. And as you can see, this is a lot closer to the array structure we are already familiar with.

XML for our site

```
<NAVIGATION>
    <MENU title='home' _x='0' _y='0' />
    <MENU title='service' _x='0' _y='20' />
    <MENU title='products' _x='0' _y='40' />
</NAVIGATION>
```

What we have here is a simple XML file, which will produce a small vertical navigation interface with three buttons in a column. Remember the text box we created? The variable name was title. So I suppose you can guess what label your buttons will have, hmm?

So, to explain what is going on here, we have a first XML node (every <tag> is a node), called NAVIGATION, which is simply the parent of everything inside these tags. < > ... </>. The first childNode of NAVIGATION is the first MENU with the attributes title='home', _x='0' and _y='0'.

To find our way through this example, here are some pointers:

- NAVIGATION – identified by myXML

- MENU home – identified by:

    myXML.firstChild
    myXML.ChildNodes[0]

- MENU products – identified by:
    myXML.ChildNodes[2]
    myXML.lastChild

myXML.childNodes will give back the complete list of childNodes, so all three tags will be in the list.

If we let myXML point to the first MENU home, with myXML = myXML.firstChild, then myXML.parentNode would point back to NAVIGATION.

It's very common to cycle through an XML structure with a `for` loop. This looks like:

```
for (var i=0; i<myXML.childNodes.length;i++) {

    trace (myXML.childNodes[i]);

}
```

The `childNodes.length` will – referring to our example – return 3, because `NAVIGATION` has three `childNodes`. So it's very simple to use XML. Just like using an array, only with a some slightly different instructions.

Maybe you noticed that the three menus don't have a closing tag. This is because

```
<TAG attribute='anything' />
```

...is the same as ...

```
<TAG attribute='anything'></TAG>.
```

If you don't use `textNodes` like this:

```
<SOMETHING>
<TEXTNODE>hello</TEXTNODE>
</SOMETHING>
```

...and you're only using attributes – as we are going to – you don't need to write the tag name again.

However, always bear in mind that `<This></THIS>` or `<this></tHiS>` aren't allowed. The cases have to match. Because of this, it's a good idea to get into the habit of always using capitals.

Another related hint is that `nodeNames` are – used and examined in Flash – case-sensitive, although attributes are not. So if you want to search an XML file for a `nodeName` like `navigation` or `menu`, it's good to have them all written in the same way.

For example:

```
if (myXML.NodeName == "Menu")
```

...and...

```
if (myXML.NodeName == "MENU")
```

...aren't the same. The first version will not find anything in our `navigation.xml` file!

9

If you like, you can also add an `XML.docTypeDecl` declaration at the top of the file, which should look like:

```
<? xml version="1.0" ?>
```

It's good practice, but Flash doesn't need or use this, so it's your choice. If you might want to send your XML file direct to a browser, you should include it.

Now let's look at the actual XML file we will be using.

Type this into any text editor:

```
<NAVIGATION>
  <MENU title='home' template='temp.swf'
➥ textfile='home.html' _x='0' _y='0'/>
  <MENU title='service' _x='0' _y='20'>
    <MENU title='service 1' _x='90' _y='0'>
      <MENU title='service 1_1' _x='90' _y='0'/>
    </MENU>
    <MENU title='service 2' _x='90' _y='20'/>
  </MENU>
  <MENU title='products' _x='0' _y='40' >
    <MENU title='product 1' _x='90' _y='0' />
    <MENU title='product 2' _x='90' _y='20' />
    <MENU title='product 3' _x='90' _y='40' />
    <MENU title='product 4' _x='90' _y='60' />
  </MENU>
  <MENU title='location' _x='0' _y='60' />
  <MENU title='contact' _x='0' _y='80' />
</NAVIGATION>
```

Don't worry about the `template` and `textfile` attributes at the moment – we will discuss them later. Here we have a basic XML structure that should be fairly self-explanatory when you think back to the simpler example we looked at earlier. A series of nested `nodeNames` and attributes is set up, and the x and y coordinates are added in to place the buttons where we want them to appear on the stage. Our Flash file will call the data from this XML document, and display it on the screen.

Functions

Now I hope you have saved your new Flash file, and your `navigation.xml` document, in the same directory, so we will go back to ActionScript.

The last step in frame 4 on the actions layer was this:

```
stop();

this.initMenu(navi_xml);
```

Now I suppose you want to know what this `initMenu` is all about, hmm? OK, here it goes. This, and all the other functions belonging to the navigation, are placed in the first frame of their own layer called functions.

So let's go through them in order.

The first function creates the navigation, by creating an empty movie clip called `Navigation` and storing the data inside it:

```
Object.prototype.initMenu = function(Menu) {
    this.id = "Navigation";
    this.createEmptyMovieClip(this.id, 1);
    name = this[id];
    this.name = name;
    this.xml_Reference = Menu;
    this.name.placeMenu(this.xml_Reference.firstChild);
};
```

The path to this movie clip will be `_level0.Navigation`, and all menu movie clips will be attached to this, for example `_level0.Navigation.menu0`.

The line `this.xml_Reference = Menu;` stores a reference (not a copy) of the loaded `navigation.xml` in `_level0.navigation.xml_Reference`. This is very important to know. When you `trace` this, you will get the referenced part of the XML file displayed. In this case it would be the whole XML file, but in fact this is only a pointer or a path.

The last line is a function call, which tells the code to place an instance of `menu` in `level0.navigation`, containing the data from the first child of our loaded XML file. If you are wondering why we need the `firstChild` tag on there, it is because our `xml_Reference` doesn't point to the first MENU tag, but the NAVIGATION tag. Flash inserts an invisible node around every XML file you load or create. This is, because you are – by XML definition – not allowed to have more than one tag on the first layer. So from scratch, we would need to write `navi_xml.firstChild.firstChild` to get to our first MENU.

9

The next function is `placeMenu`, which we just called. It builds the navigation and gives it functionality. It's quite long, so let's look at it in small sections.

First we set up the function:

```
MovieClip.prototype.placeMenu = function (Menu) {
```

A `for` loop then runs through the actions that follow for as many times as there are `childNodes` in the `Menu` (our passed `xml_Reference`):

```
for (var i = 0; i<Menu.childNodes.length; i++) {
```

Each time the loop runs, it attaches the movie clip `menu` from our library to `Navigation`, our empty movie clip:

```
this.attachMovie ("menu", "menu" +i, i);
name = this["menu" + i];
```

Remember that we set the movie clip to Export for ActionScript with a Linkage name of menu.

Next comes some code to assign functions to buttons in the newly attached menu clips:

```
name.button.onRollOver = rollover_it;
name.button.onPress = press_it;
name.button.onRelease = release_it;
name.button.onRollOut = rollout_it;
```

We'll write these functions later.

The last part of the function applies the XML properties to the newly attached movie clips:

```
var temp_xml = Menu.childNodes[i];
name.xml_Reference = temp_xml;
temp_xml.copyAttributes(name);
        }
    };
```

Here we get the number of the actual XML node we have reached in this cycle of the loop with `i`, and store it in the variable `temp_xml`. We then call the `copyAttributes` function (which we are just about to write).

This copies the given attributes to the newly created movie clip:

```
xmlnode.prototype.copyAttributes = function(name) {
  var attribArray = this.attributes;
  var dest = this[name];
  if (!dest) {
    var dest = name;
  }
  for (var i in attribArray) {
    var attrib = attribArray[i];
    if (isNaN(attrib)) {
      dest[i] = attrib;
    } else {
      dest[i] = Number(attrib);
    }
  }
};
```

We use the `prototype` function to set `copyAttributes` as working with each `xmlnode`. We pass in the name of the movie clip to attach the attributes to it.

As you can see, the function uses a small `for` loop. With a `for` loop you can loop through all properties of an object, or if we are speaking of XML, we can loop through all attributes of a given node. So if the XML node attribute being looked at is `<MENU title="home">` the loop finds the variable called `title` inside the corresponding movie clip and copies the value `home` inside `title`. So if we have something like `_x="20"` in our XML, copyAttributes will move the movie clip to x = 20.

So for example, the line:

```
<MENU title='home' _x='0' _y='0'/>
```

...in the XML will result in:

```
_level0.menu0.title = "home"
_level0.menu0._x = "0"
_level0.menu0._y = "0"
```

Cool, hmm? The XML file tells the button where to place itself. If you want, try some other Flash properties in the XML, like `_alpha` or `_rotation`. But don't get too confident with this, because we will remove these `_x` and `_y` properties later and put them, with a few modifications, into our `style.xml`. This is only for testing.

9

A funny feature of XML attributes is that they build an associative array. So it doesn't matter if you ask for title, Title or TITLE... you always get an answer. All these are the same:

```
title = myXML.attributes.title;
title = myXML.attributes.Title;
title = myXML.attributes.TITLE;
```

Now we come to the functions that give our movie clips user interaction, by coding button actions, which we attached to the buttons in the movie clips in the placeMenu function.

Let's start with the rollover_it function:

```
rollover_it = function () {
    var p = this._parent;
    if (p.xml_Reference.hasChildNodes()) {
        p.textbox.textcolor = "0x0066ff";
    } else {
        p.textbox.textcolor = "0xff6600";
    }
    p._alpha = 70;
};
```

When the button is rolled over, the function first checks to see if the MENU node in the corresponding XML to the parent movie clip, the instance of menu that the button is attached to, has any child nodes. If it does, it will change the text color to blue, and if not, it will change it to orange. This gives us a visual cue as to whether there are any sub-categories to be displayed. Either way, the alpha of the movie clip is reduced to 70 to indicate the rollover.

Then comes the release_it function:

```
release_it = function () {
    var p = this._parent;
    p.textbox.textcolor = "0x000000";
    p._alpha = 100;
};
```

When the user releases the mouse, the parent movie clip's alpha and text color will be reset.

The rollout_it function is very similar:

```
rollout_it = function () {
    var p = this._parent;
```

```
        p.textbox.textcolor = "0x000000";
        p._alpha = 100;
    };
```

Again, when the user rolls off the button, the parent's alpha and text color values will be reset.

This last function controls the actual working of the navigation, and opens nodes when a button is pressed:

```
press_it = function () {
    var p = this._parent;
    p.textbox.textcolor = "0xff0000";
    p._alpha = 100;
    if (p.xml_Reference.hasChildNodes()) {
        if (p.navi_state != "open") {
            p.checkforopenMenu(p.xml_Reference.parentNode);
            p.placeMenu(p.xml_Reference);
            p.navi_state = "open";
        } else {
            p.closeMenu(p.xml_Reference);
            p.navi_state = "close";
        }
    } else {
        p.checkforopenMenu(p.xml_Reference.parentNode);
    }
};
```

So in short, this function first checks if the pressed button has a submenu, using an `if` statement. If true, it checks if it's already open, by checking the status of the flag `navi_state`. If `navi_state` is not set to `"open"` (it's set to `"close"` or undefined) it starts a function called `checkforopenMenu` which looks to see if the user has already opened another submenu. If true, this will be closed before the new one is opened. After that the `navi_state` for the just opened submenu is set to `"open"`.

The following `else` statement deals with what happens if `navi_state` is already set to `"open"`. If this is the case, it means the user has clicked for a second time on a button with a submenu, and so the script closes the submenu again with `closeMenu`.

The final `else` statement deals with what happens when the button you just clicked doesn't have a submenu. It calls `checkforopenMenu` in case there is already a submenu open somewhere else.

Now all we have to do is code the functions to close the menus, and check for open menus.

9

The closeMenu function is very simple:

```
MovieClip.prototype.closeMenu = function(Menu) {
    for (var i = 0; i<Menu.childNodes.length; i++) {
        name = this["menu"+i];
        name.removeMovieClip();
    }
};
```

It just grabs the childNodes of the pressed button and removes them in a for loop. All other nested movie clips that are below this level are deleted too, because when you delete a parent object, all children are also deleted.

The checkforopenMenu function is a little bit more complex:

```
MovieClip.prototype.checkforopenMenu = function(Menu) {
    for (var i = 0; i<Menu.childNodes.length; i++) {
        name = this._parent["menu"+i];
        if (name.navi_state == "open") {
            for (var j = 0;
j<Menu.childNodes[i].childNodes.length; j++) {
                name.navi_state = "close";
                name["menu"+j].removeMovieClip();
            }
        }
    }
};
```

This one makes a step upwards in the navigation, and checks all siblings of the initially pressed button. If their navi_state is set to "open" it will be closed.

So at this point, we have all necessary functions to build our navigation.

Now your navigation should look like this screenshot.

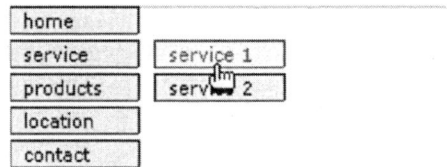

You should be able to open and collapse your submenus, and there should be a color change at rollover – orange for a dead end and blue for a button with submenus.

Styles

Now we have a basic navigation, but we are going to go much further. The `navigation.xml` still includes some data for positioning. But this was just for testing purposes. At this point, we will put all data that pertains to the design or display of the data in a special file called `style.xml`.

As we know, a good solution should separate content and design, form and function. So there will be a file containing all the necessary data we want to display, and a new file that tells us how. Just like HTML and CSS.

The new `navigation.xml` file is shown here:

```
<NAVIGATION>
    <MENU title='home' template='template.swf'
bg_template='bg_template.swf' textfile='text/home.html'/>
    <MENU title='service'>
        <MENU title='service-1' template='template.swf'
bg_template='bg_template2.swf' textfile='text/service.html'/>
        <MENU title='service-2' template='template.swf'
textfile='text/service.html'/>
    </MENU>
    <MENU title='products'>
        <MENU title='product-1' template='template.swf'
bg_template='bg_template3.swf'
textfile='text/products.html'/>
        <MENU title='product 2'>
            <MENU title='product-1' template='template.swf'
textfile='text/products.html'/>
            <MENU title='backgrounds' template='bg_template4.swf'
bg_template='bg_template2.swf'/>
            <MENU title='product 3'>
              <MENU title='product-1' template='template.swf'
textfile='text/products.html'/>
            </MENU>
        </MENU>
    </MENU>
    <MENU title='contact' template='template.swf'
bg_template='bg_template4.swf' textfile='text/contact.html'/>
    <MENU title='external link'
link='http://www.robertreich.de'/>
</NAVIGATION>
```

As you can see, this mentions the templates that we will be using later to display the actual content, but for now, the important thing to notice is that all stylistic properties have been removed.

9

That new `style.xml` is as follows:

```
<STYLES>
  <NAVIGATION>
    <MAIN start_x="0" start_y="0" dist_x="80" dist_y="0"/>
    <SUB start_x="40" start_y="16" dist_x="0" dist_y="16"/>
    <TEXTCOLOR normal = "333333" over = "FFFFFF" selected
    ➡ = "000000"/>
  </NAVIGATION>
  <TEMPLATE>
    <TEXTTEMPLATE start_x="0" start_y="0"/>
    <BGTEMPLATE start_x="0" start_y="0"/>
    <TEXTCOLOR headline="ff6600" text="333333"/>
    <HEADLINE override="0">
<FORMAT html="true" align="left" blockIdent="0" bold="0"
➡ italic="1" underline="1" size="20" indent="0" leading="0"
➡ leftMargin="0" rightMargin="0"/>
    </HEADLINE>
    <TEXT override="0">
<FORMAT html="true" align="left" blockIdent="0" bold="0"
➡ italic="0" underline="0" font="Arial" size="11" indent="0"
➡ leading="3" leftMargin="0" rightMargin="0"/>
    </TEXT>
  </TEMPLATE>
</STYLES>
```

The file is divided into two main nodes, NAVIGATION and TEMPLATE. I guess you know what NAVIGATION is for. The second node, TEMPLATE, will control the behavior and style of our text and other content, but we'll go into that in more detail in the next part.

If we look back at our neat little `copyAttributes` function, we see that there are some difficulties coming up. The function is very pleasing when you just want to have your data copied into your movie clip, but now we have some differences and specialities here. For example the nodes MAIN and SUB. Both are holding the same attribute names, but other than _x and _y, they aren't Flash properties. So to place the navigation, we now need to examine these parameters before we attach the new menu and do the positioning manually.

This means a little more work here, but at the end you will see that it is much more comfortable to just alter a starting point, `start_x`, and `start_y` and a distance `dist_x` and `dist_y`, rather than putting an _x and _y position at the tail of every menu item. This should be a *dynamic* navigation, right?

Before we embark on changing the ActionScript, we need to add some small but important graphical components to our menu movie clip in our Library.

Double-click the menu movie clip. Now you should be able to see your button, text and bg layer. Create a new layer between text and bg and call it Pointer. This will be a replacement for our rollover color change of the button's text label, when a button has submenus.

Select your Rectangle tool and draw a small square of 10x10 px in a dark color. Switch to the Free Transform tool and turn this square about 45°. The last step is to grab the Select tool, draw a rectangular marquee through the middle of it, and cut off the left side, so you have an arrow pointing to the right.

To finalize it, select your new arrow and make it a movie clip. Call this pointer, assign an instance name of pointer and make sure it is exported for ActionScript with a Linkage identifier of pointer.

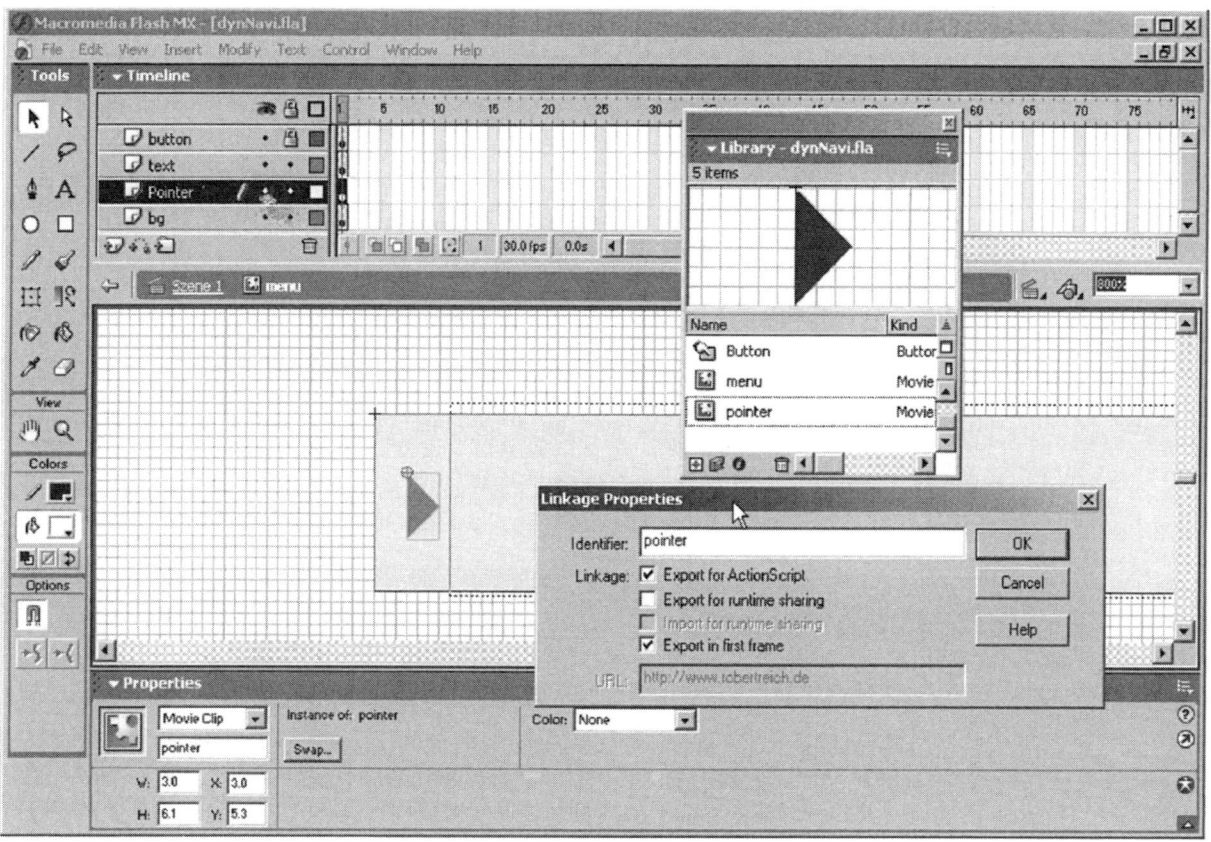

While we are at it, we will add some extra backgrounds for our navigation as well. Go back to the menu, so that you can see our four layers, select the rectangle we drew at the very beginning and make it a movie clip. Call it background and give it a Linkage identifier of background with Export for ActionScript checked.

9

Now double-click your new movie clip to get inside it. Insert two new key frames, so you end up with three key frames with the same rectangle inside.

Create a new layer above this, call it Actions and insert three empty key frames in a row. Now select these key frames, and give them the labels normal, over and selected. Also include a stop(); in every key frame as well.

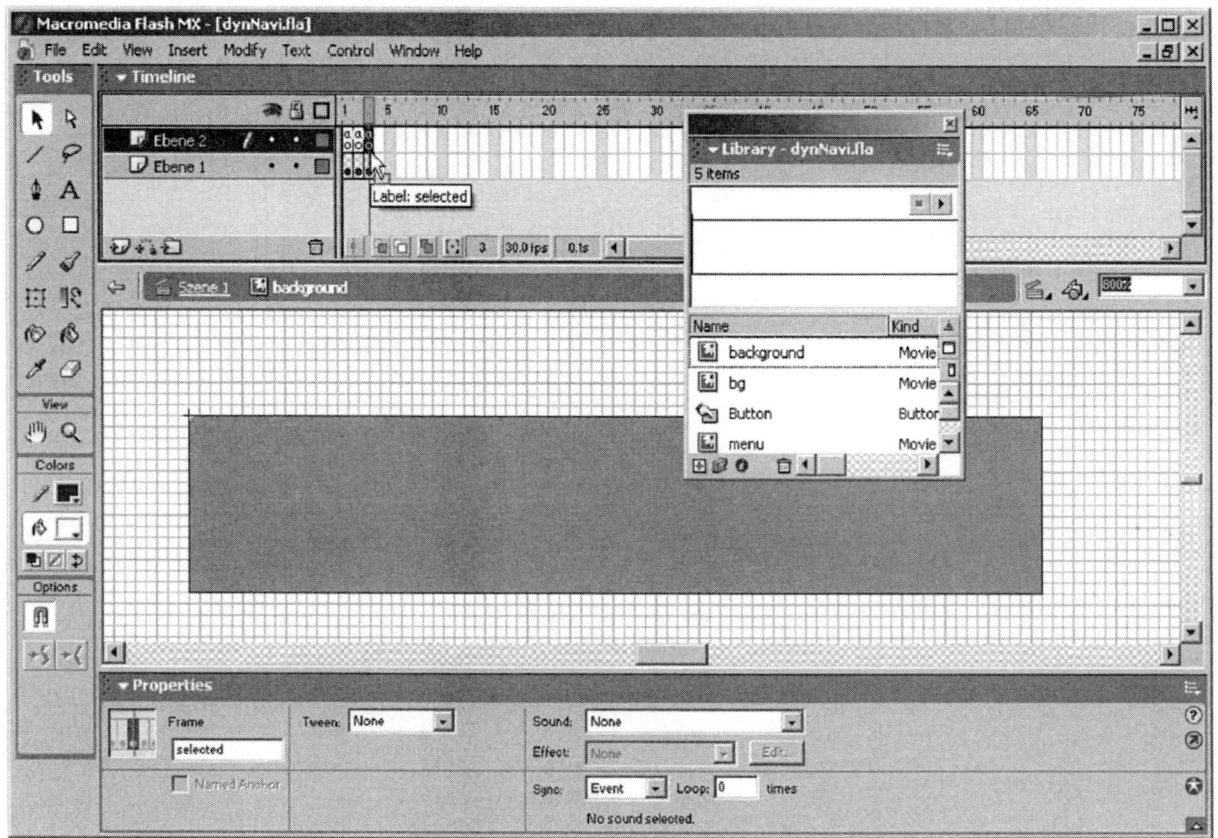

Now let's go over again and see where we have to add or fix some scripts.

In the first section, I described the functions in the order it seemed easiest to understand them, and the order they appear in makes little difference. However, as a general rule, it is good practice to list functions in the order in which they are called – otherwise you risk calling a function before it is declared. So in the part 2 files, the first thing you'll notice is that all the functions now appear to be in reverse order, so as to ensure that our code runs smoothly. The more complicated your ActionScript gets, and the more functions we use, the more important this becomes.

The first major change we have to make, is to load our new `style.xml`, so we need to change the code on the Actions layer.

In frame 1, add the new code as shown below:

```
navi_xml = new XML();
navi_xml.ignoreWhite = true;
navi_xml.load("xml/navigation.xml");

style_xml = new XML();
style_xml.ignoreWhite = true;
style_xml.load("xml/style.xml");
```

This doesn't need much explanation. One thing to note is that you should create a new folder named `xml` and place the `navigation.xml` and `style.xml` there. This isn't important yet, but we will need this later in the following subchapters. Note also that to account for this we add **xml/** to the front of our links to those XML files!

In frame 3, amend the code as shown:

```
if (navi_xml.loaded && style_xml.loaded) {
 gotoAndPlay(4);
} else {
gotoAndPlay(2);
}
```

Again, this isn't a big change – we just need to make sure that our style file is loaded too, before the movie jumps to frame 4.

Actions layer, frame 4:

```
stop();

this.initMenu(navi_xml,style_xml);
```

Here we just pass another path to the function `initMenu` – our new `style.xml`.

That was the easy part of our modifications.

9

Now let's go to our functions layer at frame 1, where all our important code resides. To follow the chain, we begin with our initMenu function, which, if you have rearranged your code as mentioned earlier, as I have, will now be at the bottom of the script:

```
Object.prototype.initMenu = function(Menu, Style) {
    this.id = "Navigation";
    this.createEmptyMovieClip(this.id, 1);
    name = this[id];
    this.name = name;
    name.xml_Reference = Menu.firstChild;
    name.xml_Style = Style.firstChild.firstChild;
    for (var i = 0; i<name.xml_Style.childNodes.length; i++)
    {
        if (name.xml_Style.childNodes[i].nodeName == "MAIN") {
          name.xml_Style_main = name.xml_Style.childNodes[i];
        }
        if (name.xml_Style.childNodes[i].nodeName == "SUB") {
          name.xml_Style_sub = name.xml_Style.childNodes[i];
        }
        if (name.xml_Style.childNodes[i].nodeName ==
        ➥ "TEXTCOLOR") {
          name.xml_Style_textcolor =
          ➥ name.xml_Style.childNodes[i];
        }
    }
    name.placeMenu(name.xml_Reference, name.xml_Style_main,
    ➥ name);
};
```

As we can see, here are some additions. First of all, the function now gets two parameters - Menu and Style. Style is just another XML reference, this time for style.xml. xml_style is the reference for it.

The next big change is a for loop which cycles through the child nodes, starting from the references we have set. It gets the nodes for our navigation, MAIN, SUB and TEXTCOLOR. These results will be stored in a reference as well, because the assignment will be done in placeMenu, as the last function call name.placeMenu(...) implies. The name variable is, as mentioned before, a path to _level0.Navigation, which means that all style references belonging to the navigation are stored in that object or movie clip, such as _level0.Navigation.xml_Style_main.

The other thing worth noting here is that the initial call of placeMenu is performed with xml_Style_main, whereas all other calls from the buttons, or, to be more exact, from our press_it button function, will be performed with xml_Style_sub. This is to get two different modes for the display of our navigation – the main buttons in a horizontal arrangement, and the submenus in a vertical order, placed under their parent.

So let's have a look at placeMenu, next up from the bottom, and see what will happen with our styles. Here is the whole function:

```
MovieClip.prototype.placeMenu = function(Menu, Style, base) {
    for (var i = 0; i<Menu.childNodes.length; i++) {
        this.attachMovie("menu", "menu"+i, i);
        name = this["menu"+i];
        name.base = base;
        name.swapDepths(100-i);
        if (!Menu.ChildNodes[i].hasChildNodes()) {
            name.pointer._visible = false;
        }
        name.textcolor_normal = parseInt
        ➥ ("0x"+base.xml_Style_textcolor.Attributes.normal);
        name.textcolor_over = parseInt
        ➥ ("0x"+base.xml_Style_textcolor.Attributes.over);
        // first init the given textColor.
        name.textbox.textColor = name.textcolor_normal;
        name.textbox.tabEnabled = false;
        // Positioning
        name.start_x = Number(Style.Attributes.start_x);
        name.start_y = Number(Style.Attributes.start_y);
        name.dist_x = Number(Style.Attributes.dist_x);
        name.dist_y = Number(Style.Attributes.dist_y);
        // fixed startpoint, menu2 has 2 * dist(x,y)
        name._x = name.start_x+(i*name.dist_x);
        name._y = name.start_y+(i*name.dist_y);
        // Assign functions to buttons
        name.button.onRollOver = rollover_it;
        name.button.onPress = press_it;
        name.button.onRelease = release_it;
        name.button.onRollOut = rollout_it;
        // apply XML properties
        var temp_xml = Menu.childNodes[i];
        name.xml_Reference = temp_xml;
        // Reference (!) to the actual XMLNode, not a copy.
        temp_xml.copyAttributes(name);
    }
};
```

9

This has grown a little as well. The first version in the **Navigation** section had much less code inside. The first thing to look at is the parameters, passed at the call – Menu, Style, base. The function is called from initMenu like this:

```
name.placeMenu(name.xml_Reference, name.xml_Style_main,
➥name);
```

...followed by:

```
name = this["menu" + i];
name.base = base;
```

xml_Reference is a path to navigation.xml, and xml_Style_main is the necessary part of style.xml. The base is a path to _level0.Navigation.

This base is a path stored in every menu button, and if necessary, passed to a function called after a mouse-click, for example. So, if I am deep inside a sub-navigation, this.base will give a path back to _level0.Navigation.

If you are now asking "but why don't I simply use _level0.Navigation?" then the answer is: "what happens to this path, if you load our navigation.swf in _level1?" With a fixed path, it might not work at all, and will certainly cause problems. With this.base, the path would automatically change to _level1.Navigation, and everything is fine.

For a closer look at this, you can test the complete script in Flash MX by pressing CTRL+SHIFT+ENTER, which – if you don't already know – starts the preview with the Debugger. This handy little thing can save you hours of bug tracking. And you can examine if your variables and properties are right where they are supposed to be.

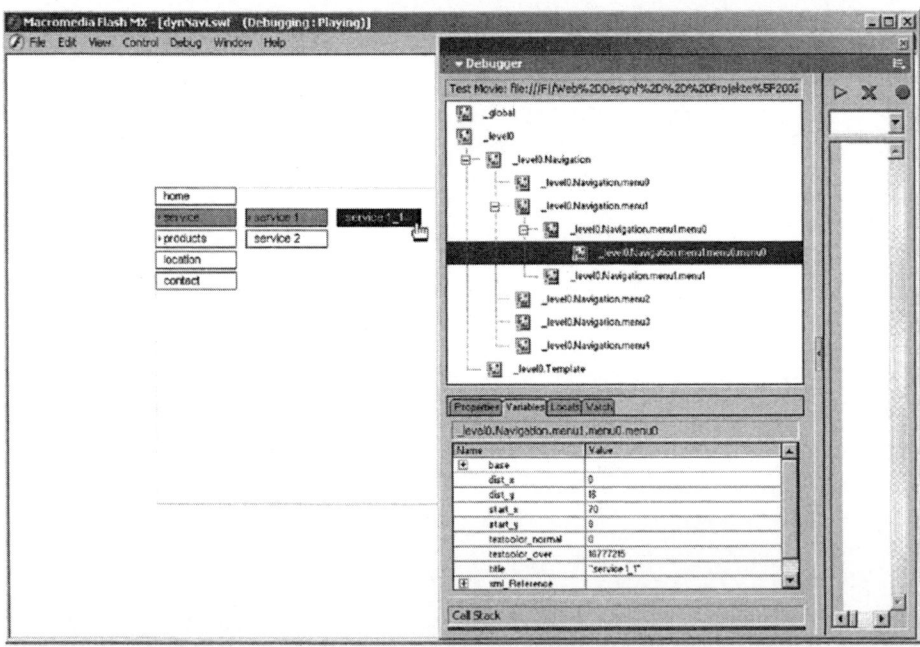

The next oddity to notice is this:

```
name.swapDepths(100-i);
```

The `for` loop counts i upwards (i++), right? So this will result in the simple fact that menu0 will have depth = 0, and menu1 depth = 1. By using swapDepths(100-i) menu0 will be at depth = 100 and the rest at 99, 98, and so on. It just looks better if a submenu is on top of its parent button.

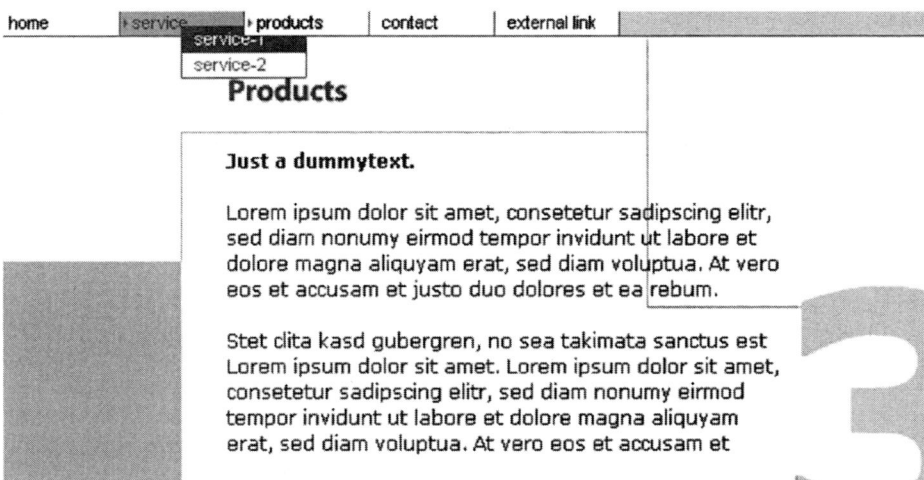

The next bit of code controls the visibility of the pointer:

```
if (!Menu.ChildNodes[i].hasChildNodes()) {
  name.pointer._visible = false;
}
```

This is an easy one, I guess. If the current menu we place has submenus, our new `pointer` will be left unchanged. By default it's visible. If not, the pointer is set to `_visible = false;`.

The next part stores the three button colors inside the `button` movie clip itself, where they can be accessed by our `press_it` function:

```
name.textcolor_normal =
➥ parseInt("0x"+base.xml_Style_textcolor.Attributes.normal);
    name.textcolor_over = parseInt
        ➥ ("0x"+base.xml_Style_textcolor.Attributes.over);
```

9

Then the color is set to normal, and we make sure the textbox cannot be selected through the user's keyboard:

```
name.textbox.textColor = name.textcolor_normal;
name.textbox.tabEnabled = false;
```

The following is the positioning:

```
name.start_x = Number(Style.Attributes.start_x);
name.start_y = Number(Style.Attributes.start_y);
name.dist_x = Number(Style.Attributes.dist_x);
name.dist_y = Number(Style.Attributes.dist_y);
name._x = name.start_x+(i*name.dist_x);
name._y = name.start_y+(i*name.dist_y);
```

Style is a variable passed by the call – a path to the NAVIGATION, MAIN or SUB node from our style.xml. The rest is simple – place the new button at the given _x and _y positions and add (i * dist).

One thing here to note – due to the fact that all sub-buttons are also sub-objects of their caller, their first _x and _y positions aren't the same as those of the main stage or timeline. They refer to their parent object. So if I press service with _x=50 and _y=50, the first sub-button takes 50,50 (viewed from the stage) for its 0,0 and adds its given distance.

For example:

```
menu1._x = 50;
menu1.menu2._x = 30;
```

Result _x for menu2, viewed from the stage, is an x position of 80.

The rest of placeMenu is unchanged.

Now let's make a small addition to our checkforopenMenu function:

```
MovieClip.prototype.checkforopenMenu = function(Menu) {
    for (var i = 0; i<Menu.childNodes.length; i++) {
        name = this._parent["menu"+i];
        if (name.navi_state == "open") {
            name.background.gotoAndStop("normal");
            name.textbox.textcolor = p.textcolor_normal;
            for (var j = 0;
j<Menu.childNodes[i].childNodes.length; j++) {
                name.navi_state = "close";
```

```
        name["menu"+j].removeMovieClip();
      }
    }
  }
};
```

This makes sure that when a menu is closed, the background and text colors are reset.

We also have to make some slight additions to our button functions, in order to have our graphical states displayed correctly.

First the longest function, press_it:

```
press_it = function () {
  var p = this._parent;
  p.textbox.textcolor = p.textcolor_normal;
  p._alpha = 100;
  p.pointer._visible = false;
  if (p.xml_Reference.hasChildNodes()) {
    p.pointer._visible = true;
    p.background.gotoAndStop("selected");
    if (p.navi_state != "open") {
      p.checkforopenMenu(p.xml_Reference.parentNode);
      p.placeMenu(p.xml_Reference, p.base.xml_Style_sub,
      ➥ p.base);
      p.navi_state = "open";
    } else {
      p.closeMenu(p.xml_Reference);
      p.navi_state = "close";
    }
  } else {
    p.pointer._visible = false;
    p.background.gotoAndStop("normal");
    p.checkforopenMenu(p.xml_Reference.parentNode);
  }
};
```

Then release_it:

```
release_it = function () {
  var p = this._parent;
  p.textbox.textcolor = p.textcolor_normal;
  p._alpha = 100;
};
```

9

Then `rollover_it`:

```
rollover_it = function () {
    var p = this._parent;
    p.background.gotoAndStop("over");
    p.textbox.textcolor = p.textcolor_over;
};
```

And finally `rollout_it`:

```
rollout_it = function () {
    var p = this._parent;
    if (p.navi_state == "open") {
        p.background.gotoAndStop("selected");
        p.textbox.textcolor = p.textcolor_selected;
    } else {
        p.textbox.textcolor = p.textcolor_normal;
        p.background.gotoAndStop("normal");
    }
    p.textbox.textcolor = p.textcolor_normal;
    p._alpha = 100;
};
```

All the changes to these functions are pretty similar. The first change is made with `p.textbox.textcolor`, where we assign `p.textcolor_normal` from our `style.xml`.

Our `placeMenu` function now gets new parameters for the style.

The rest of the changes simply deal with displaying the correct graphical elements.

The one thing left to do is to remove the part of the `copyAttributes` function that dealt with the text format. The function should now read:

```
xmlnode.prototype.copyAttributes = function(name) {
    var attribArray = this.attributes;
    var dest = this[name];
    for (var i in attribArray) {
        var attrib = attribArray[i];
        if (isNaN(attrib)) {
            dest[i] = attrib;
        } else {
            dest[i] = Number(attrib);
        }
    }
};
```

So while I grab a new coffee, you can experiment a little with your enhanced version 2 of the navigation, before we go on to the next part, which will really push us to the next level.

The templates

The two preceding sections have given you a small navigation and two XML files to play around with. But really at the moment, all this is pretty useless, as when you press a button, nothing happens. This will change in this chapter. But before I start with the code, I'll have to explain what, exactly, we are going to build, and give you a brief overview.

First of all, we need a container for all this. I mentioned this before – this will be a movie clip called `Template`, nested in our `_root`. The main structure will be the same as our `Navigation` movie clip, but with some changes in the detail.

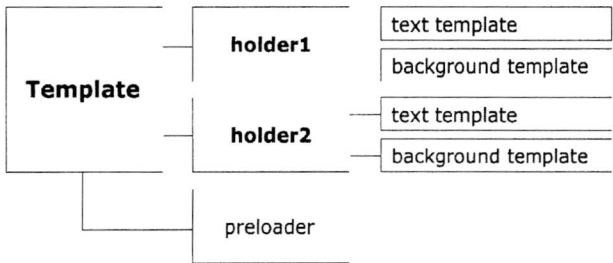

All the components we need are a text and a background template as external SWF files, two `holder` movie clips which will be created as empty movie clips, and a preloader, also created in the script.

To explain the text template, just create a new and blank file in Flash MX, make sure the stage has the same size as our navigation, 600x300 px (actually we have the ability to place our text and background templates at every position through the `style.xml`, but at this point simply match sizes), and create a second keyframe on the main timeline. Place a `stop` in the first one, and two textboxes on keyframe 2. One is for the headline and the other is for the normal text.

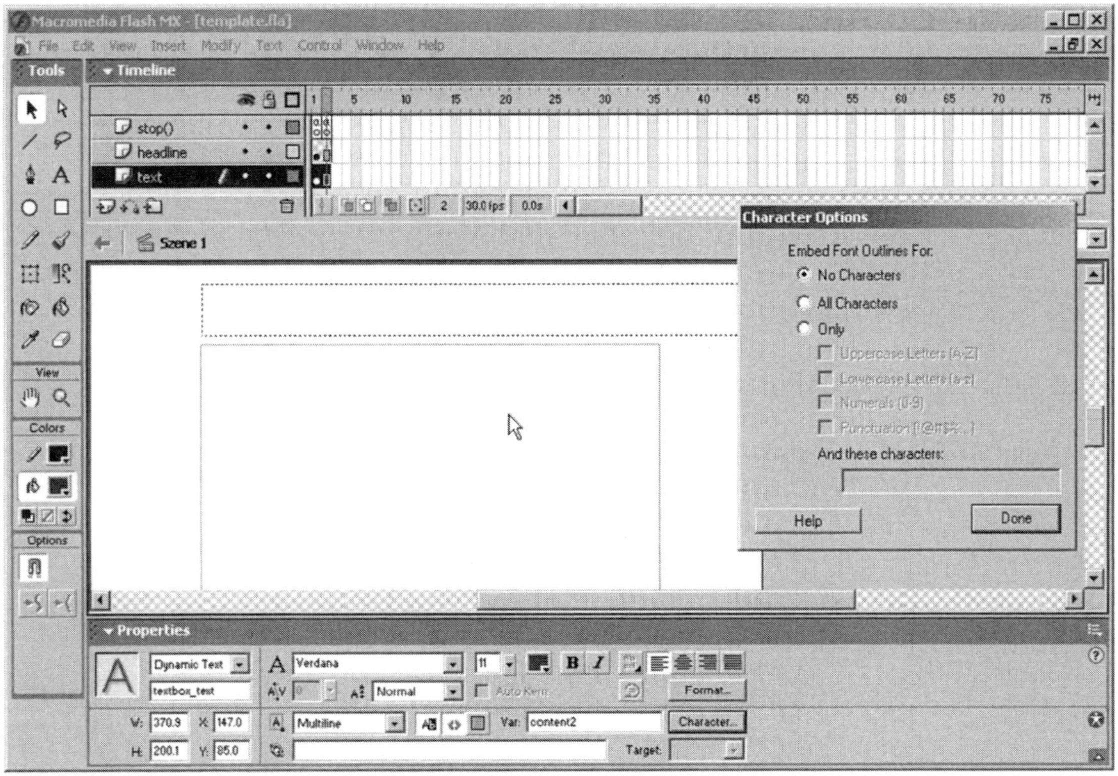

The text boxes should be named `textbox_headline`, with variable set to `content1` and `textbox_text` with variable set to `content2`. If you like, you can assign the headline with an included font, but be sure to click on the Render text as HTML button for both text boxes. As always, they need to be dynamic, because we will load text files and will use this template to display the text.

The `textbox_text` should use a system font like Arial, or Verdana with a readable size of 11 or above. If you want to use a pixel font later, be sure that the textboxes are both at exact point zero (10.0 / 20.0) positions. (Having View > Snap to pixels checked will be very handy for this.)

The background template is even more simple. Just follow the same steps as before, putting a `stop();` in the first and in the second frame, and the content started at frame 2. This is for the simple reason that when loaded, the movie won't start to play and mess around with the whole thing.

In key frame 2 you should for now just paint some squares or whatever to get visual feedback at testing that the file is loaded and was started. Here you can make say 3 different files, maybe with a fat "1", "2", etc, so you can see which `bg_template` was loaded. Save the files and call them `bg_template.swf`, `bg_template2.swf`, and so on.

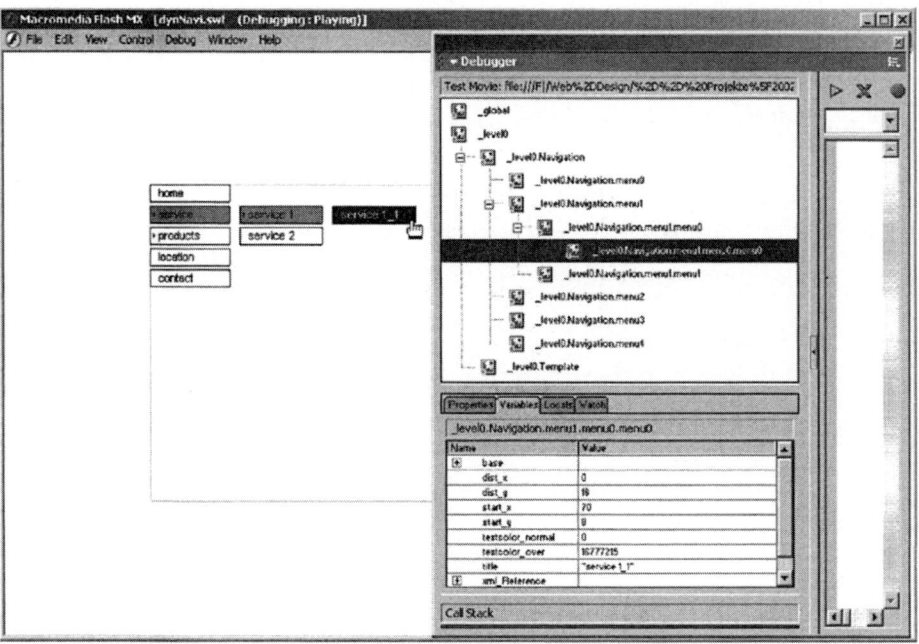

The overall idea is that when the user clicks a button in the navigation, the templates will load.

Say the node looks like this:

```
<MENU title='home' template='template.swf'
➥ bg_template='bg_template.swf' textfile='text/home.html'/>
```

`template` is our file with the text boxes, `bg_template` our background, and `text/home.html` is an HTML file which contains our headline and our normal text. That file contains the following code:

```
<table>
<h1>Home</h1>
<p>Welcome to this little page.</p>
</table>
```

It looks a little bit strange, and isn't exactly a real HTML file, but it would be displayed properly if opened in a browser. The side effect is (and the only reason to use `<table>`, `<h1>` and `<p>`) that this is also a valid XML file. One top node, 2 text nodes.

Perfect, isn't it?

So before we forget, create a folder called `text` and place this little example inside as `home.html`.

I guess you can imagine how we pick this HTML file and strip the headline and the normal text apart to put it somehow into our loaded text template. This will be done just the same way as with our `navigation.xml` and `style.xml`. The only difference is the file suffix, and that we have worked only with attributes up until now, not with textNodes.

But more on this when we come to it – we have two components left in our scheme. The word "preloader" should ring a bell, and as the name suggests, it will control how, when, and where something will be loaded and placed.

So, what the heck are these holders for?

OK. This will take a deeper look inside what happens when you click a button. Normally, on a customary HTML page, it works like this:

1. You click

2. The screen goes blank

3. You wait for the content to load

Some pages are different, but this is the usual way it goes. Maybe that's the reason why I often right-click a link and open a new browser window with the new page, continue reading on the current page, and switch to the next when the new one is loaded.

9

With Flash at our disposal, this shouldn't be common. What I really hate are huge Flash sites where I get a "Loading 200 KB" display after every button I press. And I promise you – with this system this behavior belongs to the past.

In short, the two holders "hold" the actual displayed content on the one side while the other is used to take the loading one. And the only reason for these "dummies" being between the _level0.Template and the loaded text and background is, that you can't set a loading movie clip to _visible = false. You may now be saying "but with a blank key frame and a stop at the beginning, the movies won't show up until started."

OK. That's a point, but without these holders, it would force us to give each template position a different name and a unique depth. So something like temp0, temp1, temp2 and temp3 as destinations. But where do we put the text file? We had to put it into _level0.Template, as we can't load a text file into a still loading movie either, but to be sure not to overwrite the actually displayed one, we must have two variables here as well.

This would be a hell of a mess with pointers, arrays or whatever, and very difficult not to lose the overview. But our two holders are really cool.

The loaded or displayed text is stored inside the holder, all paths are the same, except that we have to switch the holder.

That is done by thisprocess: (lets say we are in: _level0.Template)

```
...
... dynamically create empty holders + nested text and
    ➥ bg_template
...

this.holder_switch = new Array(this.holder1,
➥ this.holder2);

// number0 will be displayed, inside number1 we will load
// our files.
this.holder_switch[1]._visible = false;


...
... do the loading stuff.
...

// loading is finished -> "change" the holders.
this.holder_switch[1]._visible = true;
this.holder_switch[0]._visible = false;
this.holder_switch.reverse();
```

These are only some fragments. We have an array that's stored in our _level0.Template. This array, holder_switch consists of the paths to our two dynamically created holders. After loading is finished, we change the order inside the array, simply with Array.reverse. So next time we press a button, the loading process will be done again with the second entry of the array, holder_switch[1], but this time it's not holder2, it's holder1, due to the Array.reverse.

I hope this was accurate enough. Even if you don't understand all the little details right now, you have the broad outline and hopefully the overall picture of it. Maybe you'll understand this much better if we have a working example and you can test the example with the Debugger again, and examine what happens in the Output window if you click a button.

So let us go back to ActionScript.

First, just like with the menu, we need to initialize our code. Add the following line to the actions layer, frame 4:

```
this.initTemplate(style_xml);
this.initMenu(navi_xml,style_xml);
```

All forthcoming scripts are meant to be placed in frame 1 of our functions layer.

This function should be placed after the initMenu one:

```
Object.prototype.initTemplate = function(Style) {
   this.id = "Template";
   this.createEmptyMovieClip(this.id, 2);
   name = this[id];
   this.name = name;
   name.initDummy("holder1", 1);
   name.initDummy("holder2", 2);
   // loading display (name, depth, x, y, width, height)
   name.myTextbox("loadText", 3, 30, 50, 150, 150);
   name.holder_switch = new Array(name.holder1, name.holder2);
   name.xml_Style = Style.firstChild;
   for (var j = 0; j<name.xml_Style.childNodes.length; j++) {
      if (name.xml_Style.childNodes[j].nodeName ==
      ➡ "TEMPLATE") {
        name.xml_Style = name.xml_Style.childNodes[j];
        for (var i = 0; i<name.xml_Style.childNodes.length;
        ➡ i++) {
          if (name.xml_Style.childNodes[i].nodeName ==
          ➡ "TEXTTEMPLATE") {
            name.xml_Style_temp = name.xml_Style.childNodes[i];
          }
```

9

```
                        if (name.xml_Style.childNodes[i].nodeName ==
                     ➥ "BGTEMPLATE") {
                        name.xml_Style_bgtemp = name.xml_Style.childNodes[i];
                        }
                        if (name.xml_Style.childNodes[i].nodeName ==
                     ➥ "TEXTCOLOR") {
                        name.xml_Style_textcolor =
                     ➥ name.xml_Style.childNodes[i];
                        }
                        if (name.xml_Style.childNodes[i].nodeName ==
                     ➥ "TEXT") {
                        name.text_format = new TextFormat();
                        name.xml_Style.childNodes[i].firstChild.
                     ➥ copyAttributes(name.text_format);
                        name.text_override = Number(name.xml_Style.
                     ➥ childNodes[i].Attributes.override);
                        name.text_format.color = parseInt
                     ➥ ("0x"+name.xml_Style_textcolor.Attributes.text);
                        }
                        if (name.xml_Style.childNodes[i].nodeName ==
                     ➥ "HEADLINE") {
                        name.headline_format = new TextFormat();

                        name.xml_Style.childNodes[i].firstChild.
                     ➥ copyAttributes(name.headline_format);
                        name.headline_override = Number(name.xml_Style.
                     ➥ childNodes[i].Attributes.override);
                        name.headline_format.color = parseInt
                     ➥ ("0x"+name.xml_Style_textcolor.Attributes.headline);
                        }
                    }
                }
            }
        }
    };
```

At first glance, you might think this looks very similar to initMenu. Well, you are right. The "XML-get-my-styles-ready" part is simple copy and paste. Some minor additions for the preparation of TextFormat, but I'm sure this isn't a big thing.

Only this part is unique:

```
name.initDummy("holder1",1);
name.initDummy("holder2",2);
name.myTextbox("loadText",3,30,50,150,150);
name.holder_switch = new Array(name.holder1, name.holder2);
```

As we can see, we call the initDummy function twice, to prepare our two holders. The myTextbox function is only used to create the text box for our preloader, called loadText, with the properties *(name, depth, x, y, width, height)*

Here is the initDummy function. Place it before the initTemplate function, so that we can stay true to our practice of setting up the functions before they are called:

```
MovieClip.prototype.initDummy = function(holder, depth) {
    this.createEmptyMovieClip(holder, depth);
    this[holder].createEmptyMovieClip("template", 3);
    this[holder].createEmptyMovieClip("bg_template", 2);
    this[holder].textfile = new XML();
    this[holder].textfile.ignoreWhite = true;
};
```

The initDummy gets passed the holder name and its depth, and then it will create something like:

```
_level0.Template.holder1
_level0.Template.holder1.template
_level0.Template.holder1.bg_template
_level0.Template.holder1.textfile
```

In the second call, this looks the same, but the holder is holder2.

The myTextbox function gets all necessary data passed, and assigns some properties to that newly created text box. Put it after the copyAttributes function at the beginning of your code:

```
Object.prototype.myTextbox = function(name, depth, x, y,
width, height) {
    this.createTextField(name, depth, x, y, width, height);
    this[name].multiline = true;
    this[name].wordWrap = true;
    this[name].border = false;
    this[name].selectable = false;
    this[name].type = "dynamic";
    this[name].html = true;
};
```

So now we have a big movie clip called Template, which has some styles stored in it. There are two strange "holders" attached to this, with an empty text file as XML, and attached to these nearly empty holders, are two empty movie clips called template and bg_template... Hmm, and what now?

Yeah... now we wait, until somebody presses the button.

9

The button – where all the action starts

If you remember the Navigation and Styles parts, then you know that the navigation was working fine, but with one exception. You could expand and collapse the submenus but when clicking on a content button nothing happens.

This is the moment to change that. So let's look again at the `press_it` function and the `checkforopenMenu` function where we listen to the menu and decide what to do when the user clicks. The other button functions don't change.

First, the `press_it` function:

```
press_it = function () {
   var p = this._parent;
   p.textbox.textcolor = p.textcolor_normal;
   p._alpha = 100;
   p.pointer._visible = false;
   if (p.xml_Reference.hasChildNodes()) {
      p.pointer._visible = true;
      p.background.gotoAndStop("selected");
      p.textbox.textcolor = p.textcolor_selected;
      if (p.navi_state != "open") {
         p.checkforopenMenu(p.xml_Reference.parentNode);
         p.placeMenu(p.xml_Reference, p.base.xml_Style_sub,
         ➥p.base, p.temp_base);
         p.navi_state = "open";
      } else {
         p.closeMenu(p.xml_Reference);
         p.navi_state = "close";
      }
   } else {
      p.pointer._visible = false;
      p.background.gotoAndStop("normal");
      p.checkforopenMenu(p.xml_Reference.parentNode);
      p.temp_base.preLoad(p);
      p.base.menu0.checkforopenMenu(p.base.xml_Reference);
   }
};
```

In `press_it`, there are basically two changes. The call for `preLoad` and some strange looking call for `checkforopenMenu`. The last call is, in simple terms, to simulate pressing the home button. The `p` in the path is a pointer to the actual pressed menu button, but this menu has a variable called `base`, where the path to `_level0.Navigation` is stored. So in plain English, this is a very complex but OOP-style way to say: "I want to get `this.Navigation.menu0`".

Now let's look at the changes to checkforopenMenu:

```
MovieClip.prototype.checkforopenMenu = function(Menu) {
    for (var i = 0; i<Menu.childNodes.length; i++) {
        name = this._parent["menu"+i];
        if (name.navi_state == "open") {
            name.background.gotoAndStop("normal");
            name.textbox.textcolor = p.textcolor_normal;
            for (var j = 0;
            ➥j<Menu.childNodes[i].childNodes.length; j++) {
                name.navi_state = "close";
                name["menu"+j].removeMovieClip();
            }
        }
    }
};
```

These two new lines of code reset the button state to normal when closing an opened submenu.

So let's see what this new preLoad function does. It should be placed after the initTemplate function:

```
MovieClip.prototype.preLoad = function(menu) {
    if (menu == this.buttoncheck) {
        return;
    }
    this.buttoncheck = menu;
    if (this.all_loaded == false) {
        return;
    } else {
        this.all_loaded = false;
        clearInterval(this.Int_id);
    }
    var d = this.holder_switch[1];
    d._visible = false;
    this.initDummy(d._name, d._name.substring(d._name.length-
1));
    this.l_array = new Array();
    if (suffixCheck(menu.template, ".swf")) {
        d.template.loadMovie(menu.template);
        this.l_array.push([d.template, "template"]);
        if (suffixCheck(menu.textfile, ".htm")) {
```

9

```
            d.textfile.load(menu.textfile);
            this.l_array.push([d.textfile, "text"]);
        }
        if (suffixCheck(menu.bg_template, ".swf")) {
            d.bg_template.loadMovie(menu.bg_template);
            this.l_array.push([d.bg_template, "background"]);
        }
        this.loadStateChecker(this);
    } else {
        this.all_loaded = true;
        this.clearLoaderDisplay(this);
        if (menu.link != undefined) {
            if (suffixCheck(menu.link, "http://")) {
                getURL(menu.link, "_blank");
            } else {
                getURL("http://"+menu.link, "_blank");
            }
        } else {
            // if you step here, something
            // went really wrong... no template and no link...
            // this is a good place to put some error message to
            //the screen.
            this.all_loaded = true;
            go.crazy = true;
            //
        }
    }
};
```

Again let's look at it in small parts.

At first, there are two `if` clauses, which are for so-called security reasons:

```
if (menu == this.buttoncheck) {
    return;
}
this.buttoncheck = menu;
if (this.all_loaded == false) {
    return;
} else {
    this.all_loaded = false;
    clearInterval(this.Int_id);
}
```

First, a check in case the user pressed a content button twice. Remember the press_it function. If you expand and collapse a menu, you also press a button twice but don't pass through this function, because no content is behind that button. But if you press – for example – the home button twice, this will check it and will leave the preLoad function with a return. Even when all needed files are present in the browser cache, it isn't necessary to load this again when it's still on the screen, right?

The next if clause is much more important. What will happen, if the load is still in progress, and we select another page to load? Normally you would say, the first attempt will be overwritten. But with our two holders in mind, this will blow up the whole idea of not waiting for content. Also the real preloader, which is run by the new Flash MX setInterval function, will stop working properly, so we clear the interval.

The next block is this:

```
var d = this.holder_switch[1];
d._visible = false;
this.initDummy(d._name, d._name.substring(d._name.length-1));
this.l_array = new Array();
```

d is the path to the actual holder where we will load the new page. The initDummy is a re-initialization of d, but because the initDummy function needs a string like "holder1" and a depth, I had to extract the holder and its depth out of the path of d again, and then hide it. Only then can I re-initialize the holder and delete the old templates.

The l_array is a two-dimensional array that stores the data from the following extraction process. If, for example, a text template is assigned to the page we load, the array will push two parameters – the path, and a display name for the preloader.

```
this.l_array.push ([d.template,"template"]);
```

The first part will later be taken and with getBytesLoaded and getBytesTotal we are able to calculate the amount of loading completed. The second item is just to be shown in the preloader text box to indicate what we are loading. But actually this whole process inside the preLoad function will start the loading and then pass the array over to a second function called loadStateChecker, which will loop until all data is loaded.

Next, a function called suffixCheck, which we will look at in a minute, runs through and assigns templates to all our files, according to their file endings. We also call two other functions, loadstateChecker, and clearloaderDisplay. LoadstateChecker is the real preloader – the preLoad function has examined the data, placed a hook inside our l_array and now loadStateChecker does the rest.

9

319

If nothing happens, then no templates or text files are assigned in the `navigation.xml` for this button, but there is a good chance that there is a link defined. This is – not mentioned before – also a feature:

```
if (menu.link != undefined) {
        if (suffixCheck(menu.link, "http://")) {
          getURL(menu.link, "_blank");
        } else {
          getURL("http://"+menu.link, "_blank");
        }
```

Basically, if it is already named, go to the URL, and if not, name it:

```
<MENU title='Google.com' link='www.google.com'/>
```

...and this should work fine.

Let's have a look at the other functions we call from this code.

Place the `suffixCheck` function after the `myTextBox` function near the beginning of the code:

```
Object.prototype.suffixCheck = function(name, sfx) {
   var myString = name.toUpperCase();
   var sfx = sfx.toUpperCase();
   if (myString == undefined) {
      return false;
   }
   if (myString.indexOf(sfx) != -1) {
      return true;
   } else {
      return false;
   }
};
```

You simply pass a string like `"template.swf"` as `name` and another string, a suffix like `".swf"` and the function returns `true` or `false` if the examined file is of the right type.

This makes sure we don't load an HTML file inside a movie clip, or a SWF inside an XML node.

Next, let's look at the `loadStateChecker` function, which you'll remember I said is our real preloader. This goes at the end of your code:

```
MovieClip.prototype.loadStateChecker = function(base) {
    if (!base.timer) {
        base.Int_id = setInterval(base.loadStateChecker, 10,
        ➡base);
        base.timer = true;
        base.loadText._visible = true;
    }
    // Array -> (swf=true or text=false?),actual path,
    //destination, displaytext
    var count = 0;
    var s_count = 0;
    var loadingtext = "<font face='Arial' size='11'
    ➡color='#666666'>loading: <br>";
    for (var i = 0; i<base.l_array.length; i++) {
        s_count =
        ➡(int(base.l_array[i][0].getBytesLoaded()/base.l_array
        ➡[i][0] getBytesTotal())*100);
        count += s_count;
        loadingtext += (s_count+" >
        ➡"+base.l_array[i][1]+"<br>");
    }
    base.loadText.htmlText = (loadingtext+"state:
    ➡"+int(count/base.l_array.length)+" %</font>");
    if ((count/base.l_array.length)>=100) {
        clearInterval(base.Int_id);
        base.timer = false;
        base.Int_id = setInterval(base.clearLoaderDisplay,
        ➡1500, base);
        base.finishTemplates();
    }
};
```

First, and most important here, is the `if` clause. This is passed once, then the `timer = true` and the `setInterval` are set in the same function:

```
if (!base.timer) {
        base.Int_id =
setInterval(base.loadStateChecker,100,base);
        base.timer = true;
        base.loadText._visible = true;
    }
```

9

This is one of the most useful new features of Flash MX. You never again need a timeline and something like *gotoAndPlay(last frame)* for a loop that doesn't consume processor time.

The rest is calculating the percentage and preparing the display text. If count indicates that all is loaded, the Interval for the loop is cleared, the timer is set to false and now it's time to put the loaded text file and all the styles into use. As a small addition, the if clause sets a new setInterval, which calls clearLoaderDisplay which simply clears the display, after 1.5 seconds.

The clearLoaderDisplay function goes after the preload function:

```
MovieClip.prototype.clearLoaderDisplay = function(base) {
   base.loadText.htmlText = "";
   clearInterval(base.Int_id);
};
```

And last but not least, we have to finish and assign all to work properly. That's done with finishTemplates, which goes after the preload function:

```
MovieClip.prototype.finishTemplates = function() {
   var holder = this.holder_switch[1];
   this.xml_Style_temp.copyAttributes(holder.template);
   this.xml_Style_bgtemp.copyAttributes(holder.bg_template);
   holder.template._x = holder.template.start_x;
   holder.template._y = holder.template.start_y;
   holder.bg_template._x = holder.bg_template.start_x;
   holder.bg_template._y = holder.bg_template.start_y;
   holder.template.gotoAndPlay(2);
   holder.bg_template.gotoAndPlay(2);
   this.holder_switch[0].template.gotoAndStop(1);
   this.holder_switch[0].bg_template.gotoAndStop(1);
   this.text_format.html = true;
   this.headline_format.html = true;
   var myTextNode = holder.textfile;
   for (var j = 0; j<myTextNode.childNodes.length; j++) {
      if (myTextNode.childNodes[j].nodeName == "table") {
         myTextNode = myTextNode.childNodes[j];
      }
   }
   for (var i = 0; i<myTextNode.childNodes.length; i++) {
      if (myTextNode.childNodes[i].nodeName == "h1") {
         holder.template.textbox_headline.setTextFormat
         ➡ (this.headline_format);
         var myString = myTextNode.childNodes[i]
```

```
    ➥ .childNodes.join("");
      holder.template.content1 = preFormatText
    ➥ (this.headline_format, myString);
    }
    if (myTextNode.childNodes[i].nodeName == "p") {
      holder.template.textbox_text.
    ➥ setTextFormat(this.text_format);
      var myString = myTextNode.childNodes[i].
    ➥ childNodes.join("");
      holder.template.content2 = preFormatText
    ➥ (this.text_format, myString);
    }
    if (this.text_override) {
      holder.template.textbox_text.
    ➥ setTextFormat(this.text_format);
    }
    if (this.headline_override) {
      holder.template.textbox_headline
    ➥ .setTextFormat(this.headline_formatX);
    }
  }
  holder._visible = true;
  this.holder_switch[0]._visible = false;
  this.holder_switch.reverse();
  this.all_loaded = true;
};
```

First, we get our holder for the just loaded content. After that – as seen in placeMenu before – we assign the normal x and y settings, after passing through our copyAttributes function. In the next lines, we reset the "old" content by setting the movie clips' keyframes to the beginning with gotoAndStop(1) and start playback for the new ones.

We then get the path for the text file and extract the necessary parts for the text strings:

```
holder.template.textbox_headline.setTextFormat(this.headline_
➥ format);
      var myString =
    ➥ myTextNode.childNodes[i].childNodes.join("");
      holder.template.content1 =
    ➥ preFormatText(this.headline_format, myString);
    }
}
    if (myTextNode.childNodes[i].nodeName == "p") {
```

9

```
holder.template.textbox_text.setTextFormat
➥ (this.text_format);
var myString =
➥ myTextNode.childNodes[i].childNodes.join("");
holder.template.content2 =
➥ preFormatText(this.text_format, myString);
```

The rest of the code deals with the display of the text.

To understand what the whole idea behind this is, I have to tell you a little more about a text field and the new TextFormat function, which we will look at in a minute.

Normally, if you draw a text box onto your stage, there are some basic parameters set by default. Like a font, or the type, or a font size.

This isn't a big problem if you just want to cover or overwrite these settings with your own TextFormat, and if your loaded text has font tags, this isn't a problem either.

But if you assign your TextFormat to have your normal text formatted with your chosen font, color and so on from your style.xml and you also want the text file to keep its format, you can see this can cause a lot of trouble.

First try:

You assign your TextFormat, and then put your text inside. Result – the TextFormat is gone, replaced through the initial values (font and size) when you created the textbox, but your loaded text is formatted correctly. Hmm.

Second try:

You first load your text inside and then assign the TextFormat. Result – your TextFormat works fine, but now all font tags from your text file are gone.

Maybe – I'm really not sure – this is just caused by a stupid mistake I've made. But nevertheless I've done a small but very pleasing workaround for this. Place this just before the finishTemplates function:

```
MovieClip.prototype.preFormatText = function(tformat,
➥textstring) {
   var l = tformat.leading;
   var font = tformat.font;
   var size = tformat.size;
   var tc = tformat.color;
   var a = tformat.align;
   if (font == undefined) {
      var str = "<TEXTFORMAT LEADING='"+l+"'><P
```

```
    ➡ ALIGN='"+a+"'><FONT SIZE='"+size+"'
    ➡ COLOR='"+tc+"'>"+textstring+"</FONT></P></TEXTFORMAT>";
  } else {
    var str = "<TEXTFORMAT LEADING='"+l+"'><P
    ➡ ALIGN='"+a+"'><FONT FACE='"+font+"' SIZE='"+size+"'
    ➡ COLOR='"+tc+"'>"+textstring+"</FONT></P></TEXTFORMAT>";
  }
  return str;
};
```

So this does what I initially wanted. You pass your `TextFormat` and the loaded text as `textstring` and this places the format you have been given by the `style.xml` around the loaded text, and then puts it inside the text box. We also have two possibilities here. If you have a headline – which is commonly set with an included font – then the function doesn't touch this, it only overrides the size, color, leading and alignment. Otherwise the text box with an included font set to Arial or something would simply be empty. That is, because if `TextField.embedFonts = true`, you can't use system fonts if they aren't included in your Flash file.

Going back to the `finishTemplates` function, the last trick is this:

```
if (this.text_override) {

holder.template.textbox_text.setTextFormat(this.text_format);
    }
    if (this.headline_override) {
      holder.template.textbox_headline.
      ➡ setTextFormat(this.headline_formatX);
    }
```

If you take a look back at `style.xml`, you maybe remember the small but neat additional attributes for TEXT and HEADLINE.

```
<HEADLINE override="0"> ...
<TEXT override="0"> ...
```

If set to `"0"`, all that's described before will happen and these two `if` clauses will be passed with no change. If set to `"1"`, the `TextFormat` will be assigned again to the two textboxes and override the settings so that they exactly match to these of your `style.xml` and all additional formatting from the text files are gone.

So you can call this a simple step towards CSS for Flash!

Some other text-related thing is the new preference of Flash MX and the Flash player for **Unicode** formatted text. By default, Flash MX expects all loaded texts to be Unicode, where Version 5 worked with normal ASCII. Unicode is, in short, another format for text.

9

Or maybe this is better described as the way you define and save characters. This is a very good invention for the future, especially if your language uses special signs or letters. But to remove this feature for now, simply place this line only once in your ActionScript at the beginning of the code:

```
system.useCodepage = true;
```

There are some other small changes to make to existing functions, and then we are done.

Amend copyAttributes as follows:

```
xmlnode.prototype.copyAttributes = function(name) {
    var attribArray = this.attributes;
    var dest = this[name];
    if (!dest) {
        var dest = name;
    }
    for (var i in attribArray) {
        var attrib = attribArray[i];
        if (isNaN(attrib)) {
            dest[i] = attrib;
        } else {
            dest[i] = Number(attrib);
        }
    }
};
```

Add in a few extra lines to placeMenu:

```
MovieClip.prototype.placeMenu = function(Menu, Style, base,
➡temp_base) {
    for (var i = 0; i<Menu.childNodes.length; i++) {
        this.attachMovie("menu", "menu"+i, i);
        name = this["menu"+i];
        name.base = base;
        name.temp_base = temp_base;
        name.depth = this.depth+1;
        name.swapDepths(100-i);
        if (!Menu.ChildNodes[i].hasChildNodes()) {
            name.pointer._visible = false;
        }
        name.textcolor_normal = parseInt
        ➡ ("0x"+base.xml_Style_textcolor.Attributes.normal);
        name.textcolor_over = parseInt
```

```
➥ ("0x"+base.xml_Style_textcolor.Attributes.over);
name.textcolor_selected = parseInt
➥ ("0x"+base.xml_Style_textcolor.Attributes.selected);
name.textbox.textColor = name.textcolor_normal;
```

And change the initMenu function:

```
Object.prototype.initMenu = function(Menu, Style) {
    this.id = "Navigation";
    this.createEmptyMovieClip(this.id, 100);
    name = this[id];
    this.name = name;
    this.temp_base = this.Template;
    name.xml_Reference = Menu.firstChild;
    name.xml_Style = Style.firstChild;
    for (var j = 0; j<name.xml_Style.childNodes.length; j++)
{
        if (name.xml_Style.childNodes[j].nodeName ==
        ➥ "NAVIGATION") {
          name.xml_Style = name.xml_Style.childNodes[j];
          for (var i = 0; i<name.xml_Style.childNodes.length;
          ➥i++) {
            if (name.xml_Style.childNodes[i].nodeName ==
            ➥"MAIN") {
              name.xml_Style_main =
              ➥name.xml_Style.childNodes[i];
            }
            if (name.xml_Style.childNodes[i].nodeName == "SUB")
            ➥{
              name.xml_Style_sub =
              ➥name.xml_Style.childNodes[i];
            }
            if (name.xml_Style.childNodes[i].nodeName ==
            ➥ "TEXTCOLOR") {
              name.xml_Style_textcolor =
              ➥ name.xml_Style.childNodes[i];
            }
          }
        }
    }
    name.placeMenu(name.xml_Reference, name.xml_Style_main,
    ➥ name, temp_base);
};
```

9

327

All these changes are only minor, and reflect the changes in the external files that we are loading.

So those were the templates. As long as nothing has gone wrong, you should now have a really cool toy with lots of features to play with.

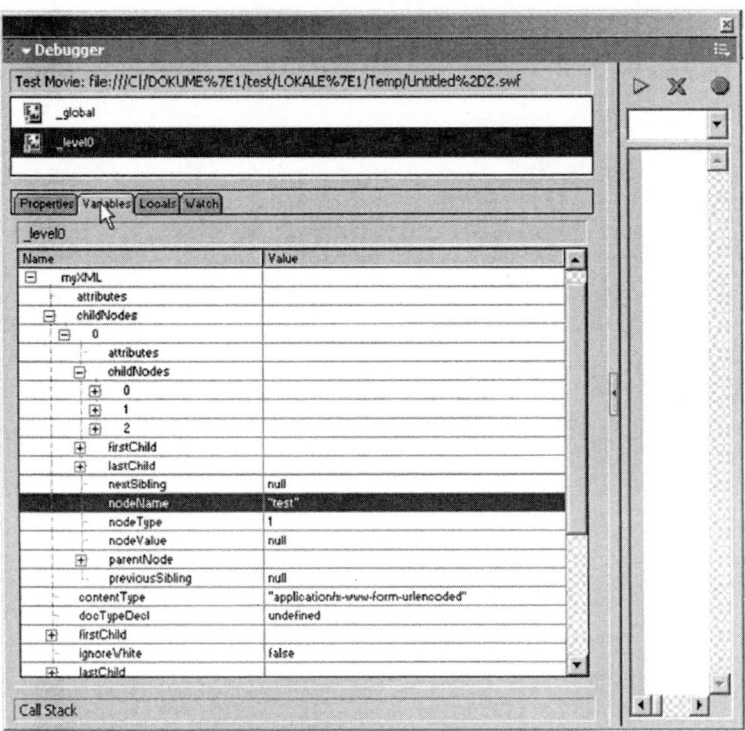

As a final tweak, you can also add some code to frame 4 of the actions layer which will automatically load the homepage for you when you open the page:

```
var home_button = this.Navigation.menu0;
this.Template.preLoad(home_button);
```

Further possibilities

This file was originally designed to use PHP to update your files while the website is still up and running. As you can see in the screenshot earlier, there is an admin link, and advice on amending your files. This would make it a completely dynamic updateable system. If you are interested in looking into this in more depth, there is a folder called `part3_final_php` included in the download files, along with a `php.pdf` document.

There are lots of other ways in which this concept could be expanded, so in this final section I'd like to share some of my ideas with you, and hopefully inspire some of your own!

Animation

Due to the complexity of this subject, I decided not to include any type of animation function. But it is something I've thought about, and so here are some starting points, ideas, improvements and also some neat little scripts, to compensate for that. Always remember, this is only a small example and the further we've gone in this chapter, the more possibilities have shown up. The navigation in particular would look nice animated.

To animate the navigation, we would first have to make some general decisions about how and where we wanted this to occur. If we want to animate when it opens, then the `press_it` or `placeMenu` functions would be the right place to do this, or at least they would be the right place to call another function to perform the animation. To animate the menu as it closes would be much more complex, because we would need to delay the `closeMenu` and `checkforopenMenu` functions, as otherwise they simply delete our movie clips and there is nothing left to animate.

Maybe something like this would give us some time for the delay:

```
base.Int_id = setInterval(this.yourAnim,1000);
```

I'm sure there is a wide range of possible ways forward and solutions ... actually I don't have a good suggestion of a simple way to do it – if I did, I'd tell you, I promise. If you come up with any useful ideas I'd be very interested to hear them, so please let me know.

Background images

With the dynamic loading capabilities of Flash MX, another good idea would be to add a third node to the `style.xml` file, where you could define some theme-based JPEG images that would be shown for every main NAVIGATION node.

```
<STYLES>
    <NAVIGATION>
    ...
    </NAVIGATION>
    <TEMPLATE>
    ...
    </TEMPLATE>
    <BACKGROUNDS>
        <PIC>bluesky.jpg</PIC>
        <PIC>flowers.jpg</PIC>
        ...
        ...
    </BACKGROUNDS>
</STYLES>
```

9

They could simply be loaded with `LoadMovie` and placed in a structure like `Template` or `Navigation`. Take the first lines of `initNavigation`, call it `initBackground`, rename the `id` and there's your basis.

There is actually a small bit of commented-out code in the `part3_final/dynNavi.fla` which you can use if you want to give this a go.

A small `for` loop could simply get every picture from XML, create a set of empty movie clips called `bg0`, `bg1`, `bg2`, and so on, and load them into it.

The `initDummy` function could be good for this, just add a `for` loop and an `if` statement where you examine the `style.xml` to cycle through all entries of `BACKGROUNDS` and you're almost finished.

The last thing would be a hook somewhere in `press_it`, where you check if you have to switch the pictures.

This could be done by the suffix, joined to the menu name. So `menu0` and all submenus would have the first theme, `menu1` the second and so on. So as the path to `_level0.Template` and `_level0.Navigation` is stored in every button, it wouldn't be a big problem to store a category or theme number in every created button.

In `initMenu`, inside the loop you'd put something like:

```
this.category = i;
```

...and inside `placeMenu`:

```
name.category = this.category;
```

This number can be extracted inside of `press_it`, and there you can change your pictures.

Sound

Of course, decent sound for the navigation is a plus. I guess the simplest way to include this is inside our `menu` movie clip in our Library. Maybe this isn't the coolest way to do this, but I don't think you'll need to change this every day, so doing this with ActionScript is possible, but could be considered overkill, if you have an extra part in your `style.xml` just to dynamically change a tiny button-click sound. But hey – if you fancy the challenge, do it. And send me that new XML code!

A sound loop is also a possibility, and I think I would approach this in a template-style way, designing a template with some controls, and then loading it somewhere. And maybe a node in `style.xml` to have the ability for x and y positioning. The rest could be done with something like `initMusic`, copy and pasted from another bit of initialization code.

XML

The ActionScript to examine our XML files is – for educational reasons – held to a more basic level than it could be, due to the fact that the documentation around XML wasn't finished with Flash 5 and it still isn't a simple issue with MX. So to make an improvement here, I would suggest a set of more general functions where you just pass a `nodeName` and you get back an array with all the hits or the path you need. Something in the style of `copyAttributes`. So you can cut down on the code in the `initMenu` and `initTemplate`.

General advice

If maybe you got the impression that, at some points in this chapter, we have made a decision in the process, and then in the next section altered this and moved to a different method, then you are right. This is maybe another thing to learn about programming in Flash, or programming in general. You should always make a good and specific plan to cover the whole project, but don't start with the smallest details, and then be afraid to change them when a different method might better suit your purposes.

First, think what you want to achieve and try to split your work into small and easy to understand pieces. Never lose focus on this master plan, but don't get bogged down in the tiny details of one area while others are still only an idea on paper. Make sure you clarify to yourself in which ways the individual pieces are connected or relying on each other, by data, function, behavior, or by their properties and variables. A flow chart can be very helpful.

If you don't have a clear idea of where you're going, you might easily fall into one of the many pitfalls that lie along the way of any programming project. But even if you do plan carefully, these pitfalls can still happen, and if you are too committed to a specific route to where you want to go, it can make it more difficult to get out of them. Remember that until you start coding, you can never have the complete overview of all the things that can go wrong.

A good example of this is that in the templates section, I ran into two lots of difficulties, firstly by creating the preloader, and secondly having some trouble with the text boxes. But because my overall plan wasn't fixed too deep, I could slip in the `holders` for the preloader, and come up with a do-it-yourself function, `TextFormat`.

So apart from hopefully showing you how you can make your Flash projects more efficient, this chapter also shows a real-world example of inventing something pretty much completely from scratch, and how it can be very handy to have a good plan that is also flexible enough to allow for a plan B.

I hope that this little trip was helpful and inspiring. Keep scripting, and allow your projects the room to grow organically.

9

INDEX

The index is arranged hierarchically, in alphabetical order, with symbols preceding the letter A. Many second-level entries also occur as first-level entries. This is to ensure that you will find the information you require however you choose to search for it.

All files refered to in the chapters are listed under Download files.

friends of ED particularly welcomes feedback on the layout and structure of this index. If you have any comments or criticisms, please contact:

feedback@friendsofED.com